尾田栄一郎

Hey, everybody! News flash! If you ingest too much sugar because of an unbalanced diet, do NOT think you can correct it by then eating too much sodium! *RAWR!!*

-Eiichiro Oda, 2003

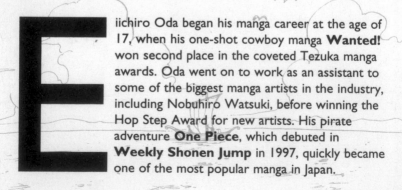

Eiichiro Oda began his manga career at the age of 17, when his one-shot cowboy manga **Wanted!** won second place in the coveted Tezuka manga awards. Oda went on to work as an assistant to some of the biggest manga artists in the industry, including Nobuhiro Watsuki, before winning the Hop Step Award for new artists. His pirate adventure **One Piece**, which debuted in **Weekly Shonen Jump** in 1997, quickly became one of the most popular manga in Japan.

ONE PIECE VOL. 31
SKYPIEA PART 8

SHONEN JUMP Manga Edition

STORY AND ART BY EIICHIRO ODA

English Adaptation/Jake Forbes
Translation/Taylor Eagle, HC Language Solutions, Inc.
Touch-up Art & Lettering/HudsonYards
Design/Sean Lee
Editor/Yuki Murashige

Published by VIZ Media, LLC
P.O. Box 77010
San Francisco, CA 94107

10 9 8 7 6 5
First printing, February 2010
Fifth printing, March 2015

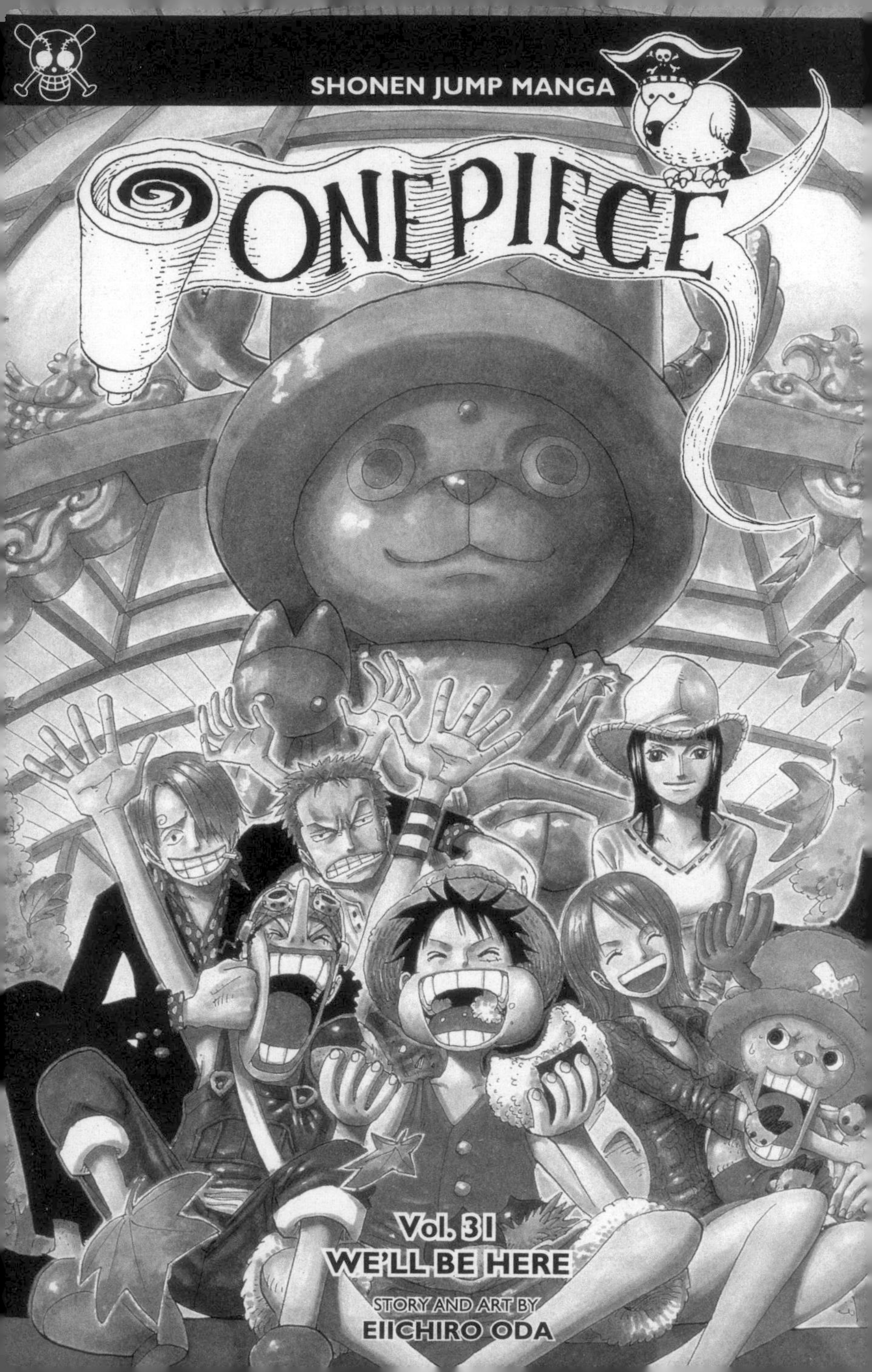
SHONEN JUMP MANGA
ONE PIECE
Vol. 31
WE'LL BE HERE
STORY AND ART BY
EIICHIRO ODA

The Shandians

The native inhabitants of Upper Yard. They're fighting to regain control of their homeland, which was seized by the Skypieans.

Wyper

Kamakiri

Braham

Genbo

Raki

Aisa

The Former Kami

"Sky Knight" Ganfor

Conis

Pagaya

The Straw Hats

Boundlessly optimistic and able to stretch like rubber, he is determined to become King of the Pirates.

Monkey D. Luffy

A former bounty hunter and master of the "three-sword" style. He aspires to be the world's greatest swordsman.

Roronoa Zolo

A thief who specializes in robbing pirates. Nami hates pirates, but Luffy convinced her to be his navigator.

Nami

A village boy with a talent for telling tall tales. His father, Yasopp, is a member of Shanks's crew.

Usopp

The bighearted cook (and ladies' man) whose dream is to find the legendary sea, the "All Blue."

Sanji

A blue-nosed man-reindeer and the ship's doctor.

Tony Tony Chopper

A mysterious woman in search of the Ponegliff on which true history is recorded.

Nico Robin

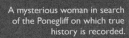

THE STORY OF ONE PIECE

Monkey D. Luffy started out as just a kid with a dream—to become the greatest pirate in history! Stirred by the tales of pirate "Red-Haired" Shanks, Luffy vowed to become a pirate himself. That was before the enchanted Devil Fruit gave Luffy the power to stretch like rubber, at the cost of being unable to swim—a serious handicap for an aspiring sea dog. Undeterred, Luffy set out to sea and recruited some crewmates—master swordsman Zolo; treasure-hunting thief Nami; lying sharp-shooter Usopp; the high-kicking chef Sanji; Chopper, the walkin' talkin' reindeer doctor; and the mysterious archaeologist Robin.

The Straw Hat pirates reach the island in the sky, Skypiea—a land ruled by the powerful Kami Eneru—but they're charged with trespassing. When the crew gets separated, Luffy, Sanji and Usopp face the tough challenges put up by the Kami's vassals, while the rest discover a shocking secret about their surroundings—mythical Upper Yard was originally part of Jaya Island! A treasure hunt for the island's legendary city of gold is in order, but before they can reach the riches the crew gets caught up in a battle between the Kami's army and the Shandians, a group of natives fighting to recapture their ancestral land. Eneru's true objective is to demolish Skypiea with all of its inhabitants as he sets off for Endless Varse, but he didn't count on one rubber man to foil his electrifying plans. Now that Luffy's arm is trapped in a huge ball of gold, Eneru is free to carry on his dastardly celebration!

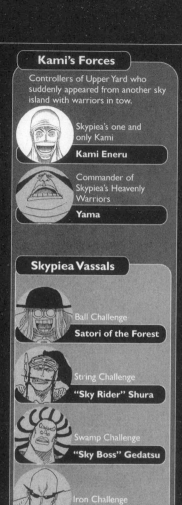

Kami's Forces

Controllers of Upper Yard who suddenly appeared from another sky island with warriors in tow.

Skypiea's one and only Kami
Kami Eneru

Commander of Skypiea's Heavenly Warriors
Yama

Skypiea Vassals

Ball Challenge
Satori of the Forest

String Challenge
"Sky Rider" Shura

Swamp Challenge
"Sky Boss" Gedatsu

Iron Challenge
"Sky Breeder" Ohm

A pirate that Luffy idolizes. Shanks gave Luffy his trademark straw hat.
"Red-Haired" Shanks

Vol. 31
We'll Be Here

CONTENTS

Chapter 286:
THE SHANDORAN DEMON

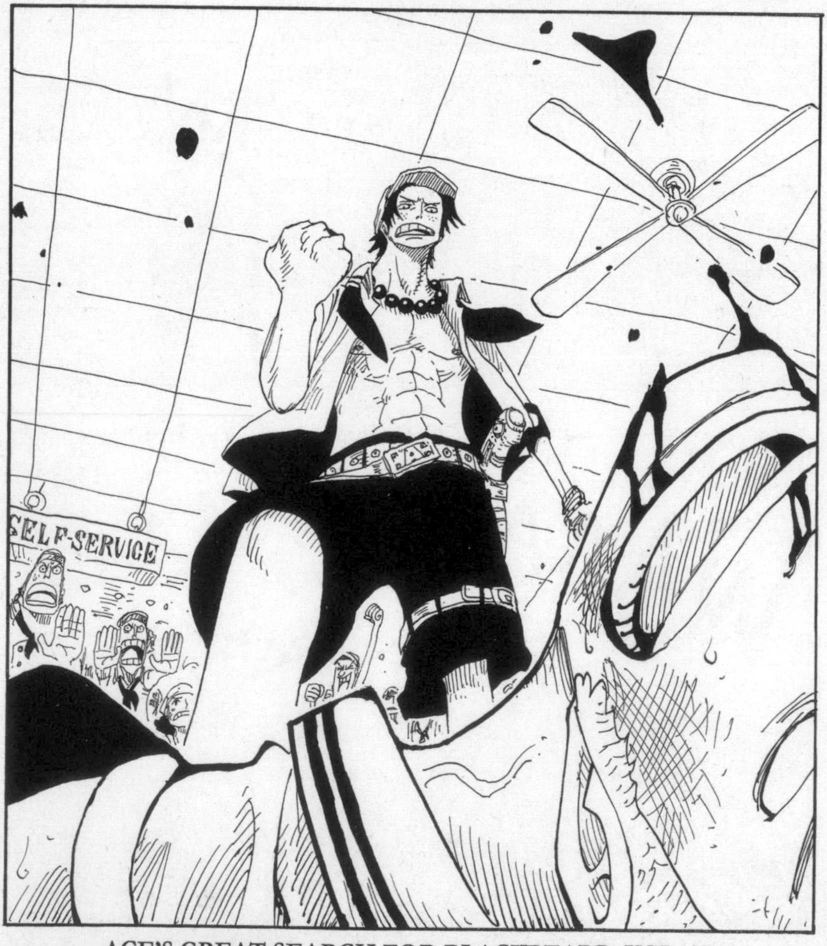
SELF-SERVICE

ACE'S GREAT SEARCH FOR BLACKBEARD, VOL. 13:
"HEARD A DISRESPECTFUL COMMENT ABOUT WHITEBEARD"

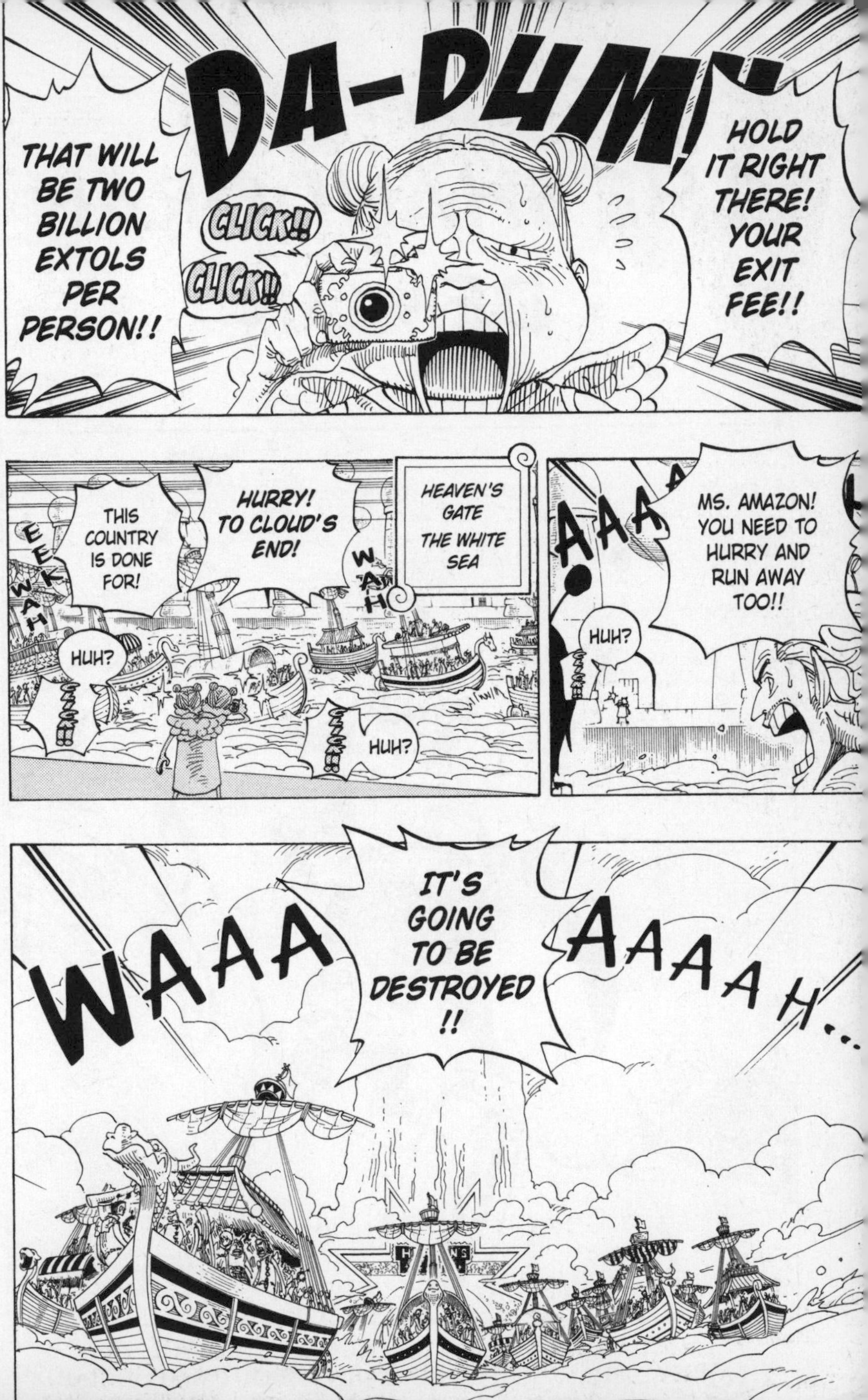
HOLD IT RIGHT THERE! YOUR EXIT FEE!!
DA-DUM
CLICK!!
CLICK!!
THAT WILL BE TWO BILLION EXTOLS PER PERSON!!
MS. AMAZON! YOU NEED TO HURRY AND RUN AWAY TOO!!
AAAA
HUH?
HEAVEN'S GATE THE WHITE SEA
HURRY! TO CLOUD'S END!
WAH
THIS COUNTRY IS DONE FOR!
EEK
WAH
HUH?
HUH?
WAAA
IT'S GOING TO BE DESTROYED!!
AAAAH...

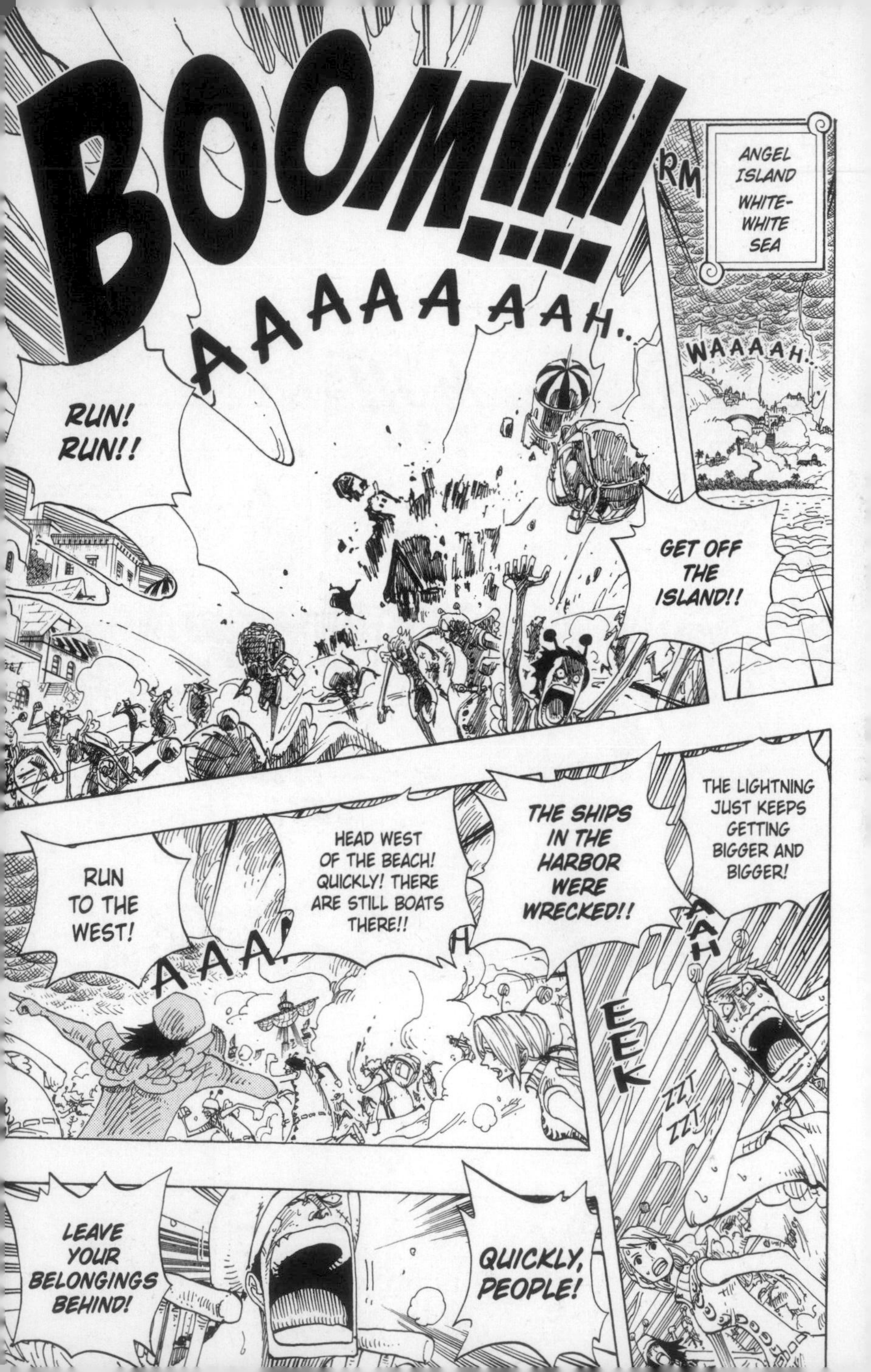
ANGEL ISLAND WHITE-WHITE SEA
RM
WAAAAH...
BOOM!!!!
AAAAAAAAH...
RUN! RUN!!
GET OFF THE ISLAND!!
THE LIGHTNING JUST KEEPS GETTING BIGGER AND BIGGER!
AAH
EEK
ZZT
ZZT
THE SHIPS IN THE HARBOR WERE WRECKED!!
HEAD WEST OF THE BEACH! QUICKLY! THERE ARE STILL BOATS THERE!!
RUN TO THE WEST!
QUICKLY, PEOPLE!
LEAVE YOUR BELONGINGS BEHIND!

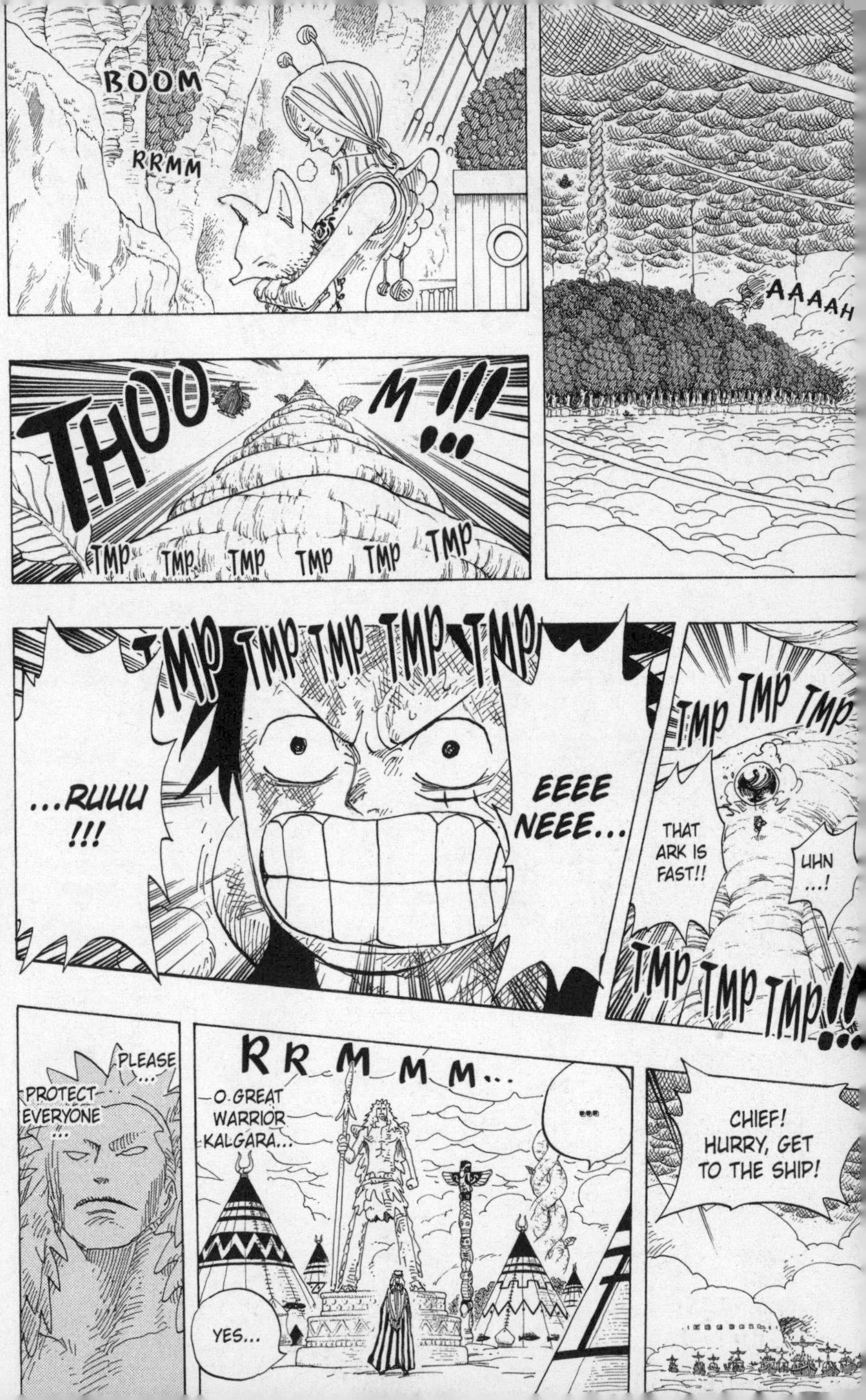
AAAAH
BOOM
RRMM
THOOM!!...
TMP TMP TMP TMP TMP TMP
TMP TMP TMP
THAT ARK IS FAST!!
UHN ...!
TMP TMP TMP!!...
TMP TMP TMP TMP TMP
EEEE NEEE...
...RUUU !!!
CHIEF! HURRY, GET TO THE SHIP!
RRMMMM...
O GREAT WARRIOR KALGARA...
...
YES...
PLEASE ...
PROTECT EVERYONE ...

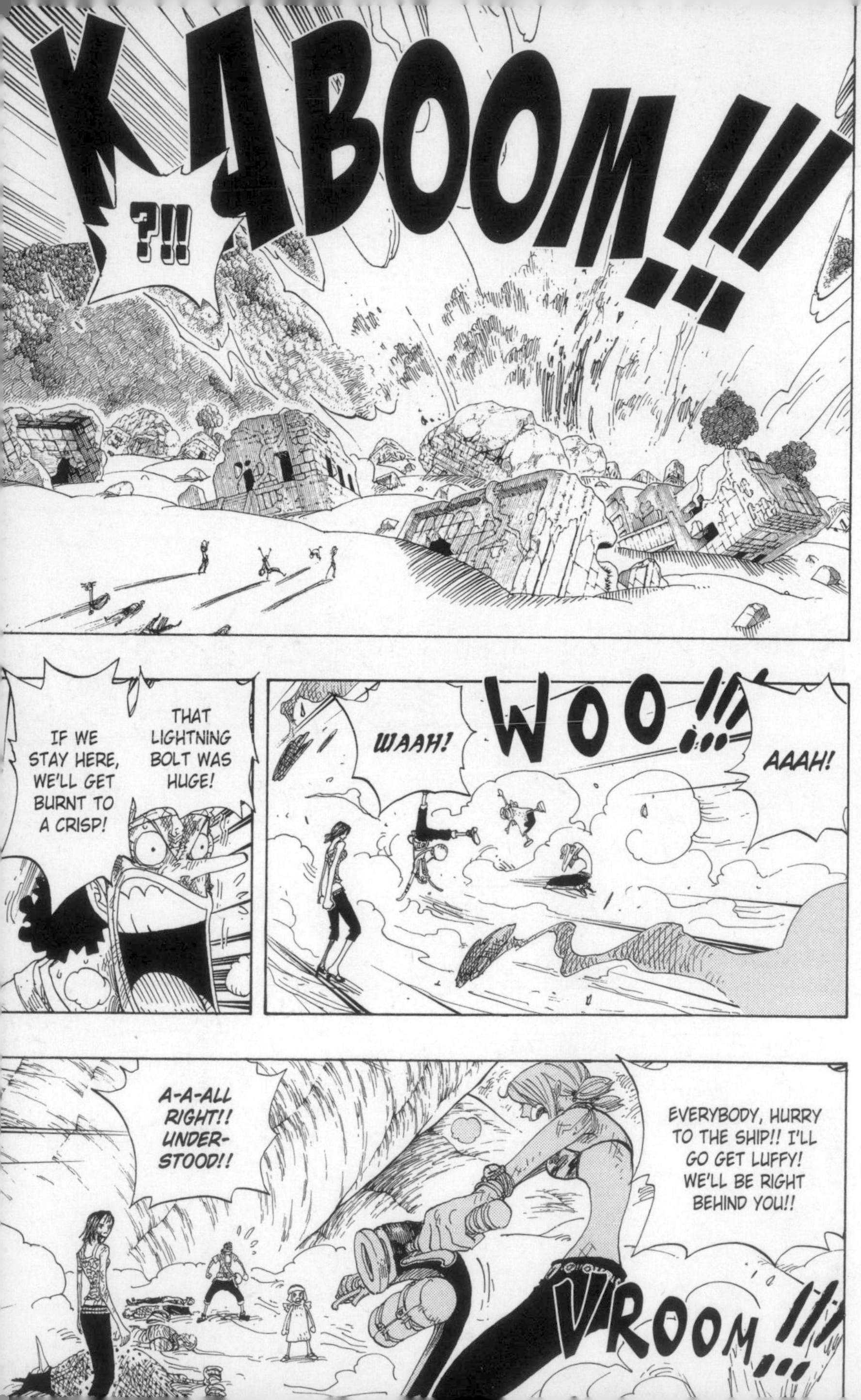
KABOOM!!!
?!!
AAAH!
WOO!!!
WAAH!
THAT LIGHTNING BOLT WAS HUGE!
IF WE STAY HERE, WE'LL GET BURNT TO A CRISP!
EVERYBODY, HURRY TO THE SHIP!! I'LL GO GET LUFFY! WE'LL BE RIGHT BEHIND YOU!!
VROOM!!!
A-A-ALL RIGHT!! UNDER-STOOD!!

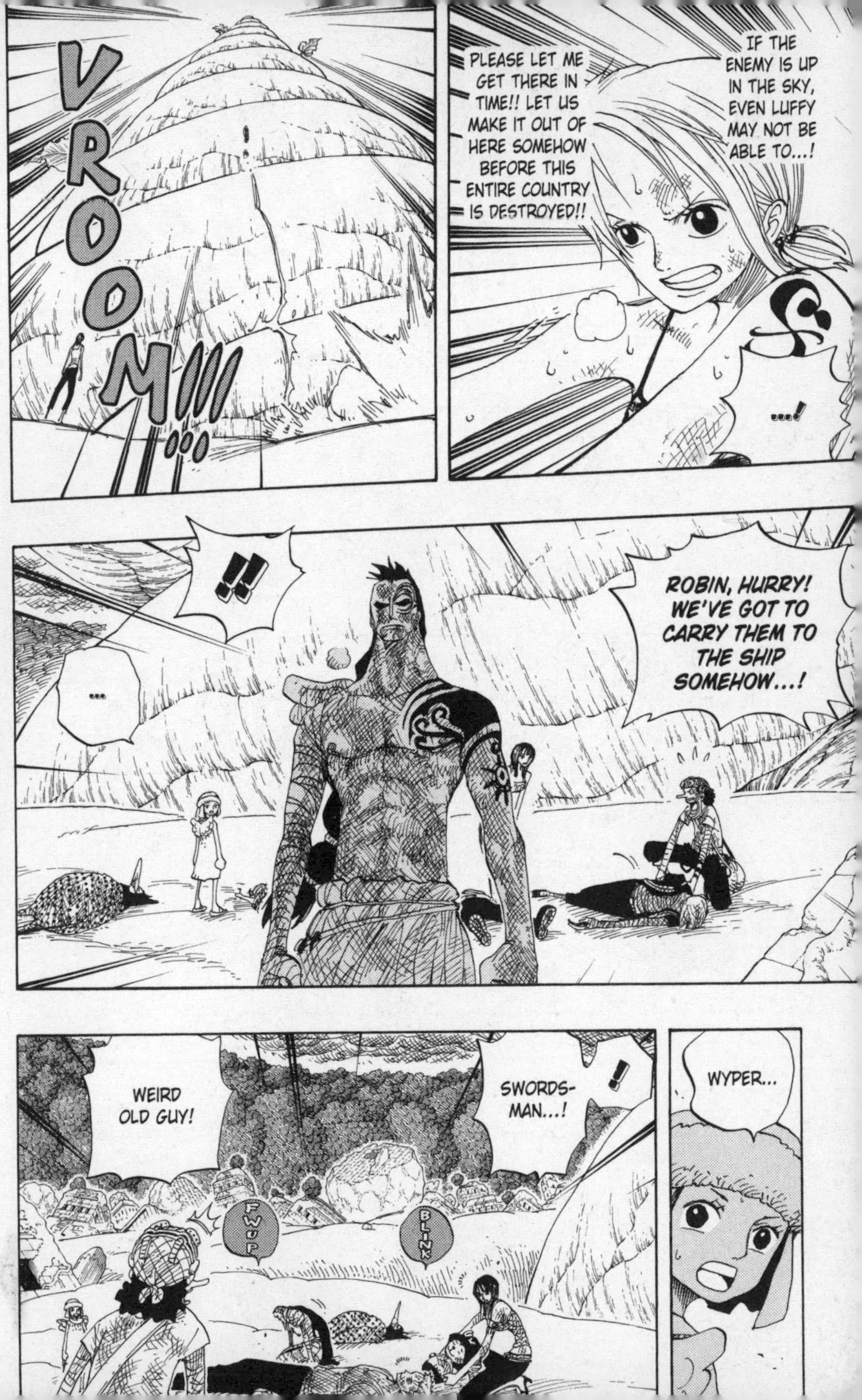
IF THE ENEMY IS UP IN THE SKY, EVEN LUFFY MAY NOT BE ABLE TO...!
PLEASE LET ME GET THERE IN TIME!! LET US MAKE IT OUT OF HERE SOMEHOW BEFORE THIS ENTIRE COUNTRY IS DESTROYED!!
...!
VROOM!!!!
ROBIN, HURRY! WE'VE GOT TO CARRY THEM TO THE SHIP SOMEHOW...!
!!
...
WYPER...
!
SWORDS-MAN...!
WEIRD OLD GUY!
BLINK
FWUP

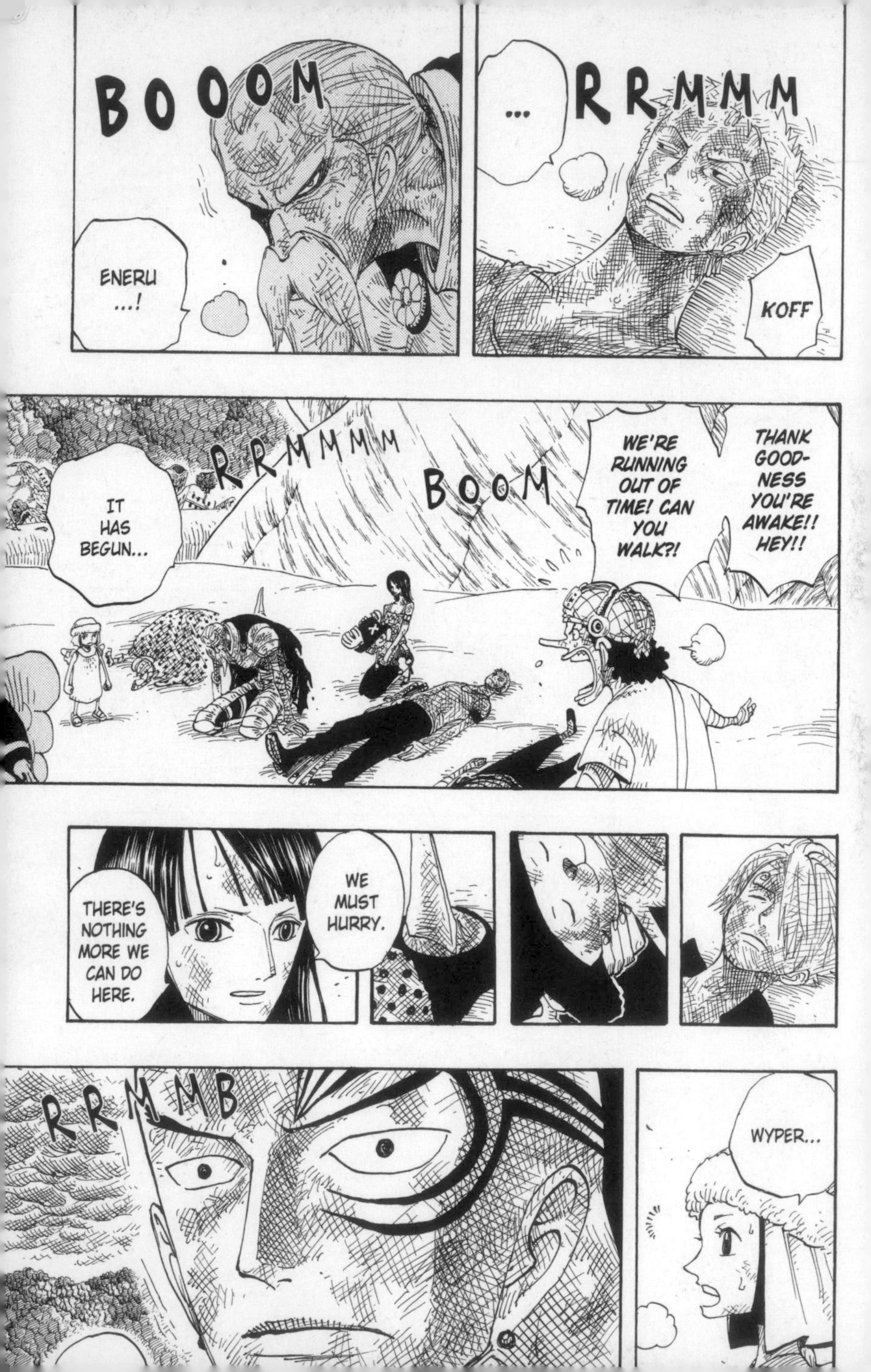
RRMMM
...
KOFF
BOOOM
ENERU ...!
THANK GOOD-NESS YOU'RE AWAKE!! HEY!!
WE'RE RUNNING OUT OF TIME! CAN YOU WALK?!
BOOM
RRMMMM
IT HAS BEGUN...
WE MUST HURRY.
THERE'S NOTHING MORE WE CAN DO HERE.
WYPER...
RRMMB

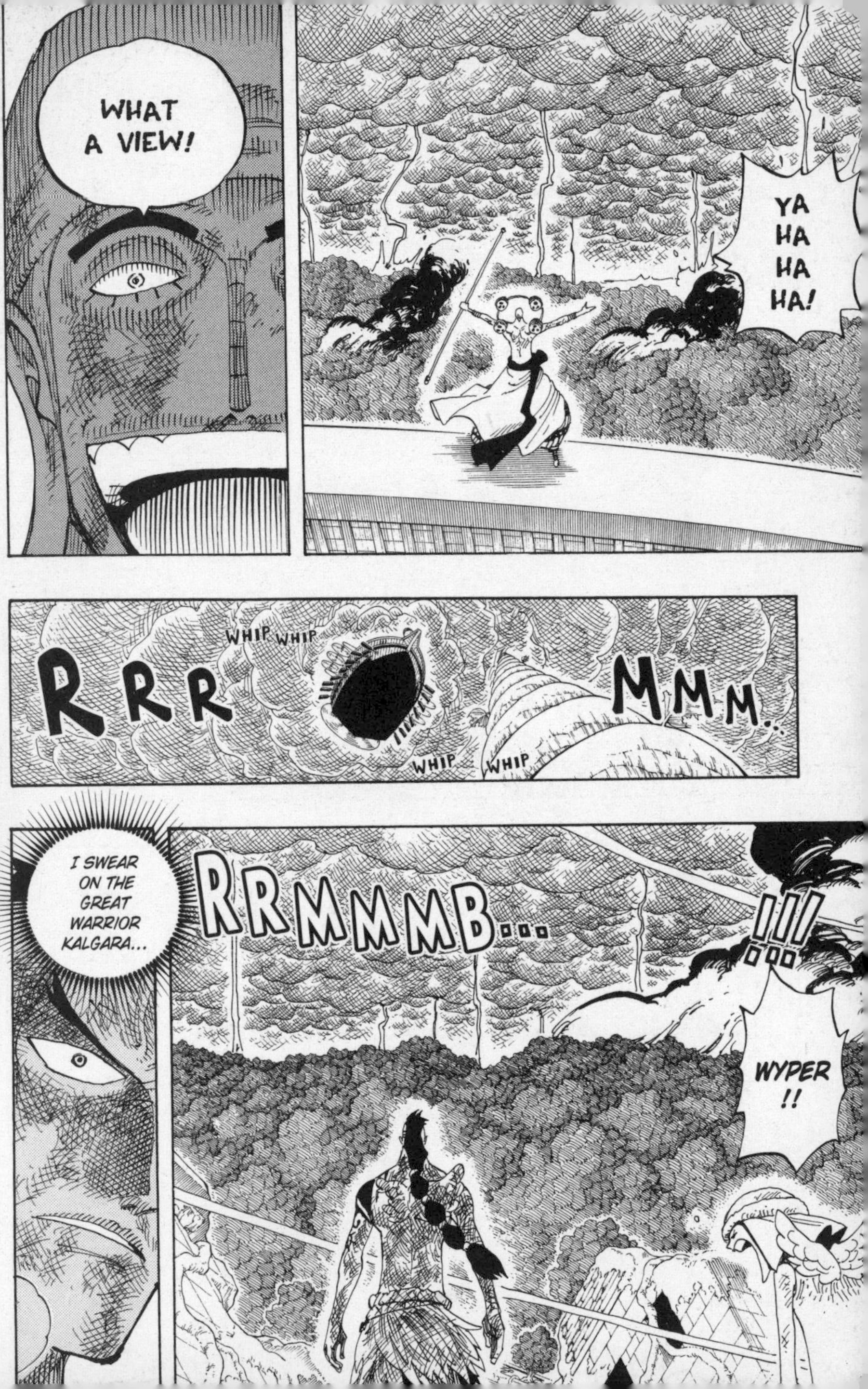
YA HA HA HA!
WHAT A VIEW!
WHIP WHIP
RRR MMM...
WHIP WHIP
RRMMMB...
!!!
WYPER !!
I SWEAR ON THE GREAT WARRIOR KALGARA...

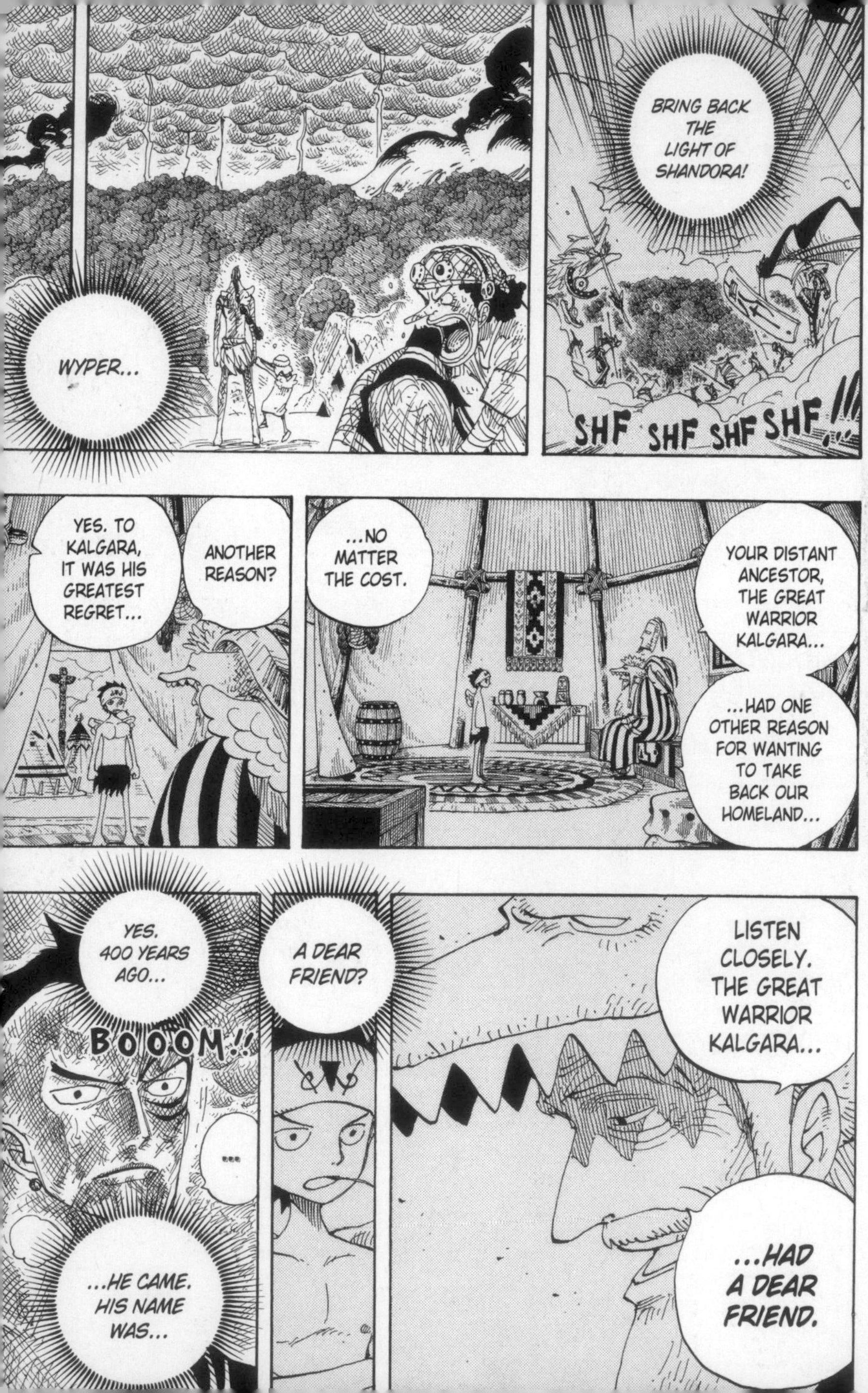
BRING BACK THE LIGHT OF SHANDORA!
SHF SHF SHF SHF!!!
WYPER...
YOUR DISTANT ANCESTOR, THE GREAT WARRIOR KALGARA...
...HAD ONE OTHER REASON FOR WANTING TO TAKE BACK OUR HOMELAND...
...NO MATTER THE COST.
ANOTHER REASON?
YES. TO KALGARA, IT WAS HIS GREATEST REGRET...
LISTEN CLOSELY. THE GREAT WARRIOR KALGARA...
...HAD A DEAR FRIEND.
A DEAR FRIEND?
YES. 400 YEARS AGO...
BOOOM!!
...
...HE CAME. HIS NAME WAS...

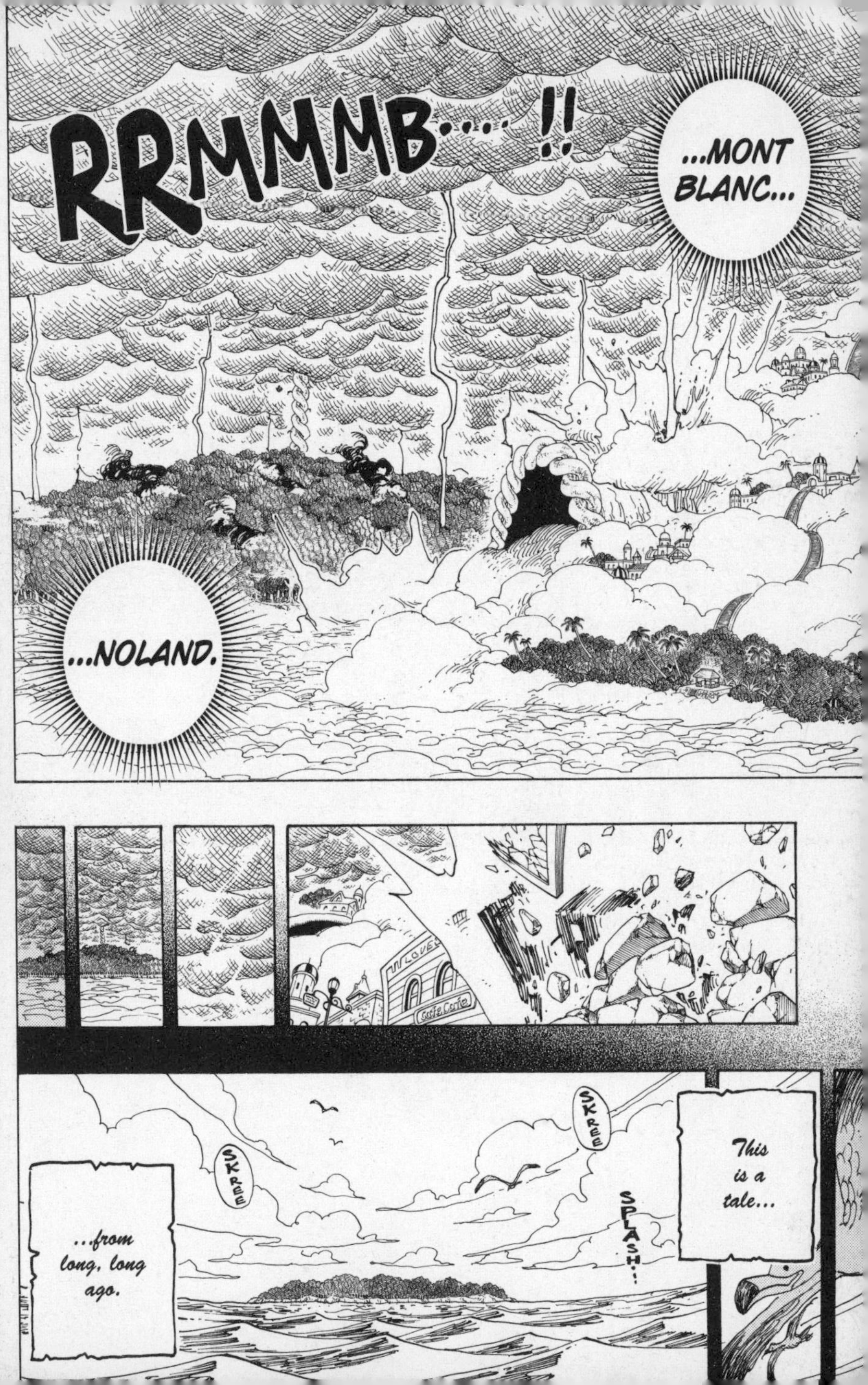
...MONT BLANC...
RRMMMB.....!!
...NOLAND.
This is a tale...
SKREE
SPLASH!!
SKREE
...from long, long ago.

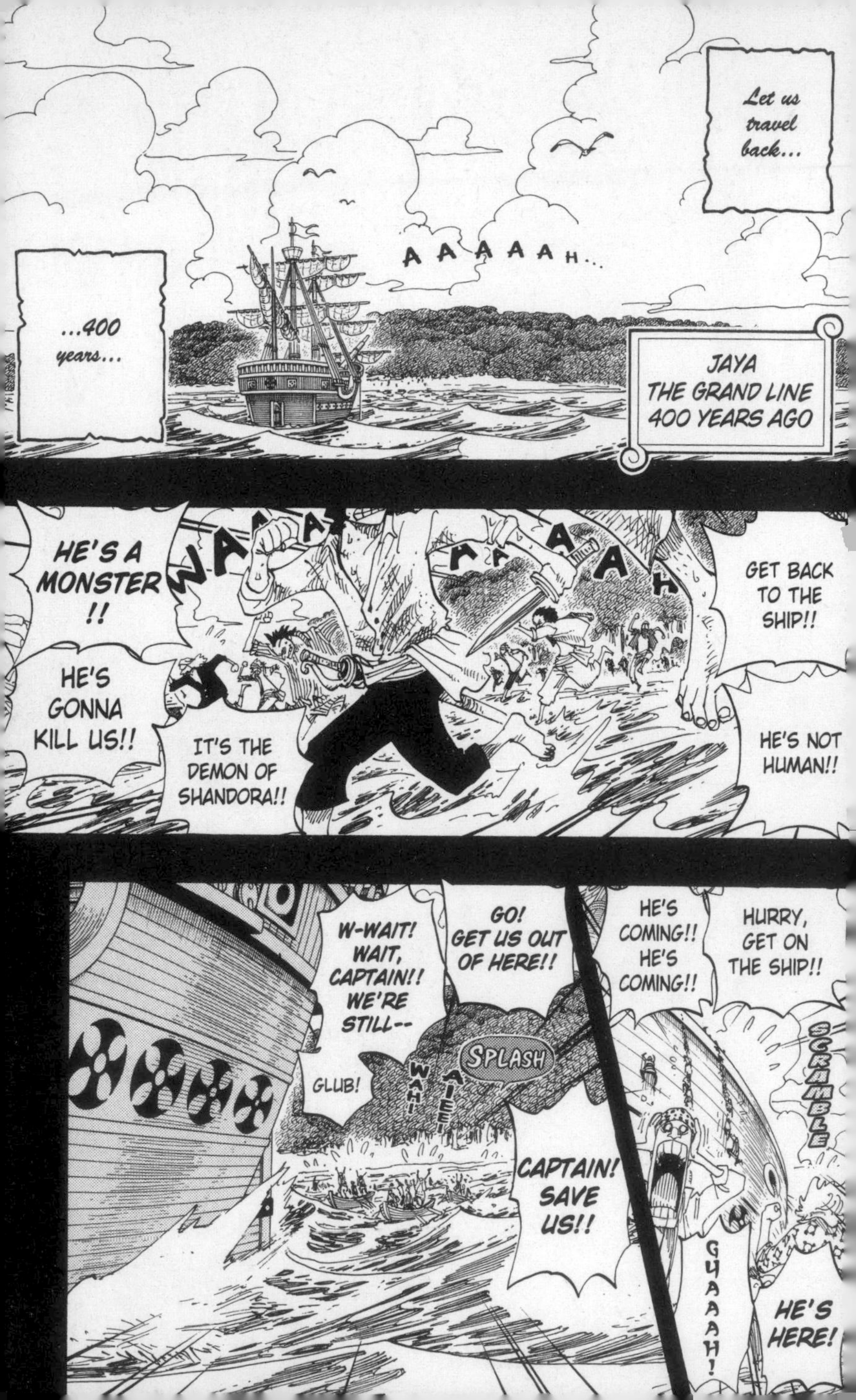
Let us travel back...
AAAAAH...
JAYA THE GRAND LINE 400 YEARS AGO
...400 years...
GET BACK TO THE SHIP!!
WAAAAAAH
HE'S A MONSTER!!
HE'S NOT HUMAN!!
IT'S THE DEMON OF SHANDORA!!
HE'S GONNA KILL US!!
HURRY, GET ON THE SHIP!!
SCRAMBLE
HE'S COMING!! HE'S COMING!!
GO! GET US OUT OF HERE!!
W-WAIT! WAIT, CAPTAIN!! WE'RE STILL--
SPLASH
AIEEE!
GLUB!
CAPTAIN! SAVE US!!
GUAAAAH!
HE'S HERE!

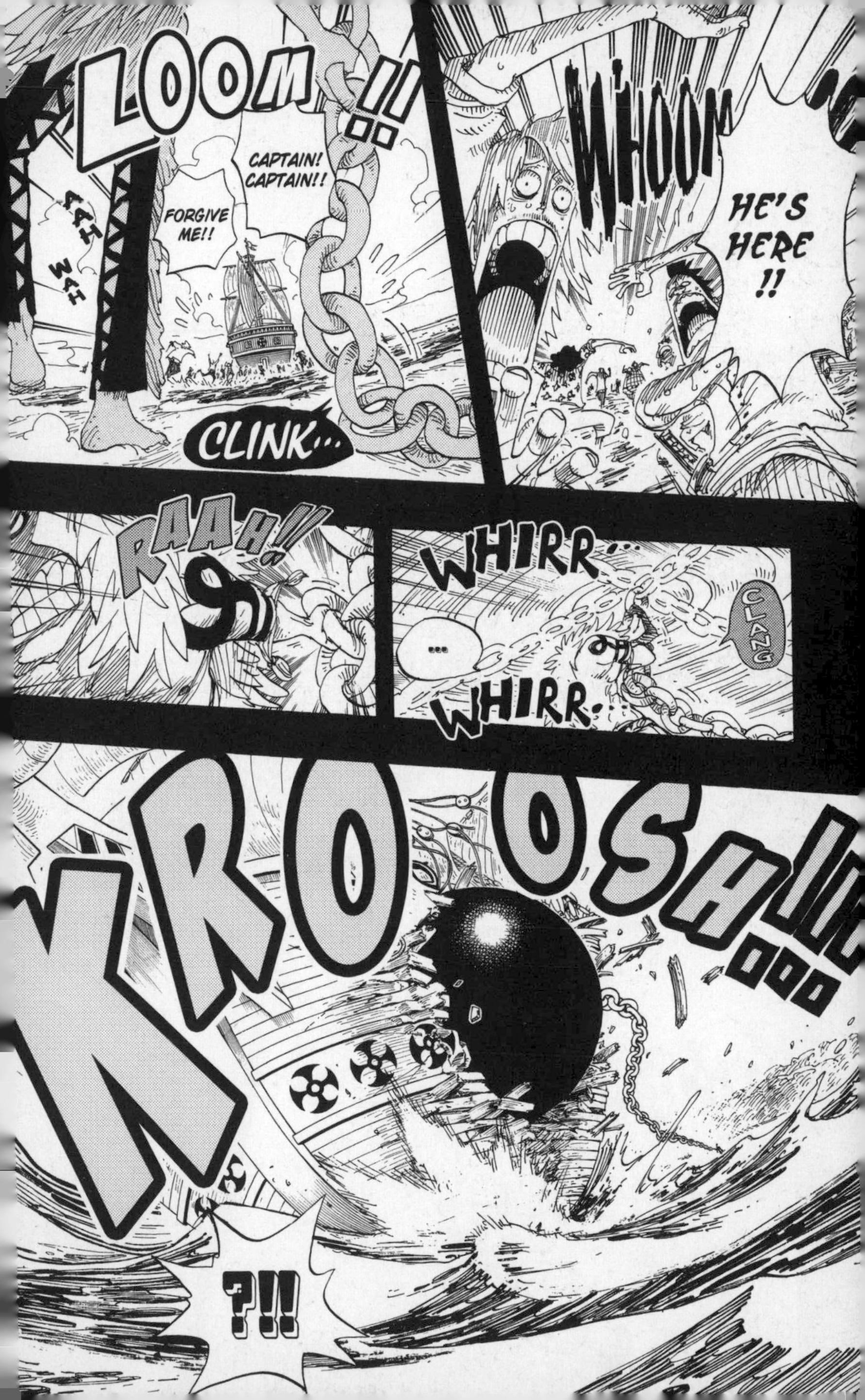

WHOOM
HE'S HERE!!
LOOM!!
CAPTAIN! CAPTAIN!!
FORGIVE ME!!
WAH WAH
CLINK...
WHIRR...
CLANG
...
WHIRR
RAAH!!
KROOSH!!
?!!

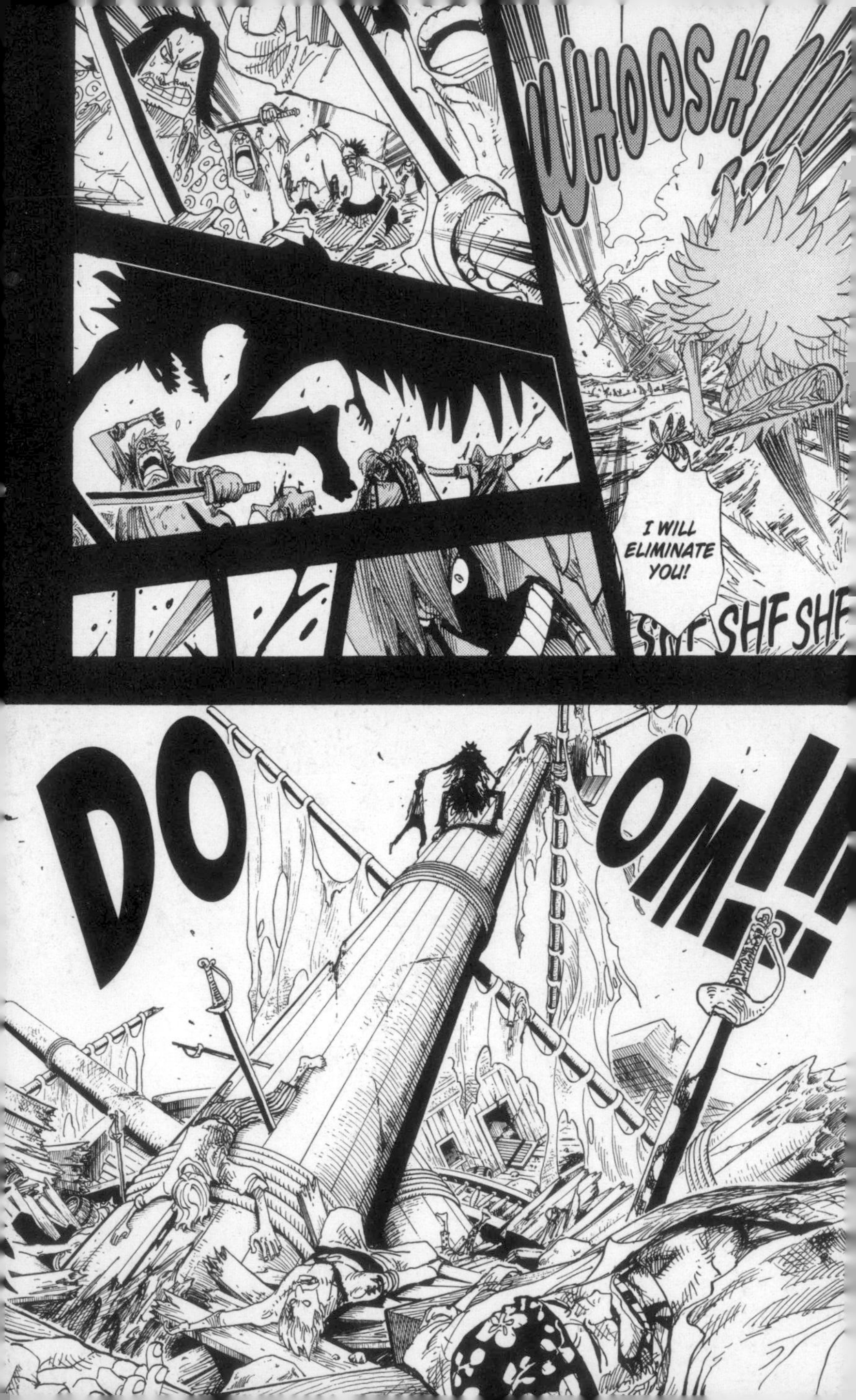
WHOOSH
I WILL ELIMINATE YOU!
SHF SHF SHF
DOOM!!

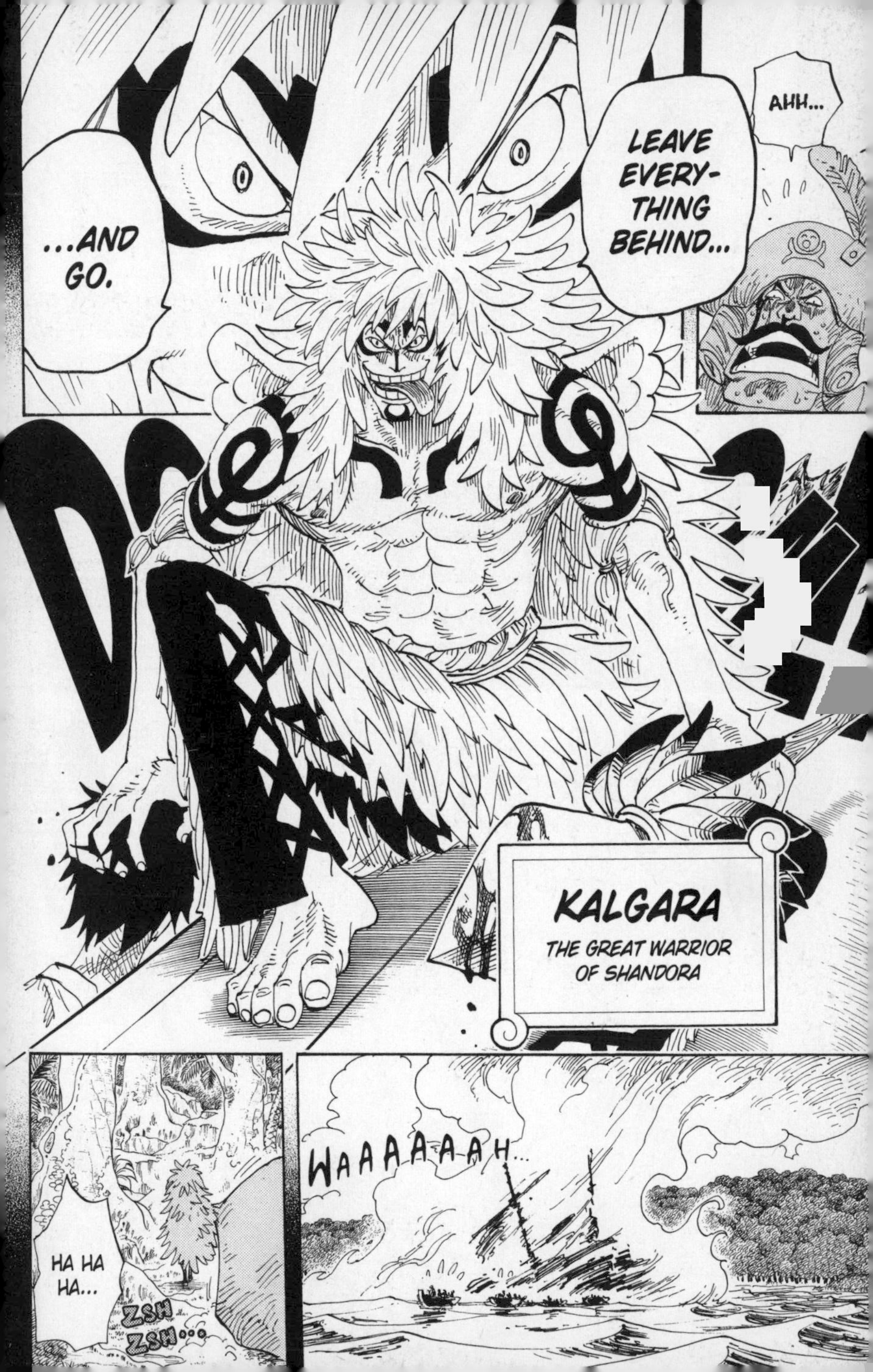
AHH...
LEAVE EVERYTHING BEHIND...
...AND GO.
KALGARA
THE GREAT WARRIOR OF SHANDORA
WAAAAAAH...
HA HA HA...
ZSH ZSH...

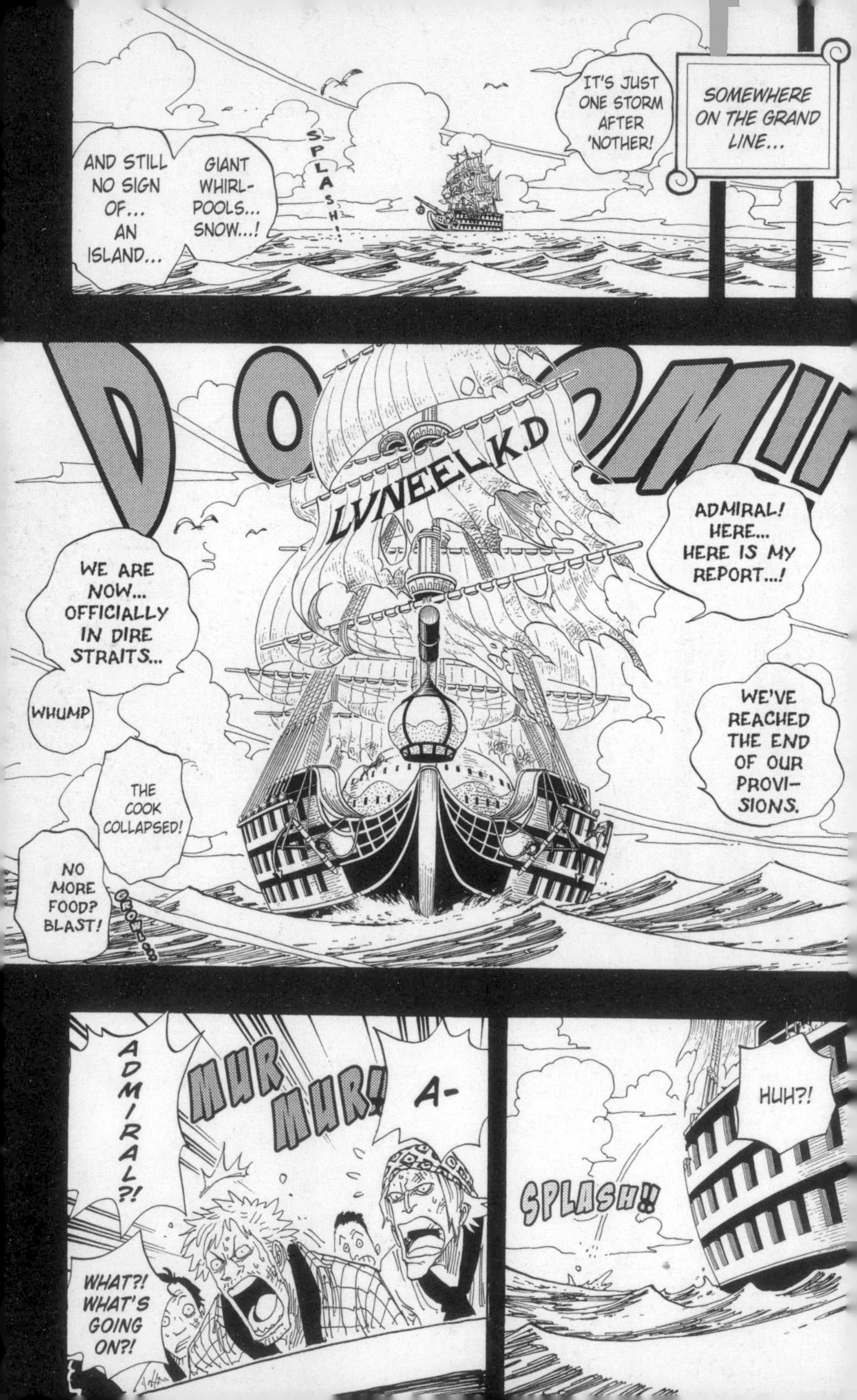
SOMEWHERE ON THE GRAND LINE...
IT'S JUST ONE STORM AFTER 'NOTHER!
SPLASH!
GIANT WHIRLPOOLS... SNOW...!
AND STILL NO SIGN OF... AN ISLAND...
DOOM!!
LVNEEL K.D
ADMIRAL! HERE... HERE IS MY REPORT...!
WE'VE REACHED THE END OF OUR PROVISIONS.
WE ARE NOW... OFFICIALLY IN DIRE STRAITS...
WHUMP
THE COOK COLLAPSED!
NO MORE FOOD? BLAST!
GROWL
HUH?!
SPLASH!!
A-
MUR MUR!
ADMIRAL?!
WHAT?! WHAT'S GOING ON?!

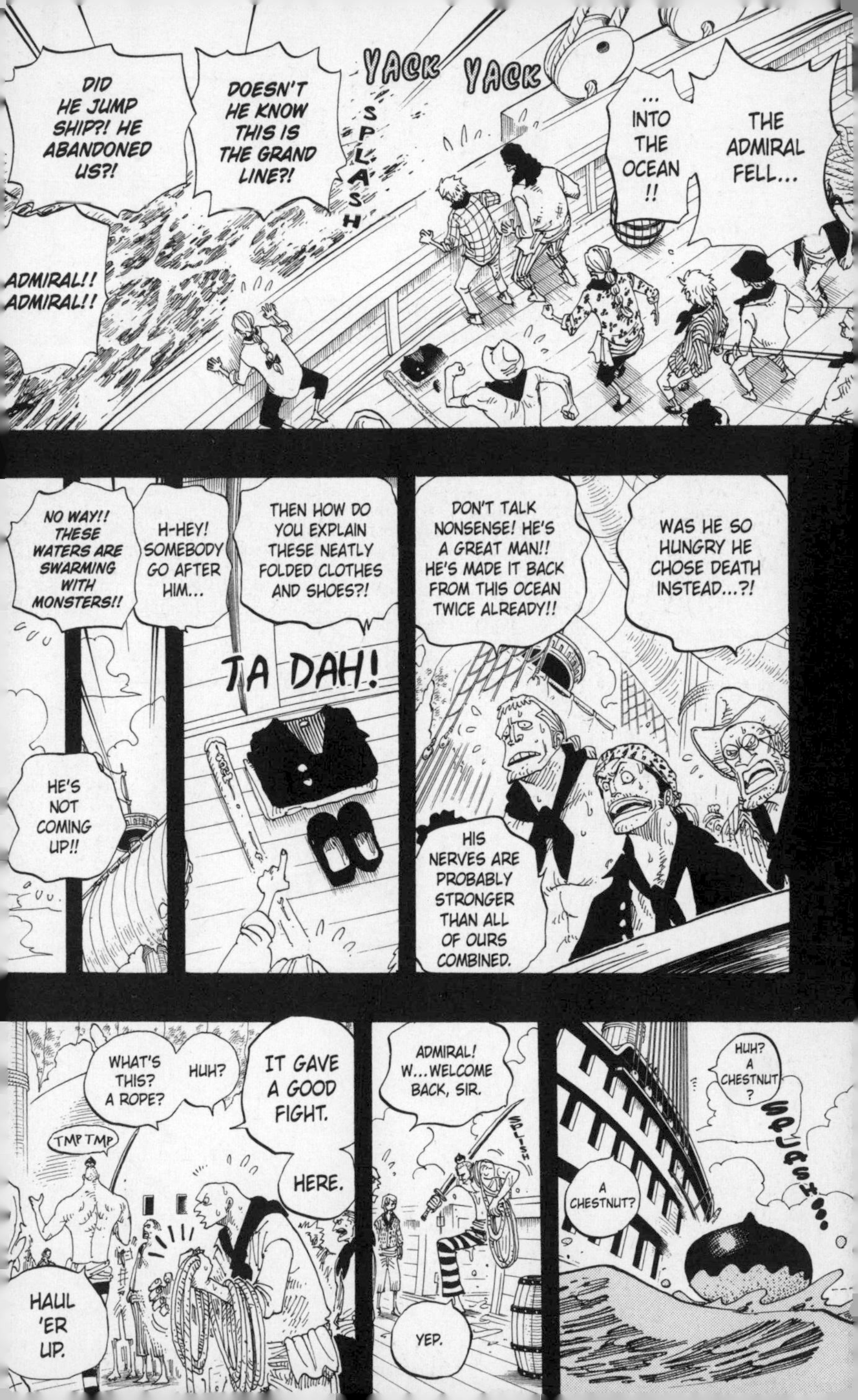
THE ADMIRAL FELL...
...INTO THE OCEAN!!
YACK YACK
SPLASH
DOESN'T HE KNOW THIS IS THE GRAND LINE?!
DID HE JUMP SHIP?! HE ABANDONED US?!
ADMIRAL!! ADMIRAL!!
WAS HE SO HUNGRY HE CHOSE DEATH INSTEAD...?!
DON'T TALK NONSENSE! HE'S A GREAT MAN!! HE'S MADE IT BACK FROM THIS OCEAN TWICE ALREADY!!
HIS NERVES ARE PROBABLY STRONGER THAN ALL OF OURS COMBINED.
THEN HOW DO YOU EXPLAIN THESE NEATLY FOLDED CLOTHES AND SHOES?!
TA DAH!
H-HEY! SOMEBODY GO AFTER HIM...
NO WAY!! THESE WATERS ARE SWARMING WITH MONSTERS!!
HE'S NOT COMING UP!!
HUH? A CHESTNUT?
SPLASH...
A CHESTNUT?
ADMIRAL! W...WELCOME BACK, SIR.
SPLISH
YEP.
IT GAVE A GOOD FIGHT.
HUH?
WHAT'S THIS? A ROPE?
TMP TMP
HERE.
HAUL 'ER UP.

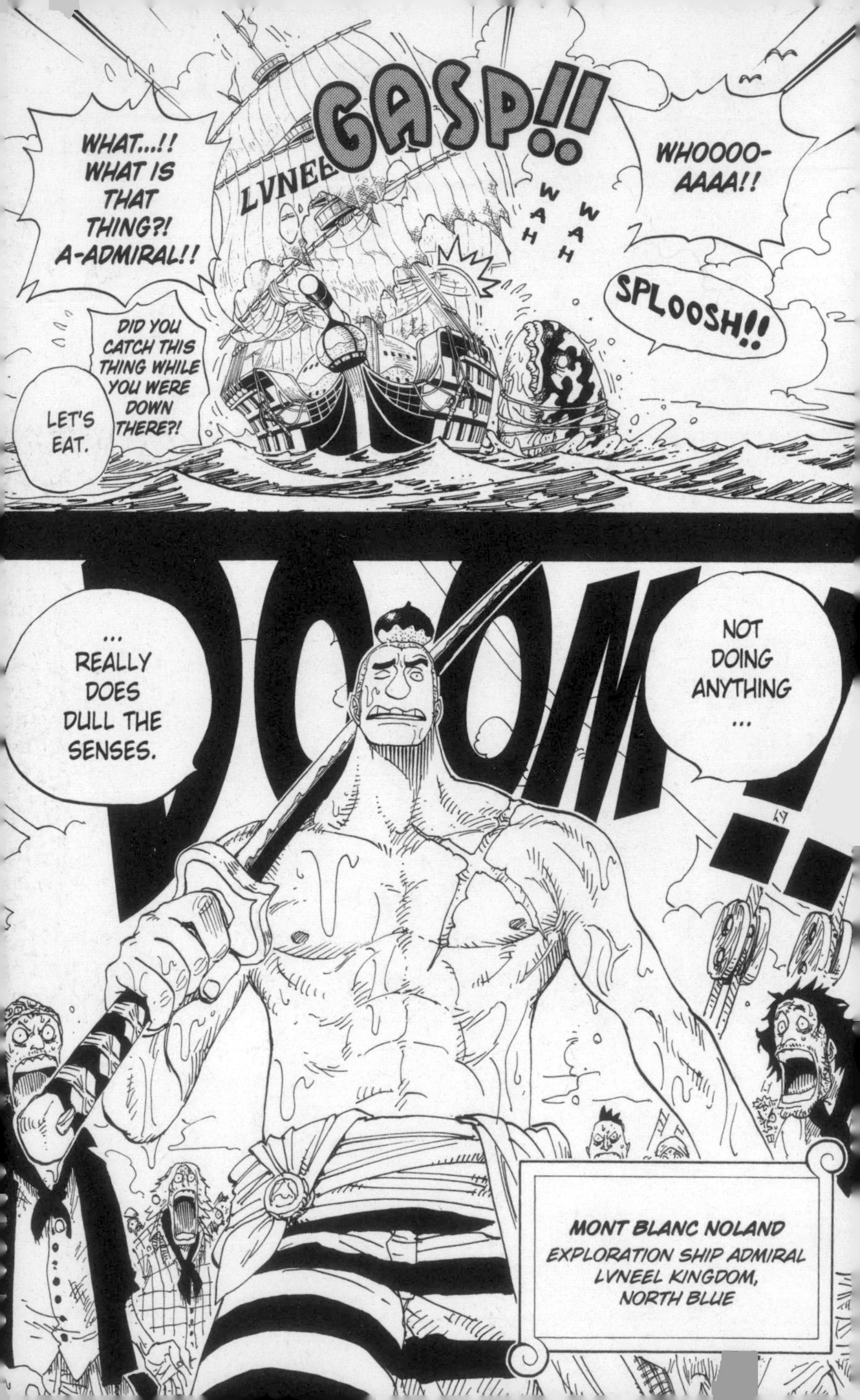
WHOOOO-AAAA!!
GASP!!
WAH WAH
WHAT...!! WHAT IS THAT THING?! A-ADMIRAL!!
SPLOOSH!!
DID YOU CATCH THIS THING WHILE YOU WERE DOWN THERE?!
LET'S EAT.
NOT DOING ANYTHING ...
... REALLY DOES DULL THE SENSES.
DOOM!!
MONT BLANC NOLAND
EXPLORATION SHIP ADMIRAL
LVNEEL KINGDOM, NORTH BLUE

Chapter 287: KAMI KILLING

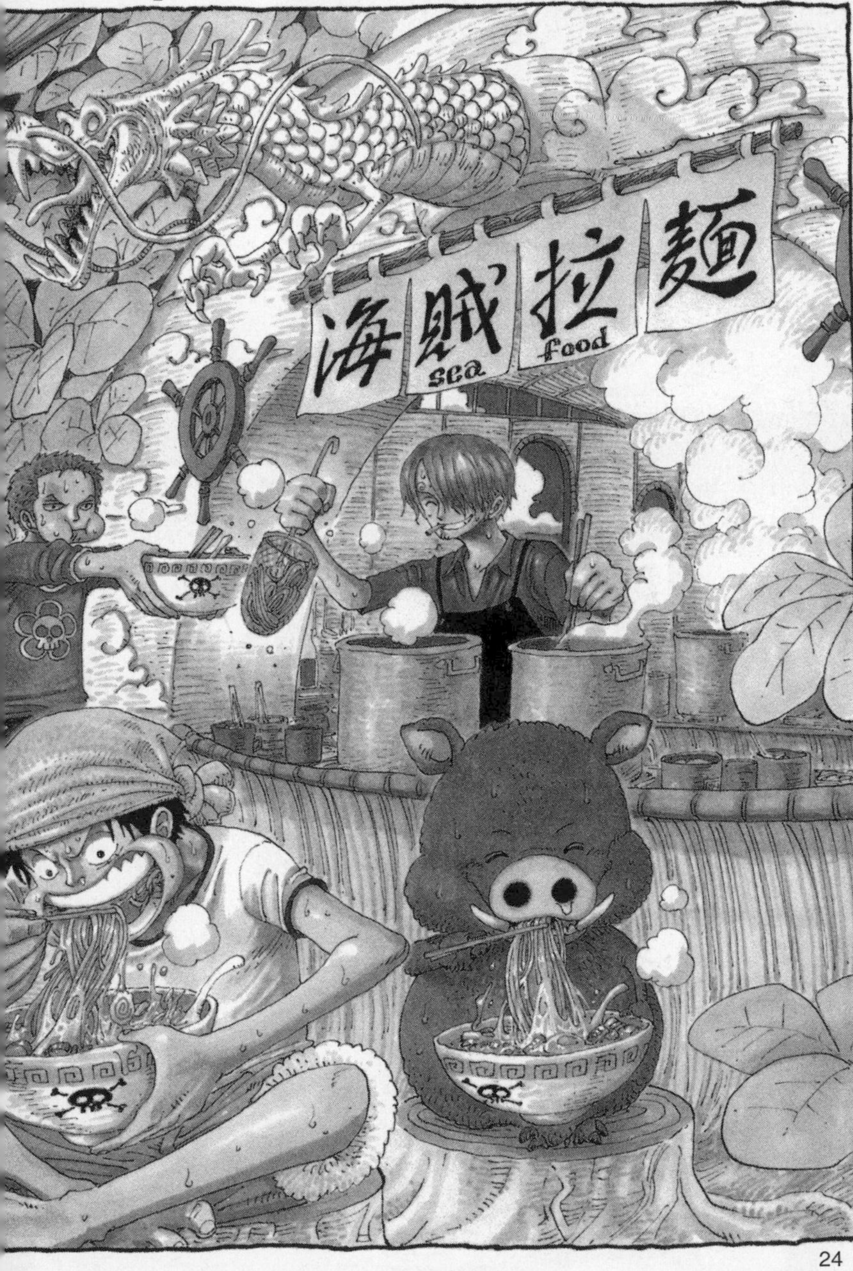
海賊拉麺
sea
food

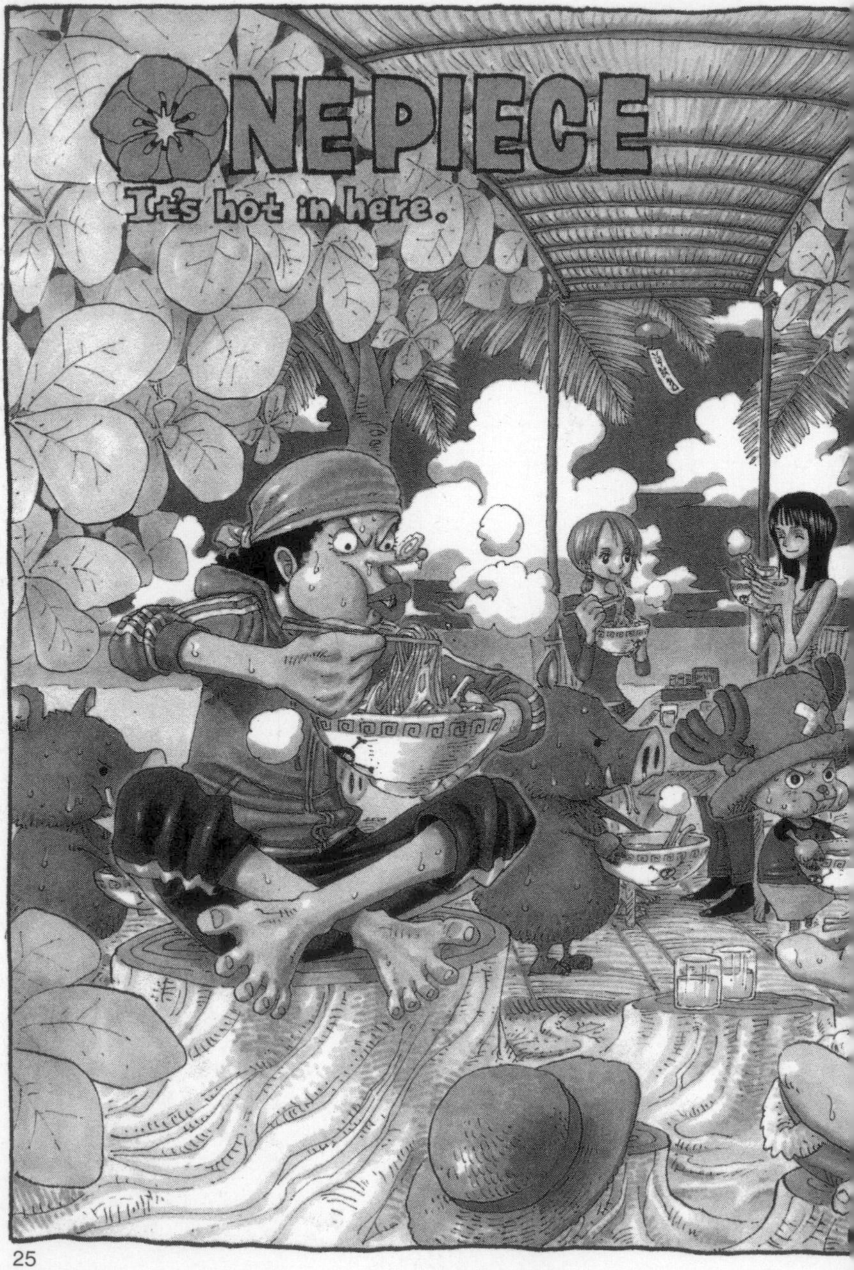
ONE PIECE
It's hot in here.

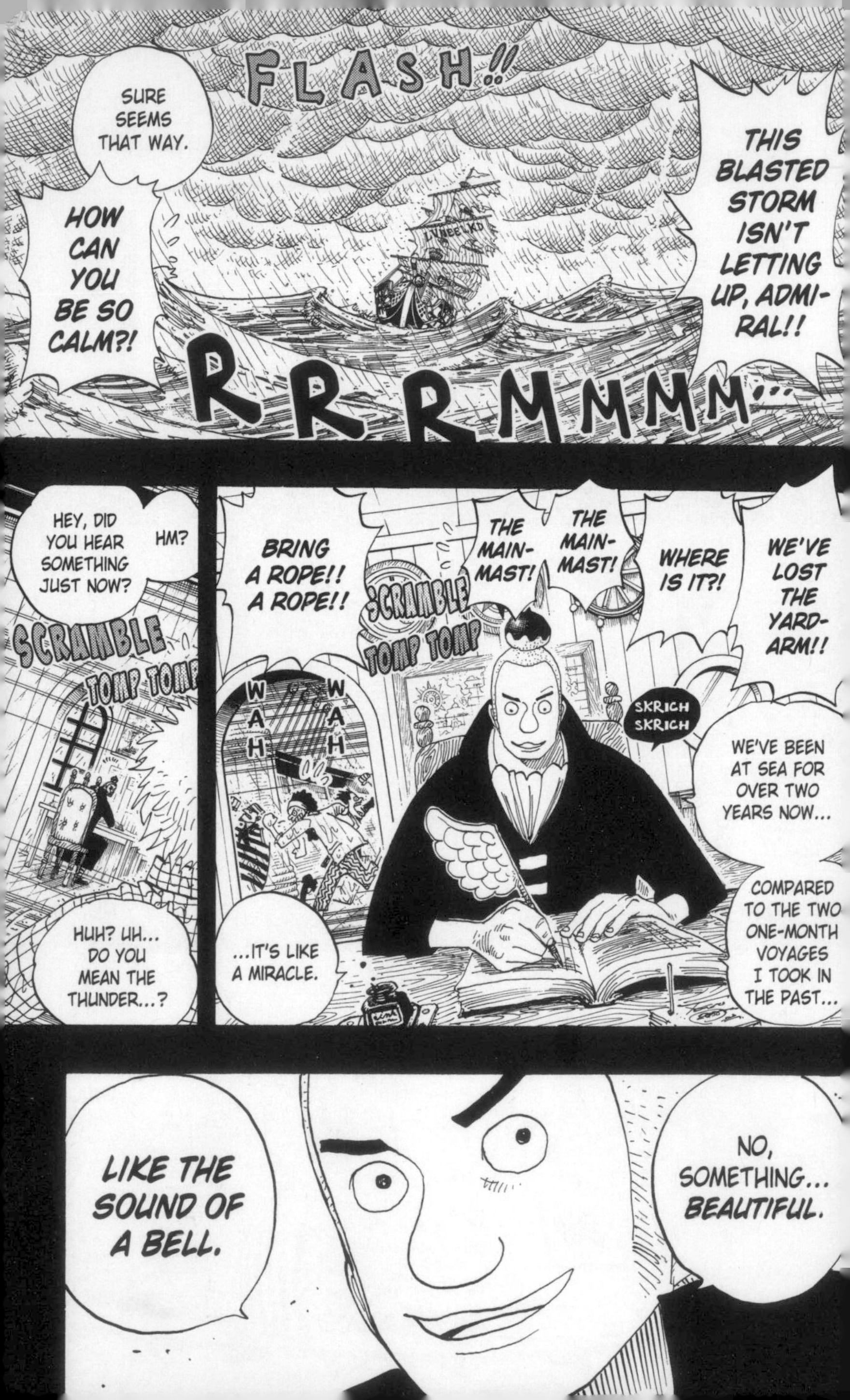
FLASH!!
THIS BLASTED STORM ISN'T LETTING UP, ADMIRAL!!
HOW CAN YOU BE SO CALM?!
SURE SEEMS THAT WAY.
RRRMMMM...
WE'VE LOST THE YARD-ARM!!
WHERE IS IT?!
THE MAIN-MAST!
THE MAIN-MAST!
BRING A ROPE!! A ROPE!!
SCRAMBLE
TOMP TOMP
WAH
WAH
SKRICH SKRICH
WE'VE BEEN AT SEA FOR OVER TWO YEARS NOW...
COMPARED TO THE TWO ONE-MONTH VOYAGES I TOOK IN THE PAST...
...IT'S LIKE A MIRACLE.
HM?
HEY, DID YOU HEAR SOMETHING JUST NOW?
SCRAMBLE
TOMP TOMP
HUH? UH... DO YOU MEAN THE THUNDER...?
NO, SOMETHING... BEAUTIFUL.
LIKE THE SOUND OF A BELL.

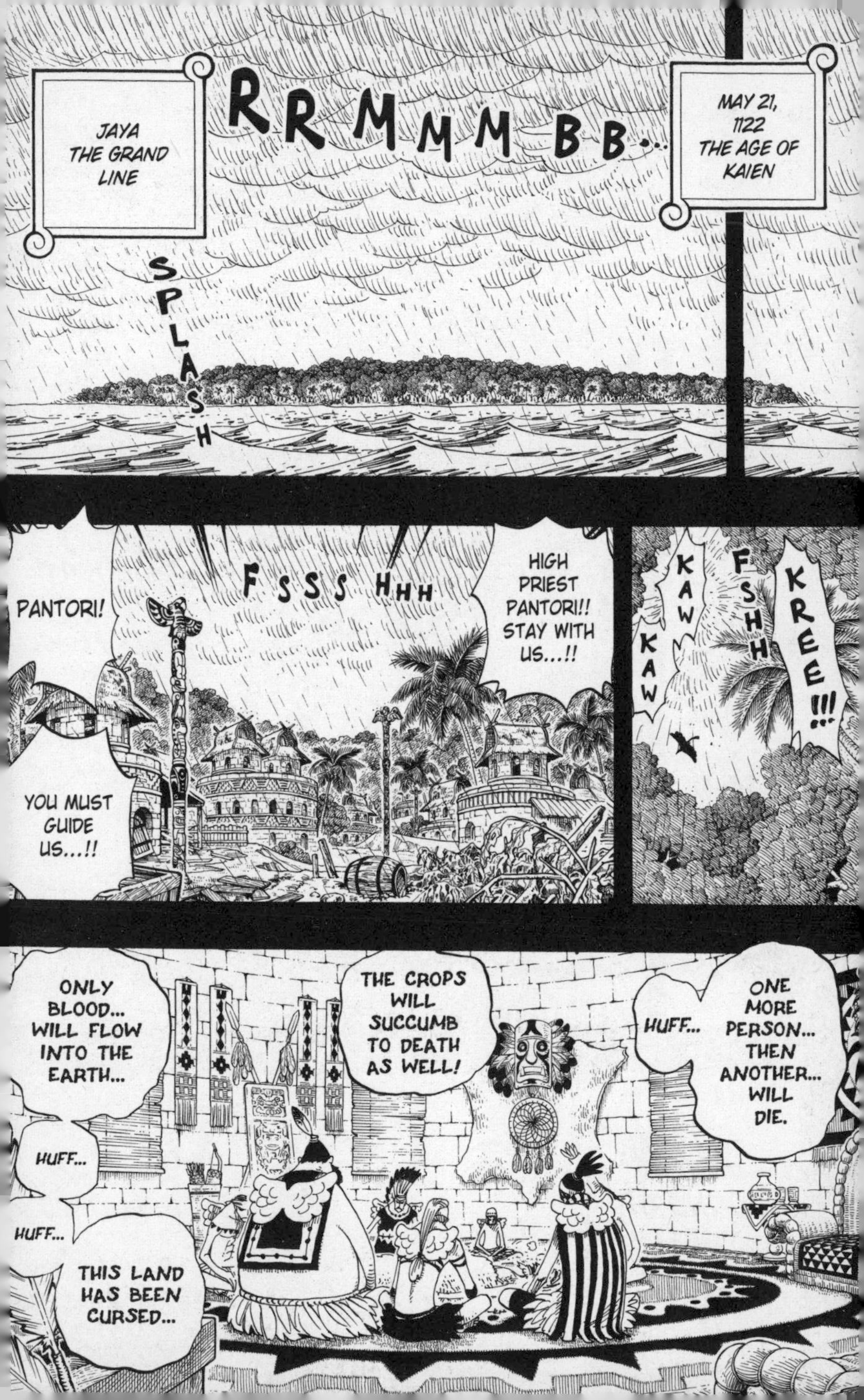
MAY 21, 1122 THE AGE OF KAIEN
JAYA THE GRAND LINE
RRMMMBB...
SPLASH
KREE!!!
FSHH
KAW
KAW
KAW
HIGH PRIEST PANTORI!! STAY WITH US...!!
FSSSHHH
PANTORI!
YOU MUST GUIDE US...!!
ONE MORE PERSON... THEN ANOTHER... WILL DIE.
HUFF...
THE CROPS WILL SUCCUMB TO DEATH AS WELL!
ONLY BLOOD... WILL FLOW INTO THE EARTH...
HUFF...
HUFF...
THIS LAND HAS BEEN CURSED...

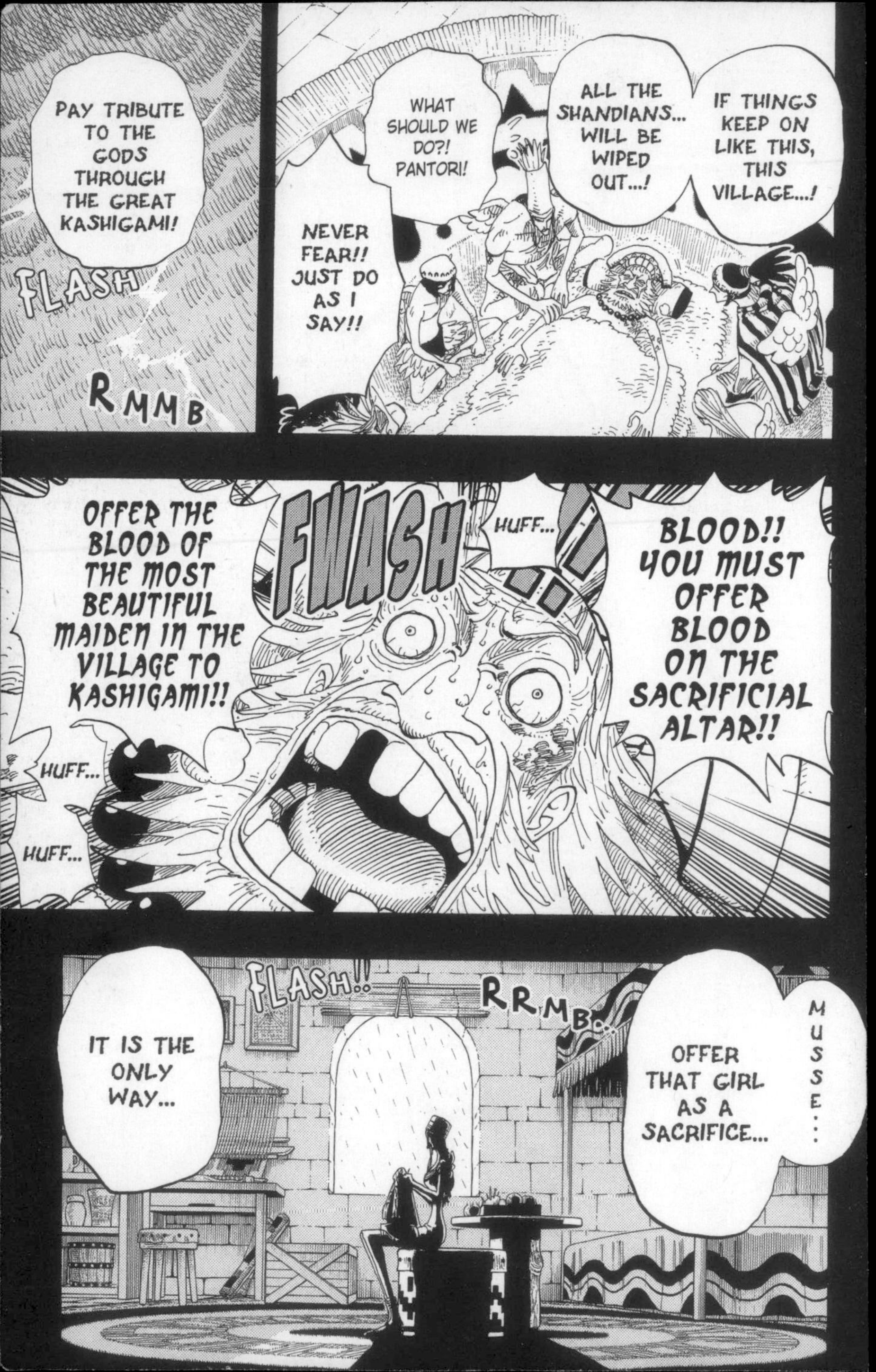
IF THINGS KEEP ON LIKE THIS, THIS VILLAGE...!
ALL THE SHANDIANS... WILL BE WIPED OUT...!
WHAT SHOULD WE DO?! PANTORI!
NEVER FEAR!! JUST DO AS I SAY!!
PAY TRIBUTE TO THE GODS THROUGH THE GREAT KASHIGAMI!
FLASH
RMMB
BLOOD!! YOU MUST OFFER BLOOD ON THE SACRIFICIAL ALTAR!!
HUFF...
FWASH
OFFER THE BLOOD OF THE MOST BEAUTIFUL MAIDEN IN THE VILLAGE TO KASHIGAMI!!
HUFF...
HUFF...
MUSSE...
OFFER THAT GIRL AS A SACRIFICE...
RRMB..
FLASH!!
IT IS THE ONLY WAY...

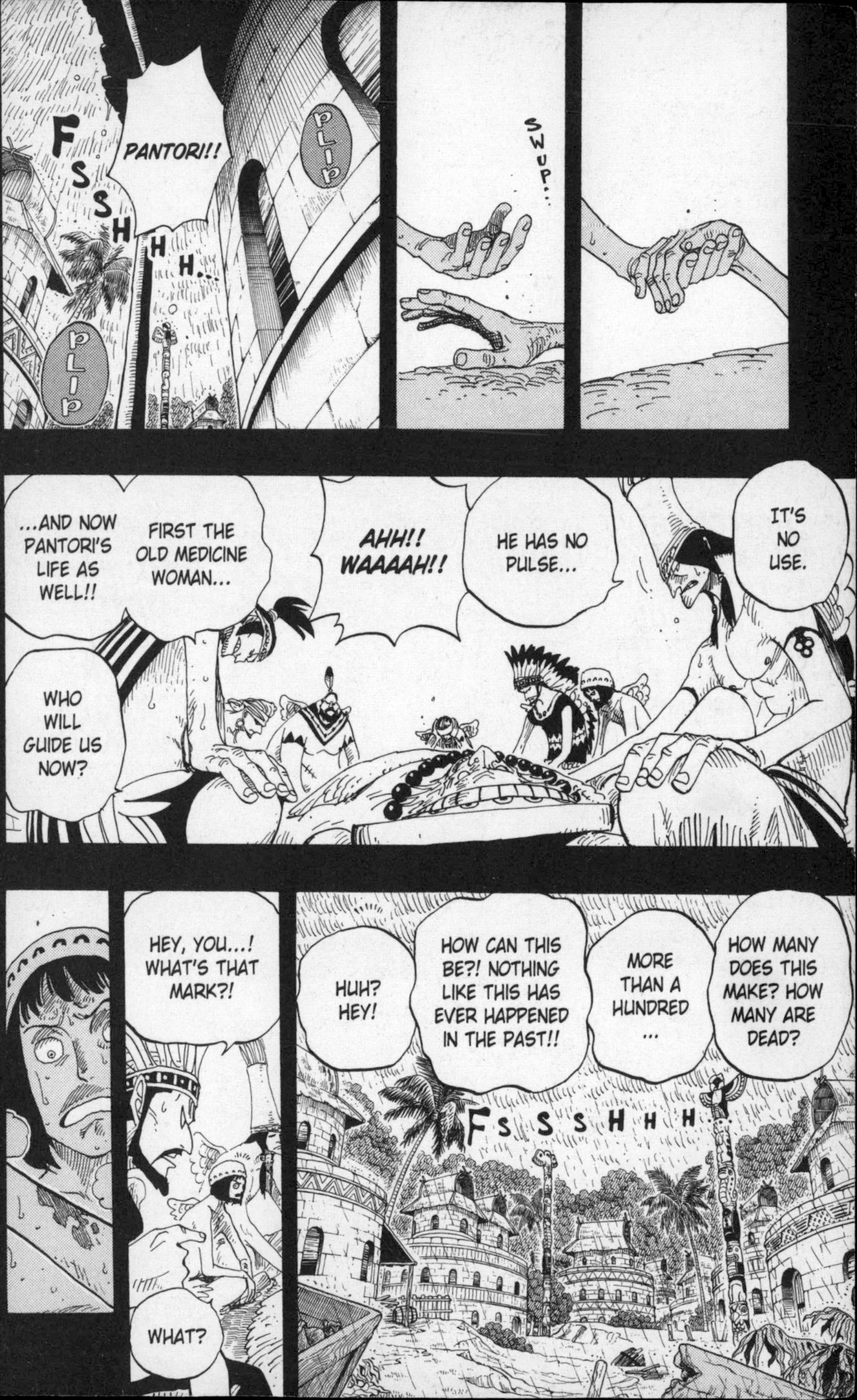
SWUP...
PANTORI!!
FSSHHH...
PLIP
PLIP
IT'S NO USE.
HE HAS NO PULSE...
AHH!! WAAAAH!!
FIRST THE OLD MEDICINE WOMAN...
...AND NOW PANTORI'S LIFE AS WELL!!
WHO WILL GUIDE US NOW?
HOW MANY DOES THIS MAKE? HOW MANY ARE DEAD?
MORE THAN A HUNDRED...
HOW CAN THIS BE?! NOTHING LIKE THIS HAS EVER HAPPENED IN THE PAST!!
HUH? HEY!
FSSSHHH
HEY, YOU...! WHAT'S THAT MARK?!
WHAT?

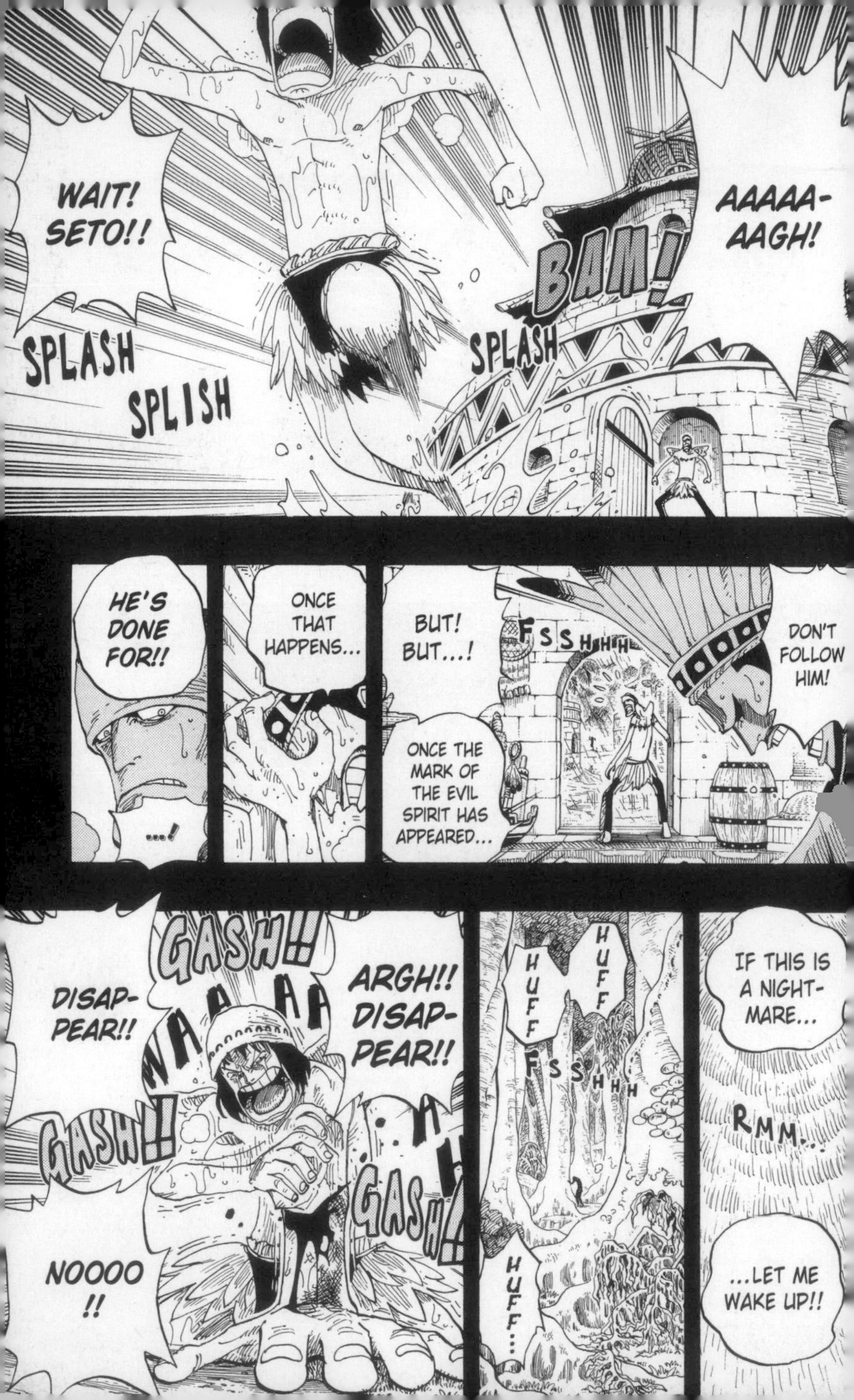
AAAAA-AAGH!
BAM!
WAIT! SETO!!
SPLASH
SPLASH
SPLISH
DON'T FOLLOW HIM!
FSSHHHH
BUT! BUT...!
ONCE THE MARK OF THE EVIL SPIRIT HAS APPEARED...
ONCE THAT HAPPENS...
HE'S DONE FOR!!
...!
IF THIS IS A NIGHT-MARE...
RMM...
...LET ME WAKE UP!!
HUFF
HUFF
FSSHHH
HUFF...
ARGH!! DISAP-PEAR!!
GASH!!
WAAAA
DISAP-PEAR!!
GASH!!
GASH!!
NOOOO!!

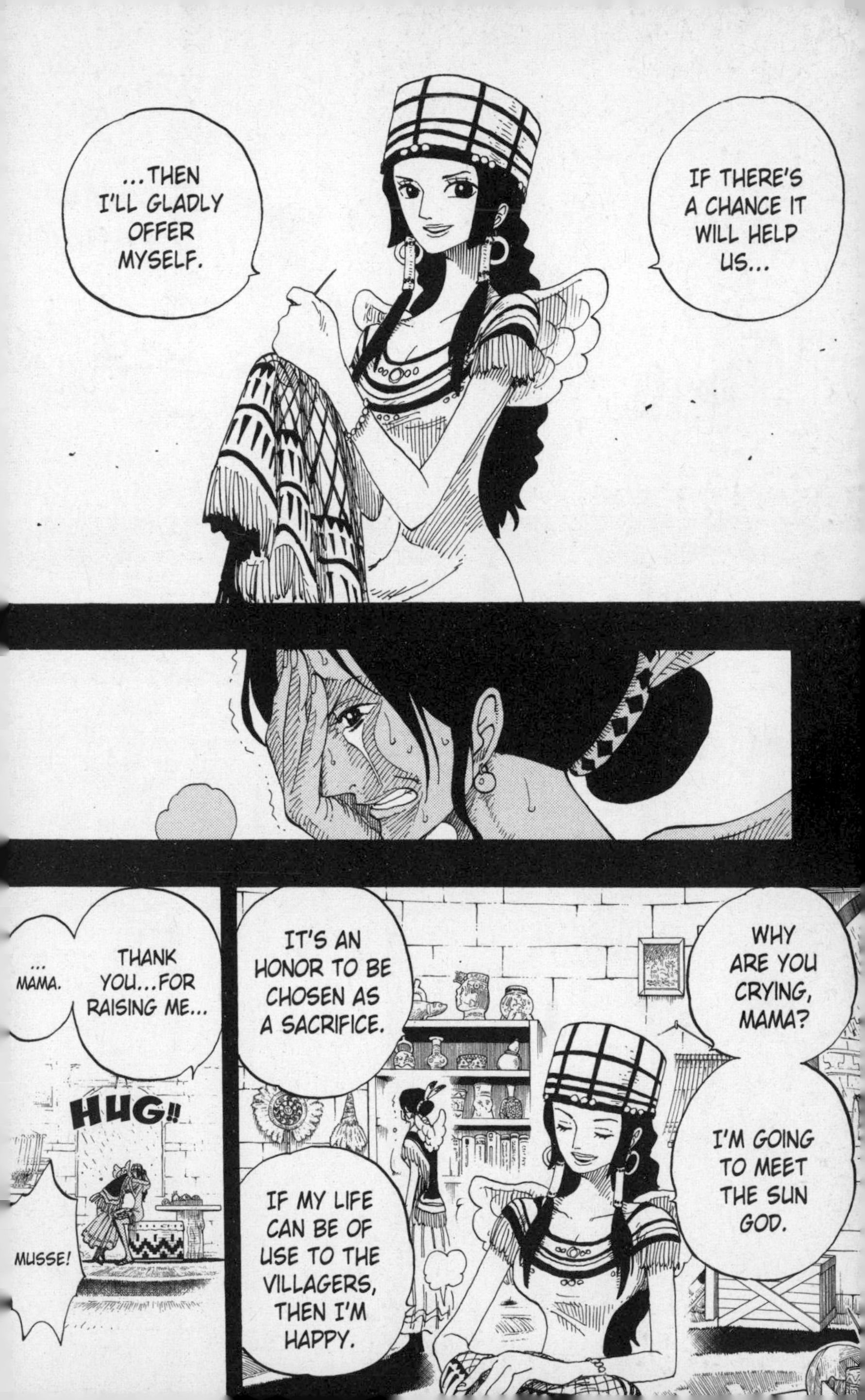
IF THERE'S A CHANCE IT WILL HELP US...
...THEN I'LL GLADLY OFFER MYSELF.
WHY ARE YOU CRYING, MAMA?
I'M GOING TO MEET THE SUN GOD.
IT'S AN HONOR TO BE CHOSEN AS A SACRIFICE.
IF MY LIFE CAN BE OF USE TO THE VILLAGERS, THEN I'M HAPPY.
THANK YOU...FOR RAISING ME...
...MAMA.
HUG!!
MUSSE!

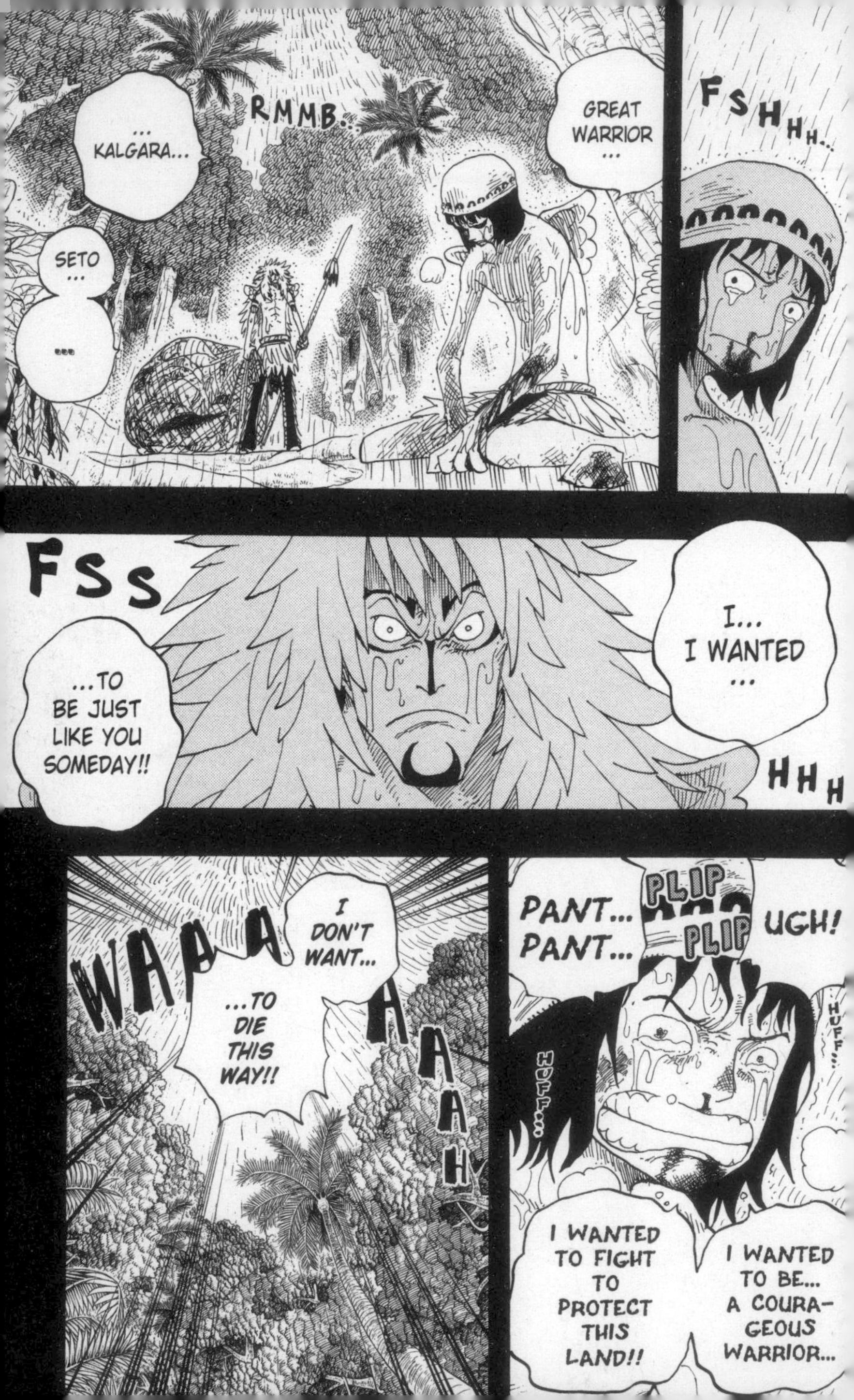
FSHHHH...
GREAT WARRIOR ...
RMMB..
... KALGARA...
SETO ...
...
I... I WANTED ...
FSS
...TO BE JUST LIKE YOU SOMEDAY!!
HHH
UGH!
PLIP PLIP
PANT... PANT...
HUFF...
HUFF...
I WANTED TO BE... A COURAGEOUS WARRIOR...
I WANTED TO FIGHT TO PROTECT THIS LAND!!
I DON'T WANT...
...TO DIE THIS WAY!!
WAAAAAAAH

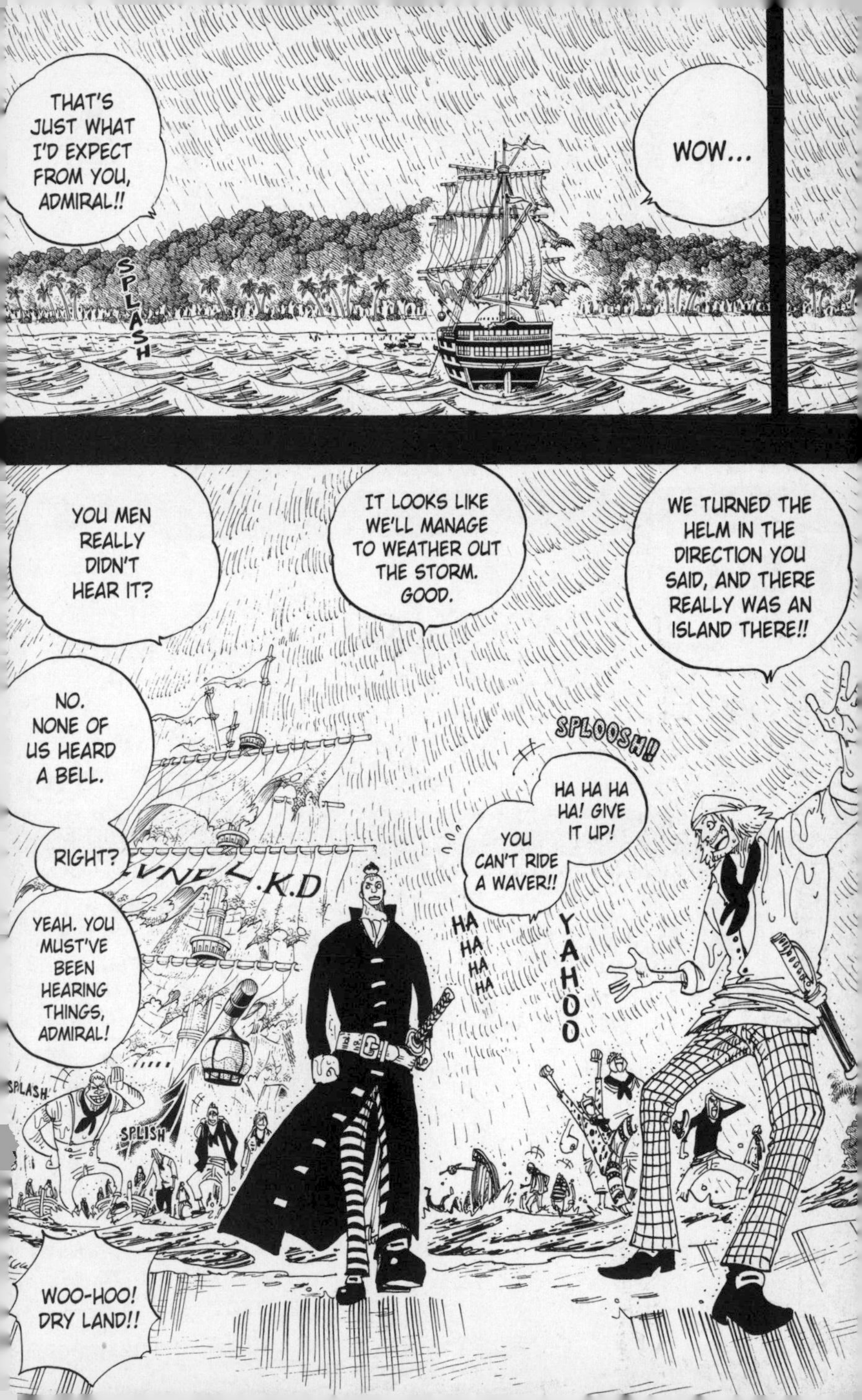
WOW...
THAT'S JUST WHAT I'D EXPECT FROM YOU, ADMIRAL!!
SPLASH
WE TURNED THE HELM IN THE DIRECTION YOU SAID, AND THERE REALLY WAS AN ISLAND THERE!!
IT LOOKS LIKE WE'LL MANAGE TO WEATHER OUT THE STORM. GOOD.
YOU MEN REALLY DIDN'T HEAR IT?
SPLOOSH!!
HA HA HA HA! GIVE IT UP!
YOU CAN'T RIDE A WAVER!!
YAHOO
HA HA HA HA
NO. NONE OF US HEARD A BELL.
RIGHT?
YEAH. YOU MUST'VE BEEN HEARING THINGS, ADMIRAL!
SPLASH
SPLISH
WOO-HOO! DRY LAND!!

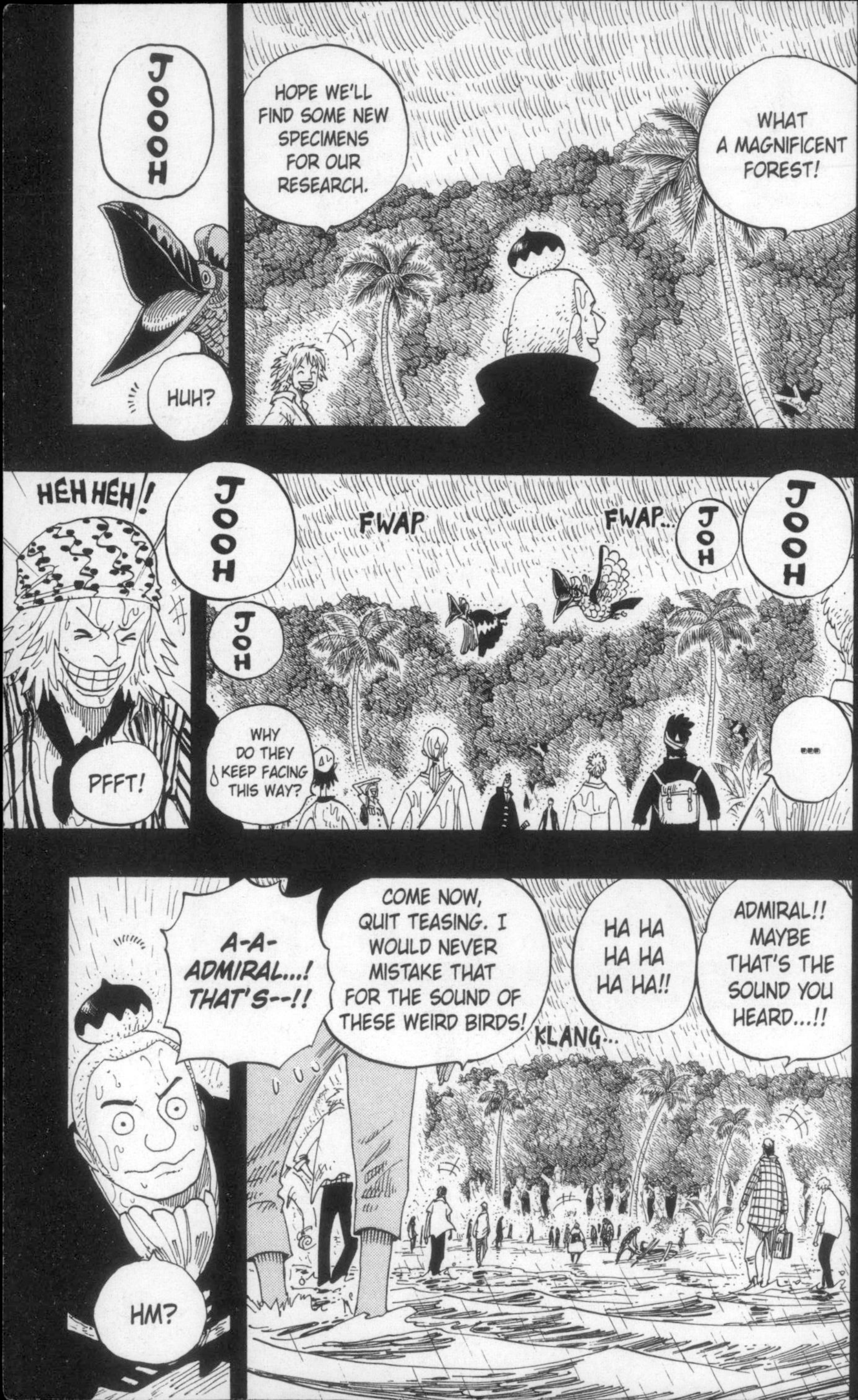
WHAT A MAGNIFICENT FOREST!
HOPE WE'LL FIND SOME NEW SPECIMENS FOR OUR RESEARCH.
JOOOH
HUH?
JOOH
JOH
FWAP...
FWAP
...
JOOH
JOH
WHY DO THEY KEEP FACING THIS WAY?
HEH HEH!!
PFFT!
ADMIRAL!! MAYBE THAT'S THE SOUND YOU HEARD...!!
HA HA HA HA HA HA!!
KLANG...
COME NOW, QUIT TEASING. I WOULD NEVER MISTAKE THAT FOR THE SOUND OF THESE WEIRD BIRDS!
A-A-ADMIRAL...! THAT'S--!!
HM?

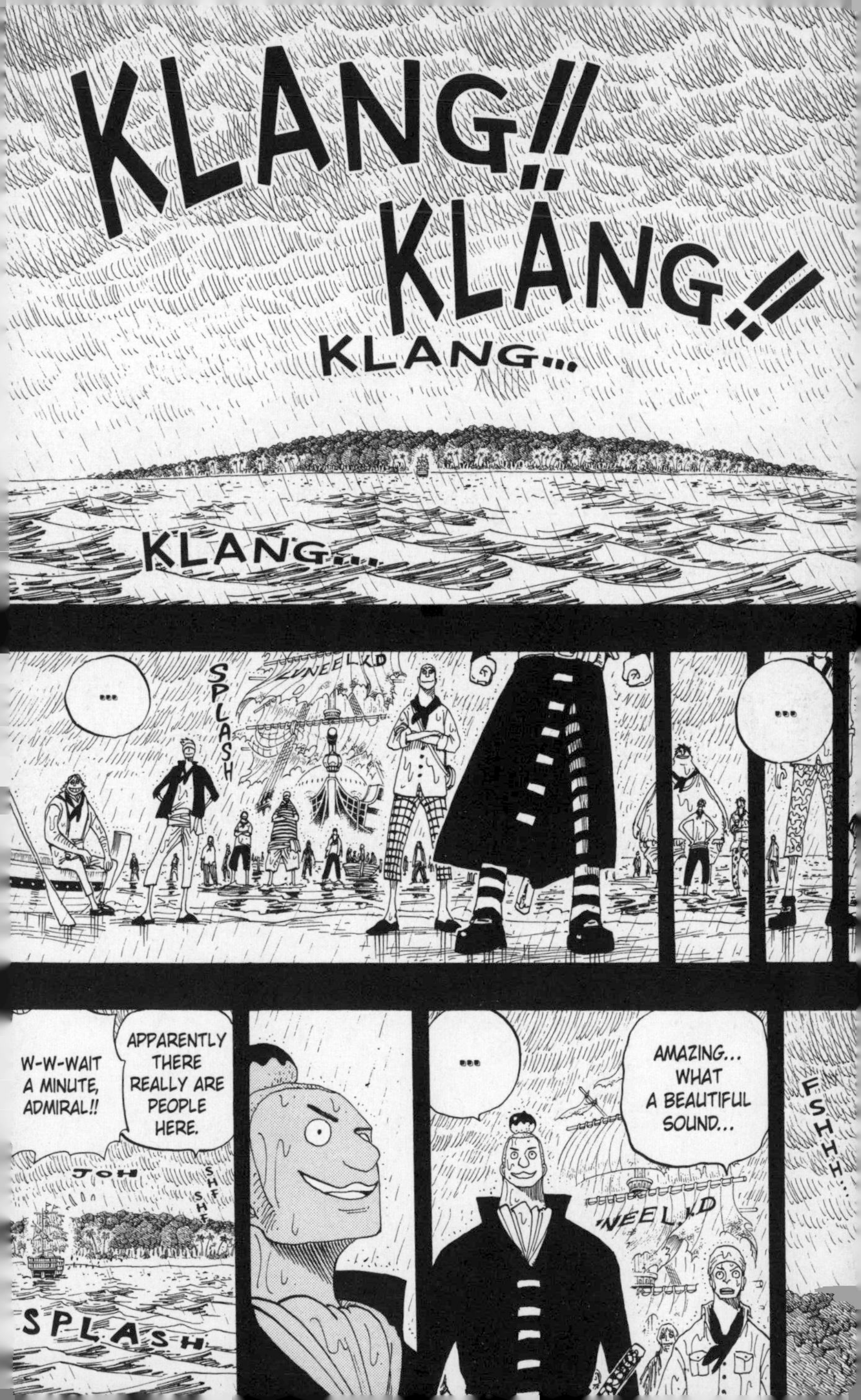
KLANG!!
KLANG!!
KLANG...
KLANG...
...
SPLASH
...
FSHHH...
AMAZING... WHAT A BEAUTIFUL SOUND...
...
APPARENTLY THERE REALLY ARE PEOPLE HERE.
W-W-WAIT A MINUTE, ADMIRAL!!
SHF SHF
JOH
SPLASH

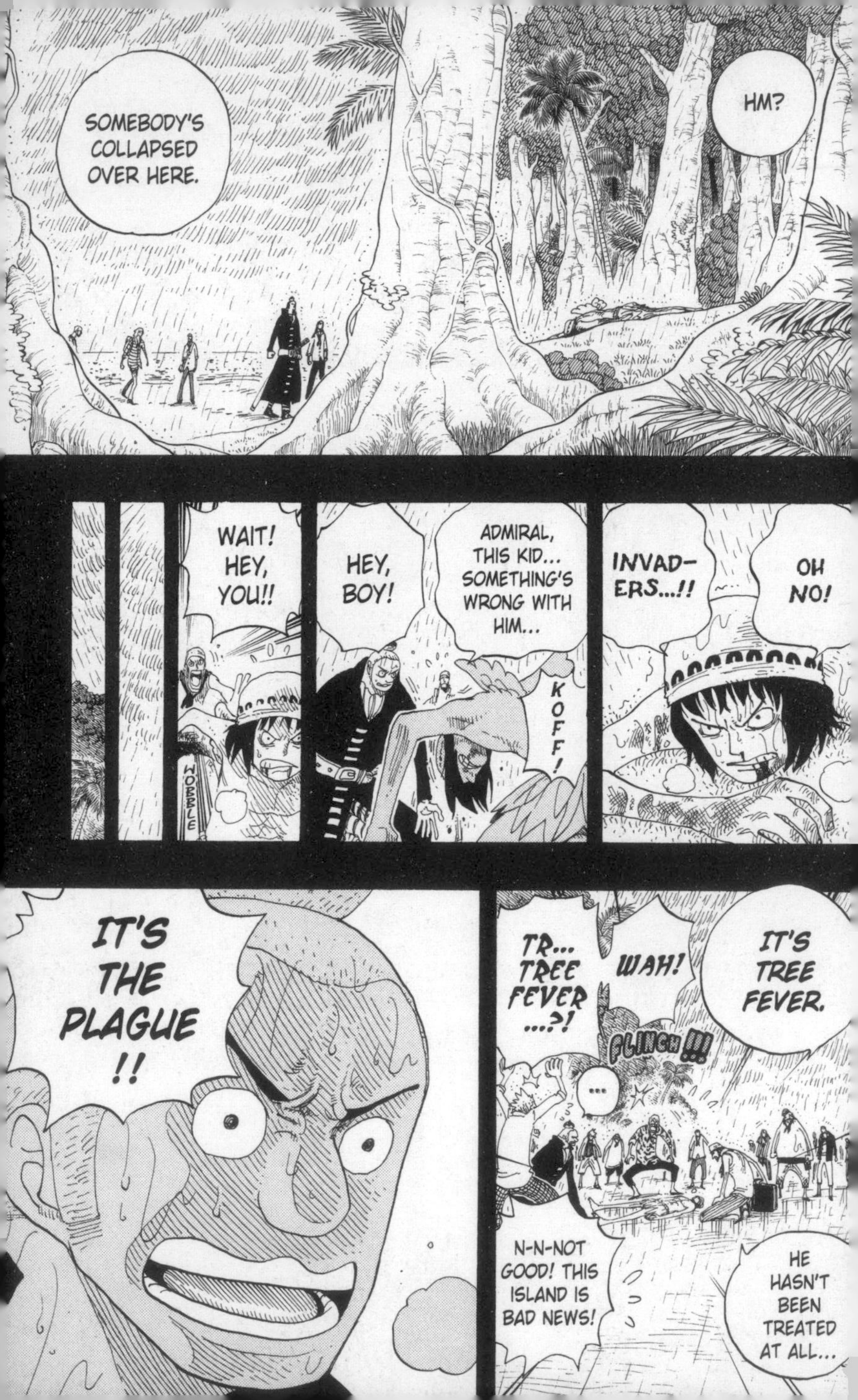
HM?
SOMEBODY'S COLLAPSED OVER HERE.
OH NO!
INVAD-ERS...!!
ADMIRAL, THIS KID... SOMETHING'S WRONG WITH HIM...
HEY, BOY!
KOFF!
WAIT! HEY, YOU!!
WOBBLE
IT'S TREE FEVER.
WAH!
TR... TREE FEVER ...?!
FLINCH!!!
...
HE HASN'T BEEN TREATED AT ALL...
N-N-NOT GOOD! THIS ISLAND IS BAD NEWS!
IT'S THE PLAGUE !!

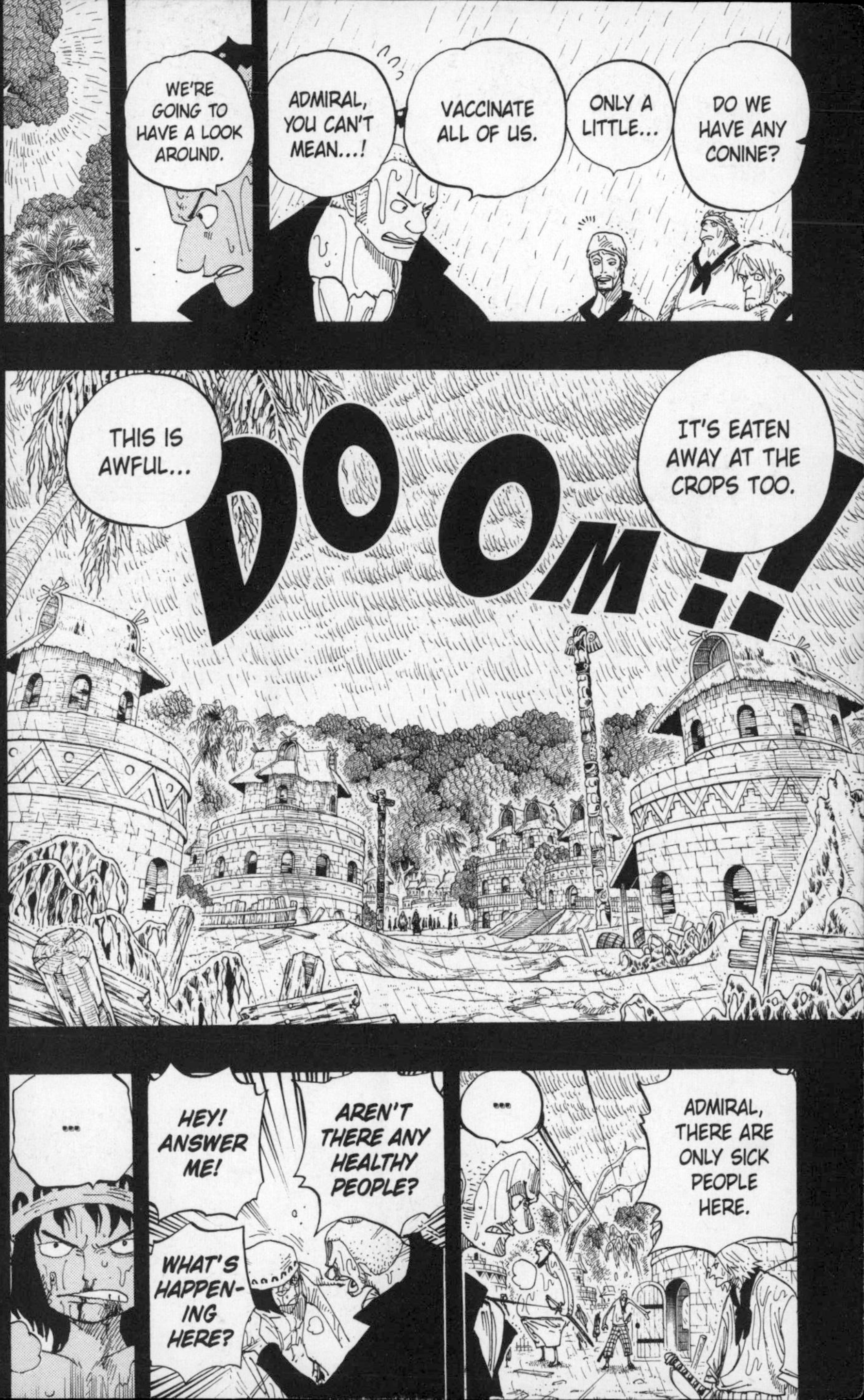
DO WE HAVE ANY CONINE?
ONLY A LITTLE...
VACCINATE ALL OF US.
ADMIRAL, YOU CAN'T MEAN...!
WE'RE GOING TO HAVE A LOOK AROUND.
IT'S EATEN AWAY AT THE CROPS TOO.
DOOM!!
THIS IS AWFUL...
ADMIRAL, THERE ARE ONLY SICK PEOPLE HERE.
...
AREN'T THERE ANY HEALTHY PEOPLE?
HEY! ANSWER ME!
WHAT'S HAPPEN-ING HERE?
...

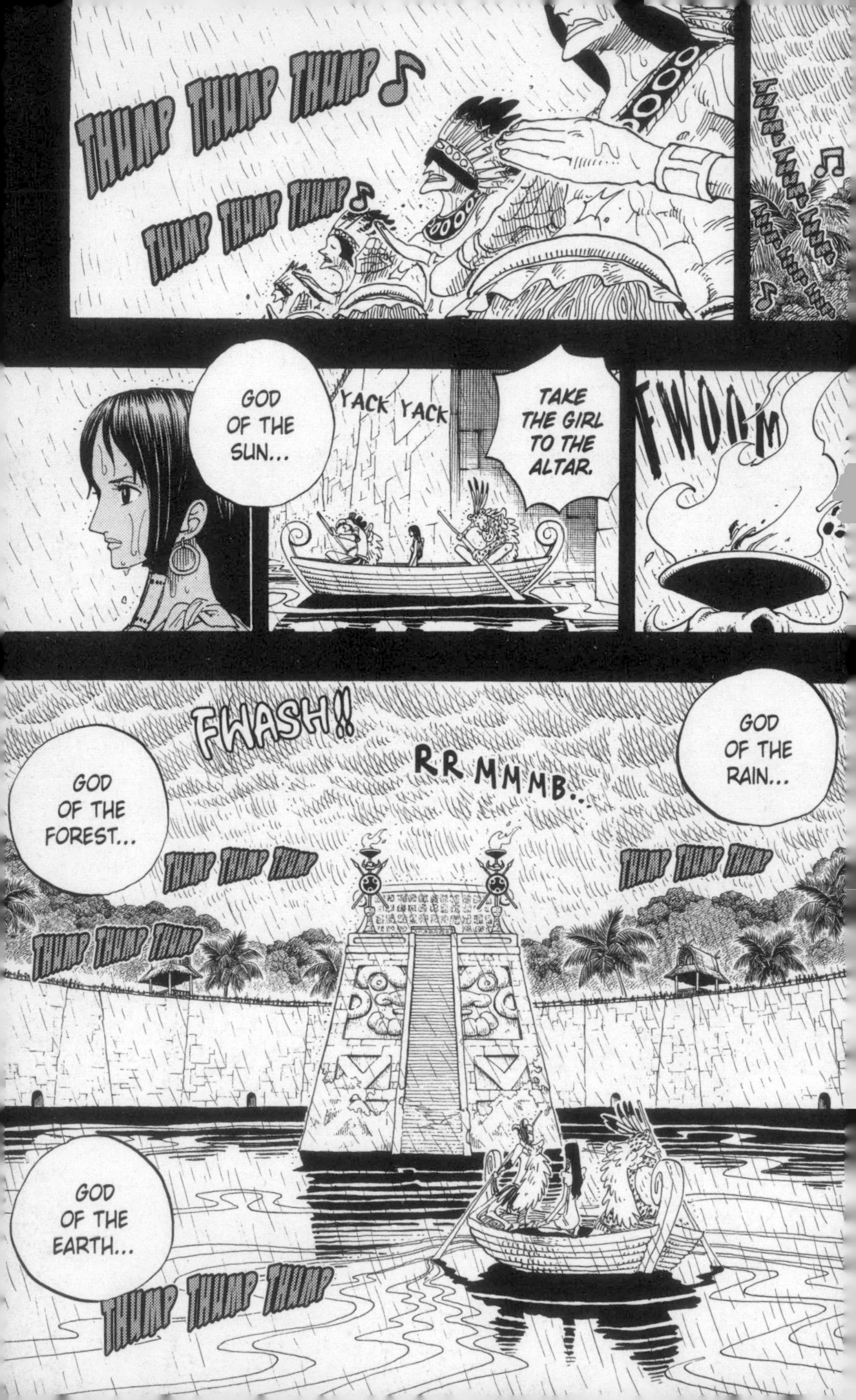
THUMP THUMP THUMP ♪
THUMP THUMP THUMP ♪
THUMP THUMP THUMP ♪
FWOOM
TAKE THE GIRL TO THE ALTAR.
YACK YACK
GOD OF THE SUN...
GOD OF THE RAIN...
THUMP THUMP THUMP
RRMMMB..
FWASH!!
GOD OF THE FOREST...
THUMP THUMP THUMP
THUMP THUMP THUMP
GOD OF THE EARTH...
THUMP THUMP THUMP

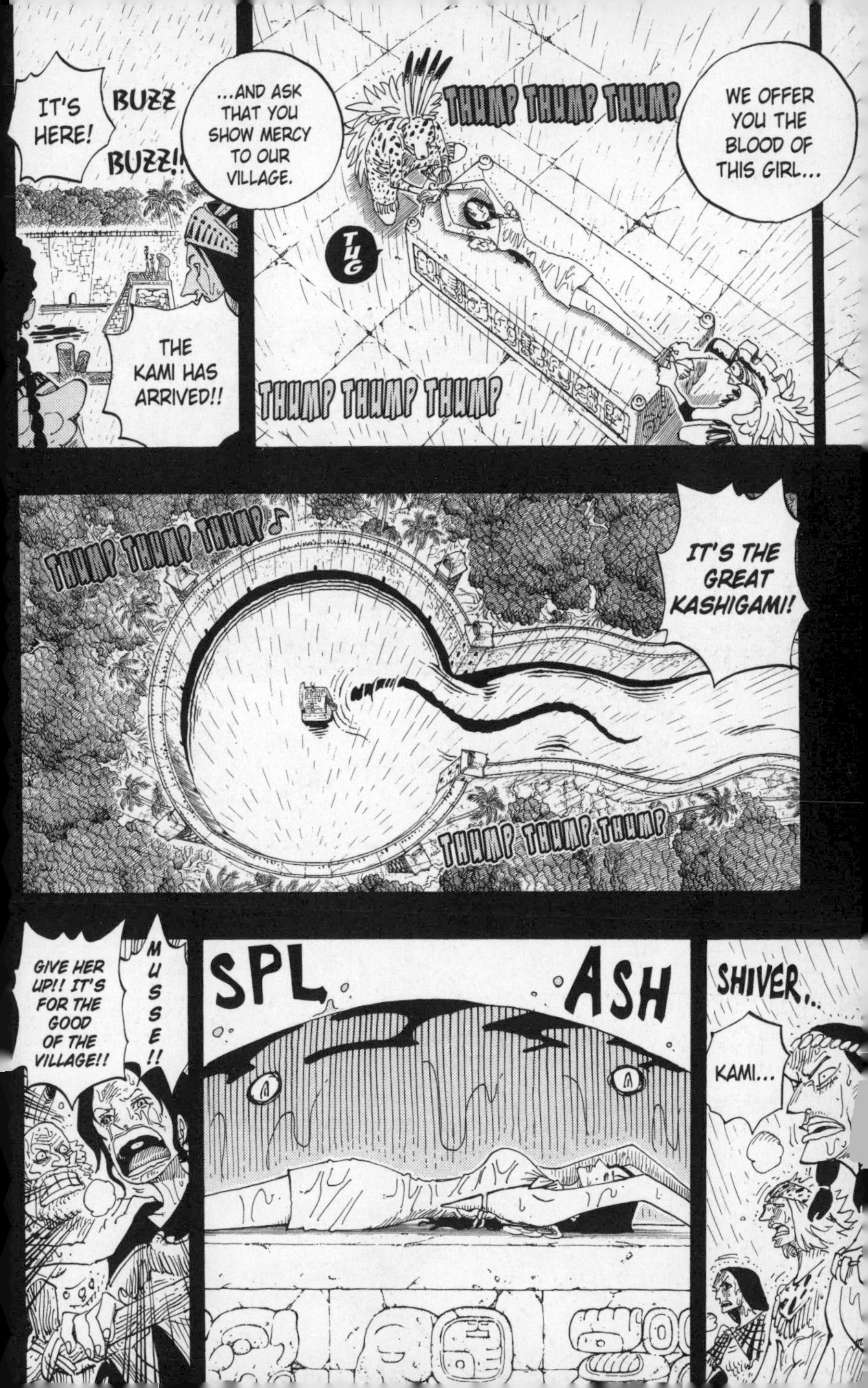
WE OFFER YOU THE BLOOD OF THIS GIRL...
THUMP THUMP THUMP
...AND ASK THAT YOU SHOW MERCY TO OUR VILLAGE.
TUG
THUMP THUMP THUMP
BUZZ BUZZ!!
IT'S HERE!
THE KAMI HAS ARRIVED!!
IT'S THE GREAT KASHIGAMI!
THUMP THUMP THUMP♪
THUMP THUMP THUMP
SHIVER...
KAMI...
ASH
SPL
MUSSE!!
GIVE HER UP!! IT'S FOR THE GOOD OF THE VILLAGE!!

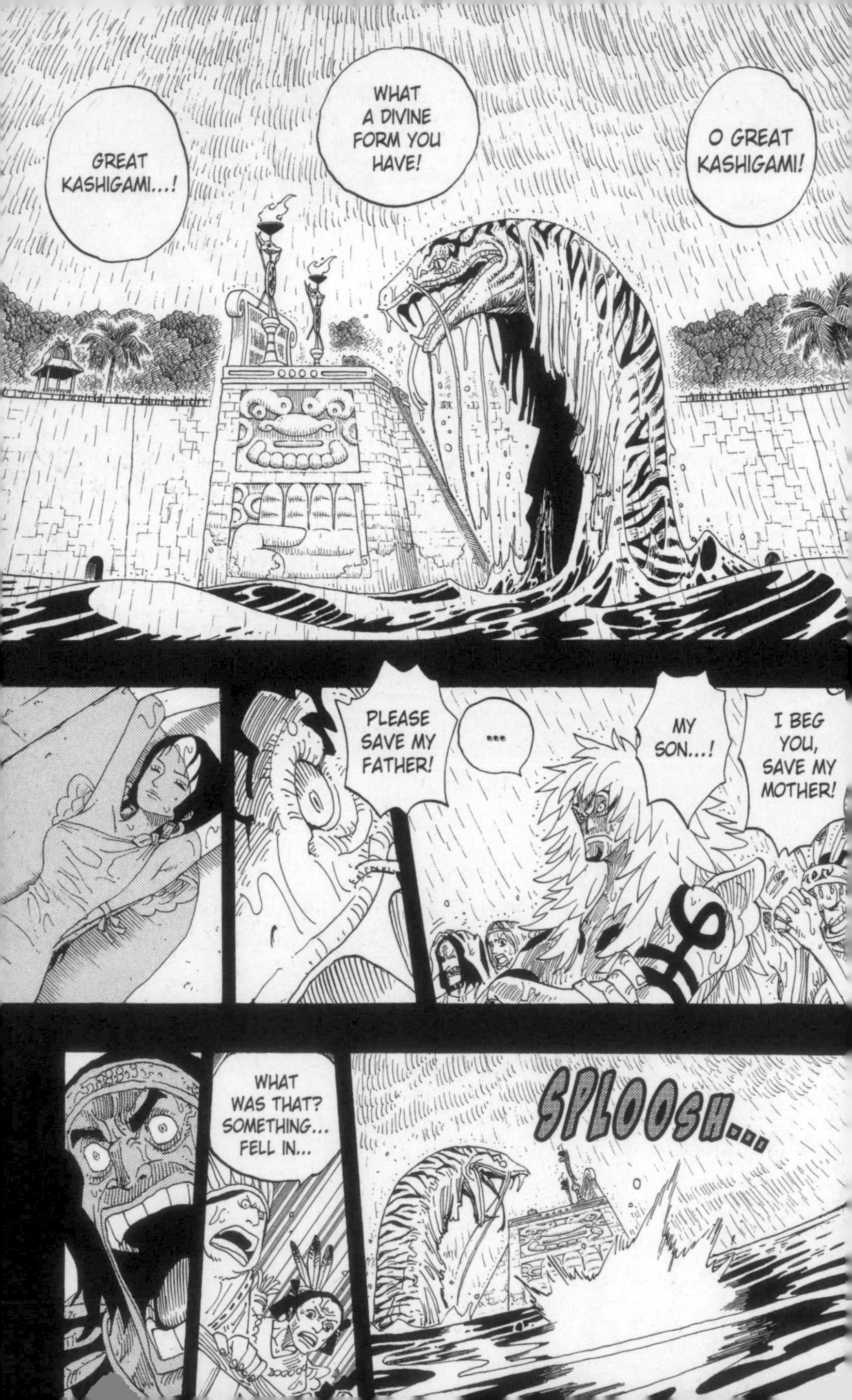
O GREAT KASHIGAMI!
WHAT A DIVINE FORM YOU HAVE!
GREAT KASHIGAMI...!
I BEG YOU, SAVE MY MOTHER!
MY SON...!
...
PLEASE SAVE MY FATHER!
SPLOOSH...
WHAT WAS THAT? SOMETHING... FELL IN...

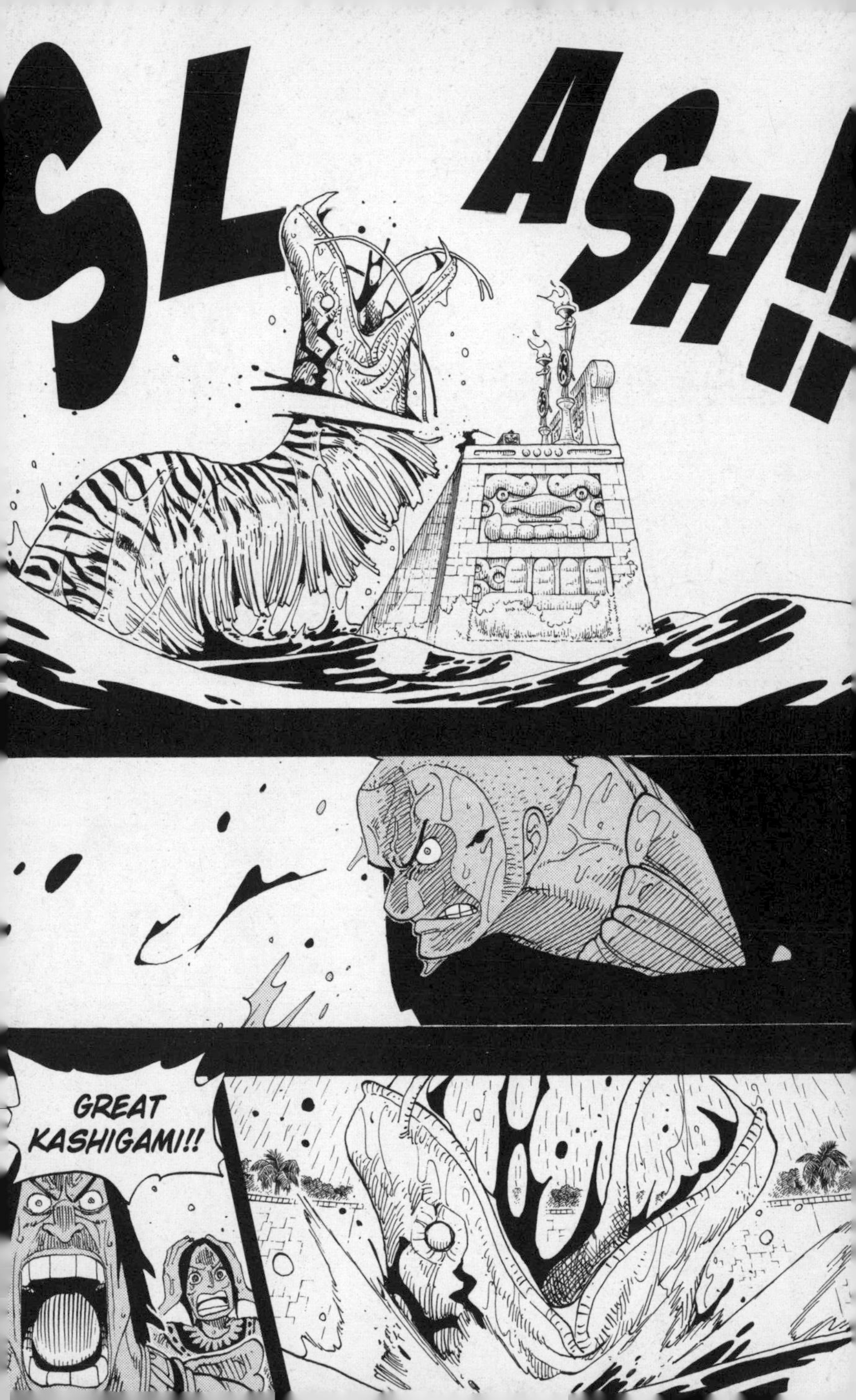
SLASH!!!
GREAT KASHIGAMI!!

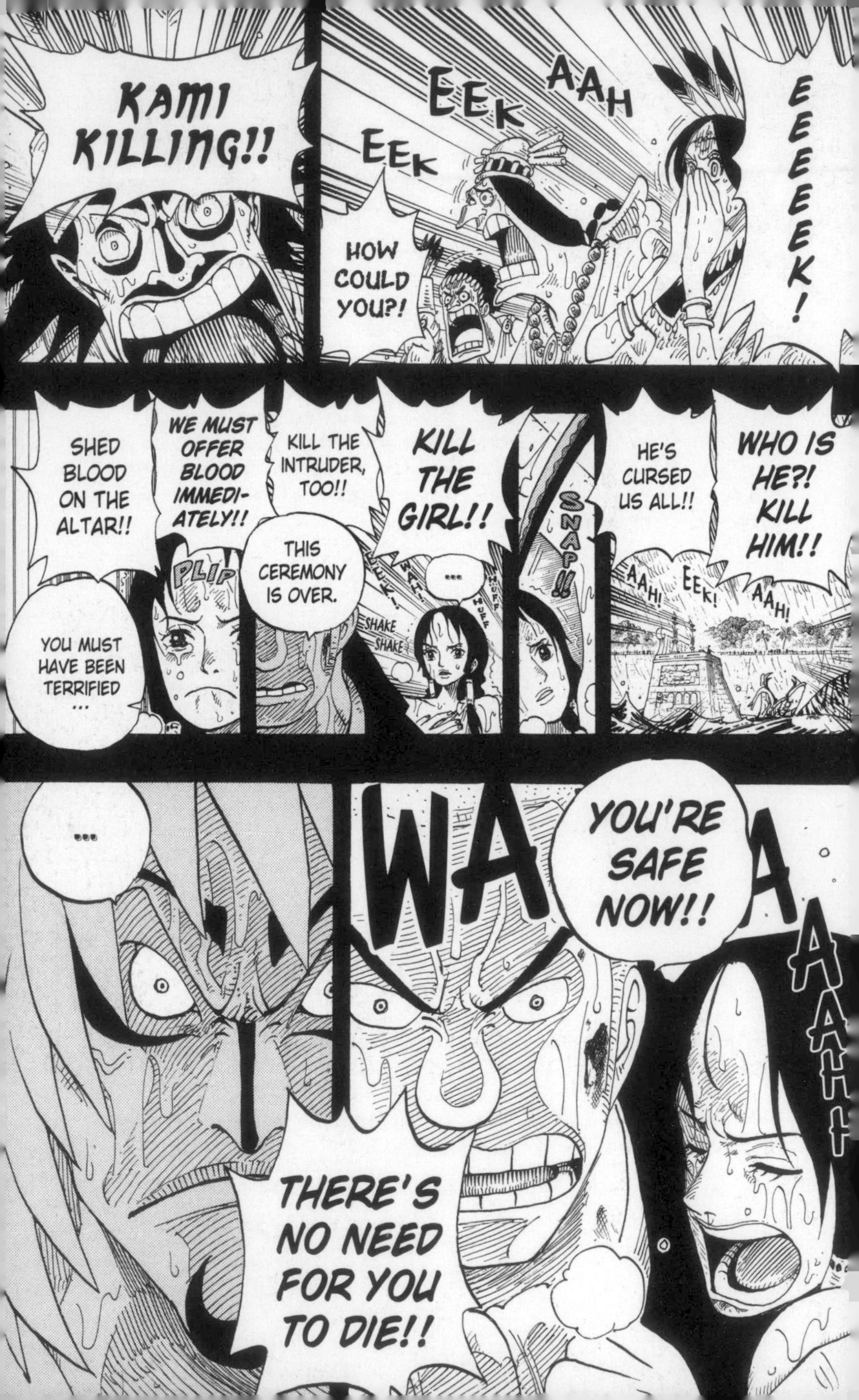
EEEEEEEK!
AAH
EEK
EEK
HOW COULD YOU?!
KAMI KILLING!!
WHO IS HE?! KILL HIM!!
HE'S CURSED US ALL!!
AAH!
EEK!
AAH!
SNAP!!
KILL THE GIRL!!
KILL THE INTRUDER, TOO!!
WE MUST OFFER BLOOD IMMEDI-ATELY!!
SHED BLOOD ON THE ALTAR!!
...
HUFF HUFF
EEK!
WAH!
SHAKE SHAKE
THIS CEREMONY IS OVER.
PLIP
YOU MUST HAVE BEEN TERRIFIED ...
WAAAAAH!
YOU'RE SAFE NOW!!
THERE'S NO NEED FOR YOU TO DIE!!
...

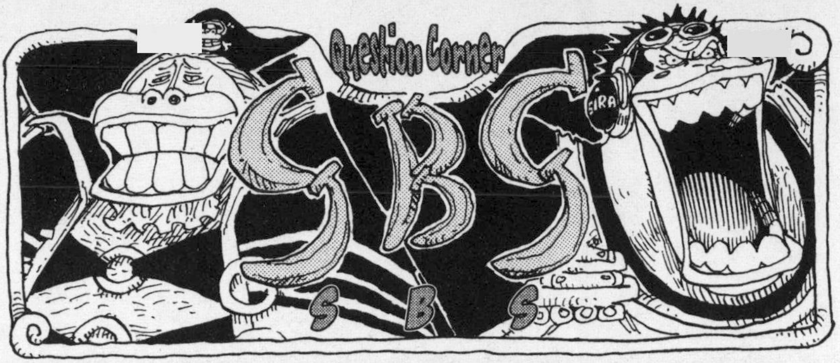
Question Corner
SBS
S B S

Oda: The Question Corner is starting! (Ta-Dah!)
All right! I said it! I really said it! I'm so excited! I bet you all thought I had given up lately, didn't you? That was naïve of you, very naïve. I've just been waiting for a chance, biding my time. Aaah... This feels great. I won't let anyone hijack this anymore! Come on, bring it on!

Reader: Oda Sensei. I've been watching *One Piece*, and I have a question. How come Luffy and Zolo and the rest don't have armpit hair?! I'm younger than Luffy, but I've got a TON of the stuff. How come they don't have armpit hair?! (sob)

--Really, why not?

Oda: Did you want me to draw that?
If everyone wants it, I'll totally draw it, you know. A lot of it too.

Q: What does Zolo's new technique, the "__ Pound Phoenix" mean?

--Tangerine

A: It's a reference to how cannons are classified, as in "12-pounder gun" and "24-pounder gun." The number refers to the weight of the cannon ball. Even with a 12-pounder gun, the weight of the cannon itself is more than a ton.
One pound = about 0.45 kilograms.
You've gotta be careful not to mix it up with "fond de veau." That one's used in French cooking.

ALSO, THE JAPANESE WORD FOR "PHOENIX" SOUNDS JUST LIKE THE WORD FOR "GUN."--ED.

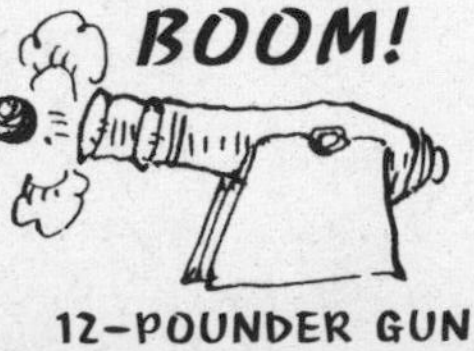
BOOM!

12-POUNDER GUN

Chapter 288:
CURSE

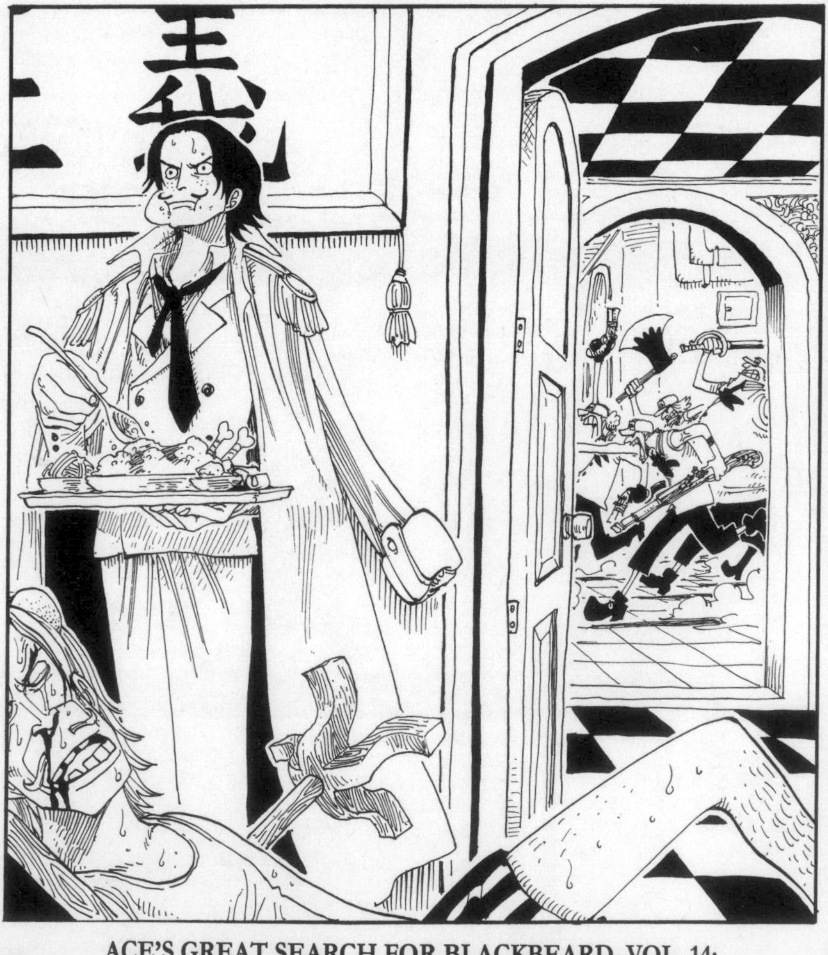

ACE'S GREAT SEARCH FOR BLACKBEARD, VOL. 14:
"THE INTRUDER, COMMANDER ACE"

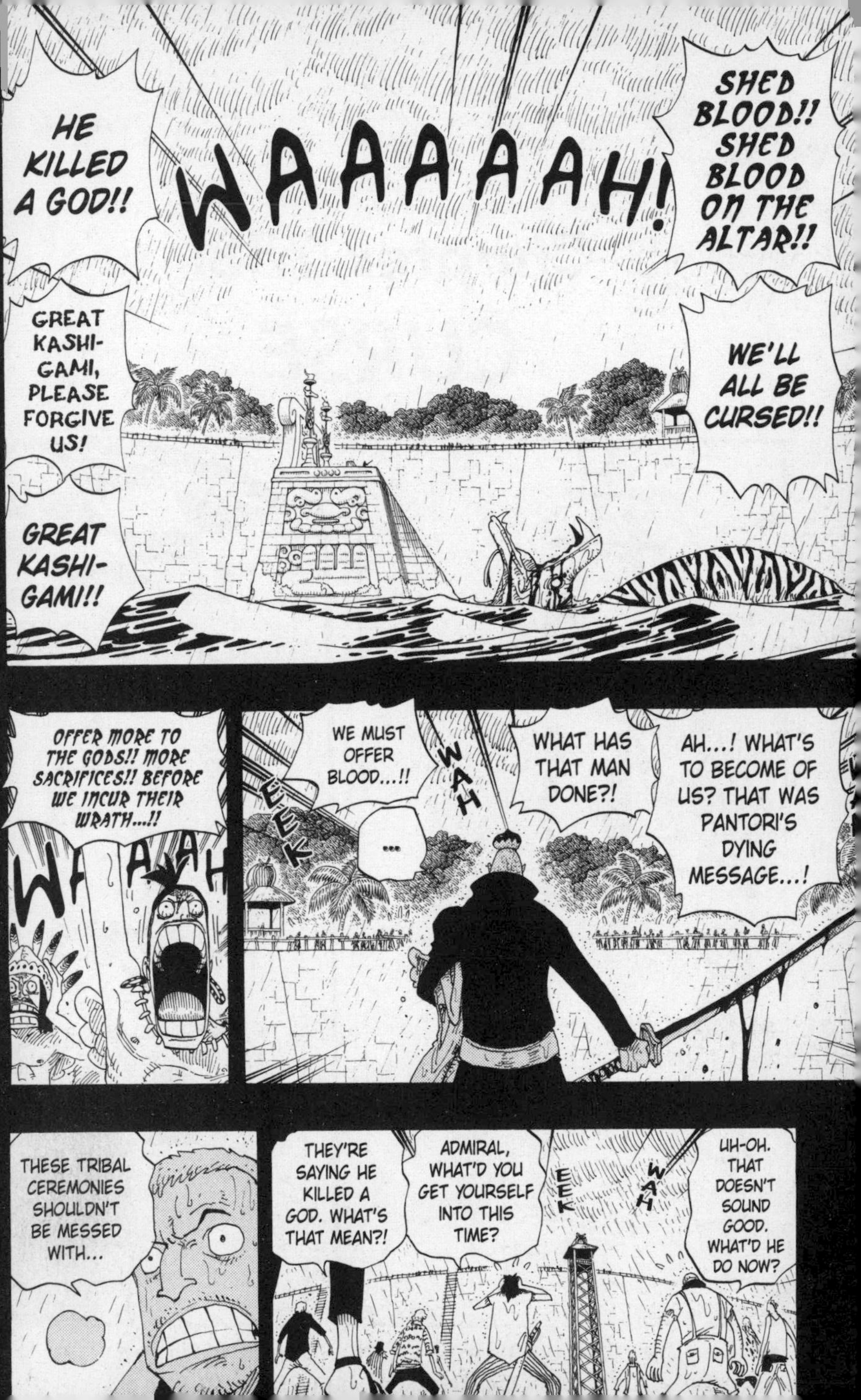
SHED BLOOD!! SHED BLOOD ON THE ALTAR!!
WAAAAAAH!
HE KILLED A GOD!!
WE'LL ALL BE CURSED!!
GREAT KASHI-GAMI, PLEASE FORGIVE US!
GREAT KASHI-GAMI!!
AH...! WHAT'S TO BECOME OF US? THAT WAS PANTORI'S DYING MESSAGE...!
WHAT HAS THAT MAN DONE?!
WAH
WE MUST OFFER BLOOD...!!
EEK
...
OFFER MORE TO THE GODS!! MORE SACRIFICES!! BEFORE WE INCUR THEIR WRATH...!!
WAAH
UH-OH. THAT DOESN'T SOUND GOOD. WHAT'D HE DO NOW?
WAH
EEK
ADMIRAL, WHAT'D YOU GET YOURSELF INTO THIS TIME?
THEY'RE SAYING HE KILLED A GOD. WHAT'S THAT MEAN?!
THESE TRIBAL CEREMONIES SHOULDN'T BE MESSED WITH...

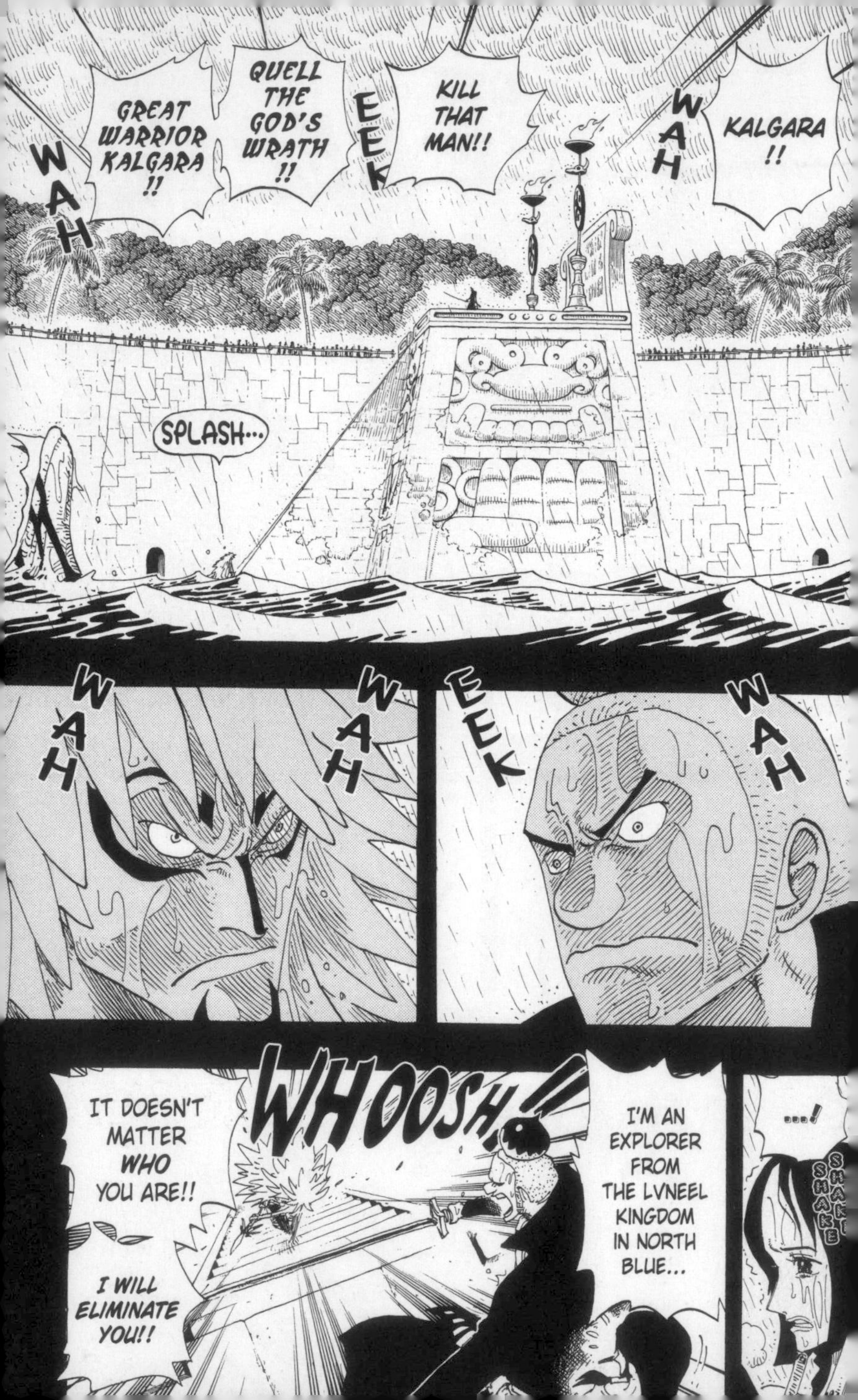
KALGARA !!
WAH
KILL THAT MAN!!
EEK
QUELL THE GOD'S WRATH !!
GREAT WARRIOR KALGARA !!
WAH
SPLASH...
WAH
EEK
WAH
WAH
...!
SHAKE SHAKE
I'M AN EXPLORER FROM THE LVNEEL KINGDOM IN NORTH BLUE...
WHOOSH!!
IT DOESN'T MATTER WHO YOU ARE!!
I WILL ELIMINATE YOU!!

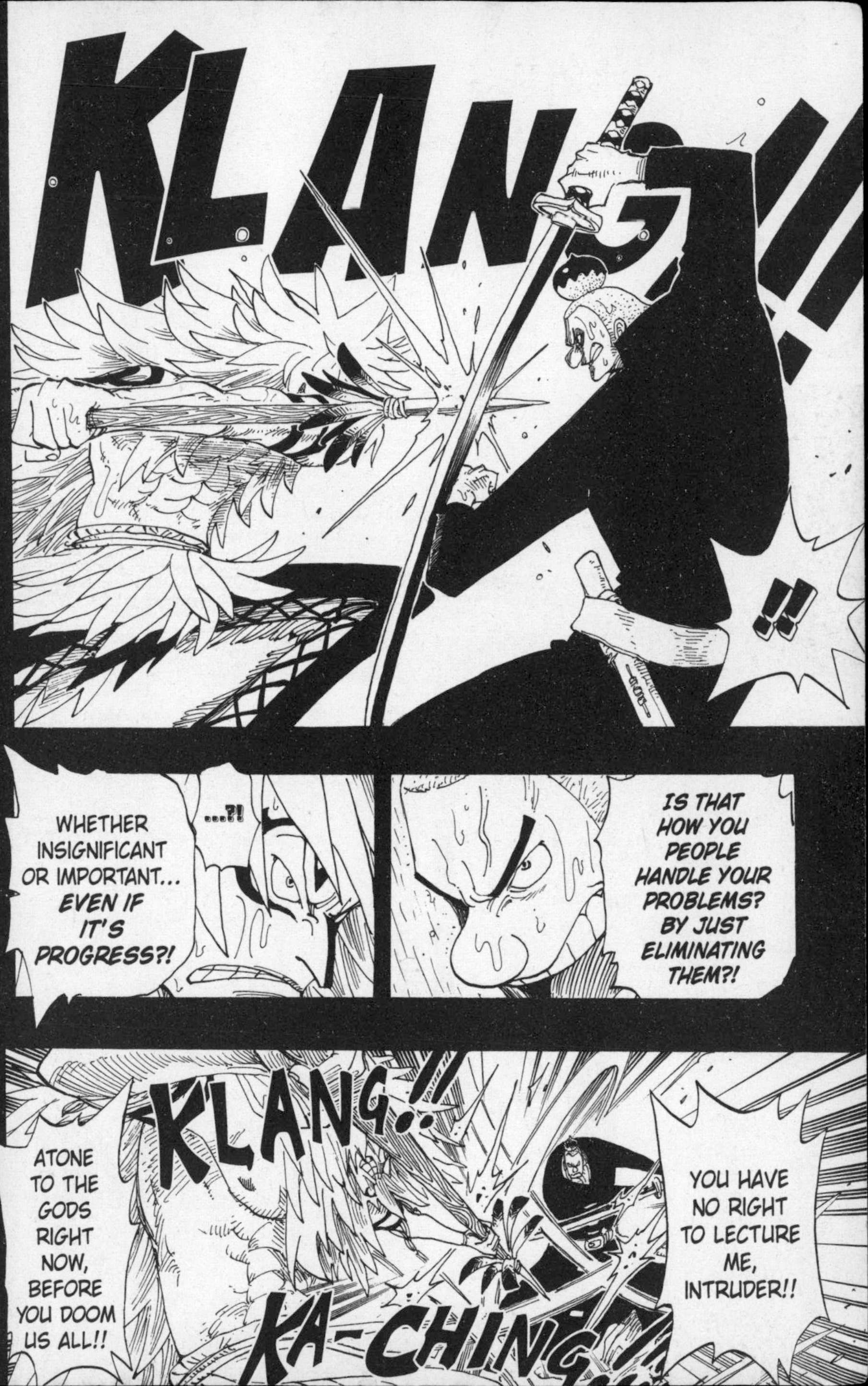
KLANG!!
!!
IS THAT HOW YOU PEOPLE HANDLE YOUR PROBLEMS? BY JUST ELIMINATING THEM?!
...?!
WHETHER INSIGNIFICANT OR IMPORTANT... EVEN IF IT'S PROGRESS?!
KLANG!!
YOU HAVE NO RIGHT TO LECTURE ME, INTRUDER!!
ATONE TO THE GODS RIGHT NOW, BEFORE YOU DOOM US ALL!!
KA-CHING!!

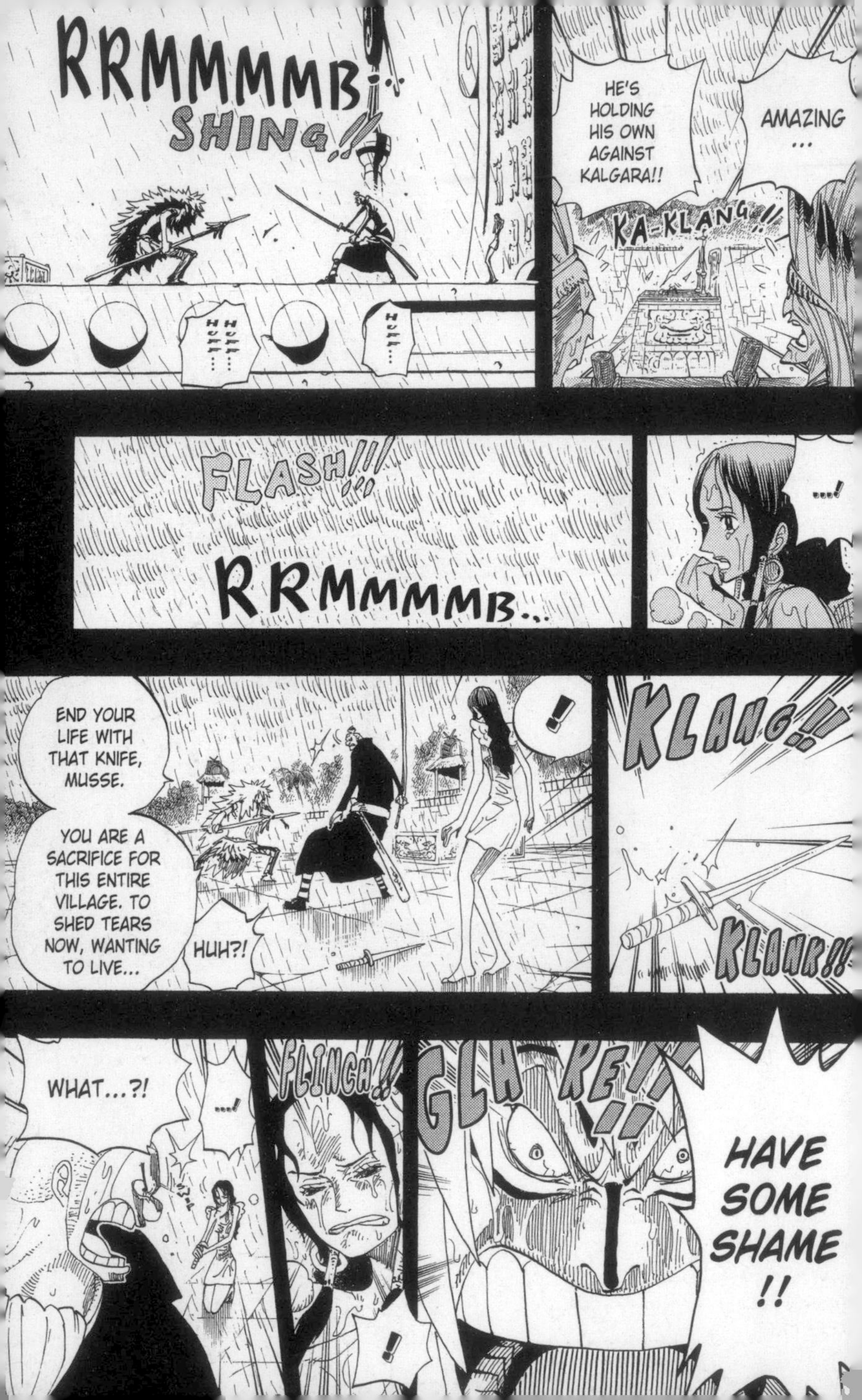
AMAZING...
HE'S HOLDING HIS OWN AGAINST KALGARA!!
KA-KLANG!!
RRMMMMMB
SHING!!
HUFF... HUFF...
HUFF...
...!
FLASH!!!
RRMMMMMB...
KLANG!!
KLINK!!
!
END YOUR LIFE WITH THAT KNIFE, MUSSE.
YOU ARE A SACRIFICE FOR THIS ENTIRE VILLAGE. TO SHED TEARS NOW, WANTING TO LIVE...
HUH?!
GLA-RE!!
HAVE SOME SHAME!!
!
FLINCH!!
WHAT...?!
...!

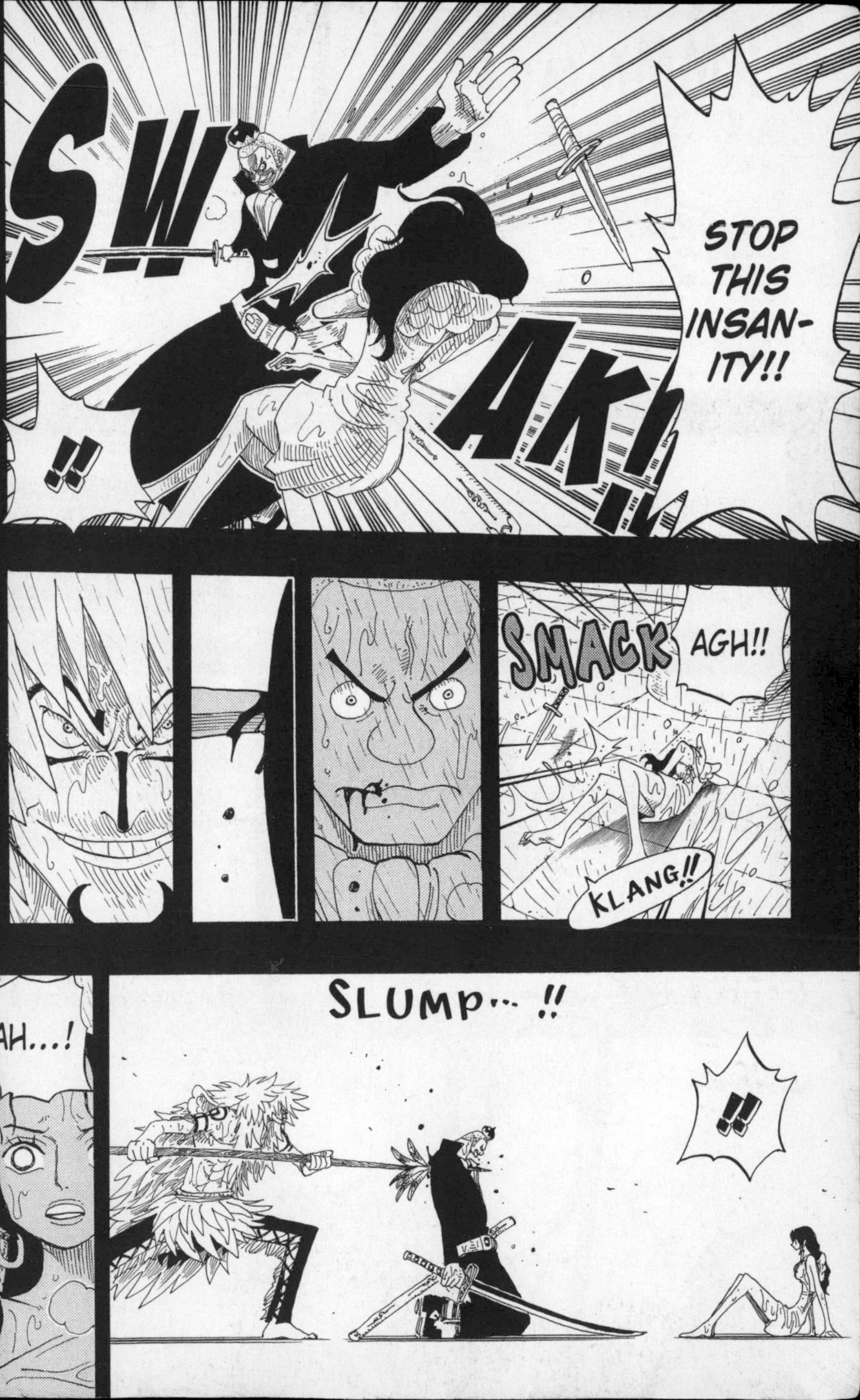
STOP THIS INSANITY!!
SWAK!!
!!
AGH!!
SMACK
KLANG!!
SLUMP... !!
!!
AH...!

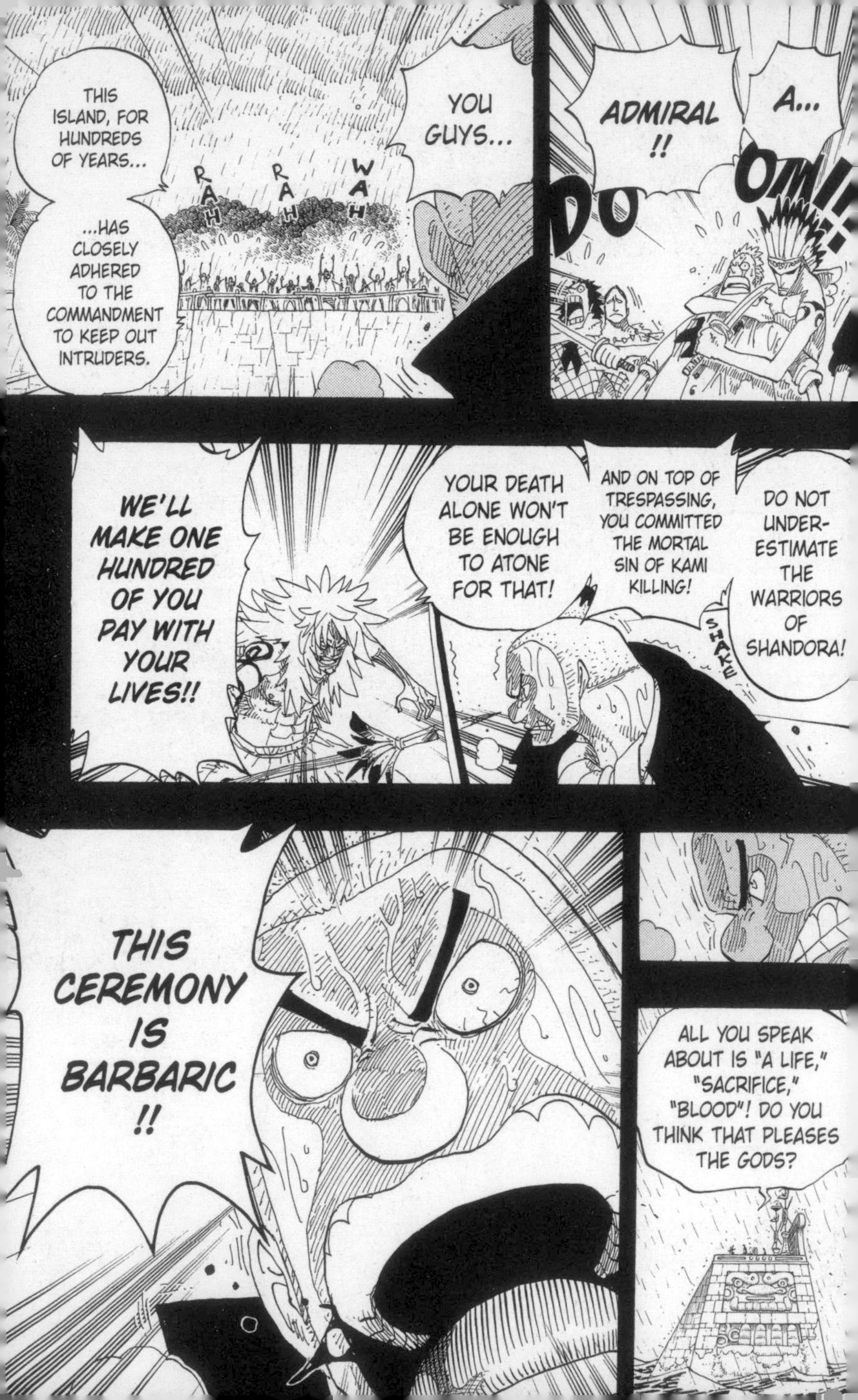
A...
ADMIRAL !!
DOOM!!
YOU GUYS...
THIS ISLAND, FOR HUNDREDS OF YEARS...
...HAS CLOSELY ADHERED TO THE COMMANDMENT TO KEEP OUT INTRUDERS.
WAH
RAH
RAH
DO NOT UNDER-ESTIMATE THE WARRIORS OF SHANDORA!
SHAKE
AND ON TOP OF TRESPASSING, YOU COMMITTED THE MORTAL SIN OF KAMI KILLING!
YOUR DEATH ALONE WON'T BE ENOUGH TO ATONE FOR THAT!
WE'LL MAKE ONE HUNDRED OF YOU PAY WITH YOUR LIVES!!
ALL YOU SPEAK ABOUT IS "A LIFE," "SACRIFICE," "BLOOD"! DO YOU THINK THAT PLEASES THE GODS?
THIS CEREMONY IS BARBARIC !!

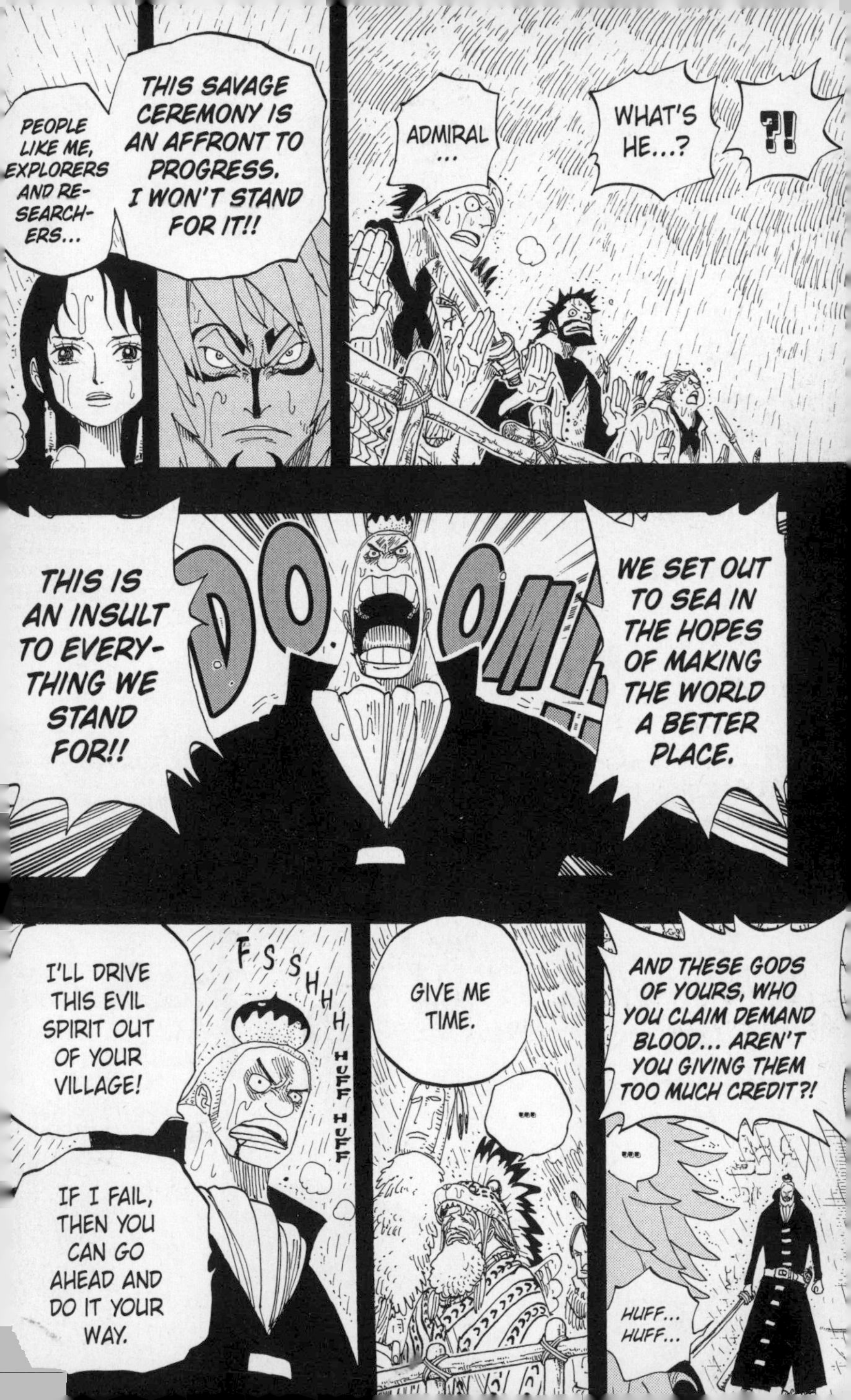
?!
WHAT'S HE...?
ADMIRAL...
THIS SAVAGE CEREMONY IS AN AFFRONT TO PROGRESS. I WON'T STAND FOR IT!!
PEOPLE LIKE ME, EXPLORERS AND RE-SEARCH-ERS...
WE SET OUT TO SEA IN THE HOPES OF MAKING THE WORLD A BETTER PLACE.
DOOM
THIS IS AN INSULT TO EVERY-THING WE STAND FOR!!
AND THESE GODS OF YOURS, WHO YOU CLAIM DEMAND BLOOD... AREN'T YOU GIVING THEM TOO MUCH CREDIT?!
...
HUFF... HUFF...
GIVE ME TIME.
...
FSSHHH
I'LL DRIVE THIS EVIL SPIRIT OUT OF YOUR VILLAGE!
HUFF HUFF
IF I FAIL, THEN YOU CAN GO AHEAD AND DO IT YOUR WAY.

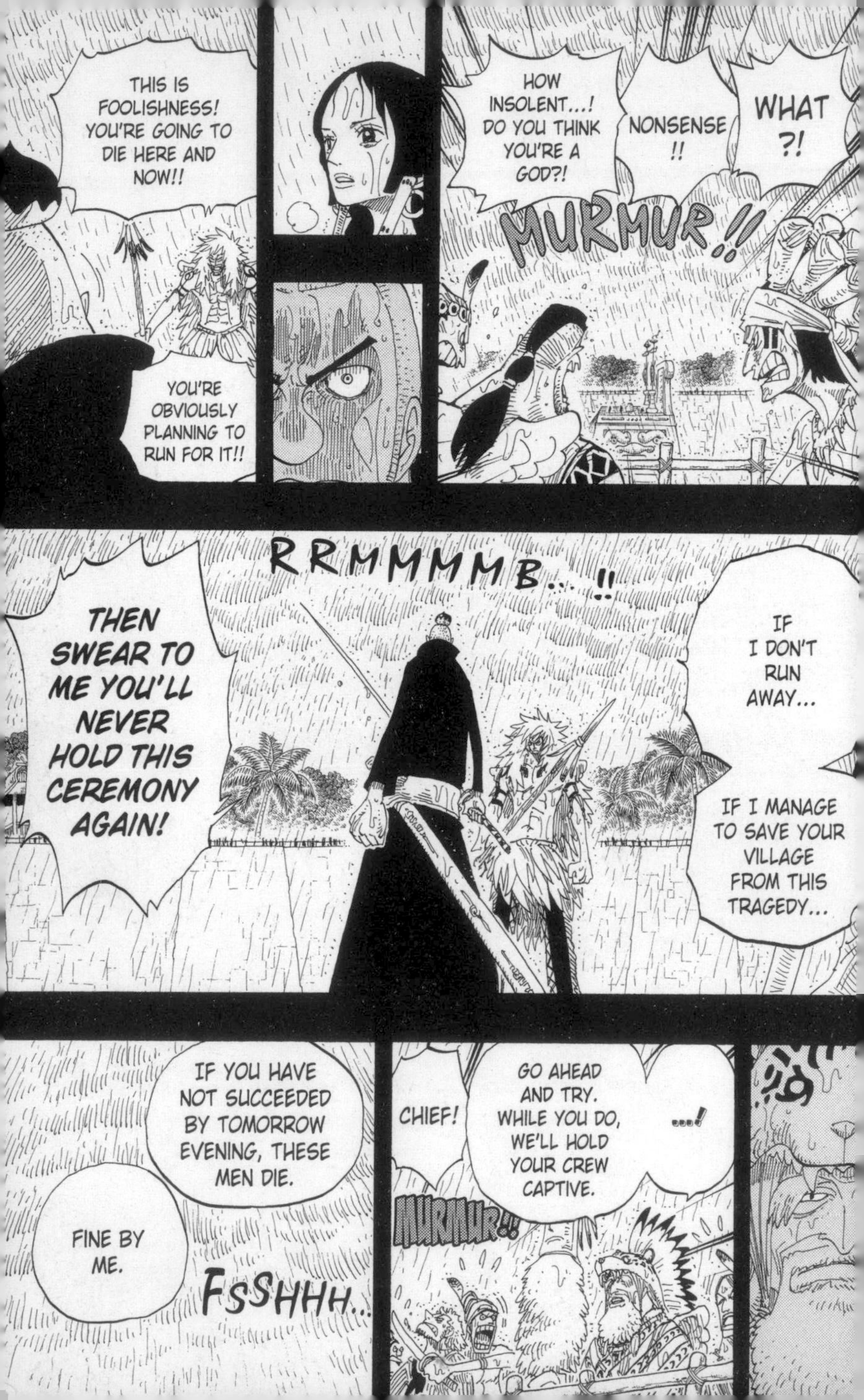
WHAT ?!
NONSENSE !!
HOW INSOLENT...! DO YOU THINK YOU'RE A GOD?!
MURMUR!!
THIS IS FOOLISHNESS! YOU'RE GOING TO DIE HERE AND NOW!!
YOU'RE OBVIOUSLY PLANNING TO RUN FOR IT!!
RRMMMMB...!!
IF I DON'T RUN AWAY...
IF I MANAGE TO SAVE YOUR VILLAGE FROM THIS TRAGEDY...
THEN SWEAR TO ME YOU'LL NEVER HOLD THIS CEREMONY AGAIN!
...!
GO AHEAD AND TRY. WHILE YOU DO, WE'LL HOLD YOUR CREW CAPTIVE.
CHIEF!
MURMUR!!
IF YOU HAVE NOT SUCCEEDED BY TOMORROW EVENING, THESE MEN DIE.
FINE BY ME.
FSSHHH...

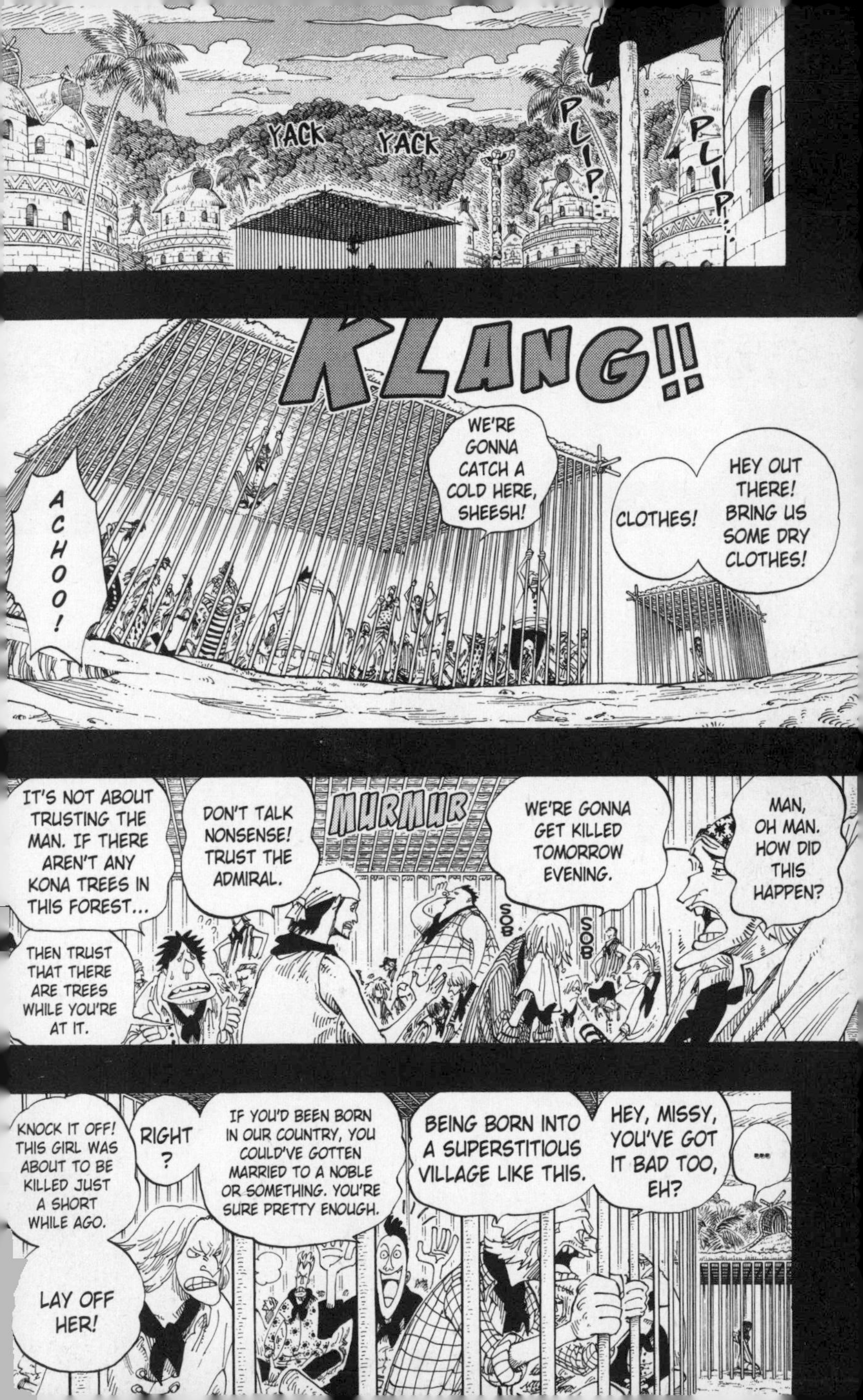
PLIP...
PLIP...
YACK
YACK
KLANG!!
HEY OUT THERE! BRING US SOME DRY CLOTHES!
CLOTHES!
WE'RE GONNA CATCH A COLD HERE, SHEESH!
ACHOO!
MAN, OH MAN. HOW DID THIS HAPPEN?
WE'RE GONNA GET KILLED TOMORROW EVENING.
SOB
SOB
MURMUR
DON'T TALK NONSENSE! TRUST THE ADMIRAL.
IT'S NOT ABOUT TRUSTING THE MAN. IF THERE AREN'T ANY KONA TREES IN THIS FOREST...
THEN TRUST THAT THERE ARE TREES WHILE YOU'RE AT IT.
...
HEY, MISSY, YOU'VE GOT IT BAD TOO, EH?
BEING BORN INTO A SUPERSTITIOUS VILLAGE LIKE THIS.
IF YOU'D BEEN BORN IN OUR COUNTRY, YOU COULD'VE GOTTEN MARRIED TO A NOBLE OR SOMETHING. YOU'RE SURE PRETTY ENOUGH.
RIGHT?
KNOCK IT OFF! THIS GIRL WAS ABOUT TO BE KILLED JUST A SHORT WHILE AGO.
LAY OFF HER!

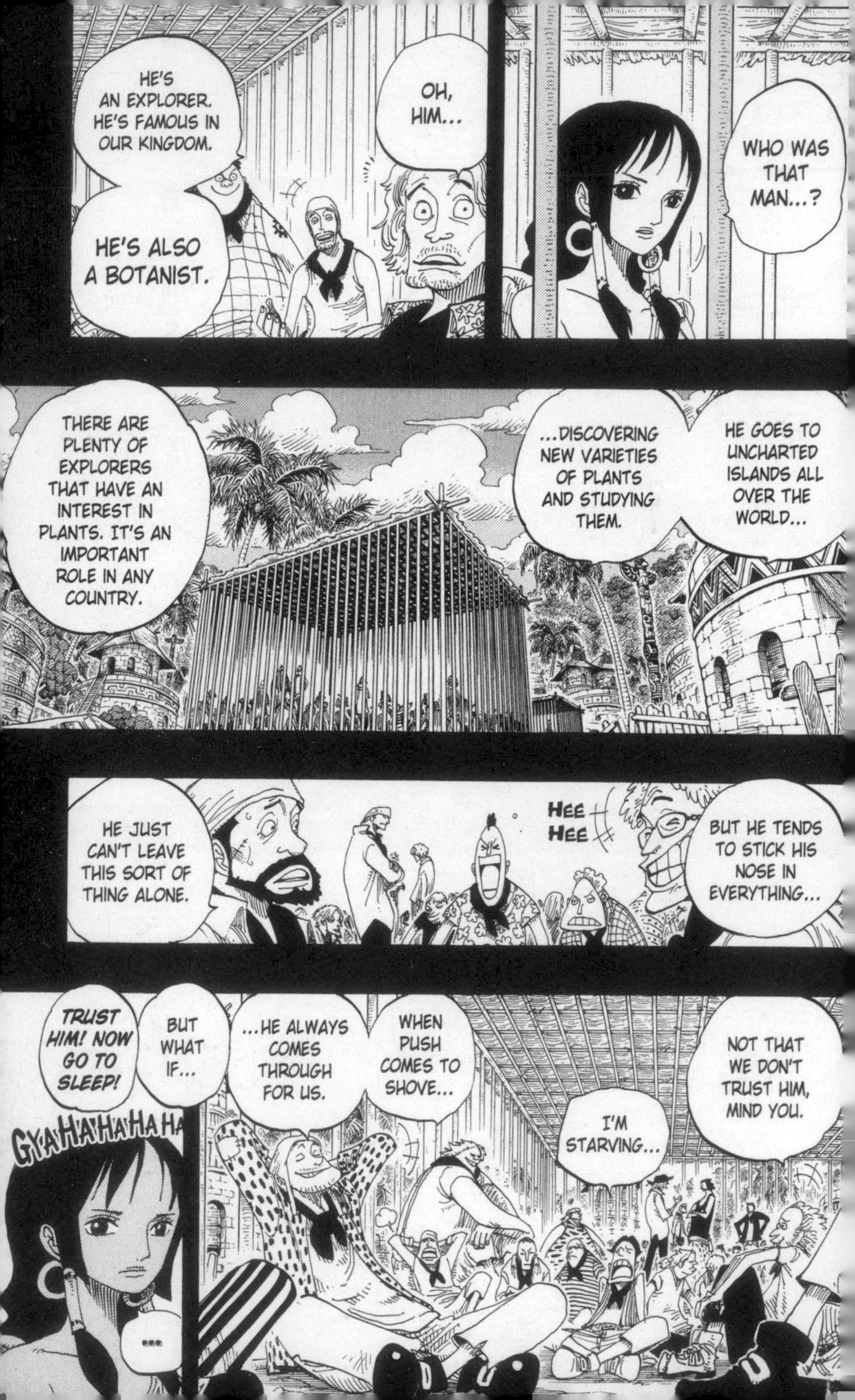
WHO WAS THAT MAN...?
OH, HIM...
HE'S AN EXPLORER. HE'S FAMOUS IN OUR KINGDOM.
HE'S ALSO A BOTANIST.
HE GOES TO UNCHARTED ISLANDS ALL OVER THE WORLD...
...DISCOVERING NEW VARIETIES OF PLANTS AND STUDYING THEM.
THERE ARE PLENTY OF EXPLORERS THAT HAVE AN INTEREST IN PLANTS. IT'S AN IMPORTANT ROLE IN ANY COUNTRY.
BUT HE TENDS TO STICK HIS NOSE IN EVERYTHING...
HEE HEE
HE JUST CAN'T LEAVE THIS SORT OF THING ALONE.
NOT THAT WE DON'T TRUST HIM, MIND YOU.
I'M STARVING...
WHEN PUSH COMES TO SHOVE...
...HE ALWAYS COMES THROUGH FOR US.
BUT WHAT IF...
TRUST HIM! NOW GO TO SLEEP!
GYAHAHAHAHA
...

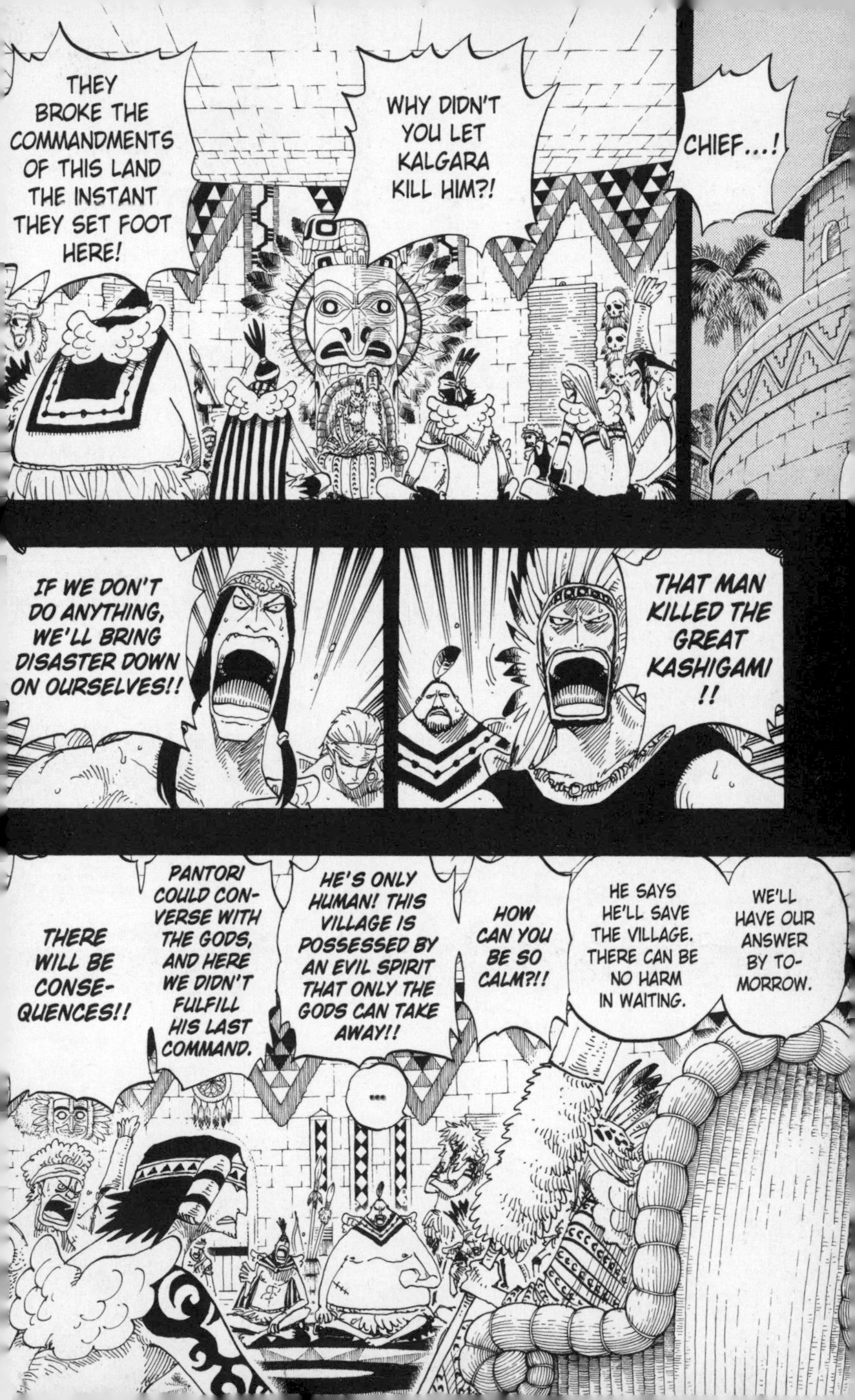
CHIEF...!
WHY DIDN'T YOU LET KALGARA KILL HIM?!
THEY BROKE THE COMMANDMENTS OF THIS LAND THE INSTANT THEY SET FOOT HERE!
THAT MAN KILLED THE GREAT KASHIGAMI !!
IF WE DON'T DO ANYTHING, WE'LL BRING DISASTER DOWN ON OURSELVES!!
WE'LL HAVE OUR ANSWER BY TOMORROW.
HE SAYS HE'LL SAVE THE VILLAGE. THERE CAN BE NO HARM IN WAITING.
HOW CAN YOU BE SO CALM?!!
HE'S ONLY HUMAN! THIS VILLAGE IS POSSESSED BY AN EVIL SPIRIT THAT ONLY THE GODS CAN TAKE AWAY!!
PANTORI COULD CONVERSE WITH THE GODS, AND HERE WE DIDN'T FULFILL HIS LAST COMMAND.
THERE WILL BE CONSEQUENCES!!
...

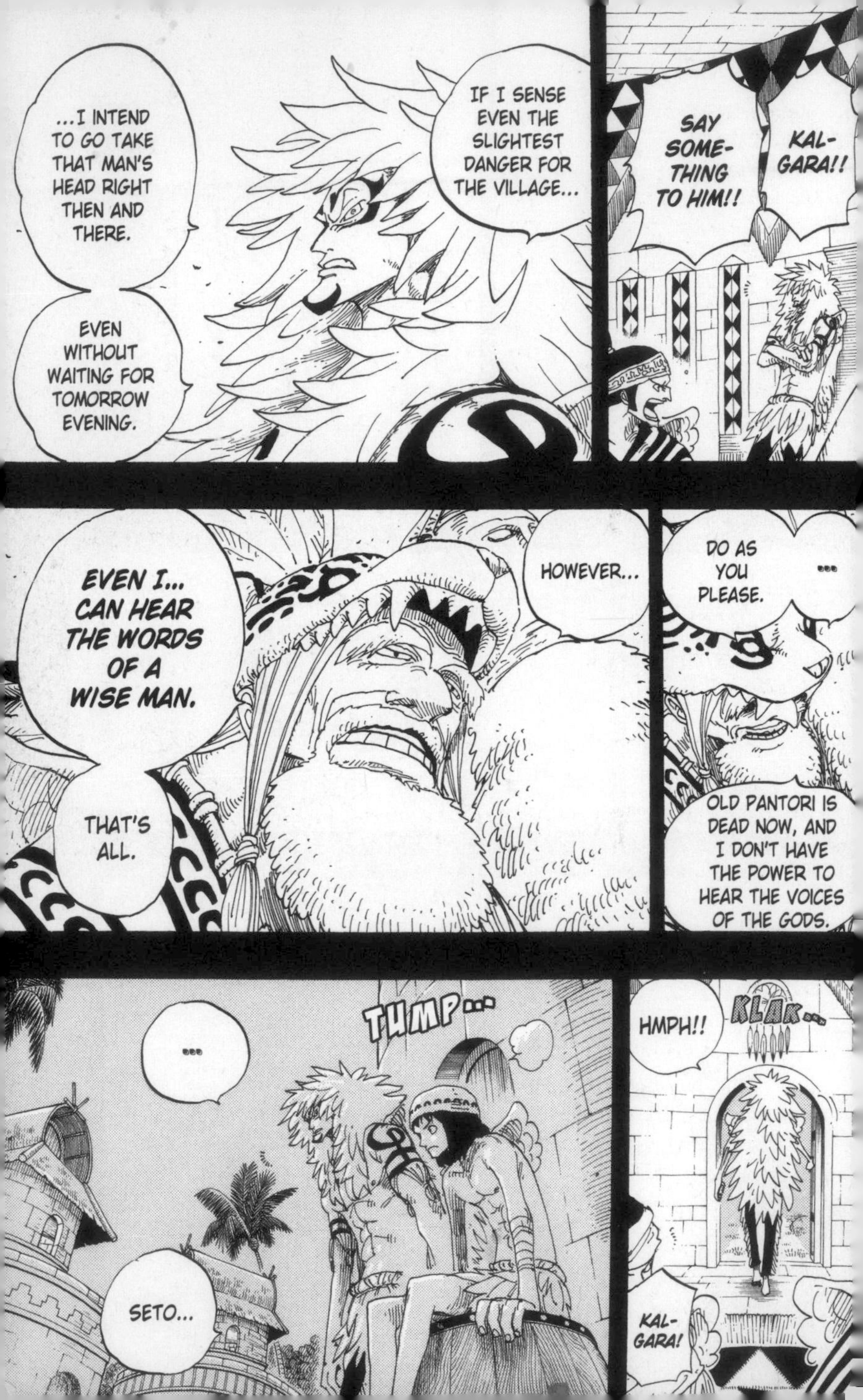
KAL-GARA!!
SAY SOME-THING TO HIM!!
IF I SENSE EVEN THE SLIGHTEST DANGER FOR THE VILLAGE...
...I INTEND TO GO TAKE THAT MAN'S HEAD RIGHT THEN AND THERE.
EVEN WITHOUT WAITING FOR TOMORROW EVENING.
...
DO AS YOU PLEASE.
OLD PANTORI IS DEAD NOW, AND I DON'T HAVE THE POWER TO HEAR THE VOICES OF THE GODS.
HOWEVER...
EVEN I... CAN HEAR THE WORDS OF A WISE MAN.
THAT'S ALL.
KLAK...
HMPH!!
KAL-GARA!
TUMP...
...
SETO...

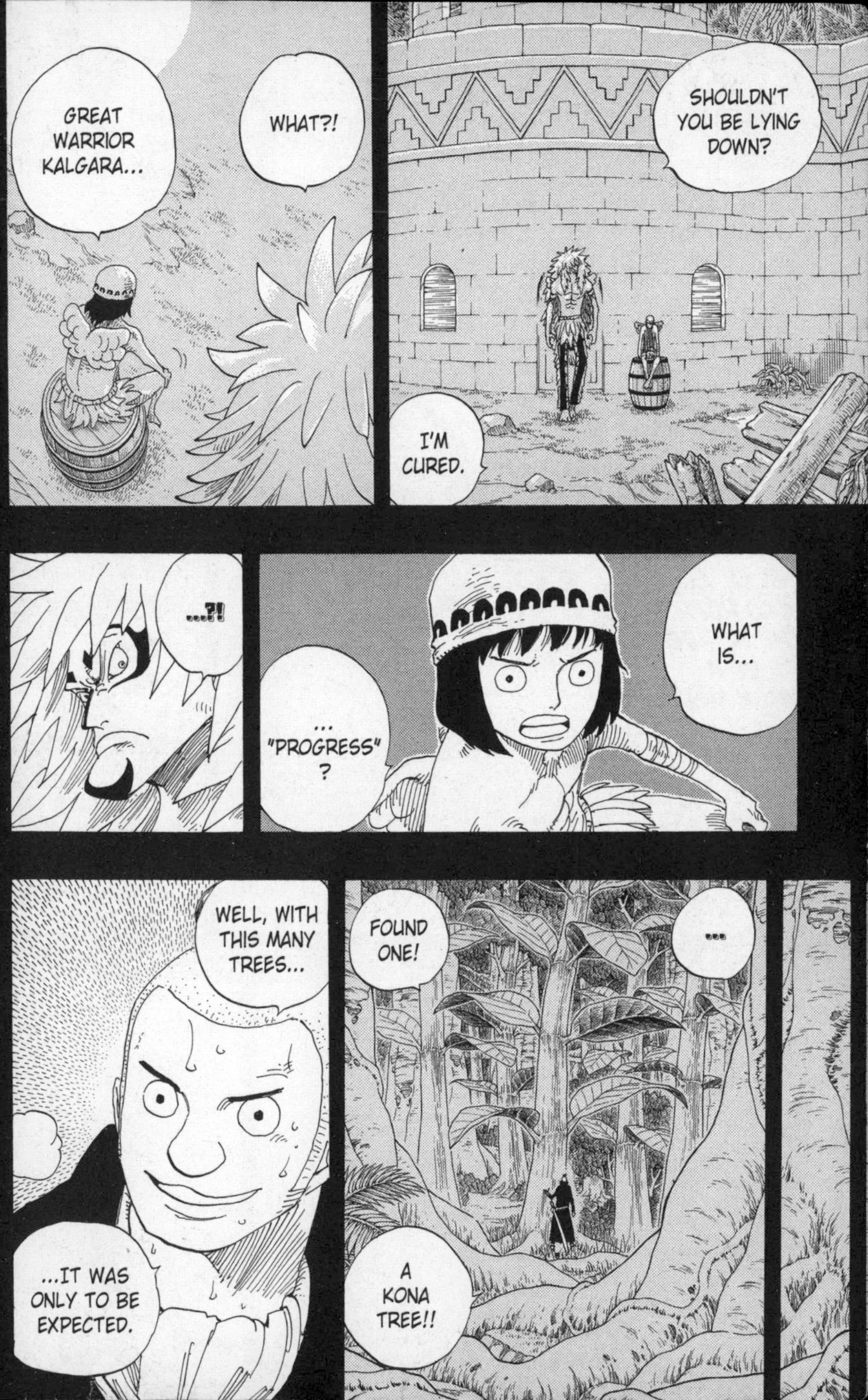
SHOULDN'T YOU BE LYING DOWN?
I'M CURED.
GREAT WARRIOR KALGARA...
WHAT?!
WHAT IS...
..."PROGRESS"?
...?!
...
FOUND ONE!
A KONA TREE!!
WELL, WITH THIS MANY TREES...
...IT WAS ONLY TO BE EXPECTED.

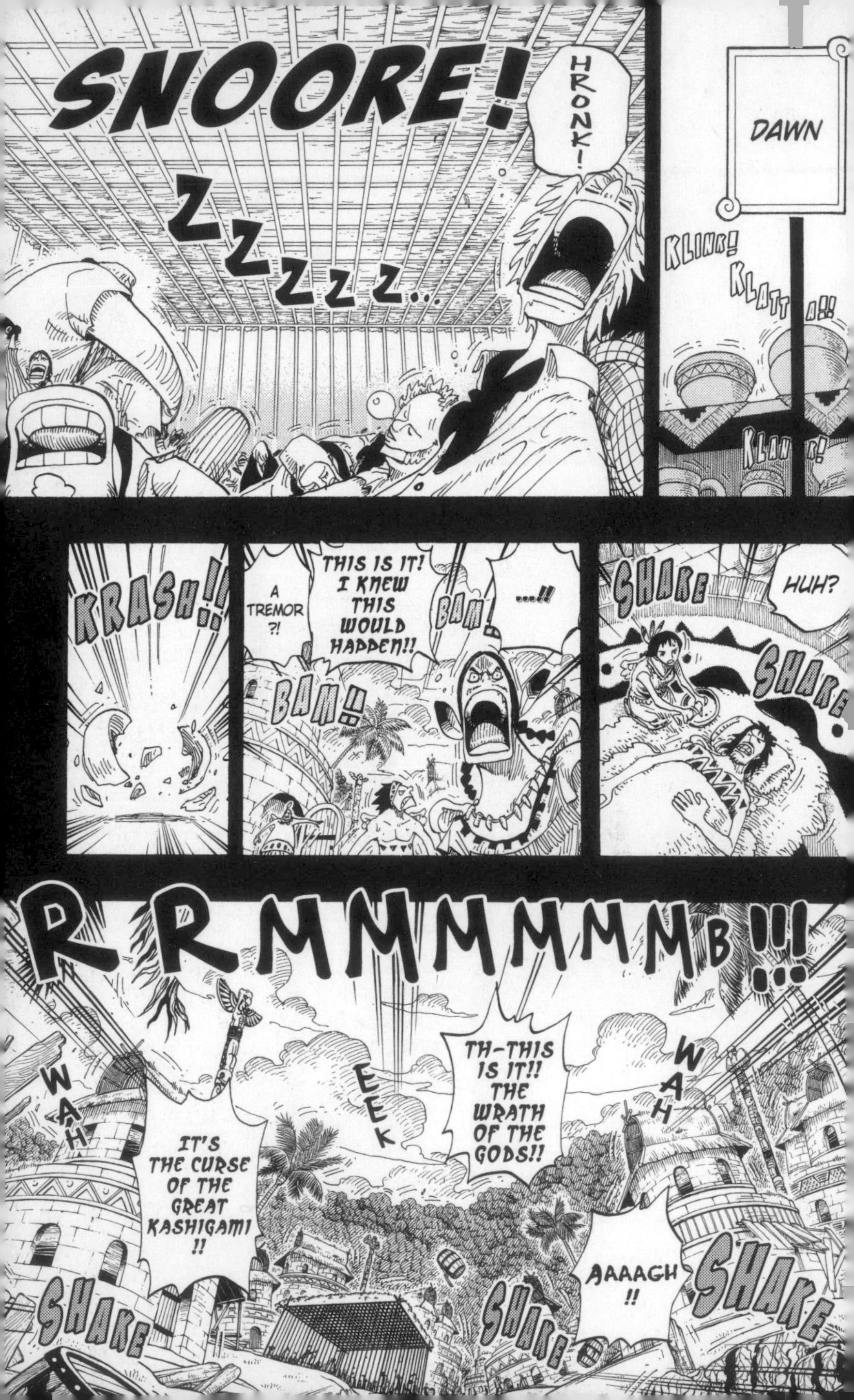
DAWN
KLINK!
HRONK!
SNOORE!
ZZZZZZ...
HUH?
SHAKE
SHAKE
...!!
BAM!
THIS IS IT! I KNEW THIS WOULD HAPPEN!!
A TREMOR ?!
BAM!!
KRASH!!
RRMMMMMMB!!!
WAH
TH-THIS IS IT!! THE WRATH OF THE GODS!!
EEEK
IT'S THE CURSE OF THE GREAT KASHIGAMI !!
WAH
SHAKE
AAAAGH !!
SHAKE
SHAKE

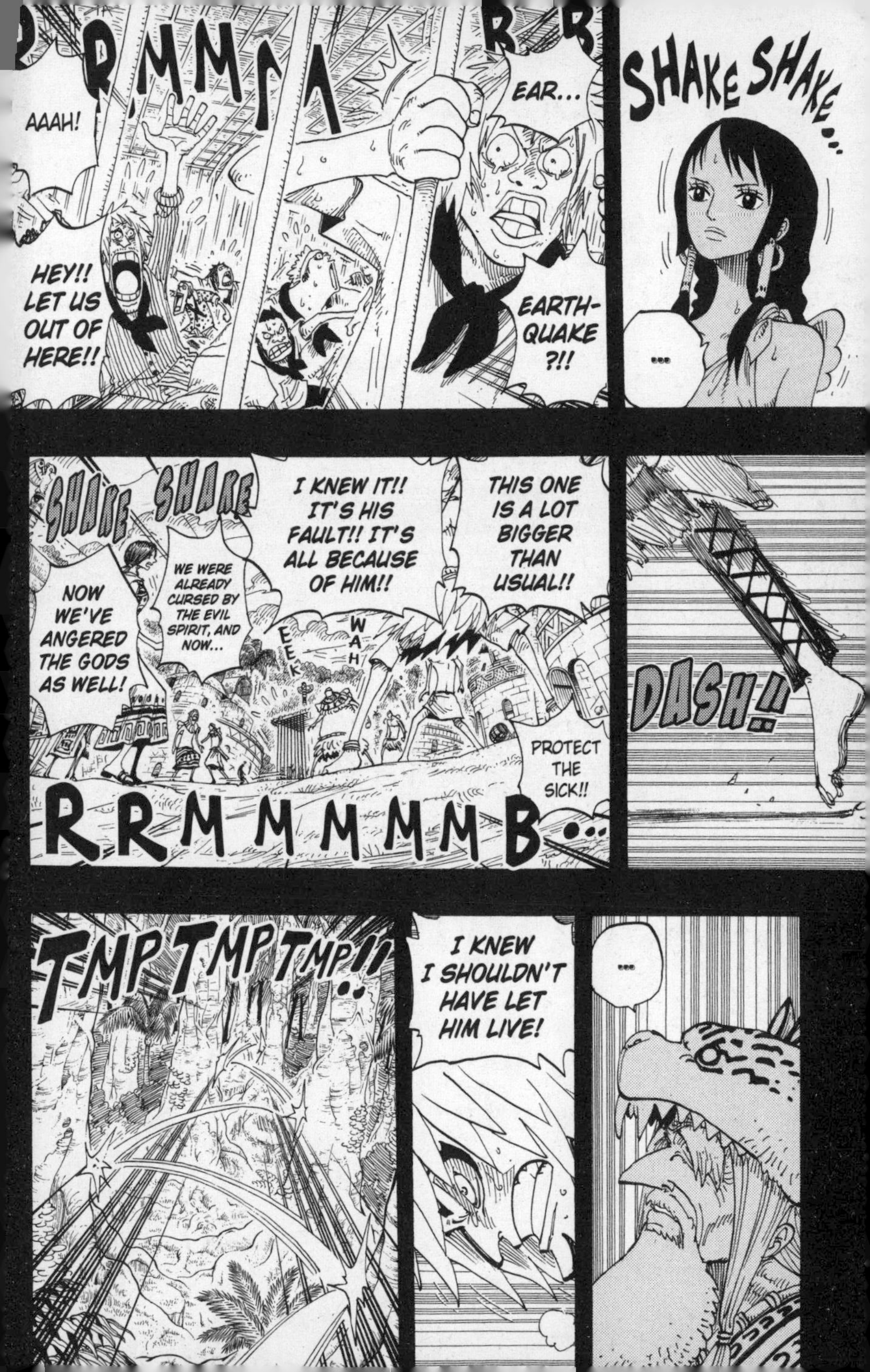
SHAKE SHAKE...
...
EAR...
EARTH-QUAKE?!!
HEY!! LET US OUT OF HERE!!
AAAH!
DASH!!
THIS ONE IS A LOT BIGGER THAN USUAL!!
I KNEW IT!! IT'S HIS FAULT!! IT'S ALL BECAUSE OF HIM!!
WE WERE ALREADY CURSED BY THE EVIL SPIRIT, AND NOW...
NOW WE'VE ANGERED THE GODS AS WELL!
SHAKE SHAKE
WAH
EEK
PROTECT THE SICK!!
RRMMMMMB...
...
I KNEW I SHOULDN'T HAVE LET HIM LIVE!
TMP TMP TMP!!

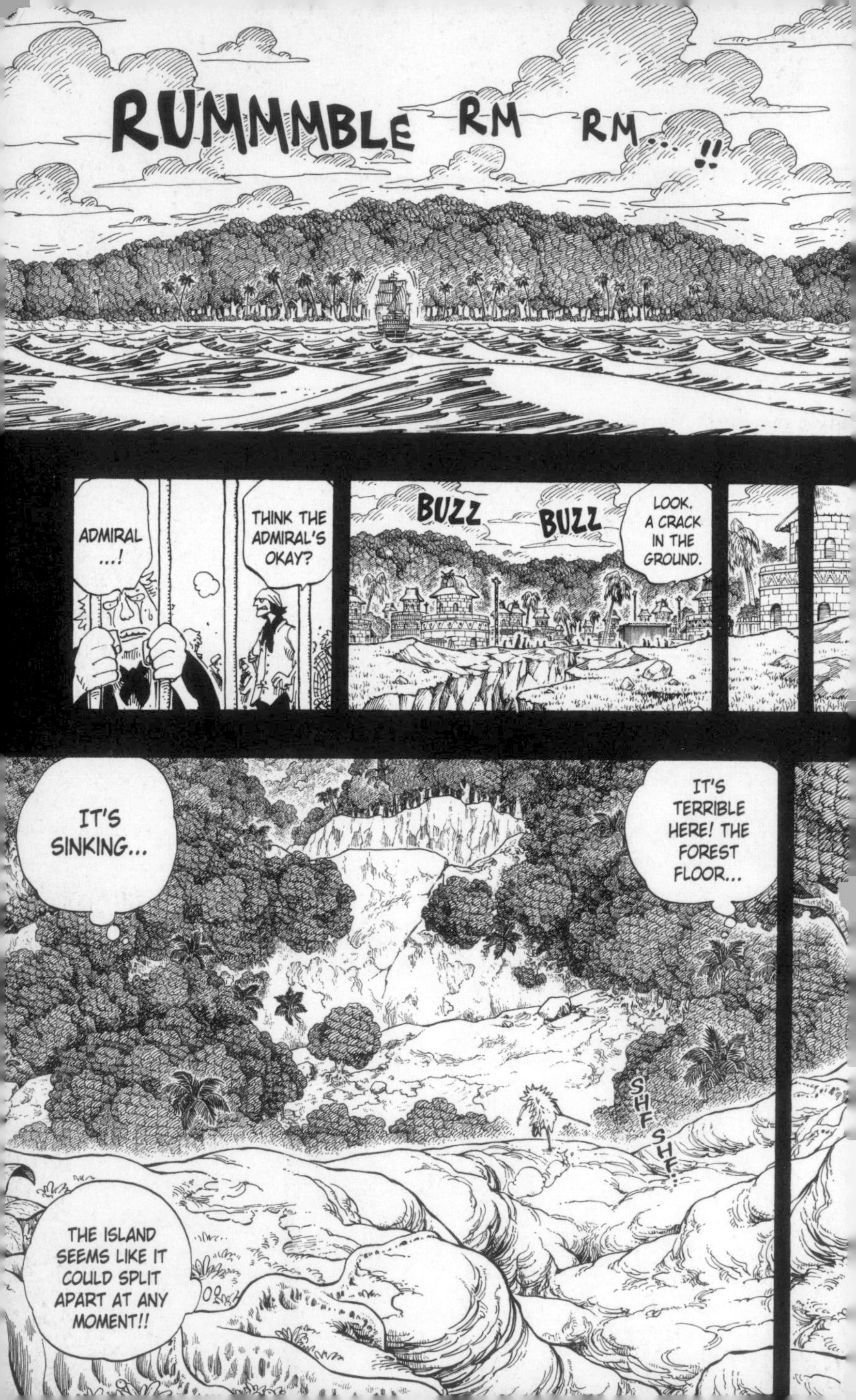
RUMMMBLE RM RM...!!
BUZZ BUZZ
LOOK. A CRACK IN THE GROUND.
THINK THE ADMIRAL'S OKAY?
ADMIRAL ...!
IT'S TERRIBLE HERE! THE FOREST FLOOR...
IT'S SINKING...
SHF SHF...
THE ISLAND SEEMS LIKE IT COULD SPLIT APART AT ANY MOMENT!!

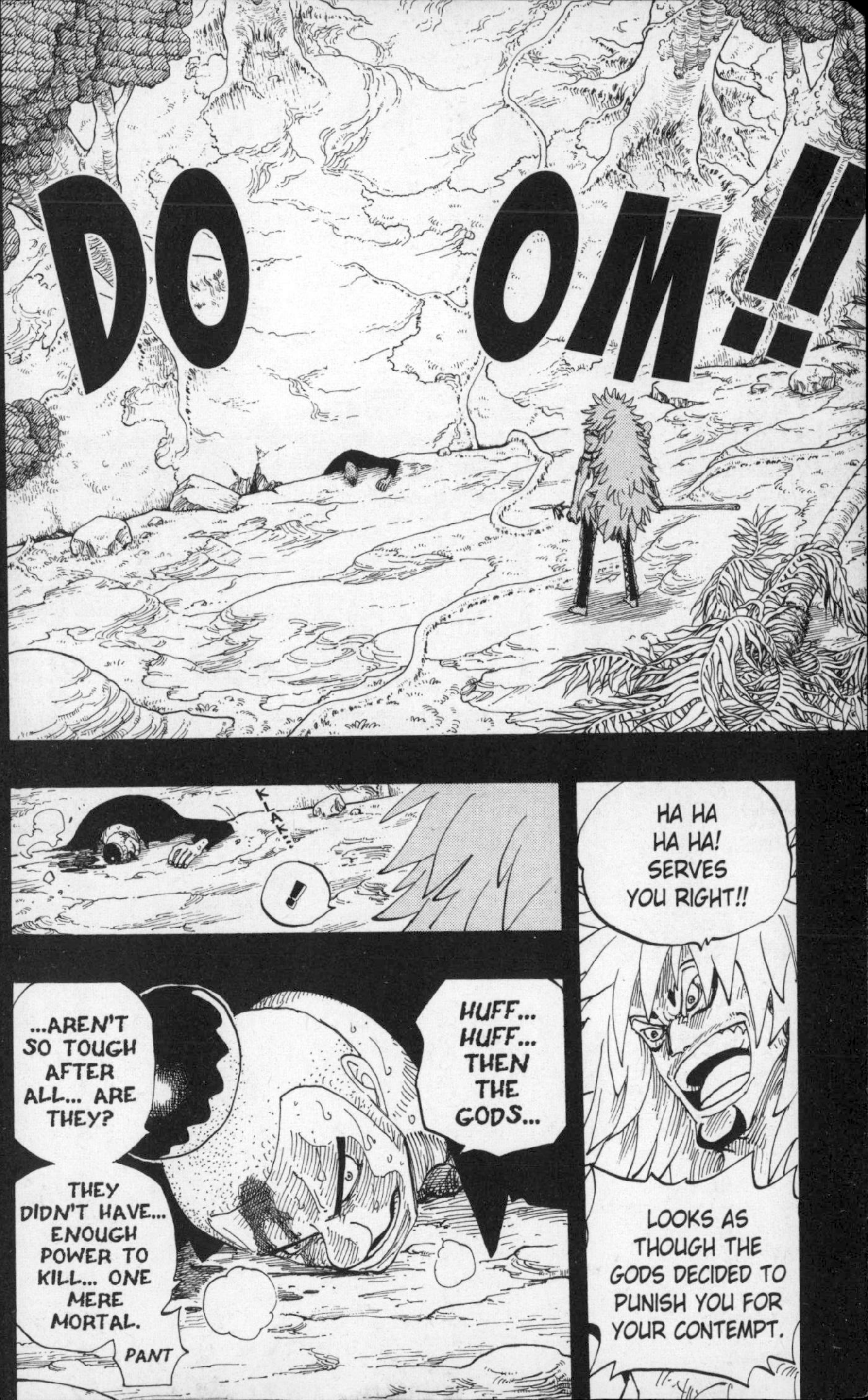
DO OM!!
HA HA HA HA! SERVES YOU RIGHT!!
LOOKS AS THOUGH THE GODS DECIDED TO PUNISH YOU FOR YOUR CONTEMPT.
KLAK...
!
HUFF... HUFF... THEN THE GODS...
...AREN'T SO TOUGH AFTER ALL... ARE THEY?
THEY DIDN'T HAVE... ENOUGH POWER TO KILL... ONE MERE MORTAL.
PANT

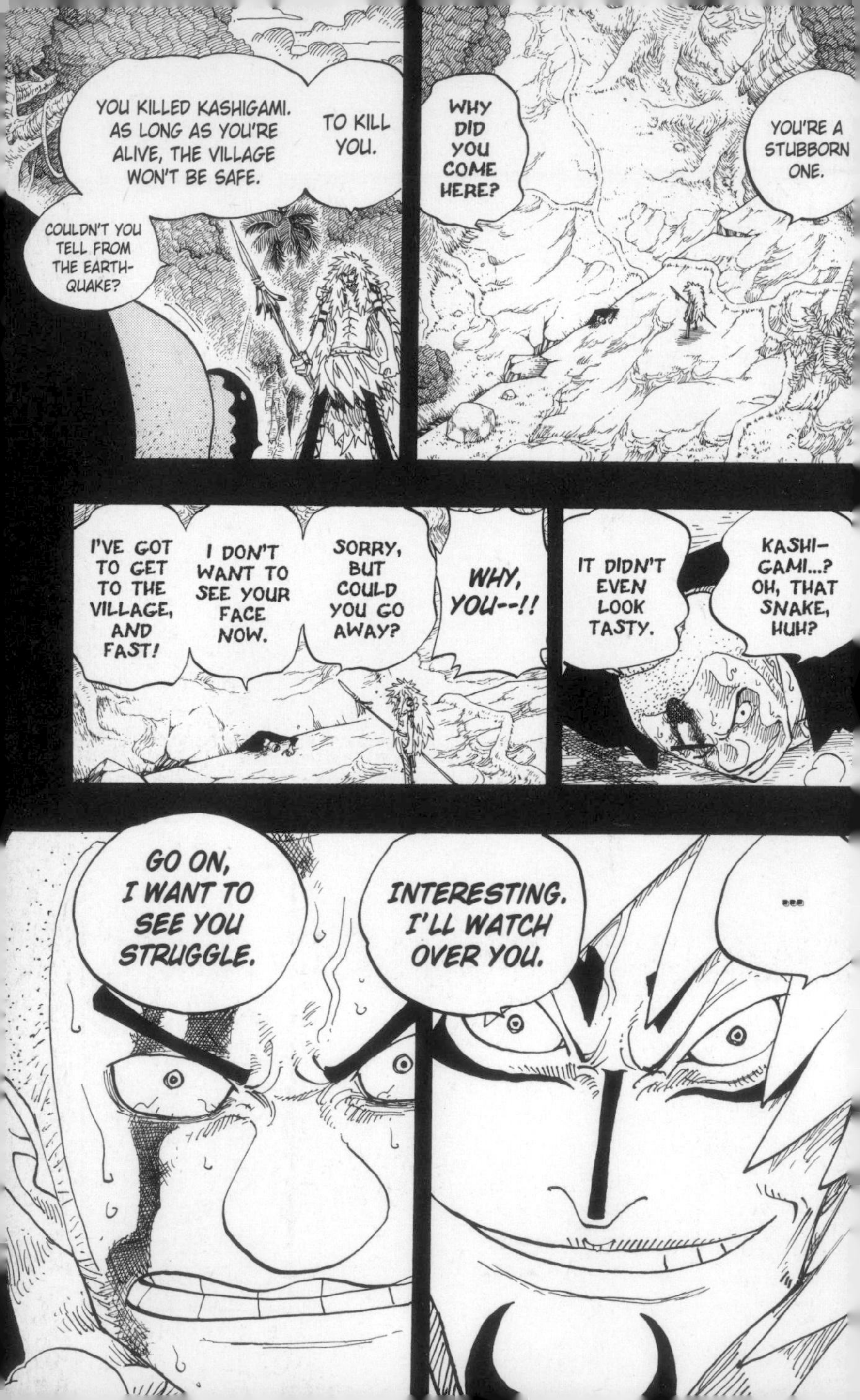
YOU'RE A STUBBORN ONE.
WHY DID YOU COME HERE?
TO KILL YOU.
YOU KILLED KASHIGAMI. AS LONG AS YOU'RE ALIVE, THE VILLAGE WON'T BE SAFE.
COULDN'T YOU TELL FROM THE EARTH-QUAKE?
KASHI-GAMI...? OH, THAT SNAKE, HUH?
IT DIDN'T EVEN LOOK TASTY.
WHY, YOU--!!
SORRY, BUT COULD YOU GO AWAY?
I DON'T WANT TO SEE YOUR FACE NOW.
I'VE GOT TO GET TO THE VILLAGE, AND FAST!
...
INTERESTING. I'LL WATCH OVER YOU.
GO ON, I WANT TO SEE YOU STRUGGLE.

Chapter 289:
FULL MOON

SIGN SAYS "JUSTICE IN MODERATION" --ED.

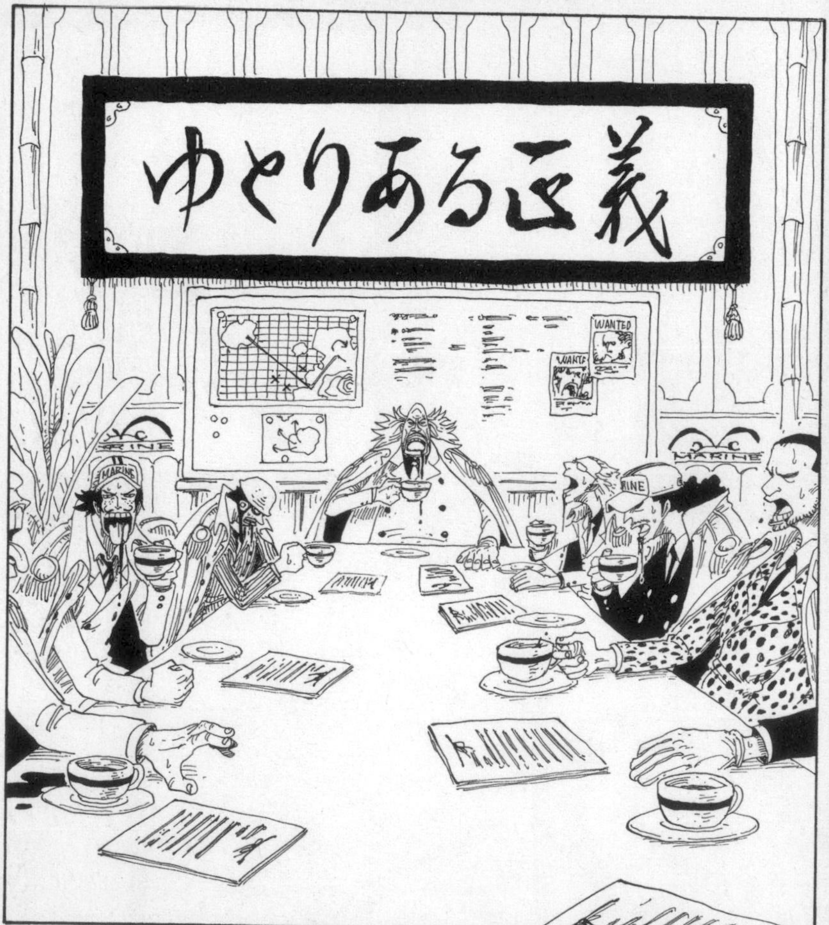
ゆとりある正義
WANTED
MARINE
MARINE

ACE'S GREAT SEARCH FOR BLACKBEARD, VOL. 15:
"MILITARY COURT COFFEE IS BITTER"

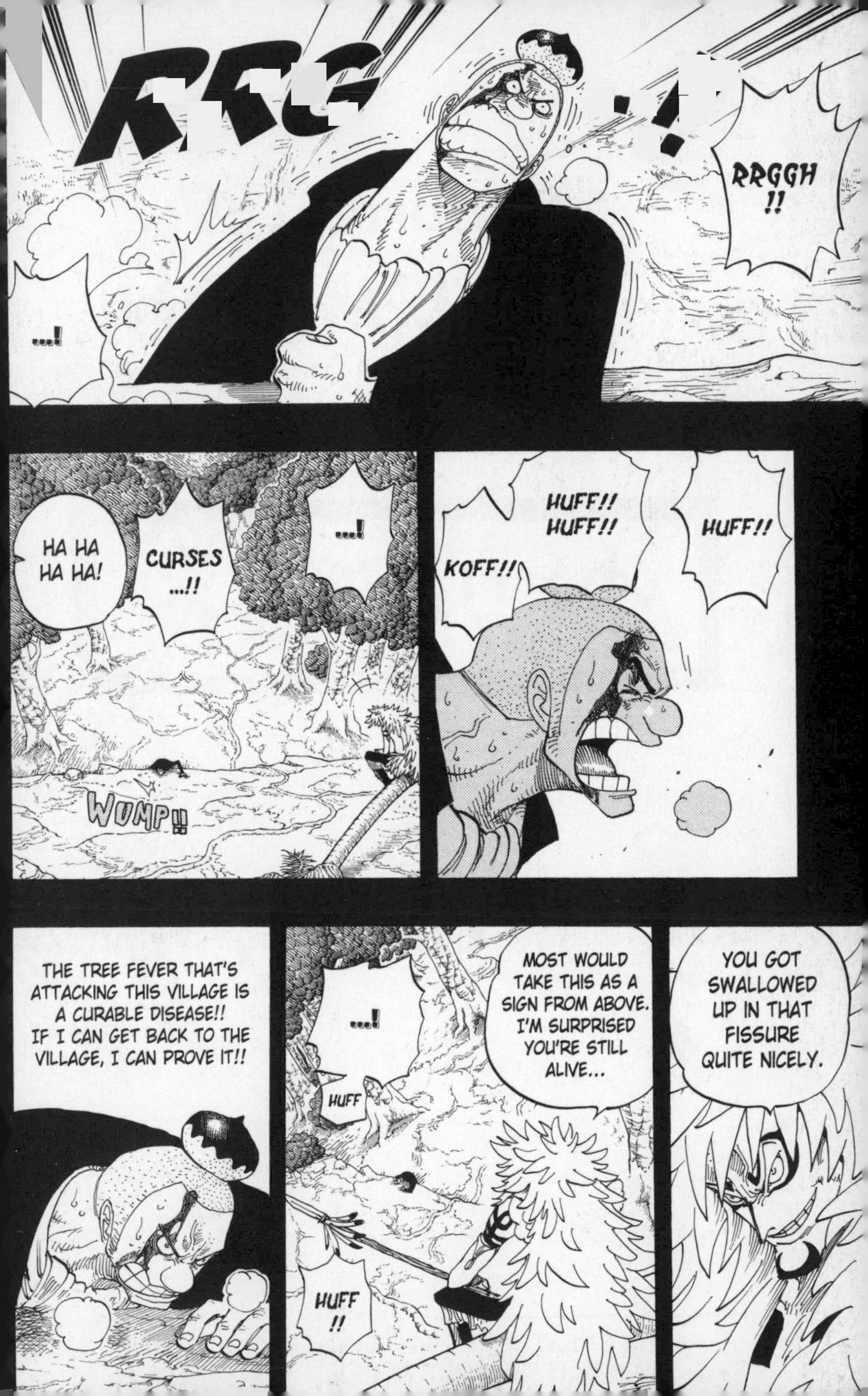
RRGGH !!
...!
HUFF!!
HUFF!! HUFF!!
KOFF!!
...!
CURSES ...!!
HA HA HA HA!
WUMP!!
YOU GOT SWALLOWED UP IN THAT FISSURE QUITE NICELY.
MOST WOULD TAKE THIS AS A SIGN FROM ABOVE. I'M SURPRISED YOU'RE STILL ALIVE...
...!
HUFF
HUFF !!
THE TREE FEVER THAT'S ATTACKING THIS VILLAGE IS A CURABLE DISEASE!! IF I CAN GET BACK TO THE VILLAGE, I CAN PROVE IT!!

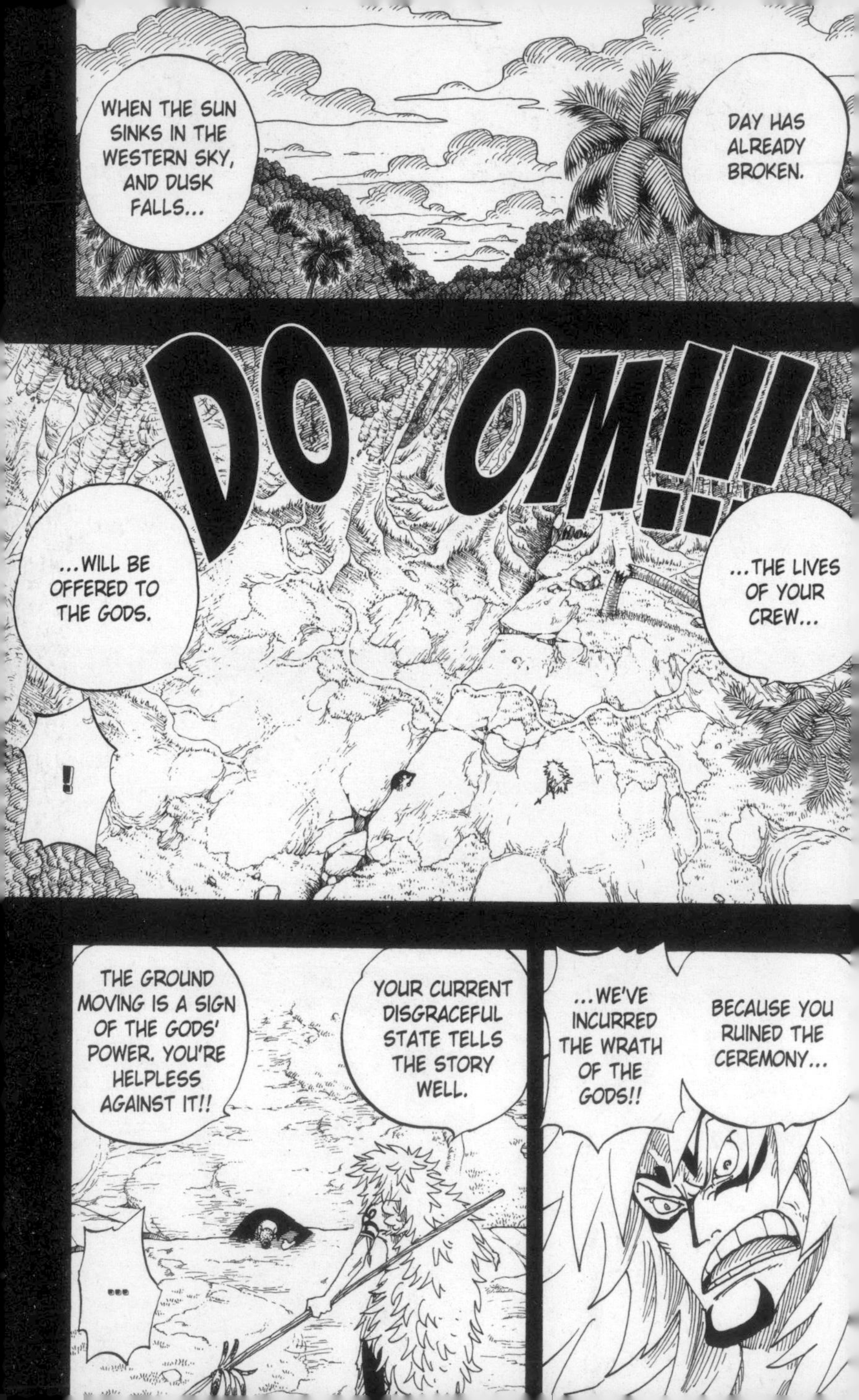
DAY HAS ALREADY BROKEN.
WHEN THE SUN SINKS IN THE WESTERN SKY, AND DUSK FALLS...
DOOM!!!
...THE LIVES OF YOUR CREW...
...WILL BE OFFERED TO THE GODS.
!
BECAUSE YOU RUINED THE CEREMONY...
...WE'VE INCURRED THE WRATH OF THE GODS!!
YOUR CURRENT DISGRACEFUL STATE TELLS THE STORY WELL.
THE GROUND MOVING IS A SIGN OF THE GODS' POWER. YOU'RE HELPLESS AGAINST IT!!
...

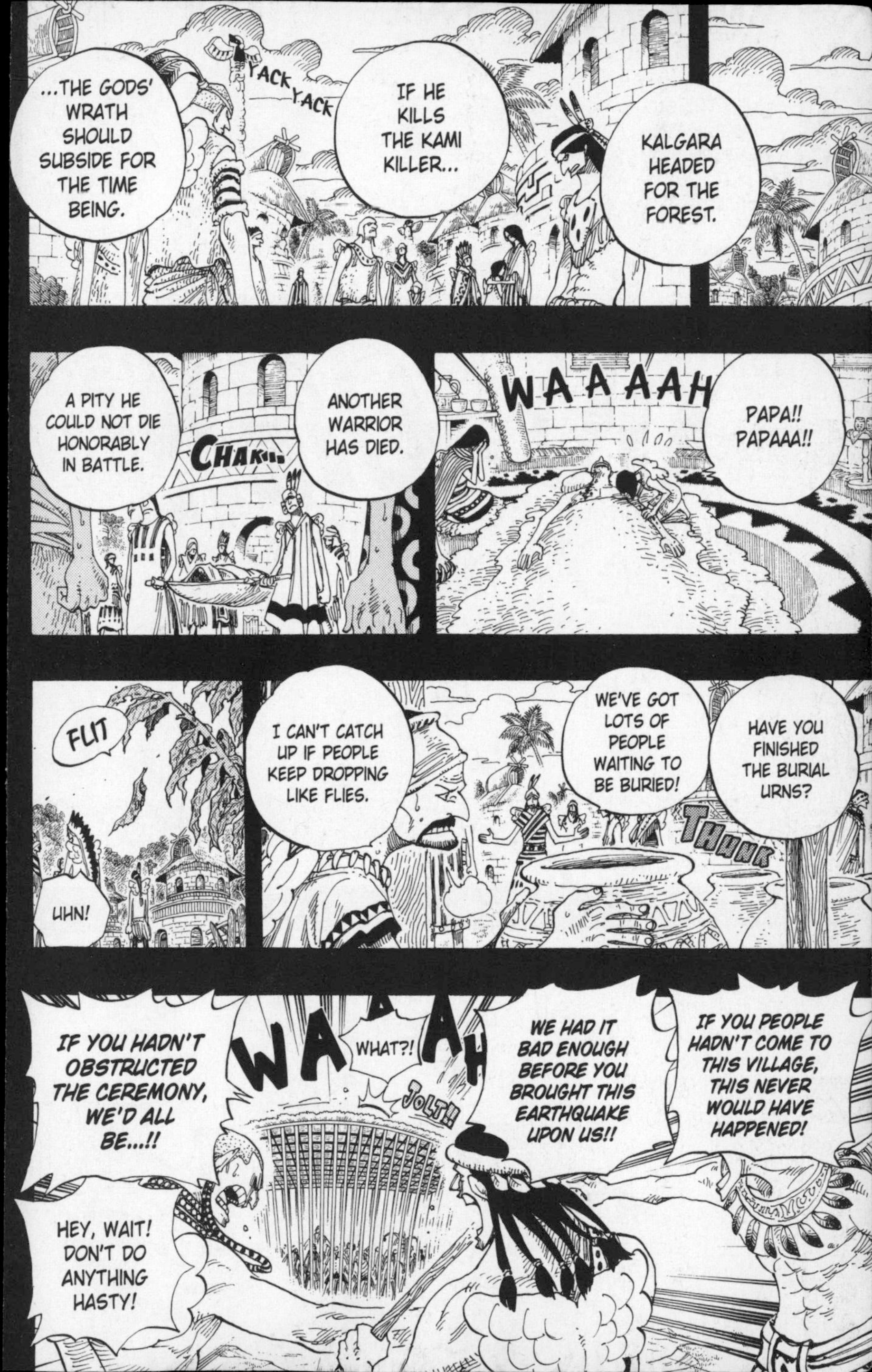
KALGARA HEADED FOR THE FOREST.
IF HE KILLS THE KAMI KILLER...
YACK YACK
...THE GODS' WRATH SHOULD SUBSIDE FOR THE TIME BEING.
PAPA!! PAPAAA!!
WAAAAH
ANOTHER WARRIOR HAS DIED.
CHAK...
A PITY HE COULD NOT DIE HONORABLY IN BATTLE.
HAVE YOU FINISHED THE BURIAL URNS?
WE'VE GOT LOTS OF PEOPLE WAITING TO BE BURIED!
THUNK
I CAN'T CATCH UP IF PEOPLE KEEP DROPPING LIKE FLIES.
FLIT
UHN!
IF YOU PEOPLE HADN'T COME TO THIS VILLAGE, THIS NEVER WOULD HAVE HAPPENED!
WE HAD IT BAD ENOUGH BEFORE YOU BROUGHT THIS EARTHQUAKE UPON US!!
WAAAH
WHAT?!
JOLT!!
IF YOU HADN'T OBSTRUCTED THE CEREMONY, WE'D ALL BE...!!
HEY, WAIT! DON'T DO ANYTHING HASTY!

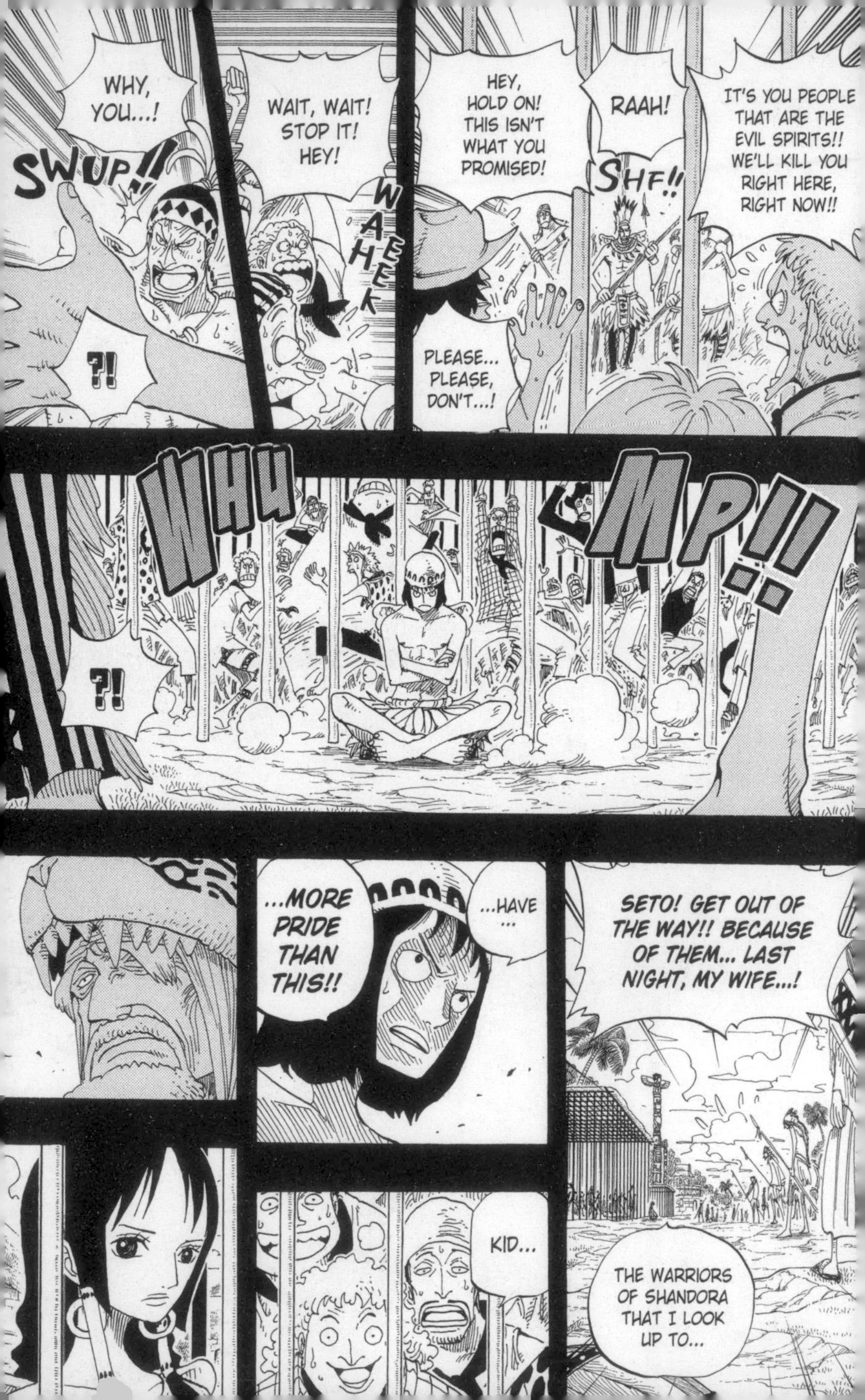
IT'S YOU PEOPLE THAT ARE THE EVIL SPIRITS!! WE'LL KILL YOU RIGHT HERE, RIGHT NOW!!
RAAH!
SHF!!
HEY, HOLD ON! THIS ISN'T WHAT YOU PROMISED!
PLEASE... PLEASE, DON'T...!
WAIT, WAIT! STOP IT! HEY!
WAHEEK
WHY, YOU...!
SWUP!!
?!
WHUMP!!
?!
SETO! GET OUT OF THE WAY!! BECAUSE OF THEM... LAST NIGHT, MY WIFE...!
THE WARRIORS OF SHANDORA THAT I LOOK UP TO...
...HAVE ...
...MORE PRIDE THAN THIS!!
KID...

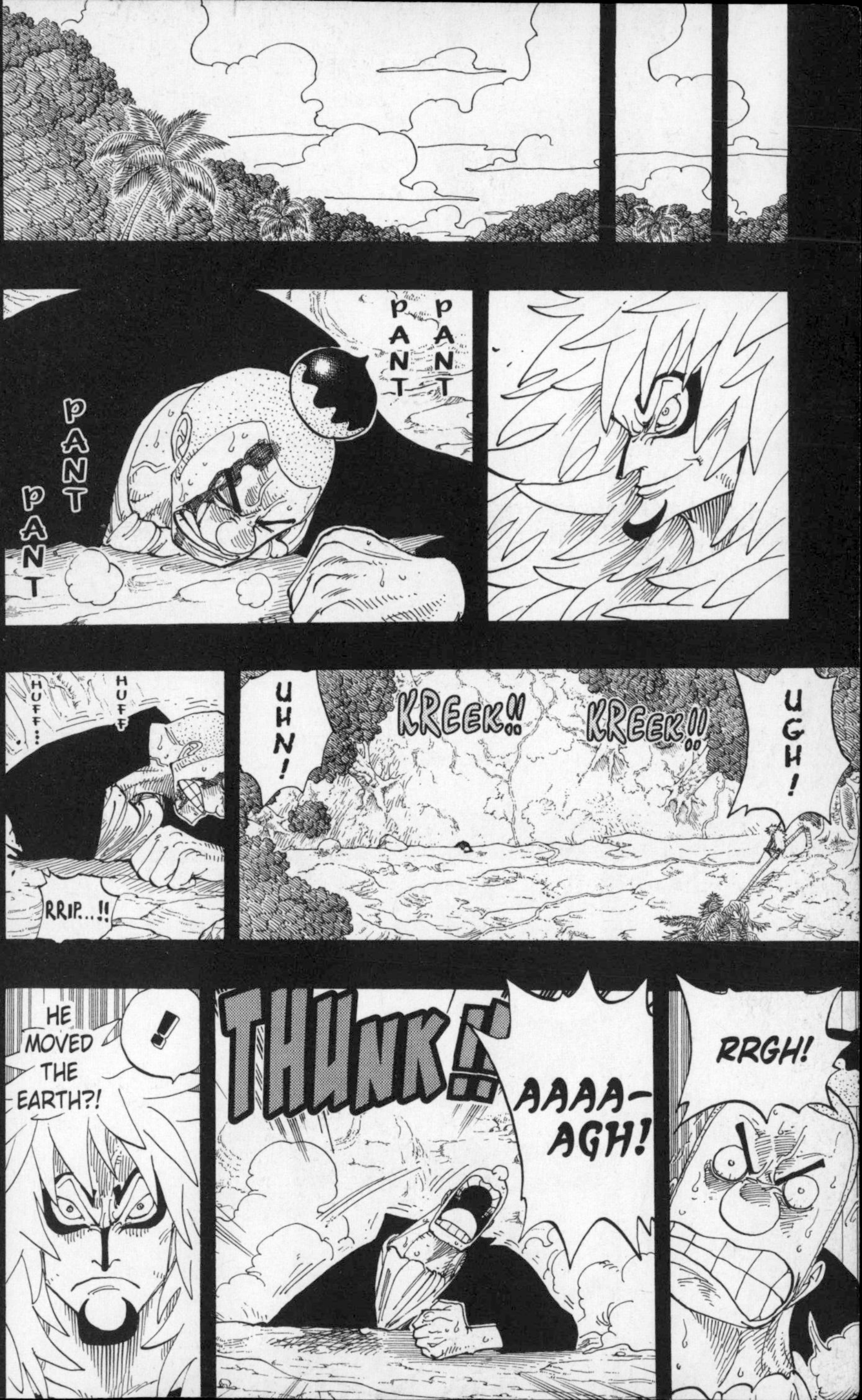
pANT pANT
pANT pANT
UGH!
KREEK!!
KREEK!!
UHN!
HUFF HUFF...
RRIP...!!
RRGH!
THUNK!!
AAAA-AGH!
!
HE MOVED THE EARTH?!

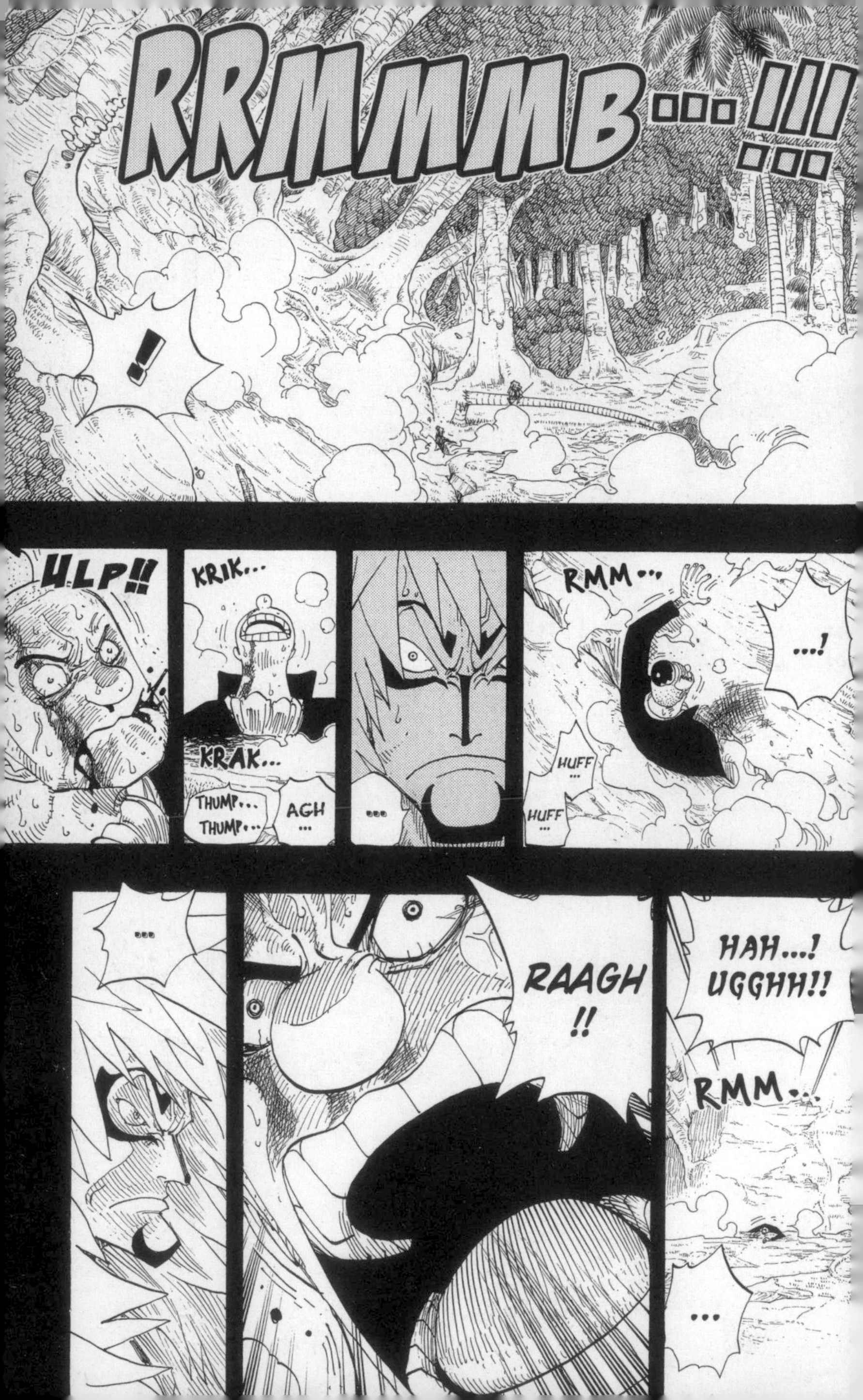
RRMMMB...!!!
!
RMM...
...!
HUFF...
HUFF...
...
KRIK...
KRAK...
AGH...
THUMP...
THUMP...
ULP!!
HAH...! UGGHH!!
RMM...
...
RAAGH !!
...

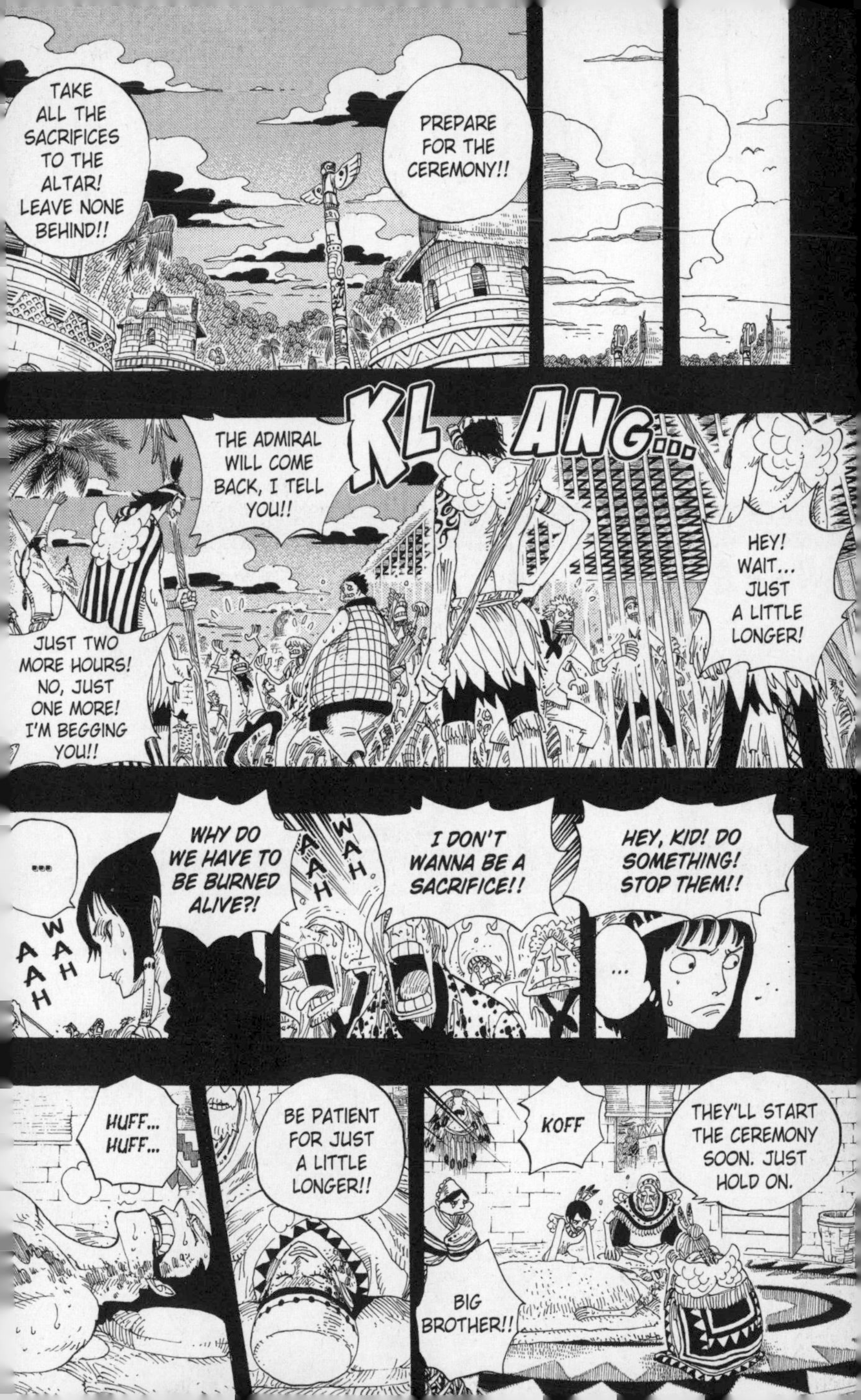
PREPARE FOR THE CEREMONY!!
TAKE ALL THE SACRIFICES TO THE ALTAR! LEAVE NONE BEHIND!!
HEY! WAIT... JUST A LITTLE LONGER!
KLANG...
THE ADMIRAL WILL COME BACK, I TELL YOU!!
JUST TWO MORE HOURS! NO, JUST ONE MORE! I'M BEGGING YOU!!
HEY, KID! DO SOMETHING! STOP THEM!!
...
I DON'T WANNA BE A SACRIFICE!!
WAH AAH
WHY DO WE HAVE TO BE BURNED ALIVE?!
...
WAH AAH
THEY'LL START THE CEREMONY SOON. JUST HOLD ON.
KOFF
BIG BROTHER!!
BE PATIENT FOR JUST A LITTLE LONGER!!
HUFF... HUFF...

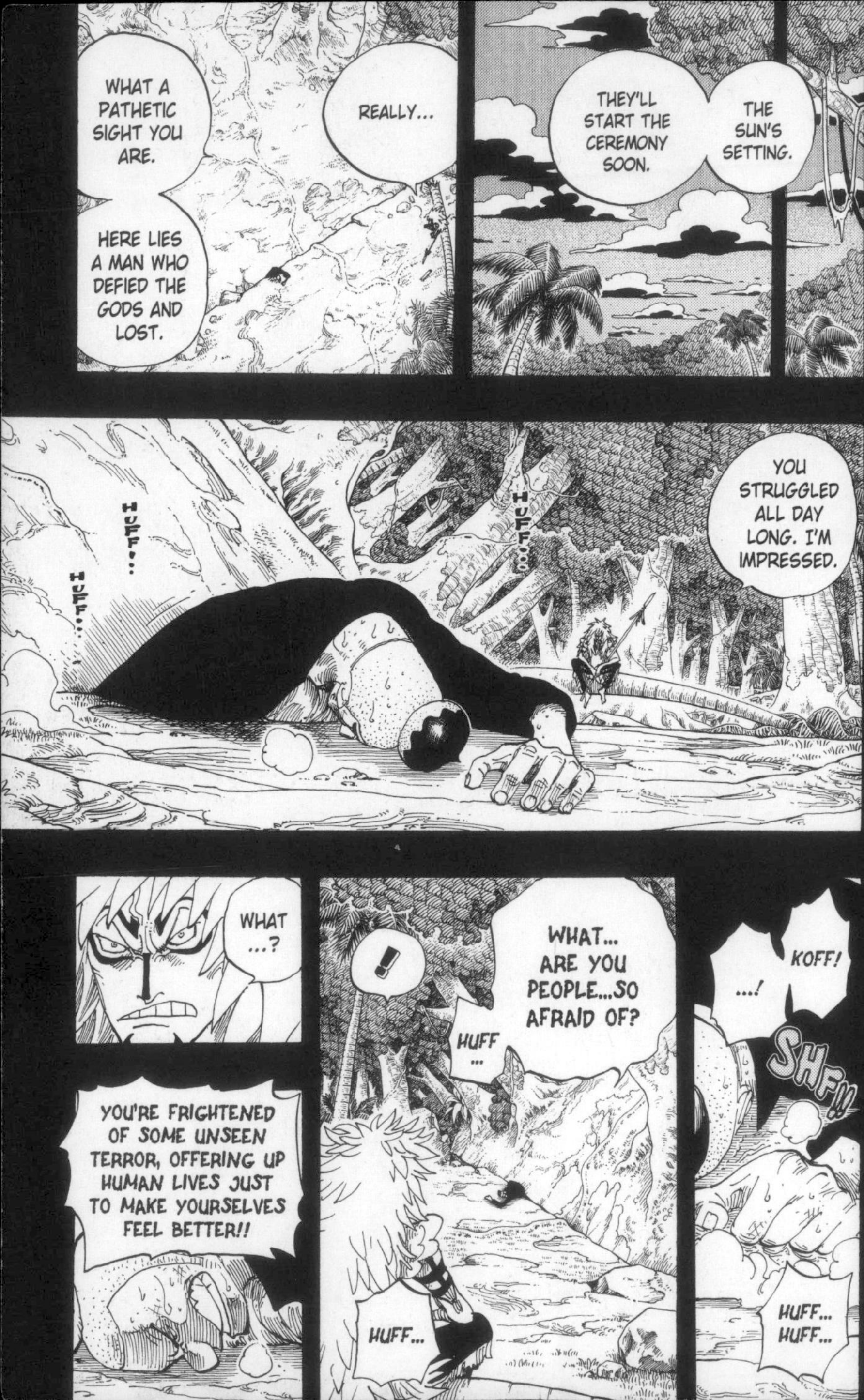

THE SUN'S SETTING.
THEY'LL START THE CEREMONY SOON.
REALLY...
WHAT A PATHETIC SIGHT YOU ARE.
HERE LIES A MAN WHO DEFIED THE GODS AND LOST.
YOU STRUGGLED ALL DAY LONG. I'M IMPRESSED.
HUFF...
HUFF...
HUFF...
KOFF!
...!
SHF!!
HUFF... HUFF...
WHAT... ARE YOU PEOPLE...SO AFRAID OF?
!
HUFF...
HUFF...
WHAT ...?
YOU'RE FRIGHTENED OF SOME UNSEEN TERROR, OFFERING UP HUMAN LIVES JUST TO MAKE YOURSELVES FEEL BETTER!!

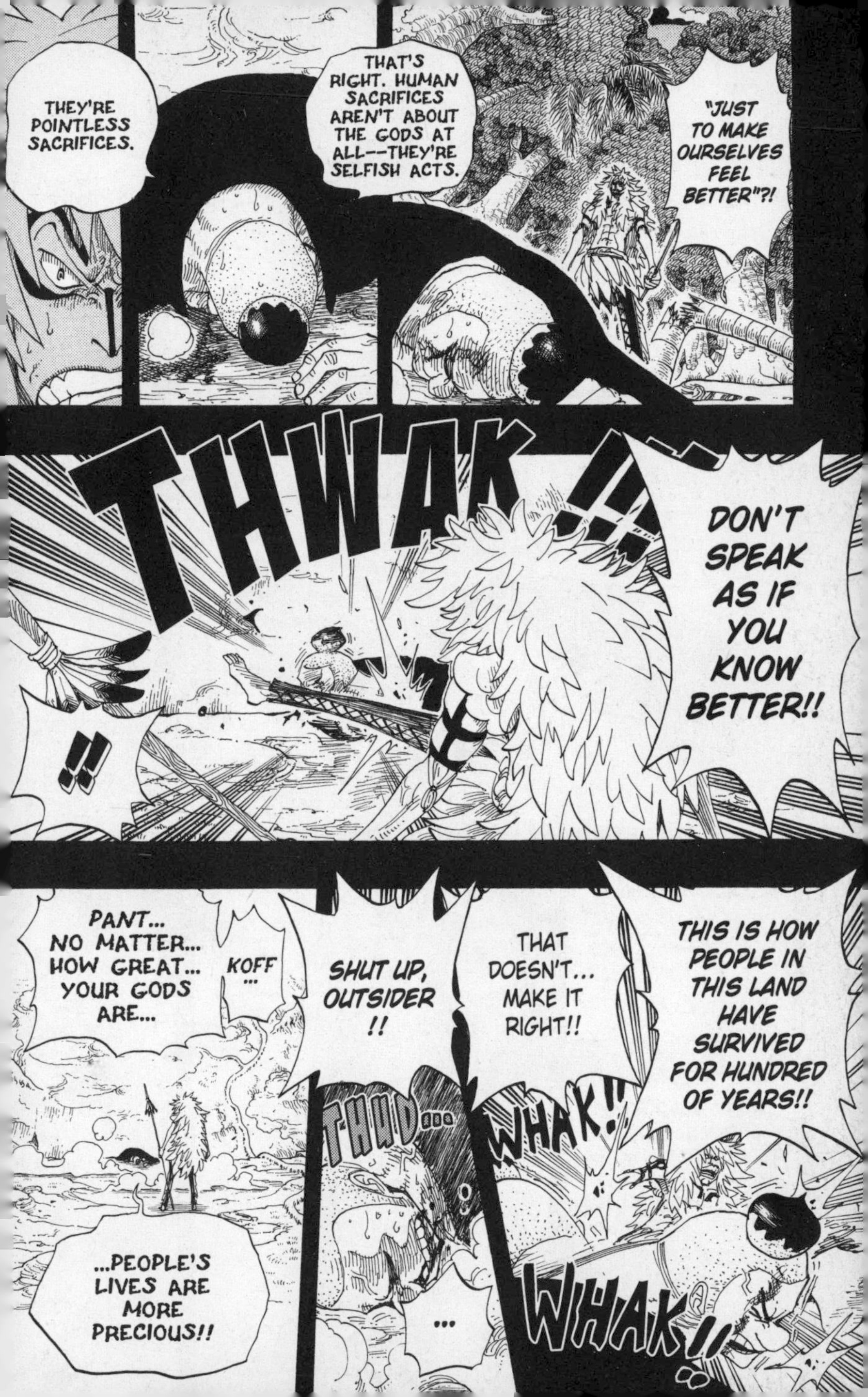
"JUST TO MAKE OURSELVES FEEL BETTER"?!
THAT'S RIGHT. HUMAN SACRIFICES AREN'T ABOUT THE GODS AT ALL--THEY'RE SELFISH ACTS.
THEY'RE POINTLESS SACRIFICES.
THWAK!!
DON'T SPEAK AS IF YOU KNOW BETTER!!
!!
THIS IS HOW PEOPLE IN THIS LAND HAVE SURVIVED FOR HUNDRED OF YEARS!!
WHAK!!
WHAK!!
THAT DOESN'T... MAKE IT RIGHT!!
SHUT UP, OUTSIDER!!
THUD...
...
KOFF...
PANT... NO MATTER... HOW GREAT... YOUR GODS ARE...
...PEOPLE'S LIVES ARE MORE PRECIOUS!!

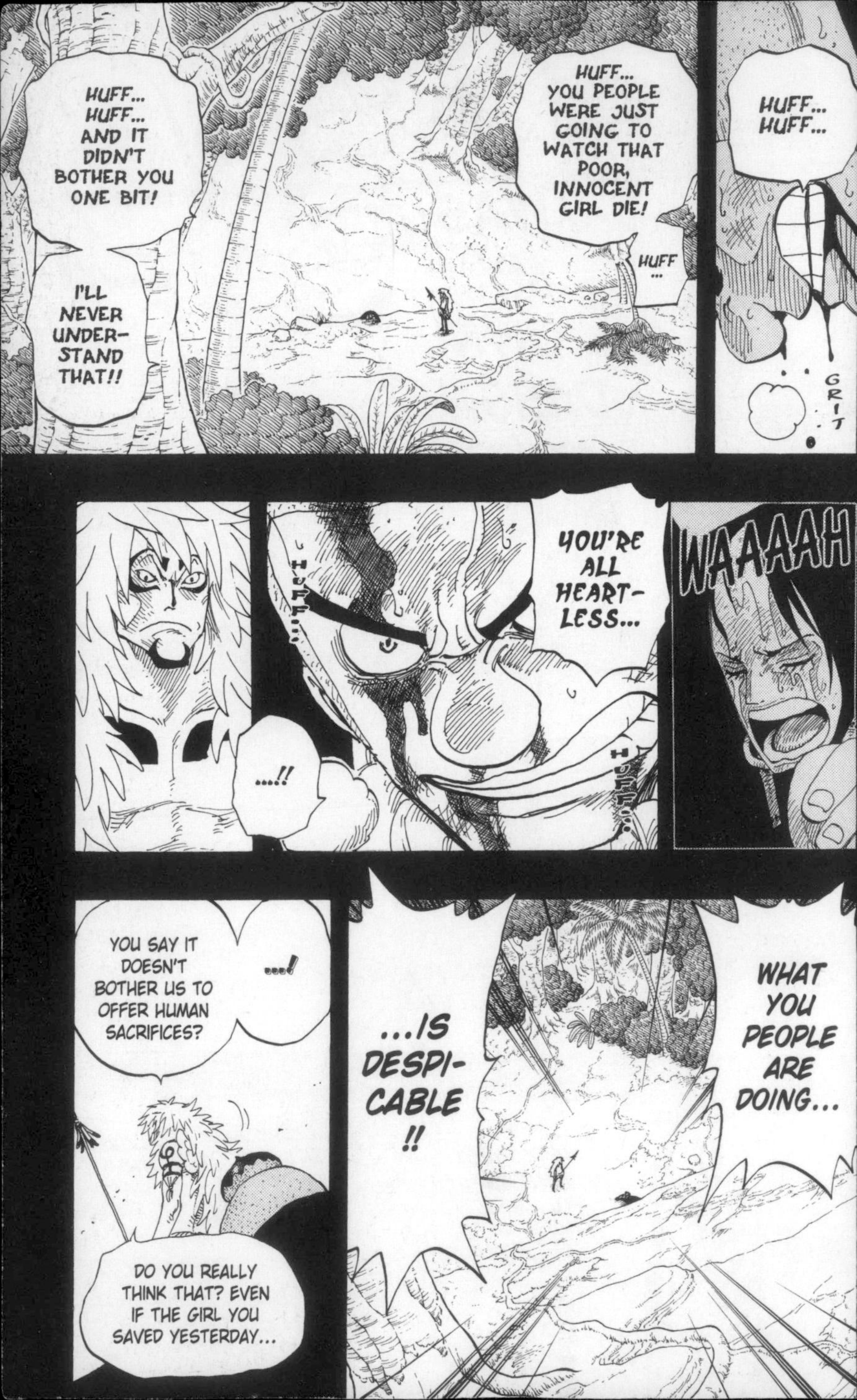
HUFF... HUFF...
GRIT
HUFF... YOU PEOPLE WERE JUST GOING TO WATCH THAT POOR, INNOCENT GIRL DIE!
HUFF...
HUFF... HUFF... AND IT DIDN'T BOTHER YOU ONE BIT!
I'LL NEVER UNDER-STAND THAT!!
WAAAAH
YOU'RE ALL HEART-LESS...
HUFF...
HUFF...
....!!
WHAT YOU PEOPLE ARE DOING...
...IS DESPI-CABLE !!
...!
YOU SAY IT DOESN'T BOTHER US TO OFFER HUMAN SACRIFICES?
DO YOU REALLY THINK THAT? EVEN IF THE GIRL YOU SAVED YESTERDAY...

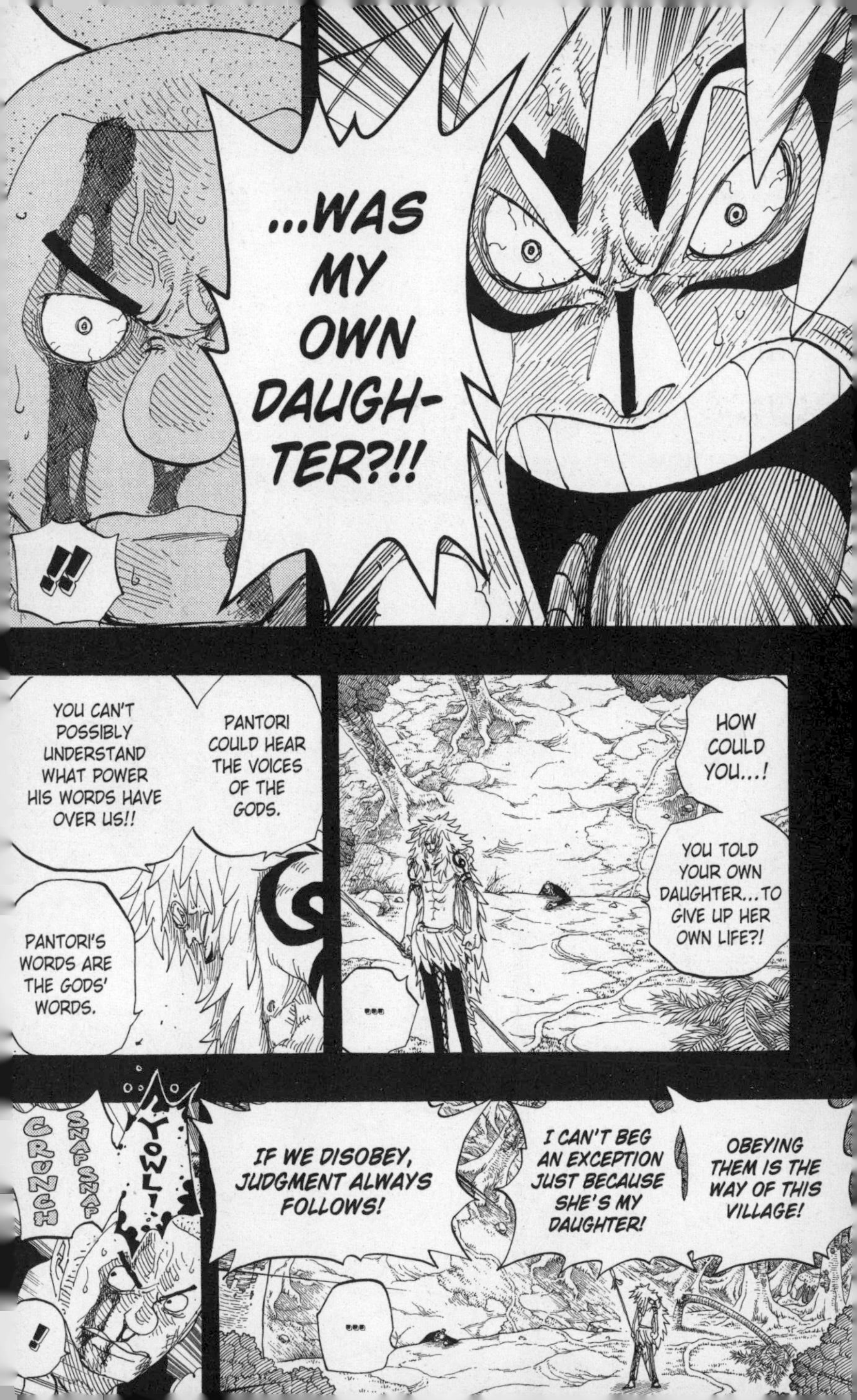
...WAS MY OWN DAUGHTER?!!
!!
HOW COULD YOU...!
YOU TOLD YOUR OWN DAUGHTER...TO GIVE UP HER OWN LIFE?!
...
PANTORI COULD HEAR THE VOICES OF THE GODS.
YOU CAN'T POSSIBLY UNDERSTAND WHAT POWER HIS WORDS HAVE OVER US!!
PANTORI'S WORDS ARE THE GODS' WORDS.
OBEYING THEM IS THE WAY OF THIS VILLAGE!
I CAN'T BEG AN EXCEPTION JUST BECAUSE SHE'S MY DAUGHTER!
IF WE DISOBEY, JUDGMENT ALWAYS FOLLOWS!
...
YOWL!!
SNAP SNAP
CRUNCH
!

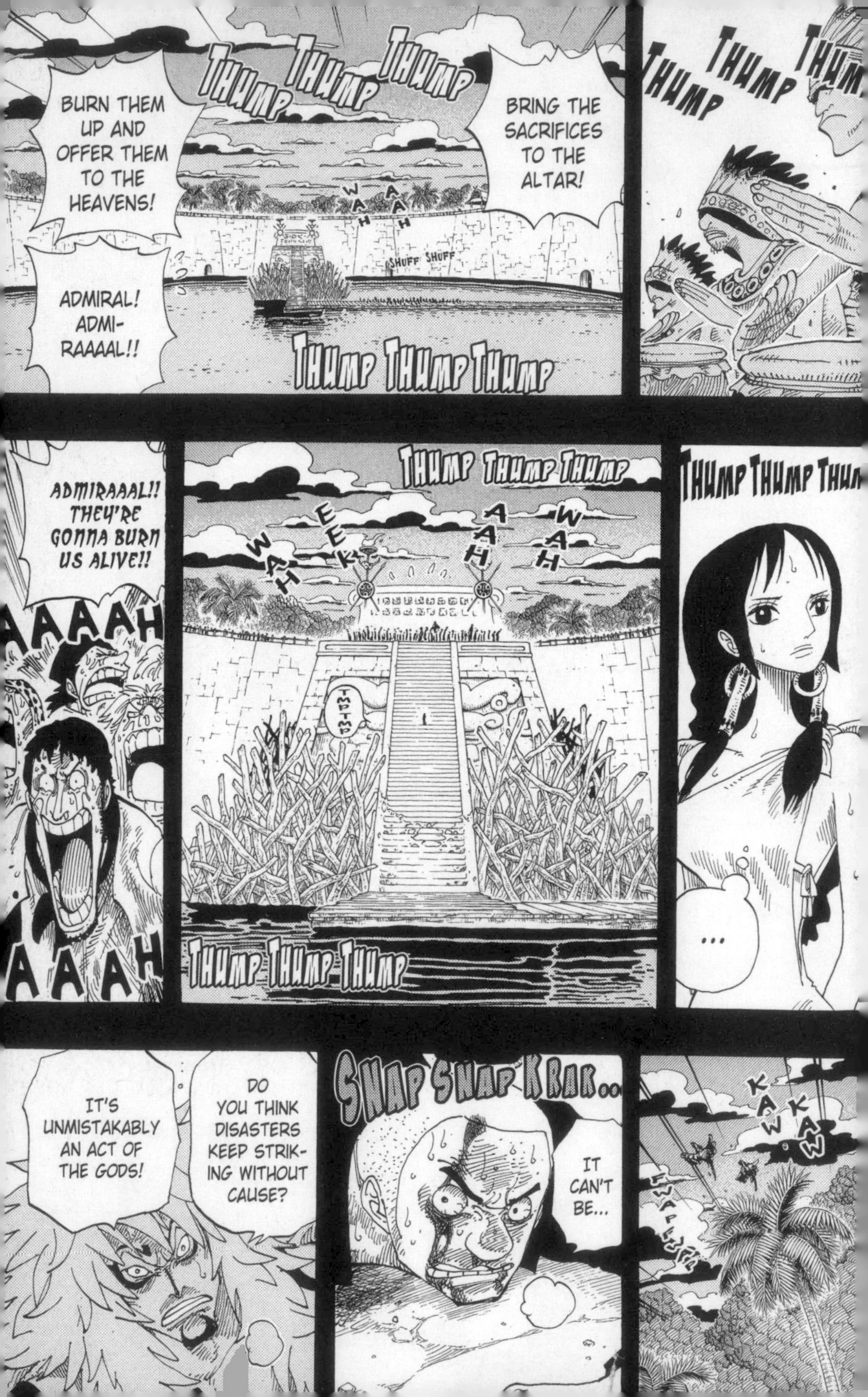
THUMP THUMP THUMP
BRING THE SACRIFICES TO THE ALTAR!
THUMP THUMP THUMP
BURN THEM UP AND OFFER THEM TO THE HEAVENS!
WAAAH
SHUFF SHUFF
ADMIRAL! ADMI-RAAAAL!!
THUMP THUMP THUMP
THUMP THUMP THUM
...
THUMP THUMP THUMP
WAAH
AAH
EEEK
WAH
THUMP THUMP THUMP
ADMIRAAAL!! THEY'RE GONNA BURN US ALIVE!!
AAAAH
AAAAH!!
KAKAW
SNAP SNAP KRAK...
IT CAN'T BE...
DO YOU THINK DISASTERS KEEP STRIK-ING WITHOUT CAUSE?
IT'S UNMISTAKABLY AN ACT OF THE GODS!

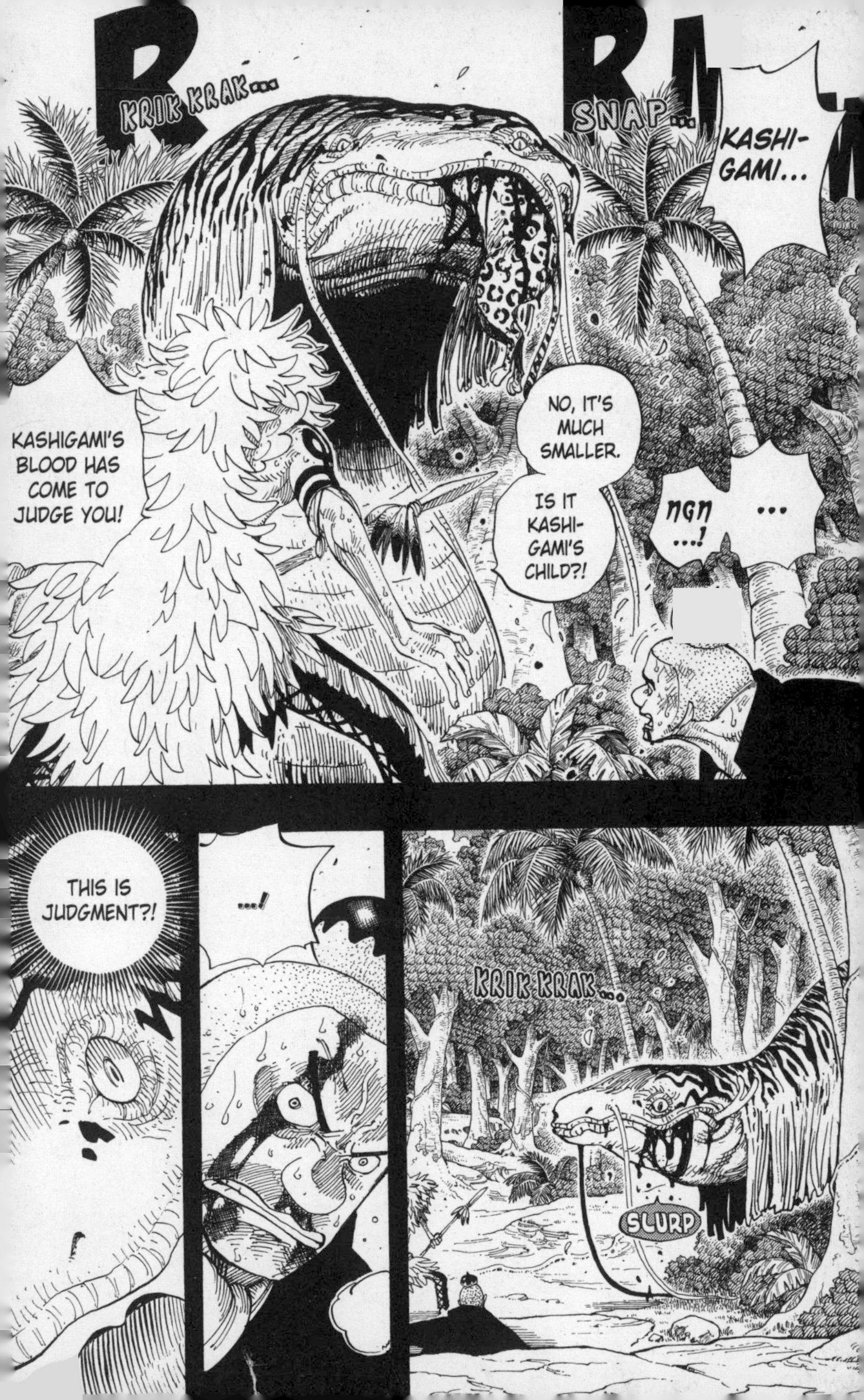
SNAP...
KASHI-GAMI...
...
ngn...!
NO, IT'S MUCH SMALLER.
IS IT KASHI-GAMI'S CHILD?!
KRIK KRAK...
KASHIGAMI'S BLOOD HAS COME TO JUDGE YOU!
KRIK KRAK...
SLURP
...!
THIS IS JUDGMENT?!

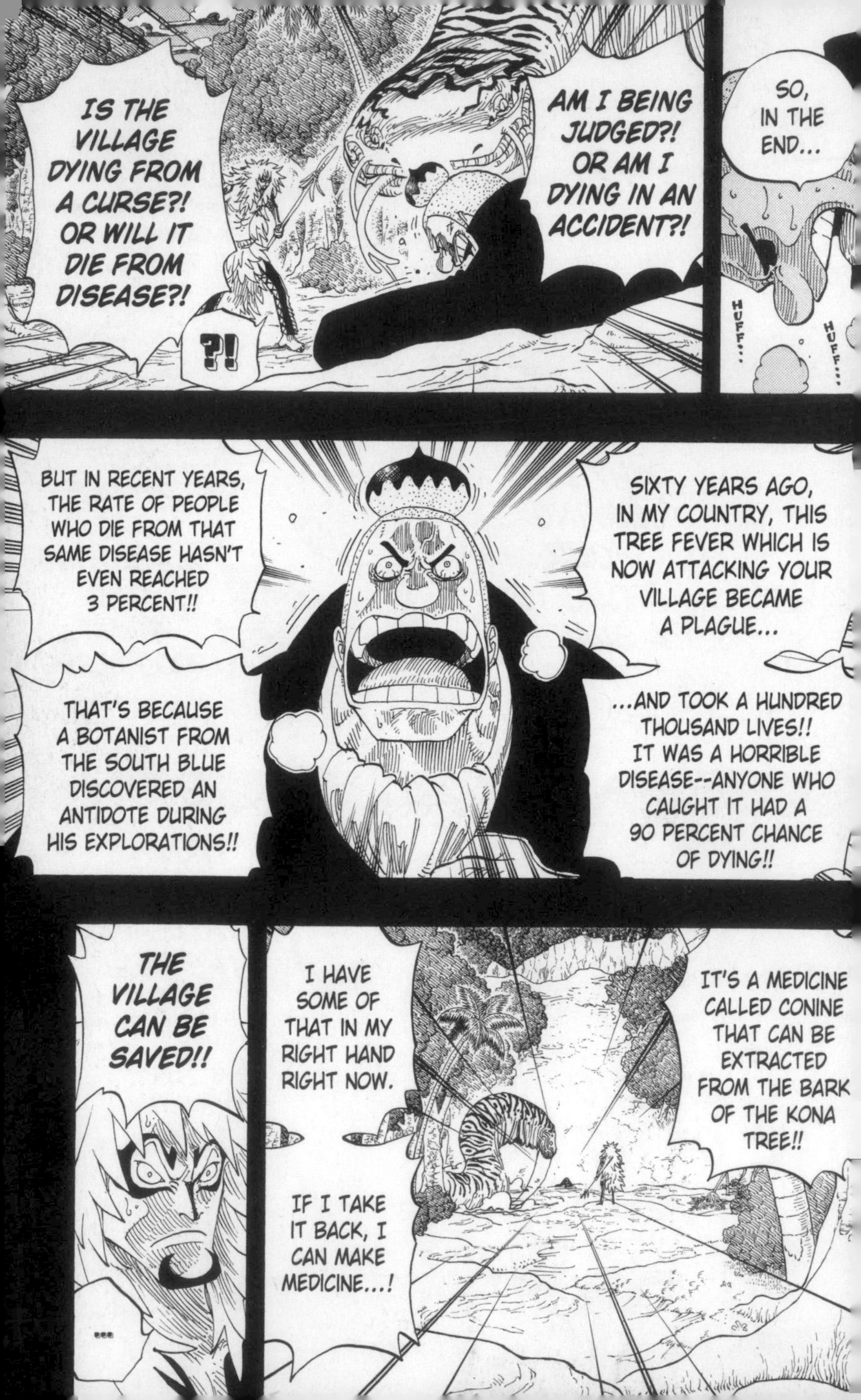
SO, IN THE END...
HUFF...
HUFF...
AM I BEING JUDGED?! OR AM I DYING IN AN ACCIDENT?!
IS THE VILLAGE DYING FROM A CURSE?! OR WILL IT DIE FROM DISEASE?!
?!
SIXTY YEARS AGO, IN MY COUNTRY, THIS TREE FEVER WHICH IS NOW ATTACKING YOUR VILLAGE BECAME A PLAGUE...
...AND TOOK A HUNDRED THOUSAND LIVES!! IT WAS A HORRIBLE DISEASE--ANYONE WHO CAUGHT IT HAD A 90 PERCENT CHANCE OF DYING!!
BUT IN RECENT YEARS, THE RATE OF PEOPLE WHO DIE FROM THAT SAME DISEASE HASN'T EVEN REACHED 3 PERCENT!!
THAT'S BECAUSE A BOTANIST FROM THE SOUTH BLUE DISCOVERED AN ANTIDOTE DURING HIS EXPLORATIONS!!
IT'S A MEDICINE CALLED CONINE THAT CAN BE EXTRACTED FROM THE BARK OF THE KONA TREE!!
I HAVE SOME OF THAT IN MY RIGHT HAND RIGHT NOW.
IF I TAKE IT BACK, I CAN MAKE MEDICINE...!
THE VILLAGE CAN BE SAVED!!
...

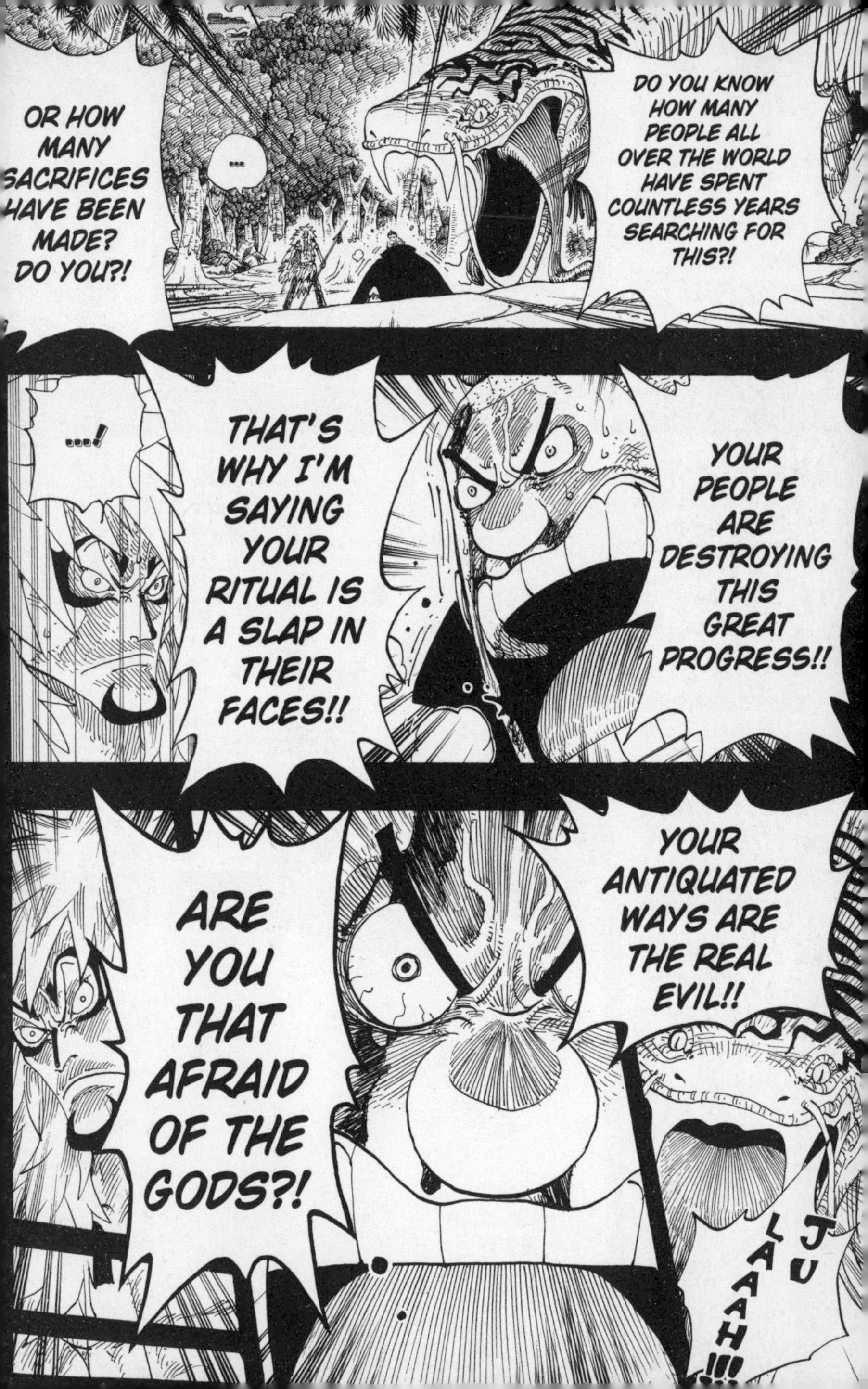
DO YOU KNOW HOW MANY PEOPLE ALL OVER THE WORLD HAVE SPENT COUNTLESS YEARS SEARCHING FOR THIS?!
...
OR HOW MANY SACRIFICES HAVE BEEN MADE? DO YOU?!
YOUR PEOPLE ARE DESTROYING THIS GREAT PROGRESS!!
THAT'S WHY I'M SAYING YOUR RITUAL IS A SLAP IN THEIR FACES!!
...!
YOUR ANTIQUATED WAYS ARE THE REAL EVIL!!
JU
LAAAAH!!!
ARE YOU THAT AFRAID OF THE GODS?!

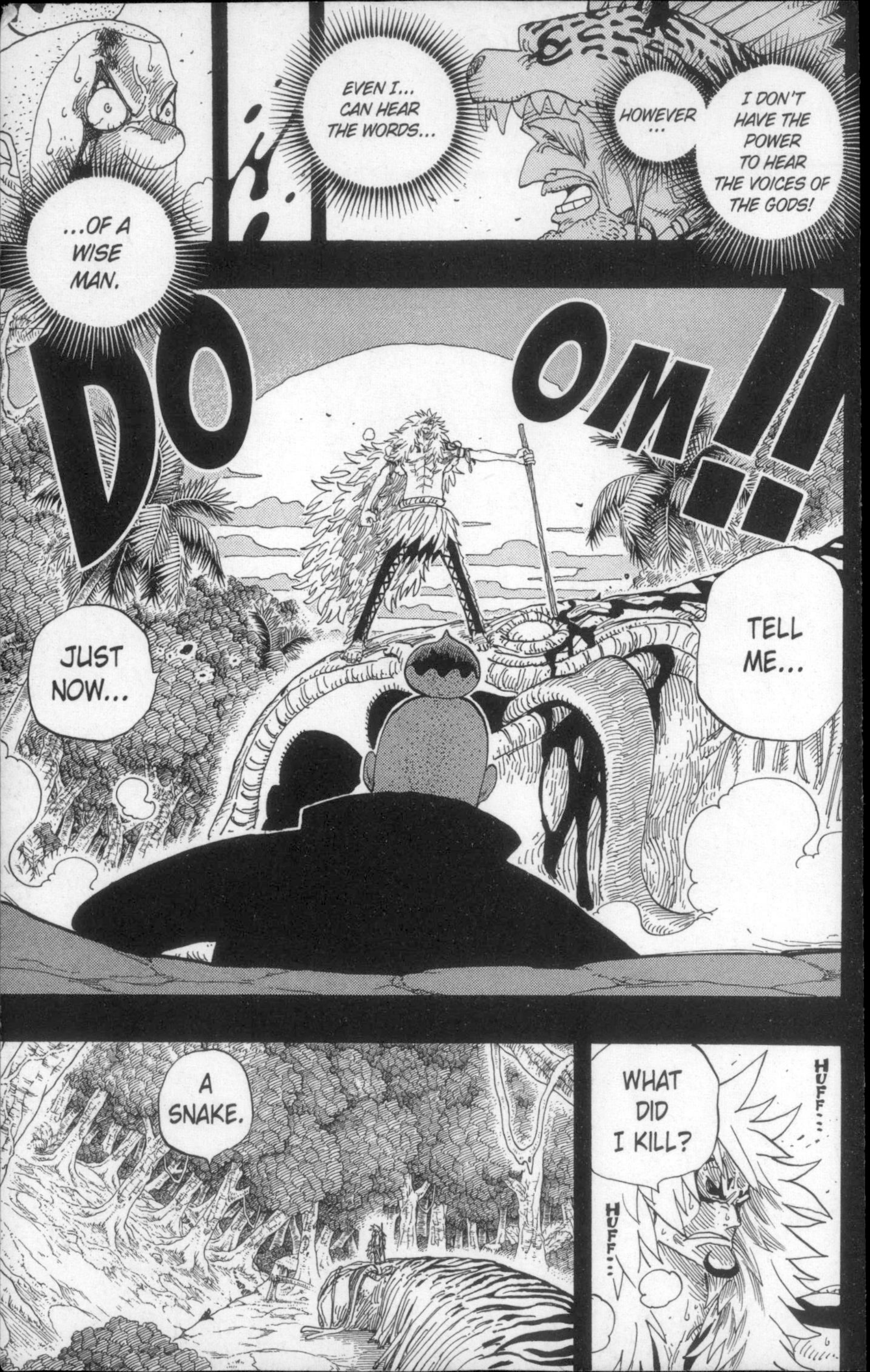

I DON'T HAVE THE POWER TO HEAR THE VOICES OF THE GODS!
HOWEVER ...
EVEN I... CAN HEAR THE WORDS...
...OF A WISE MAN.
DOOM!!
TELL ME...
JUST NOW...
HUFF...
HUFF...
WHAT DID I KILL?
A SNAKE.

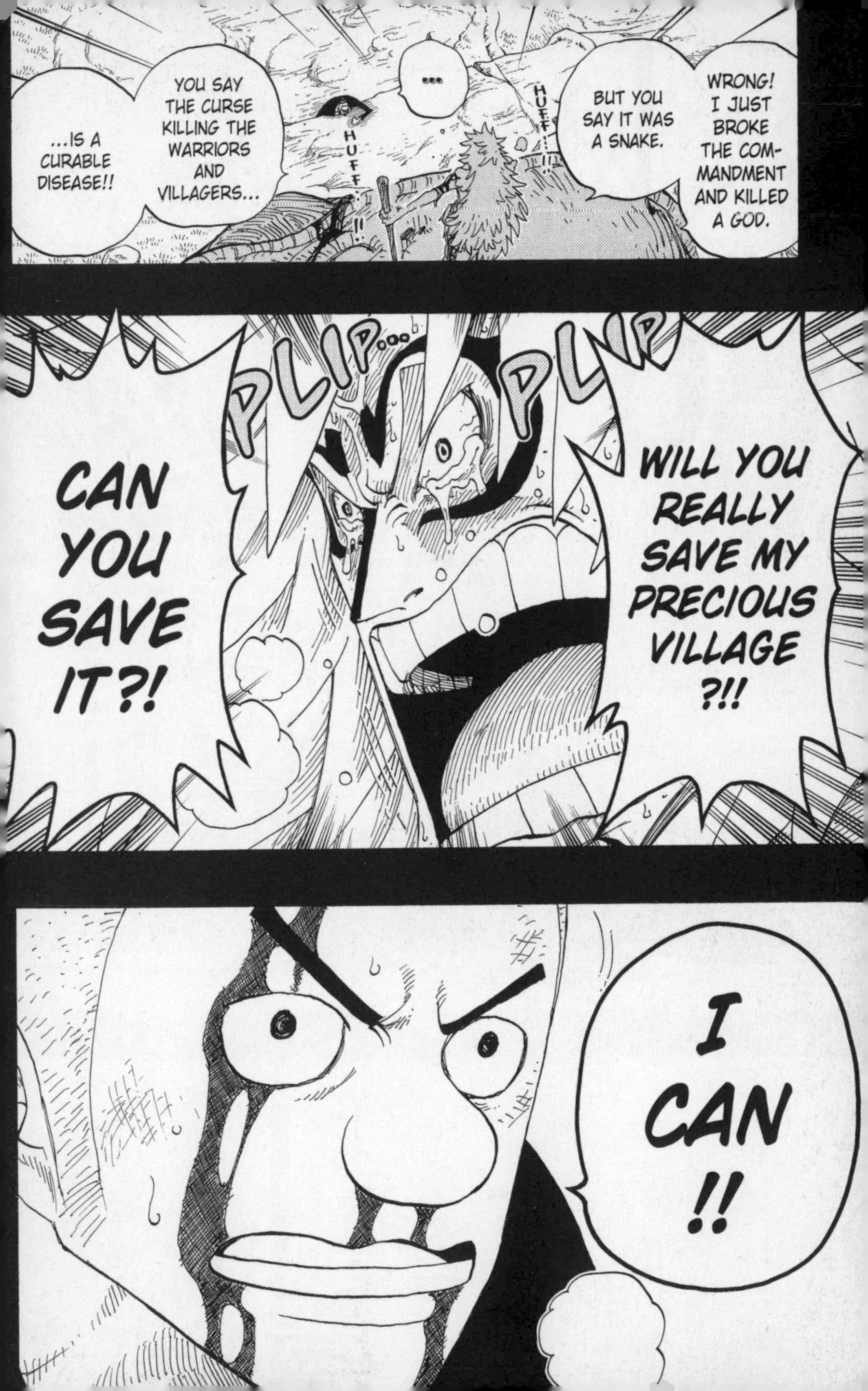
WRONG! I JUST BROKE THE COMMANDMENT AND KILLED A GOD.
BUT YOU SAY IT WAS A SNAKE.
HUFF...!!
HUFF...!!
...
YOU SAY THE CURSE KILLING THE WARRIORS AND VILLAGERS...
...IS A CURABLE DISEASE!!
PLIP
PLIP...
WILL YOU REALLY SAVE MY PRECIOUS VILLAGE ?!!
CAN YOU SAVE IT?!
I CAN !!

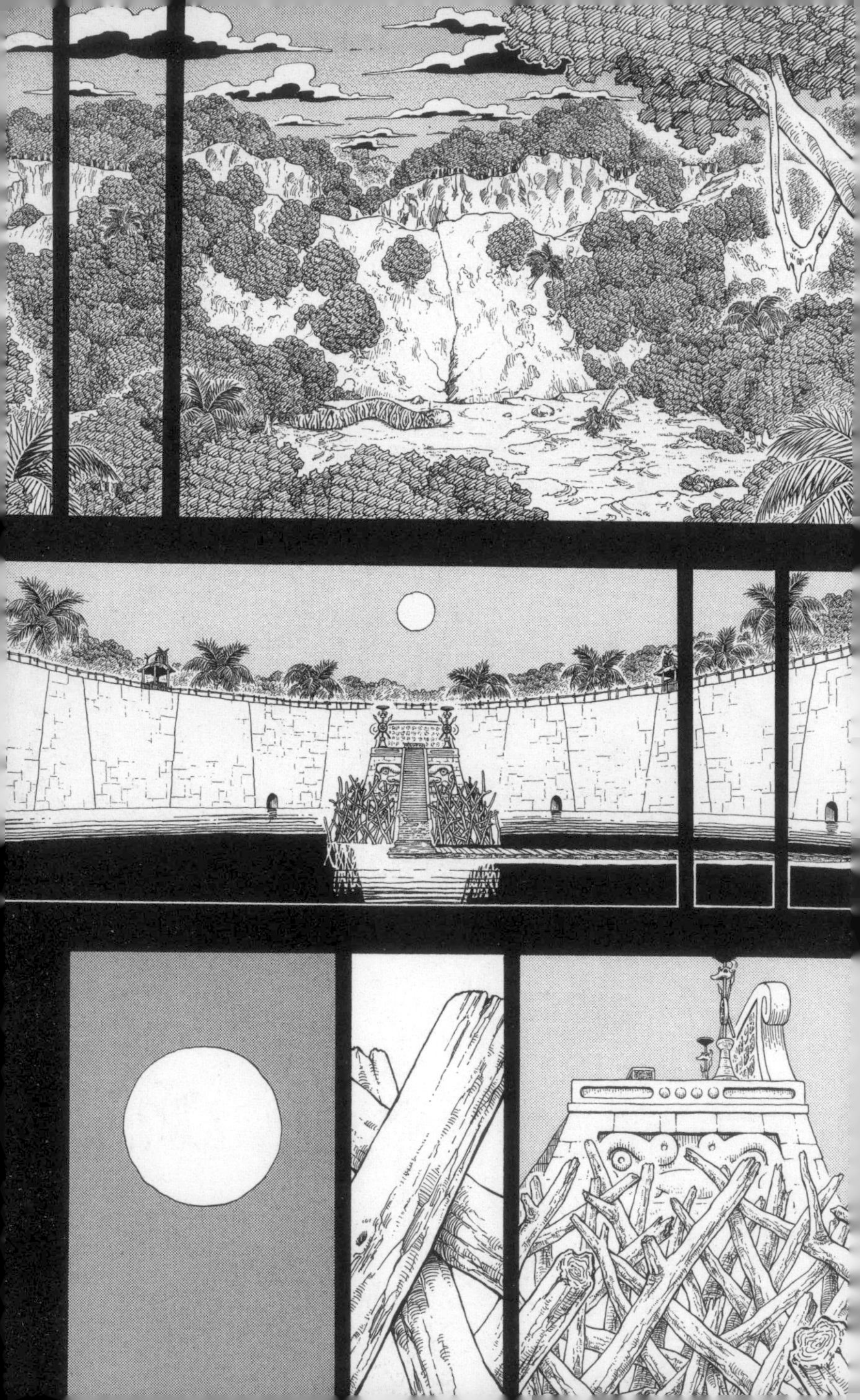

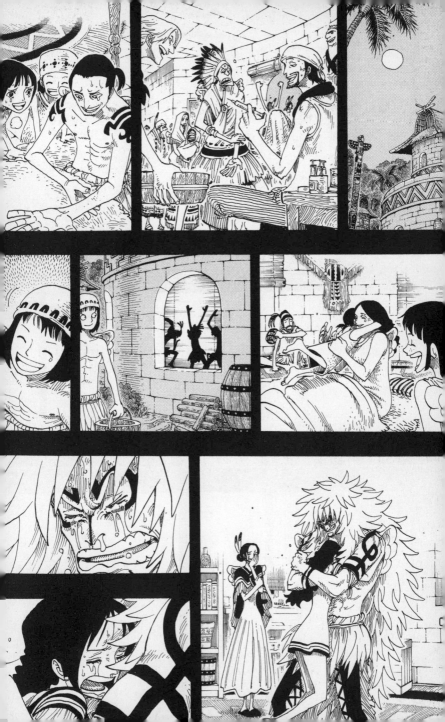

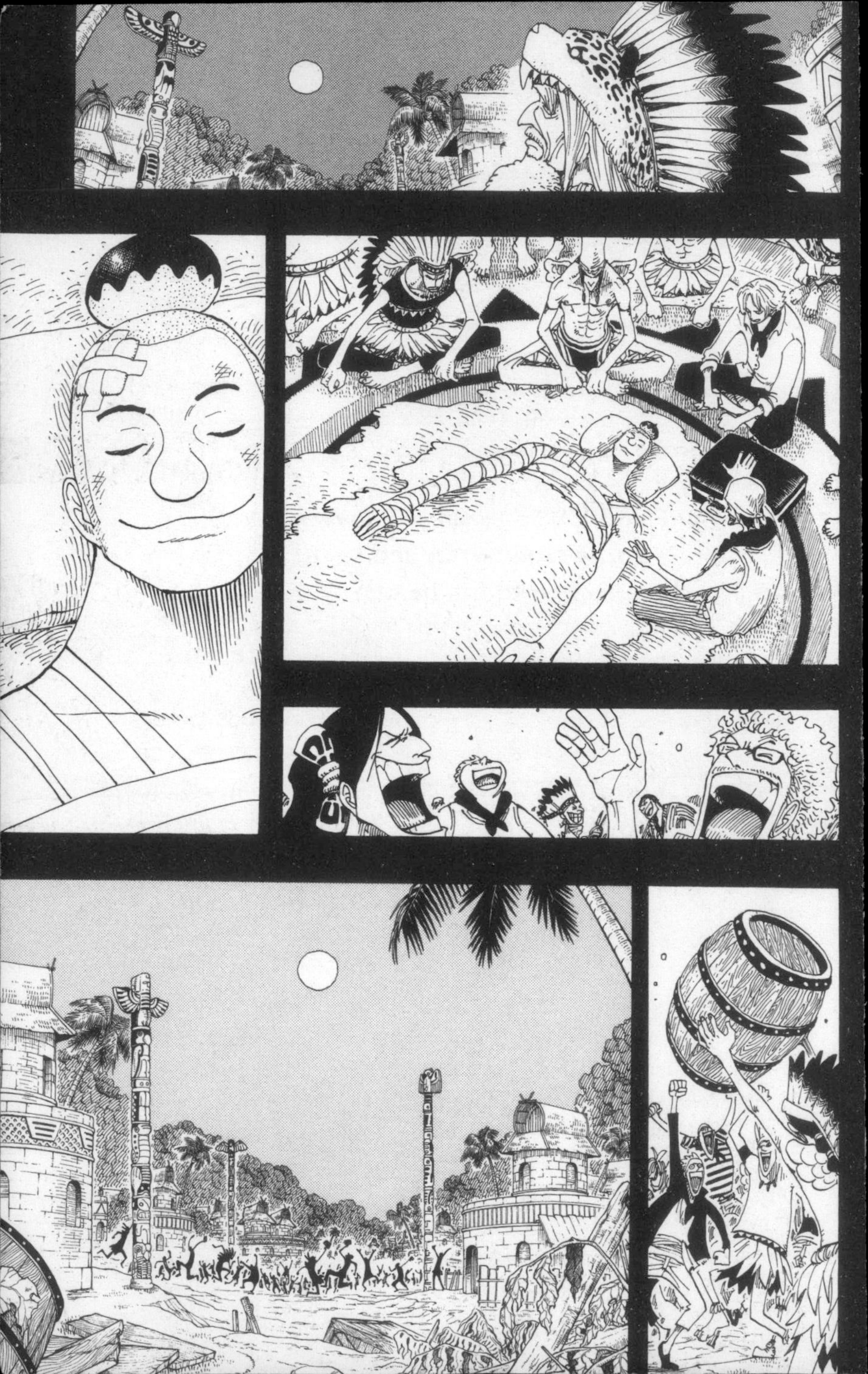

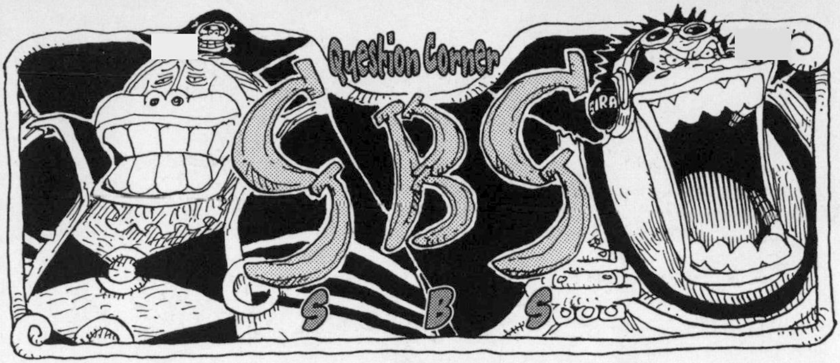
Question Corner
SBS
S B S

Q: Oda Sensei, it's nice to meet you! I always enjoy reading your work. Let me get right to the point. There's something that I want to say very badly. It's about this. →

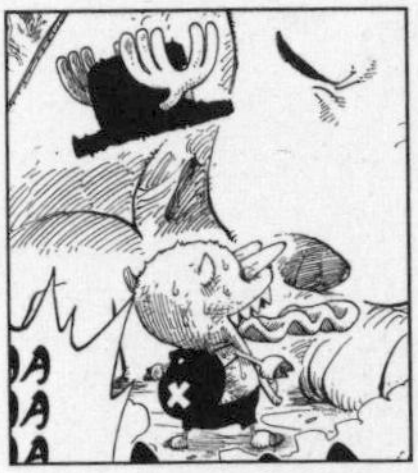

"Aww, Chopper's head is so round and cute."

--*No, that's not it!* What I really want to say is, ***"Chopper's horns aren't attached to his hat! They're attached to his head!"***

Please explain this. I'd appreciate it very much.

--Jewelweed

A: Well. I got a mountain of postcards pointing this one out. The one thing I can say to everyone is: **The truth isn't limited to what you can see.** Chopper was so startled at the time that even his horns jumped up in amazement. He altered his body to communicate that to us. In a way, that may have been his own sort of coolness, don't you think? In a way! That may, uh... have been his...own sort of, um, cool... don't...you think...? OK, next!

Q: On the opening picture for chapter 284, "Sorry," you drew a very adorable dog smoking a cigarette. Even coming from you, Oda Sensei, this is unforgivable. Are you trying to make dogs unhealthy? Well?

--Member #17
The Society for the Protection of Animals

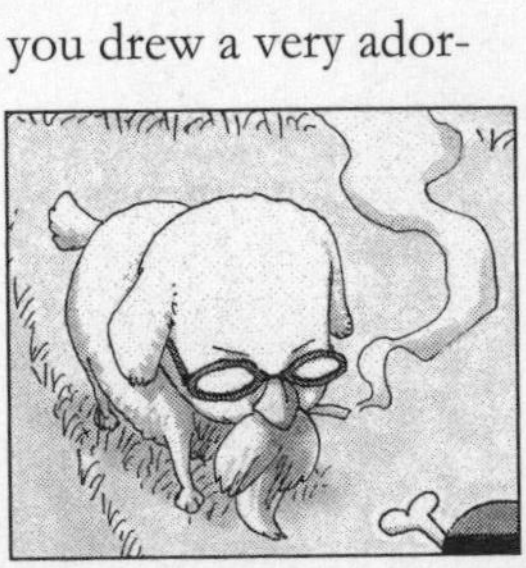

A: Oh, I wasn't paying close enough attention... I'm terribly sorry. I'll give Sanji a good talking to over this. That guy!

Chapter 290:

THE LIGHT OF SHANDORA

SIGN SAYS "NAVAL COFFEE" --ED.

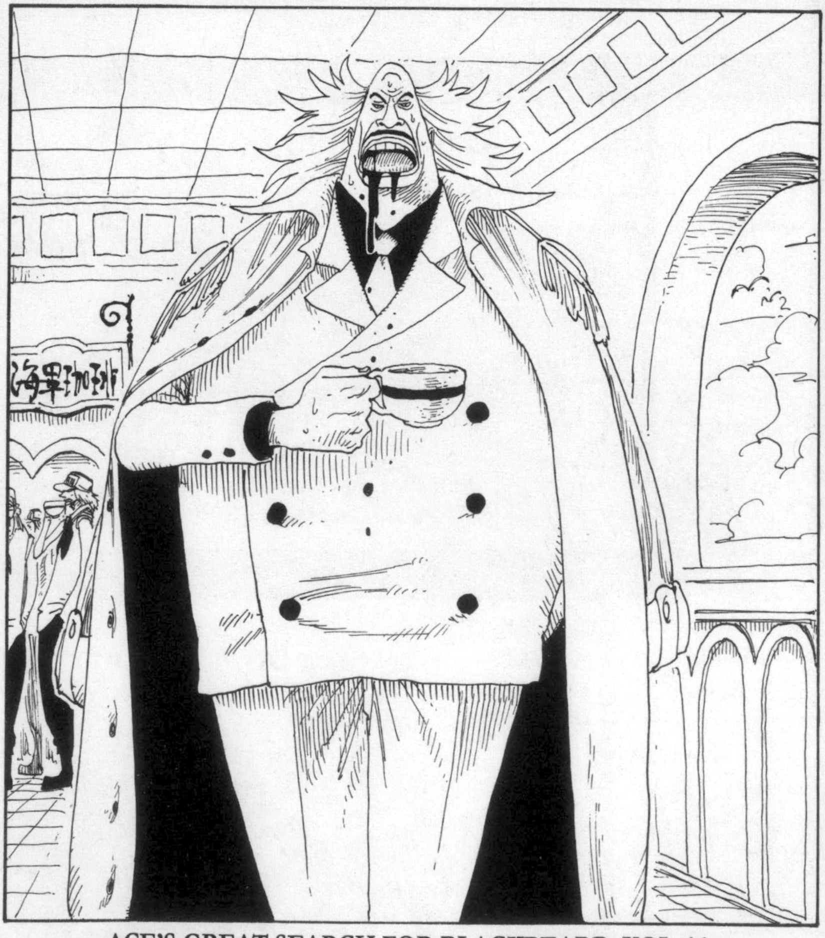
海軍珈琲

ACE'S GREAT SEARCH FOR BLACKBEARD, VOL. 16:
"VICE ADMIRAL KOMILLE DISLIKES THE BASE'S BITTER COFFEE"

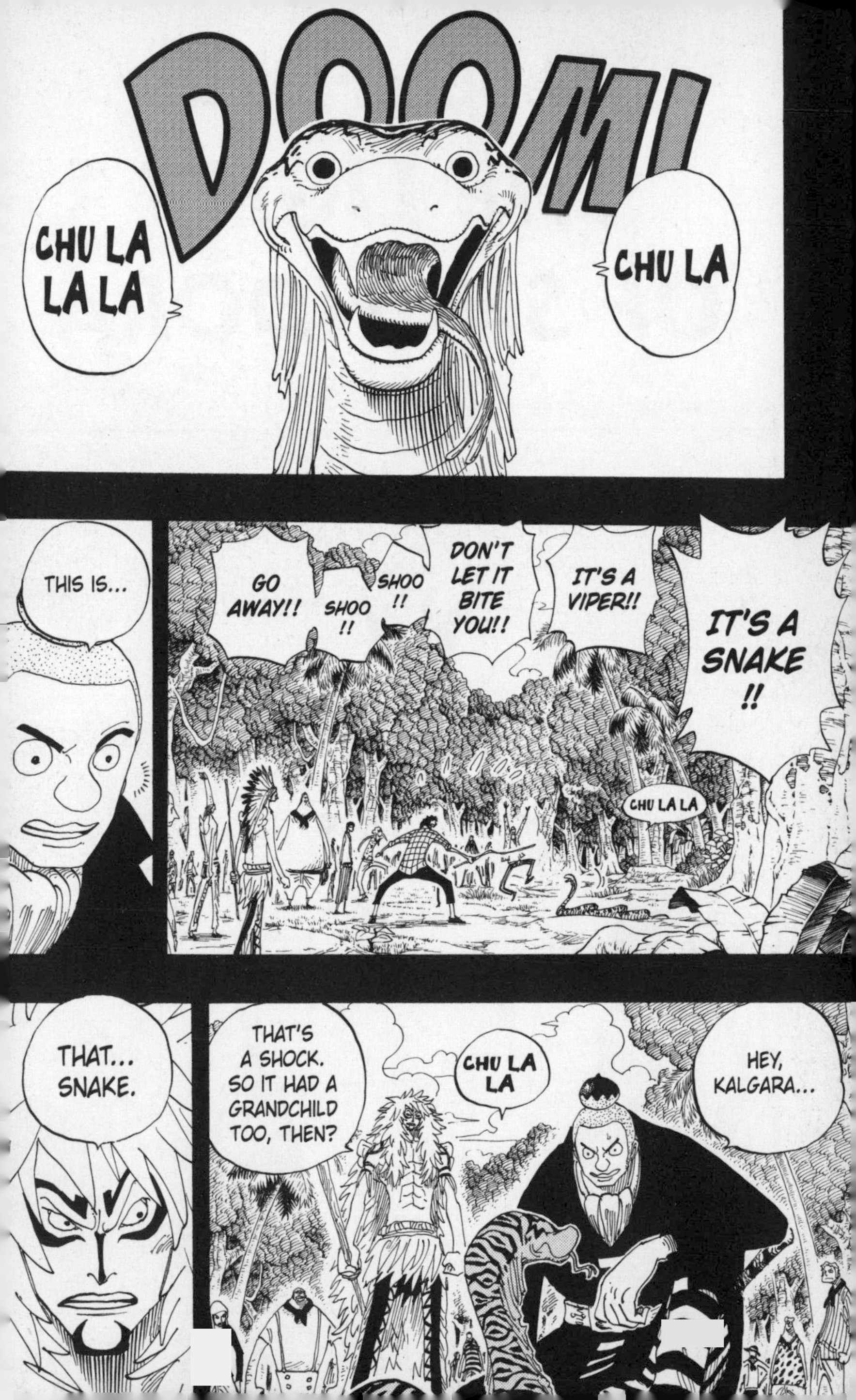
DOOM!
CHU LA
CHU LA LA LA
IT'S A SNAKE!!
IT'S A VIPER!!
DON'T LET IT BITE YOU!!
SHOO!!
SHOO!!
GO AWAY!!
CHU LA LA
THIS IS...
HEY, KALGARA...
CHU LA LA
THAT'S A SHOCK. SO IT HAD A GRANDCHILD TOO, THEN?
THAT... SNAKE.

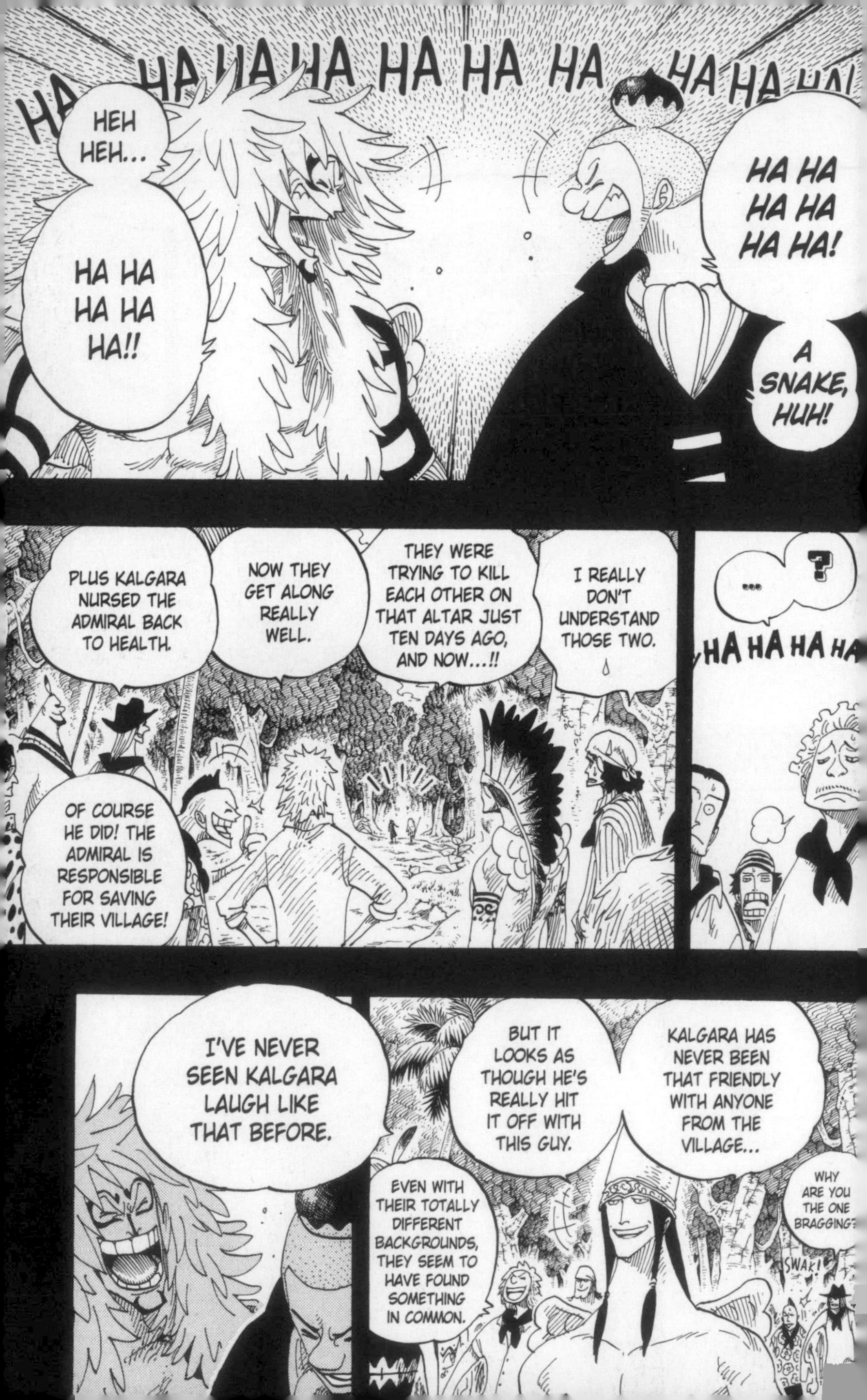
HA HA HA HA HA HA HA HA HA
HA HA HA HA HA HA!
A SNAKE, HUH!
HEH HEH...
HA HA HA HA HA!!
...?
HA HA HA HA
I REALLY DON'T UNDERSTAND THOSE TWO.
THEY WERE TRYING TO KILL EACH OTHER ON THAT ALTAR JUST TEN DAYS AGO, AND NOW...!!
NOW THEY GET ALONG REALLY WELL.
PLUS KALGARA NURSED THE ADMIRAL BACK TO HEALTH.
OF COURSE HE DID! THE ADMIRAL IS RESPONSIBLE FOR SAVING THEIR VILLAGE!
KALGARA HAS NEVER BEEN THAT FRIENDLY WITH ANYONE FROM THE VILLAGE...
BUT IT LOOKS AS THOUGH HE'S REALLY HIT IT OFF WITH THIS GUY.
WHY ARE YOU THE ONE BRAGGING?
SWAK!
EVEN WITH THEIR TOTALLY DIFFERENT BACKGROUNDS, THEY SEEM TO HAVE FOUND SOMETHING IN COMMON.
I'VE NEVER SEEN KALGARA LAUGH LIKE THAT BEFORE.

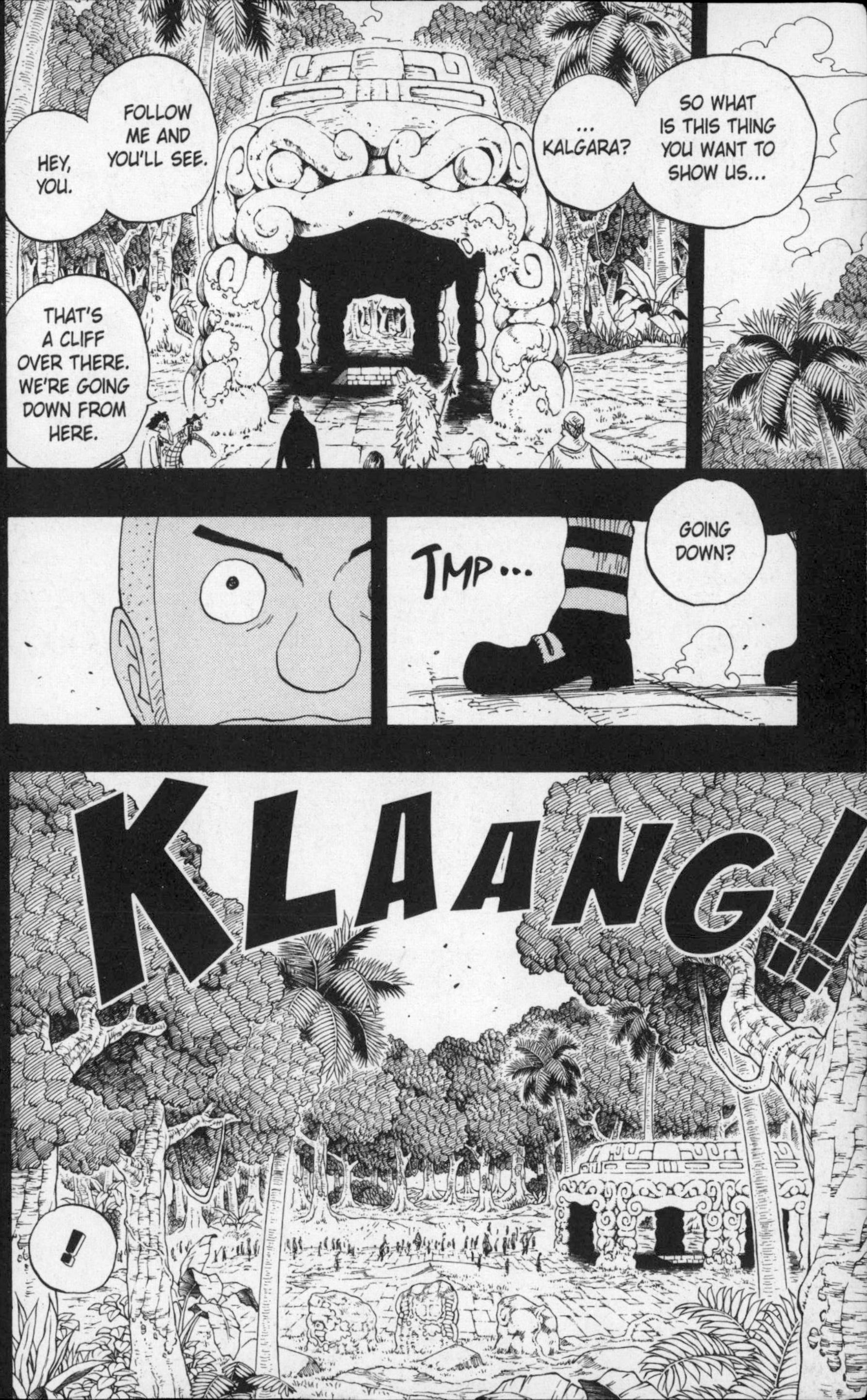
SO WHAT IS THIS THING YOU WANT TO SHOW US...
... KALGARA?
FOLLOW ME AND YOU'LL SEE.
HEY, YOU.
THAT'S A CLIFF OVER THERE. WE'RE GOING DOWN FROM HERE.
GOING DOWN?
TMP...
KLAANG!!
!

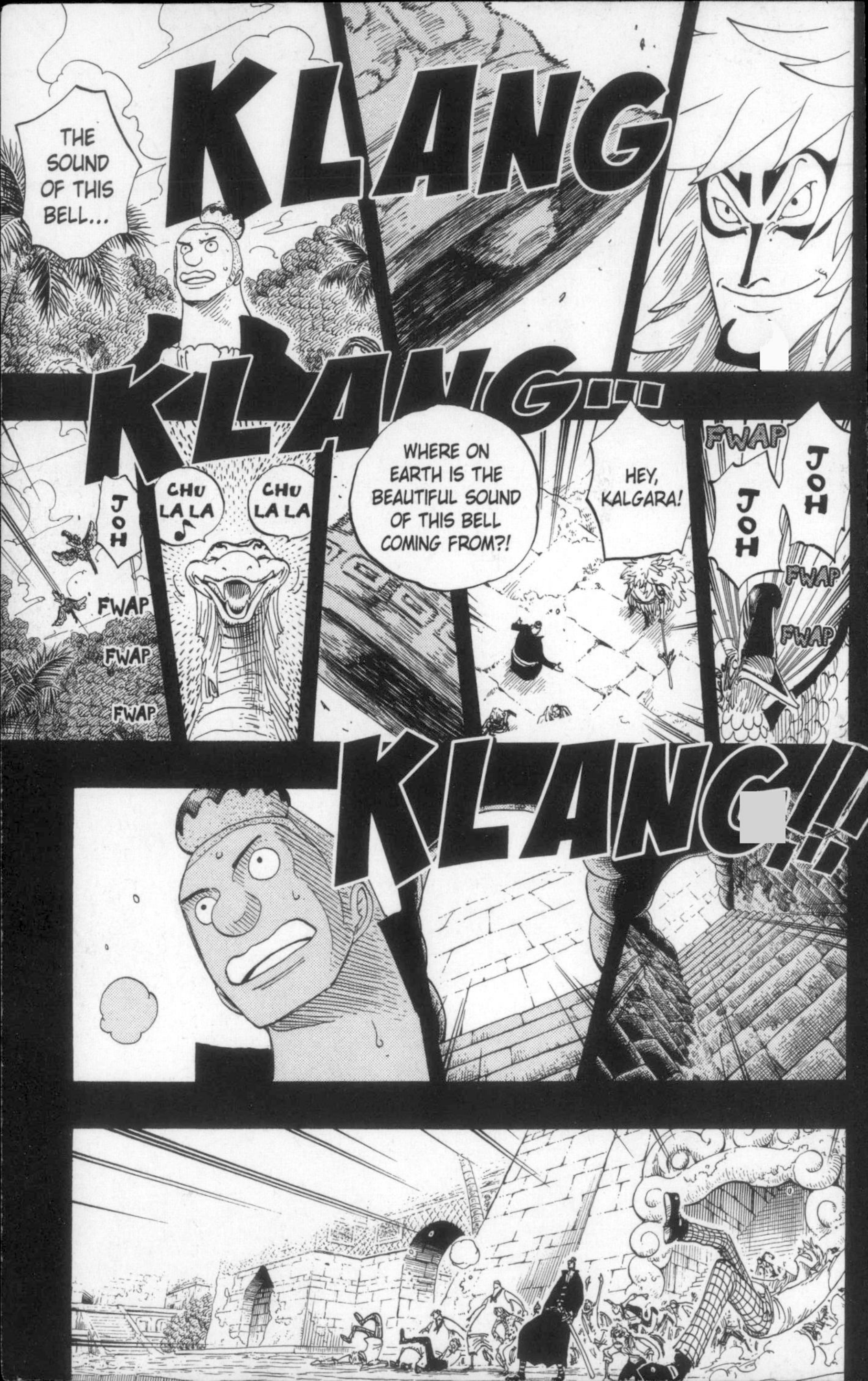
KLANG
THE SOUND OF THIS BELL...
KLANG...
HEY, KALGARA!
JOH JOH
FWAP
FWAP
FWAP
WHERE ON EARTH IS THE BEAUTIFUL SOUND OF THIS BELL COMING FROM?!
CHU LA LA
CHU LA LA
JOH
FWAP
FWAP
FWAP
KLANG!!

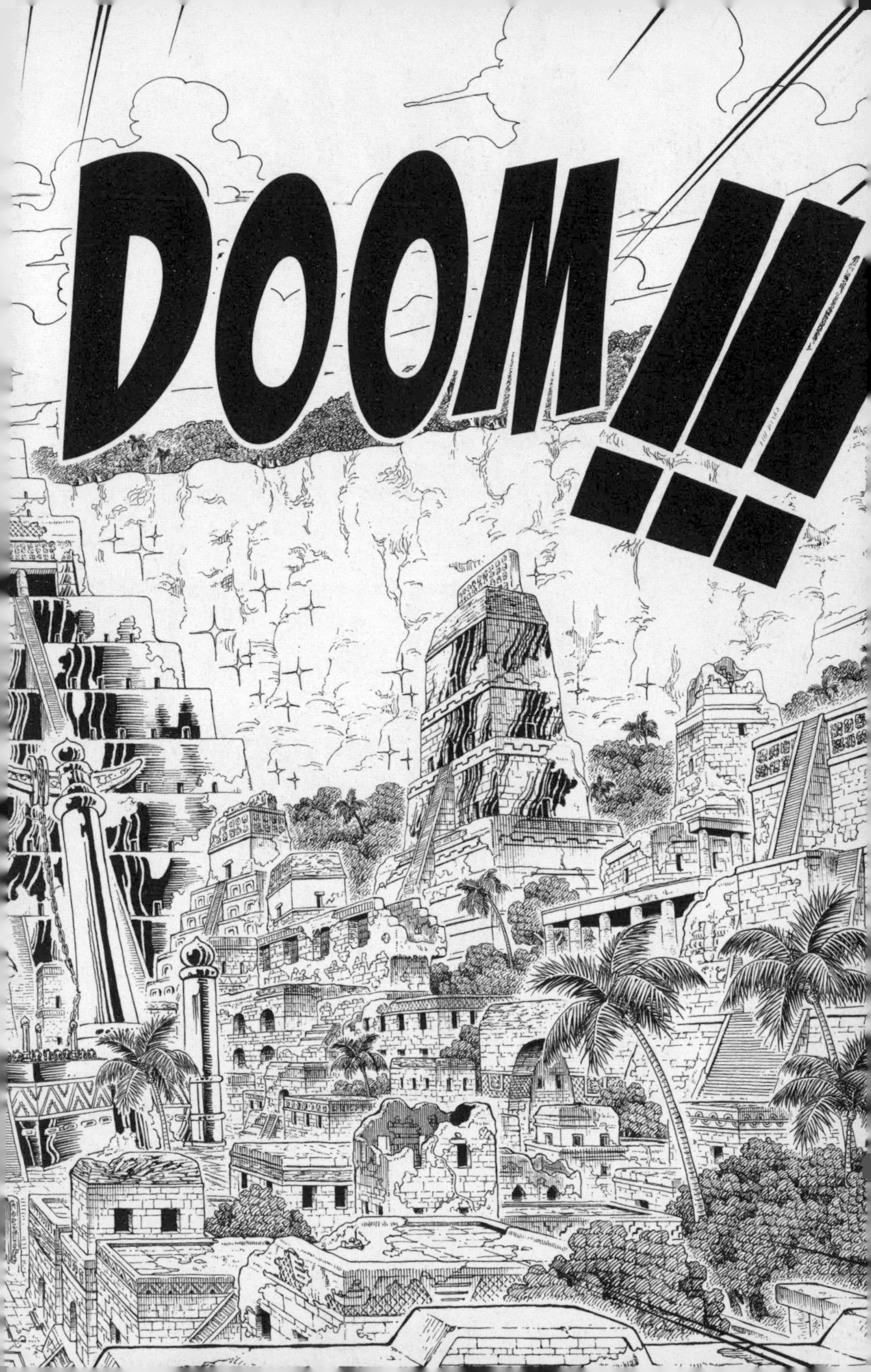
DOOM!!!

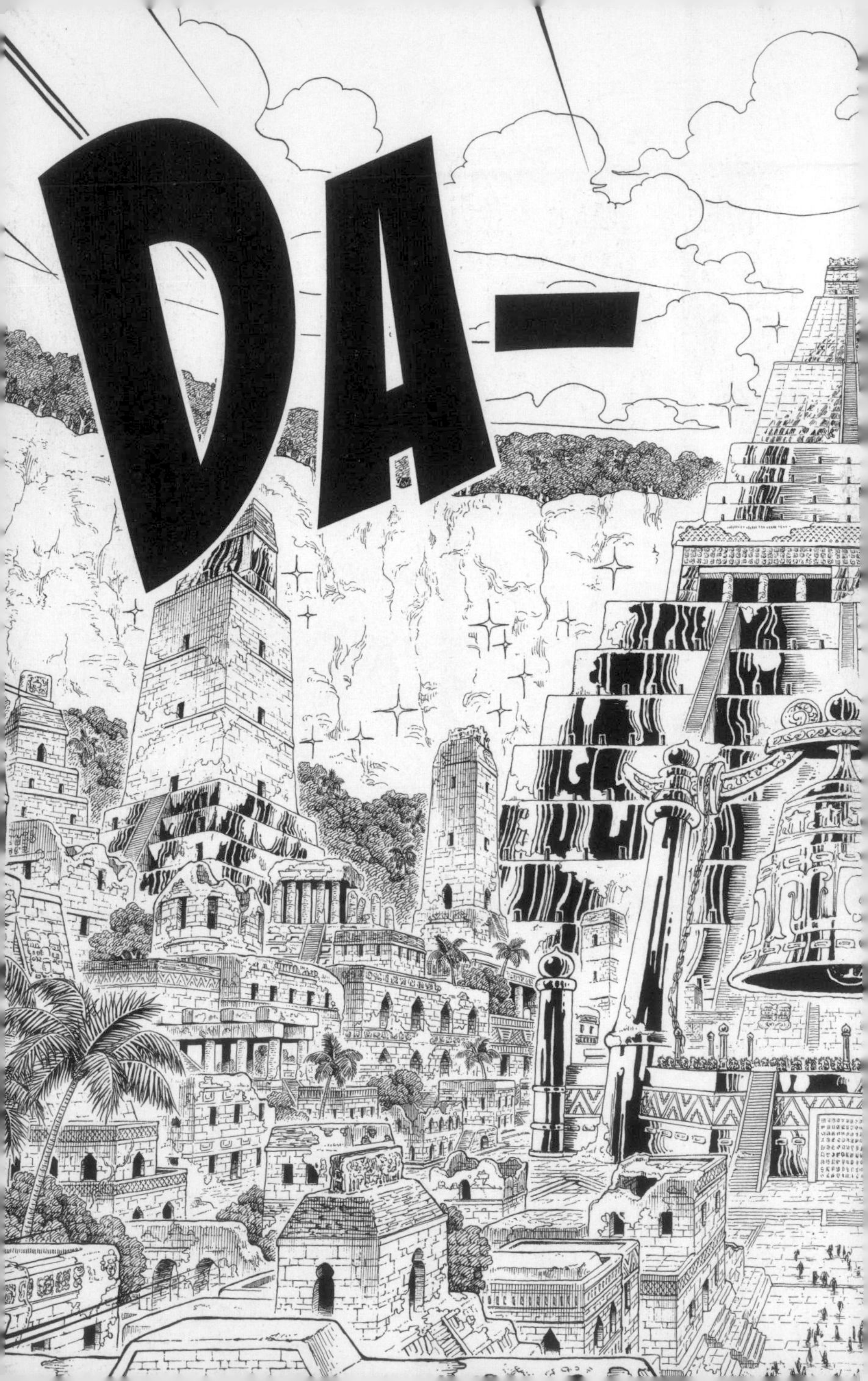
DA-

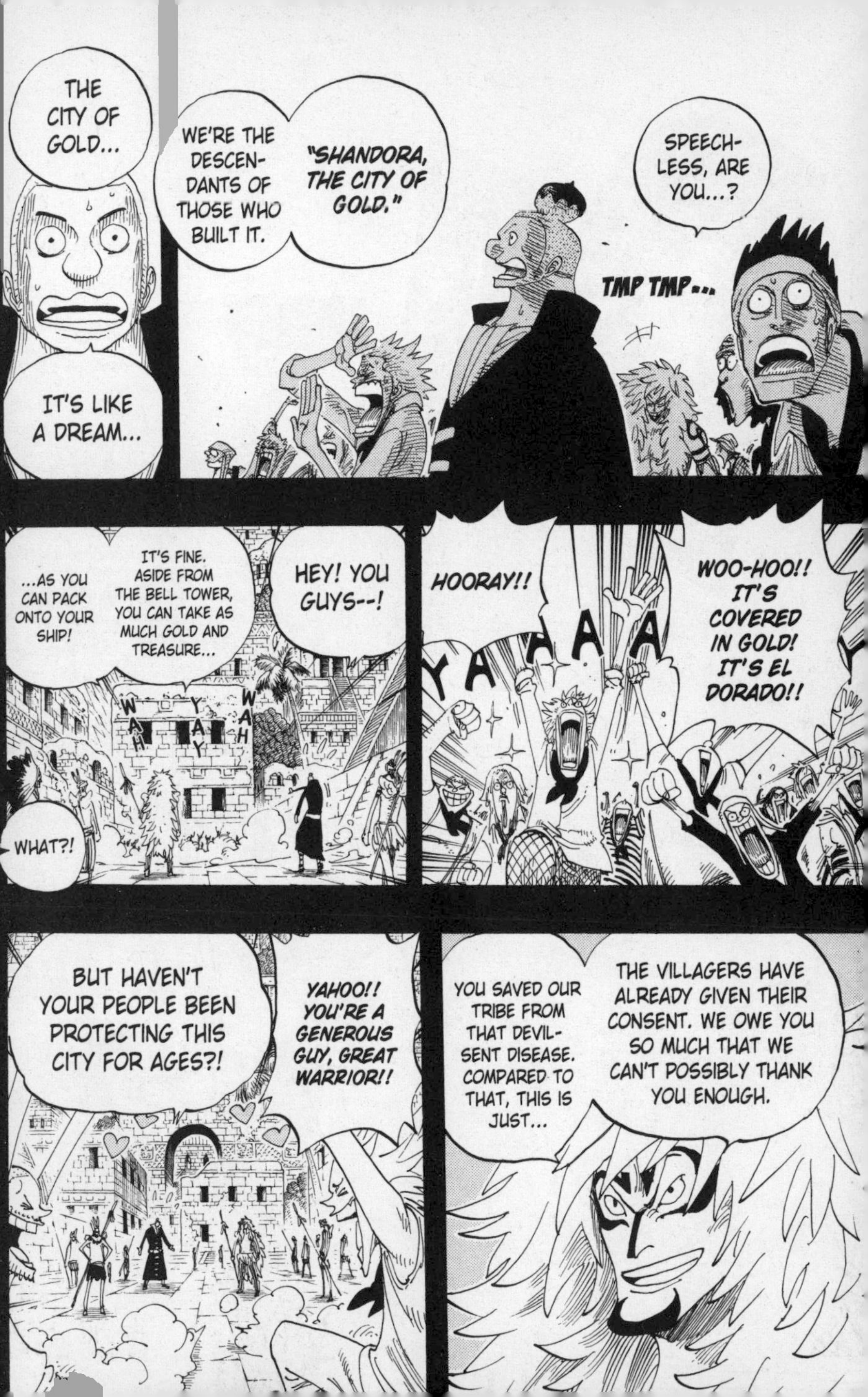
SPEECHLESS, ARE YOU...?
TMP TMP...
"SHANDORA, THE CITY OF GOLD."
WE'RE THE DESCENDANTS OF THOSE WHO BUILT IT.
THE CITY OF GOLD...
IT'S LIKE A DREAM...
WOO-HOO!! IT'S COVERED IN GOLD! IT'S EL DORADO!!
HOORAY!!
YAAAAA
HEY! YOU GUYS--!
IT'S FINE. ASIDE FROM THE BELL TOWER, YOU CAN TAKE AS MUCH GOLD AND TREASURE...
...AS YOU CAN PACK ONTO YOUR SHIP!
WAH
YAY
WAH
WHAT?!
THE VILLAGERS HAVE ALREADY GIVEN THEIR CONSENT. WE OWE YOU SO MUCH THAT WE CAN'T POSSIBLY THANK YOU ENOUGH.
YOU SAVED OUR TRIBE FROM THAT DEVIL-SENT DISEASE. COMPARED TO THAT, THIS IS JUST...
YAHOO!! YOU'RE A GENEROUS GUY, GREAT WARRIOR!!
BUT HAVEN'T YOUR PEOPLE BEEN PROTECTING THIS CITY FOR AGES?!

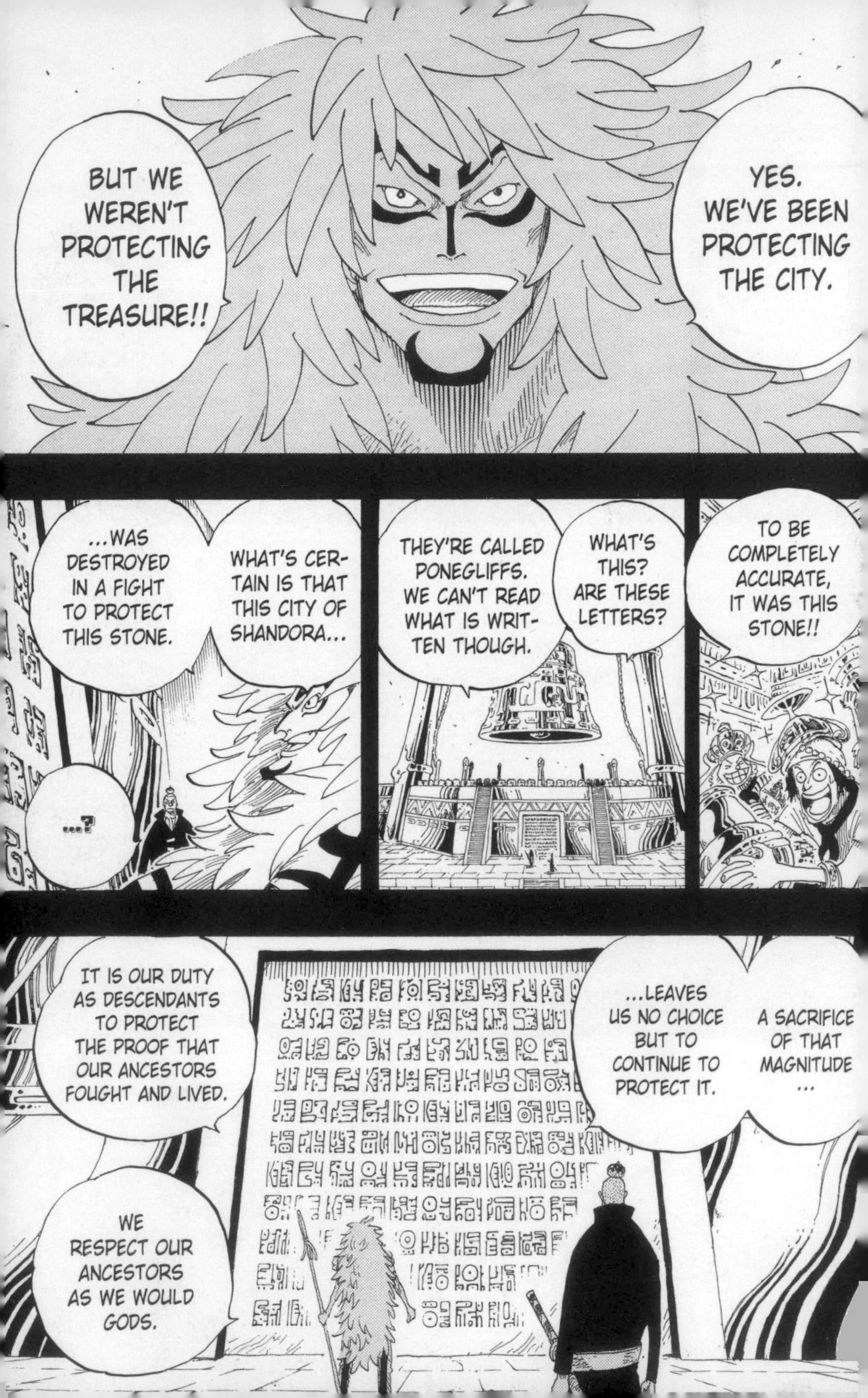
YES. WE'VE BEEN PROTECTING THE CITY.
BUT WE WEREN'T PROTECTING THE TREASURE!!
TO BE COMPLETELY ACCURATE, IT WAS THIS STONE!!
WHAT'S THIS? ARE THESE LETTERS?
THEY'RE CALLED PONEGLIFFS. WE CAN'T READ WHAT IS WRITTEN THOUGH.
WHAT'S CERTAIN IS THAT THIS CITY OF SHANDORA...
...WAS DESTROYED IN A FIGHT TO PROTECT THIS STONE.
...?
A SACRIFICE OF THAT MAGNITUDE ...
...LEAVES US NO CHOICE BUT TO CONTINUE TO PROTECT IT.
IT IS OUR DUTY AS DESCENDANTS TO PROTECT THE PROOF THAT OUR ANCESTORS FOUGHT AND LIVED.
WE RESPECT OUR ANCESTORS AS WE WOULD GODS.

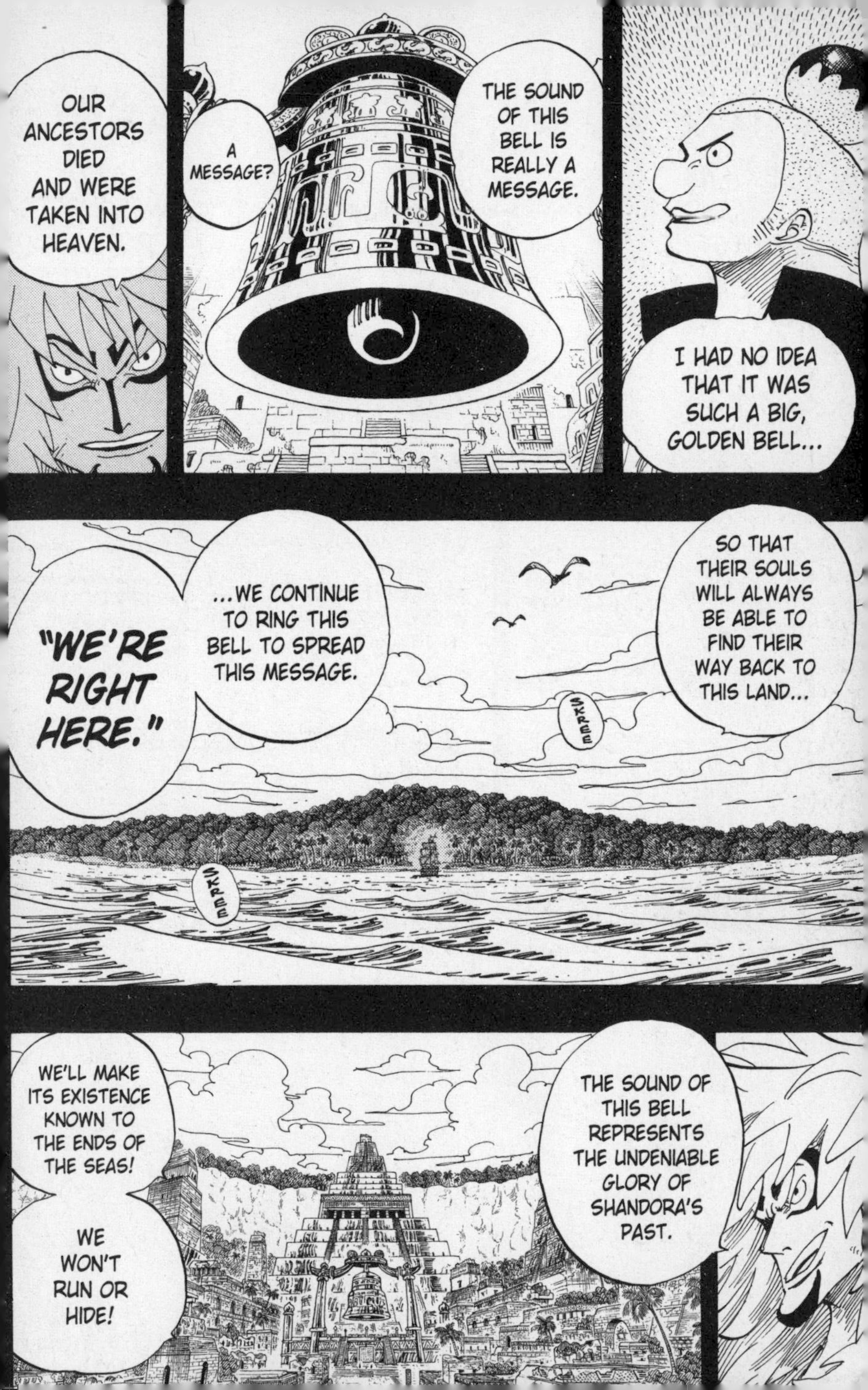
I HAD NO IDEA THAT IT WAS SUCH A BIG, GOLDEN BELL...
THE SOUND OF THIS BELL IS REALLY A MESSAGE.
A MESSAGE?
OUR ANCESTORS DIED AND WERE TAKEN INTO HEAVEN.
SO THAT THEIR SOULS WILL ALWAYS BE ABLE TO FIND THEIR WAY BACK TO THIS LAND...
SKREE
...WE CONTINUE TO RING THIS BELL TO SPREAD THIS MESSAGE.
"WE'RE RIGHT HERE."
SKREE
THE SOUND OF THIS BELL REPRESENTS THE UNDENIABLE GLORY OF SHANDORA'S PAST.
WE'LL MAKE ITS EXISTENCE KNOWN TO THE ENDS OF THE SEAS!
WE WON'T RUN OR HIDE!

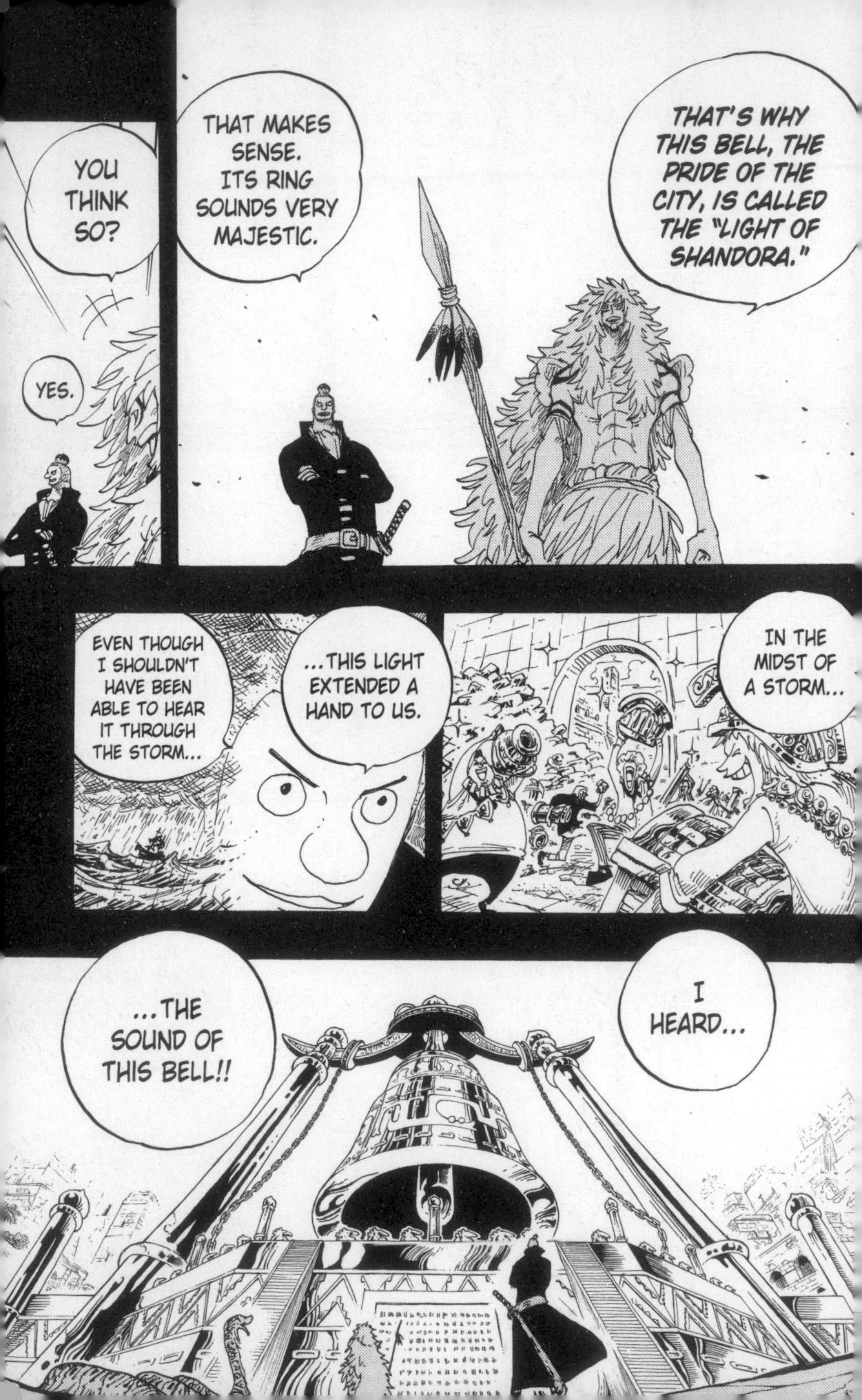
THAT'S WHY THIS BELL, THE PRIDE OF THE CITY, IS CALLED THE "LIGHT OF SHANDORA."
THAT MAKES SENSE. ITS RING SOUNDS VERY MAJESTIC.
YOU THINK SO?
YES.
IN THE MIDST OF A STORM...
EVEN THOUGH I SHOULDN'T HAVE BEEN ABLE TO HEAR IT THROUGH THE STORM...
...THIS LIGHT EXTENDED A HAND TO US.
I HEARD...
...THE SOUND OF THIS BELL!!

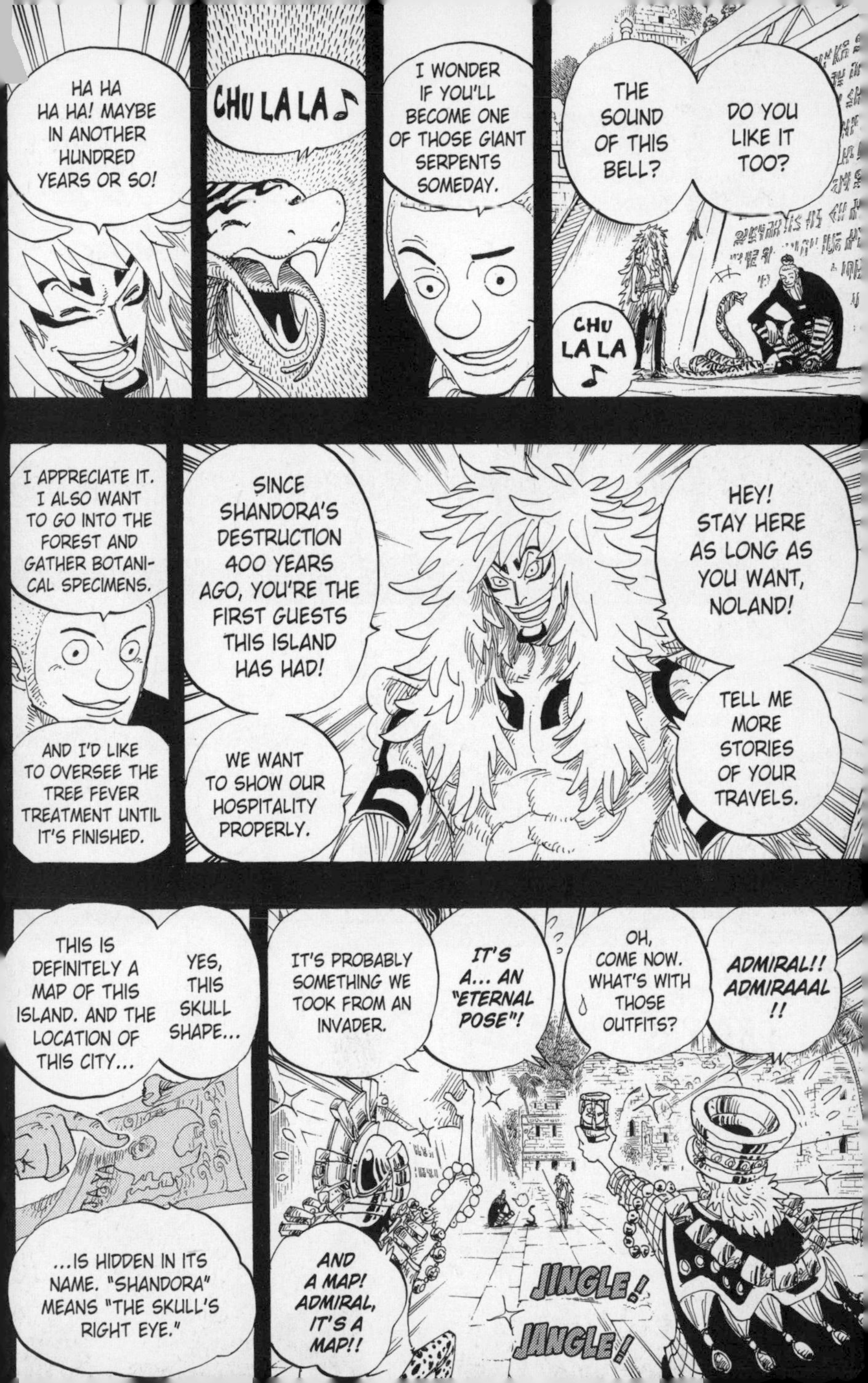
DO YOU LIKE IT TOO?
THE SOUND OF THIS BELL?
CHU LA LA ♪
I WONDER IF YOU'LL BECOME ONE OF THOSE GIANT SERPENTS SOMEDAY.
CHU LA LA ♪
HA HA HA HA! MAYBE IN ANOTHER HUNDRED YEARS OR SO!
HEY! STAY HERE AS LONG AS YOU WANT, NOLAND!
SINCE SHANDORA'S DESTRUCTION 400 YEARS AGO, YOU'RE THE FIRST GUESTS THIS ISLAND HAS HAD!
TELL ME MORE STORIES OF YOUR TRAVELS.
WE WANT TO SHOW OUR HOSPITALITY PROPERLY.
I APPRECIATE IT. I ALSO WANT TO GO INTO THE FOREST AND GATHER BOTANICAL SPECIMENS.
AND I'D LIKE TO OVERSEE THE TREE FEVER TREATMENT UNTIL IT'S FINISHED.
ADMIRAL!! ADMIRAAAL !!
OH, COME NOW. WHAT'S WITH THOSE OUTFITS?
IT'S A... AN "ETERNAL POSE"!
IT'S PROBABLY SOMETHING WE TOOK FROM AN INVADER.
AND A MAP! ADMIRAL, IT'S A MAP!!
JINGLE!
JANGLE!
YES, THIS SKULL SHAPE...
THIS IS DEFINITELY A MAP OF THIS ISLAND. AND THE LOCATION OF THIS CITY...
...IS HIDDEN IN ITS NAME. "SHANDORA" MEANS "THE SKULL'S RIGHT EYE."

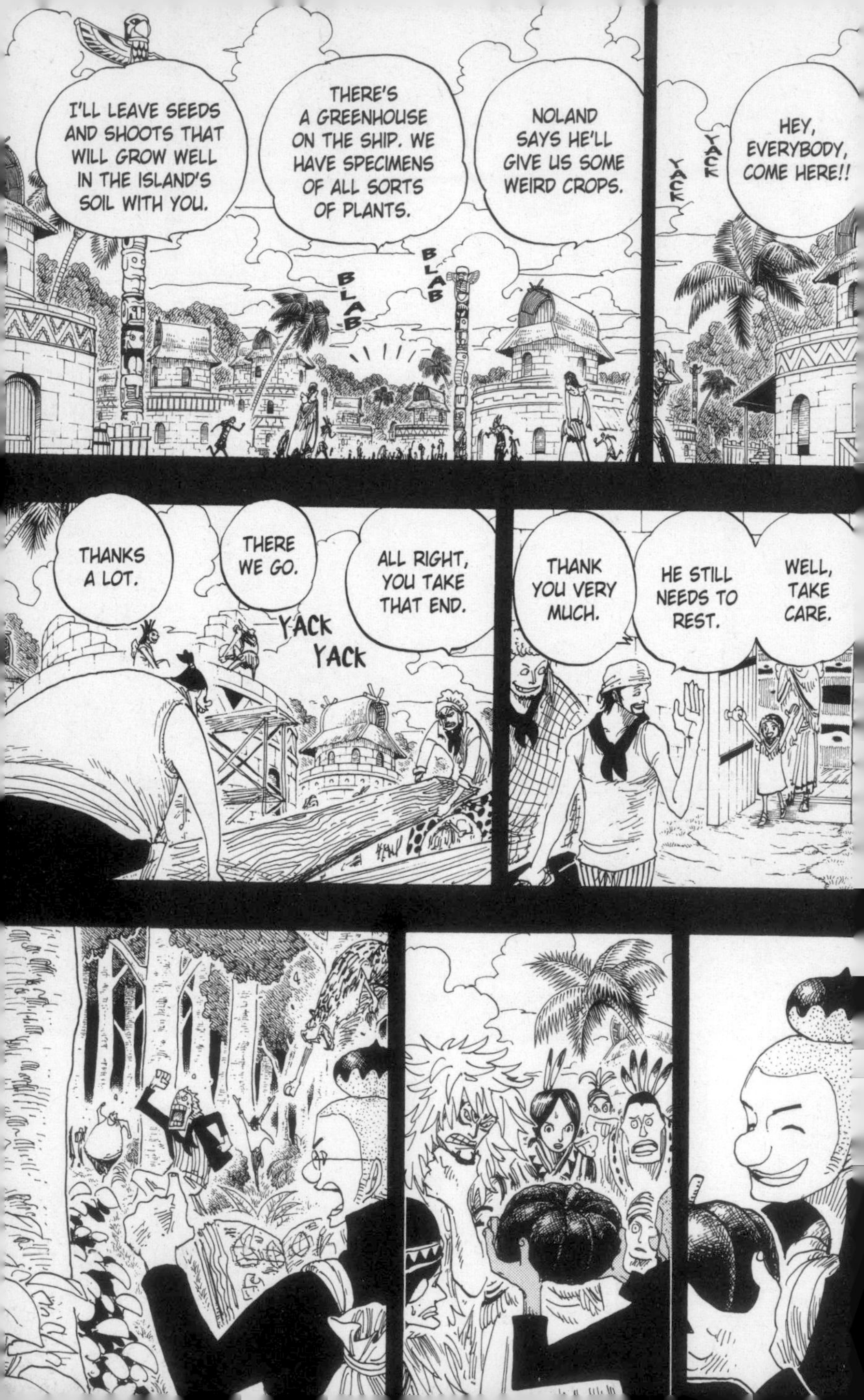
YACK
YACK
HEY, EVERYBODY, COME HERE!!
NOLAND SAYS HE'LL GIVE US SOME WEIRD CROPS.
BLAB
THERE'S A GREENHOUSE ON THE SHIP. WE HAVE SPECIMENS OF ALL SORTS OF PLANTS.
BLAB
I'LL LEAVE SEEDS AND SHOOTS THAT WILL GROW WELL IN THE ISLAND'S SOIL WITH YOU.
WELL, TAKE CARE.
HE STILL NEEDS TO REST.
THANK YOU VERY MUCH.
ALL RIGHT, YOU TAKE THAT END.
YACK YACK
THERE WE GO.
THANKS A LOT.

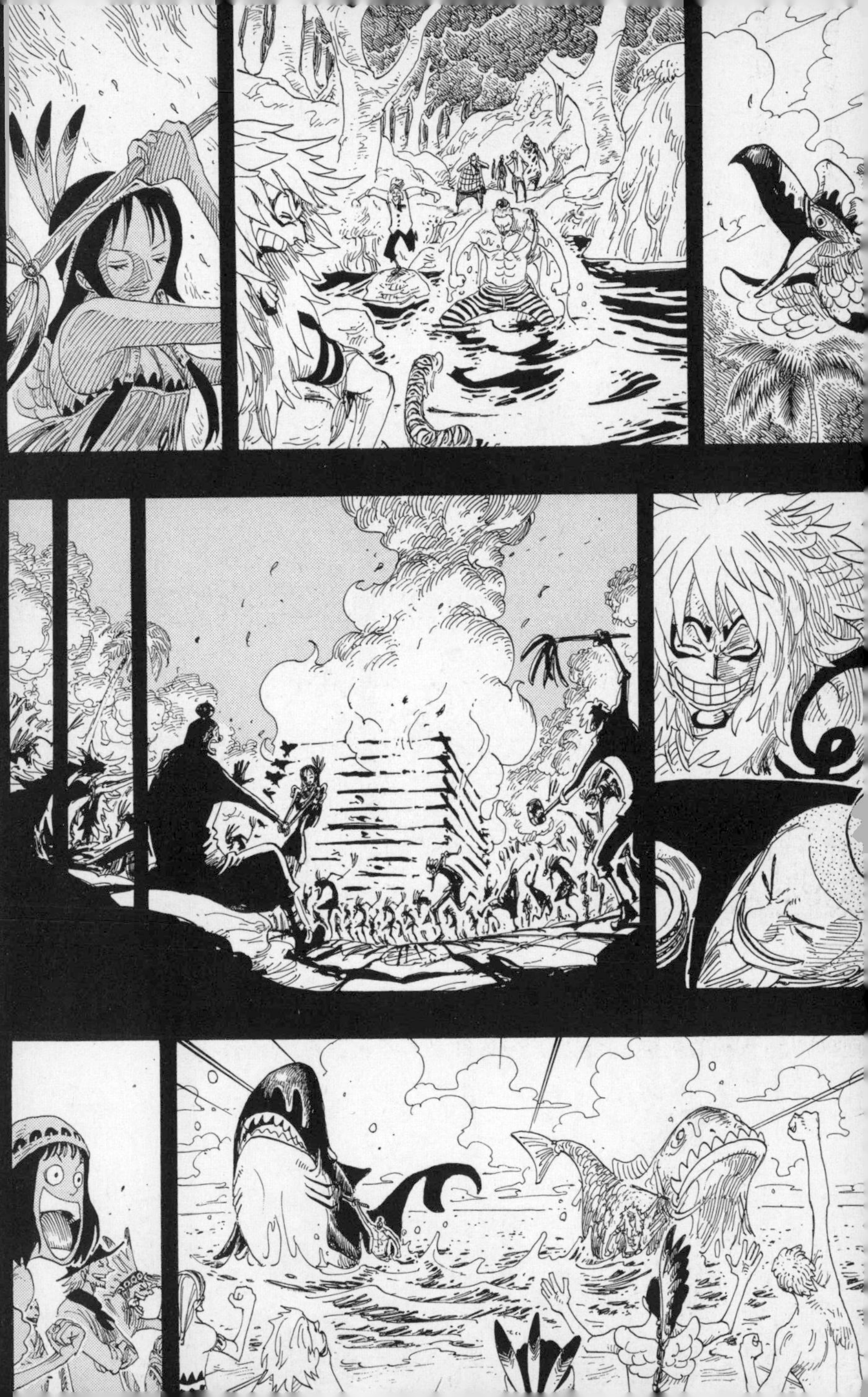

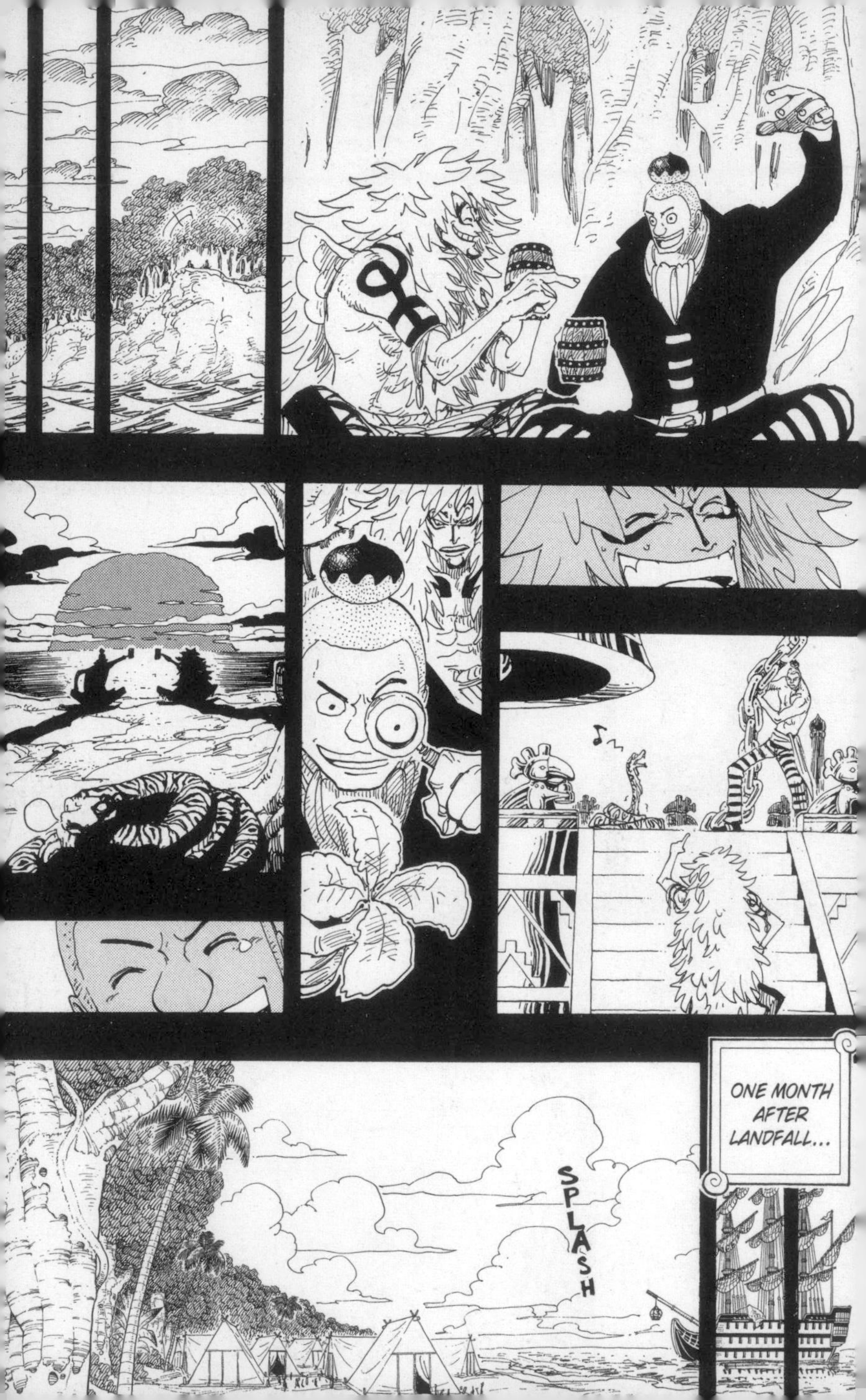
ONE MONTH AFTER LANDFALL...
SPLASH

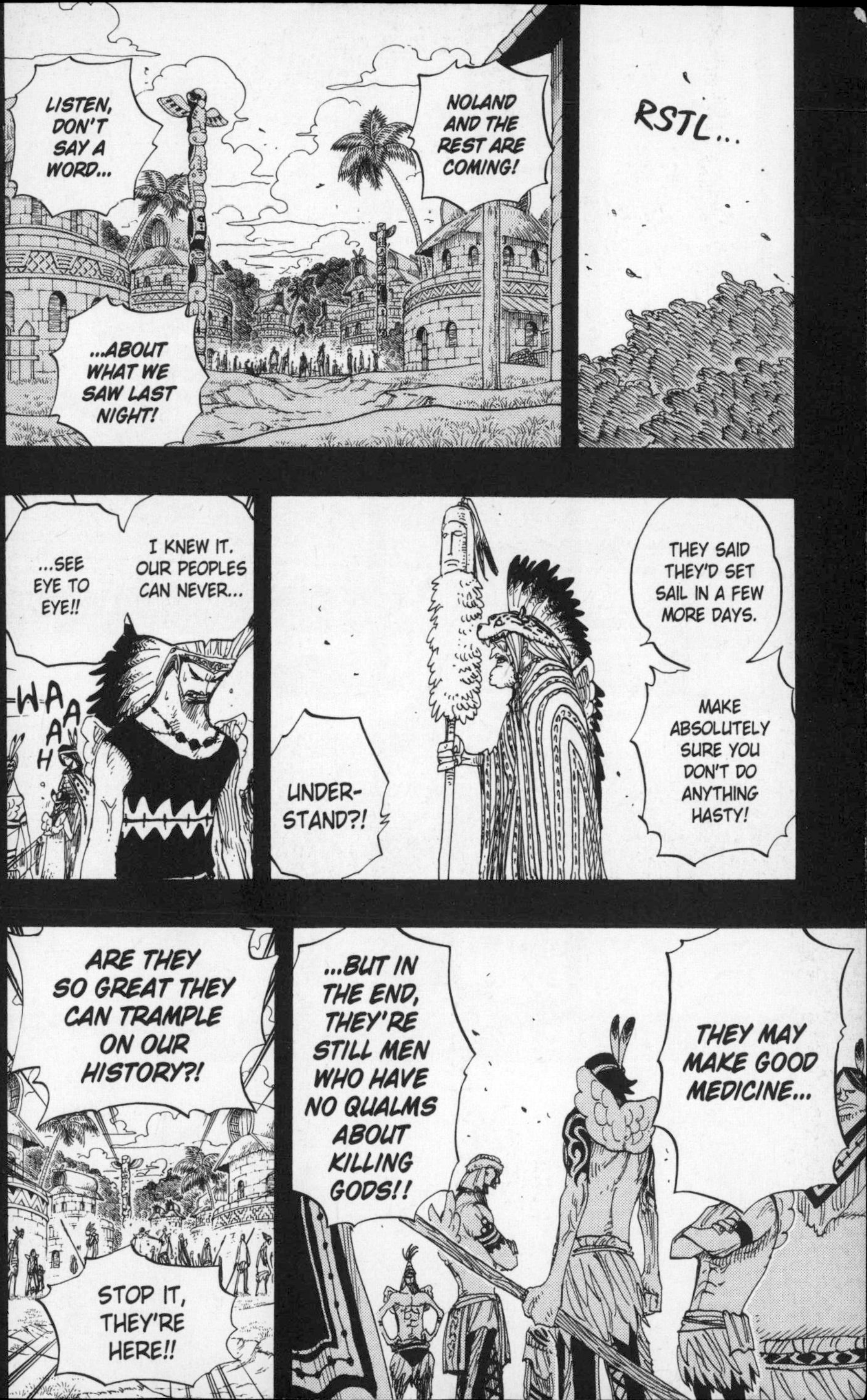
RSTL...
NOLAND AND THE REST ARE COMING!
LISTEN, DON'T SAY A WORD...
...ABOUT WHAT WE SAW LAST NIGHT!
THEY SAID THEY'D SET SAIL IN A FEW MORE DAYS.
MAKE ABSOLUTELY SURE YOU DON'T DO ANYTHING HASTY!
UNDER-STAND?!
I KNEW IT. OUR PEOPLES CAN NEVER...
...SEE EYE TO EYE!!
WAAAH
THEY MAY MAKE GOOD MEDICINE...
...BUT IN THE END, THEY'RE STILL MEN WHO HAVE NO QUALMS ABOUT KILLING GODS!!
ARE THEY SO GREAT THEY CAN TRAMPLE ON OUR HISTORY?!
STOP IT, THEY'RE HERE!!

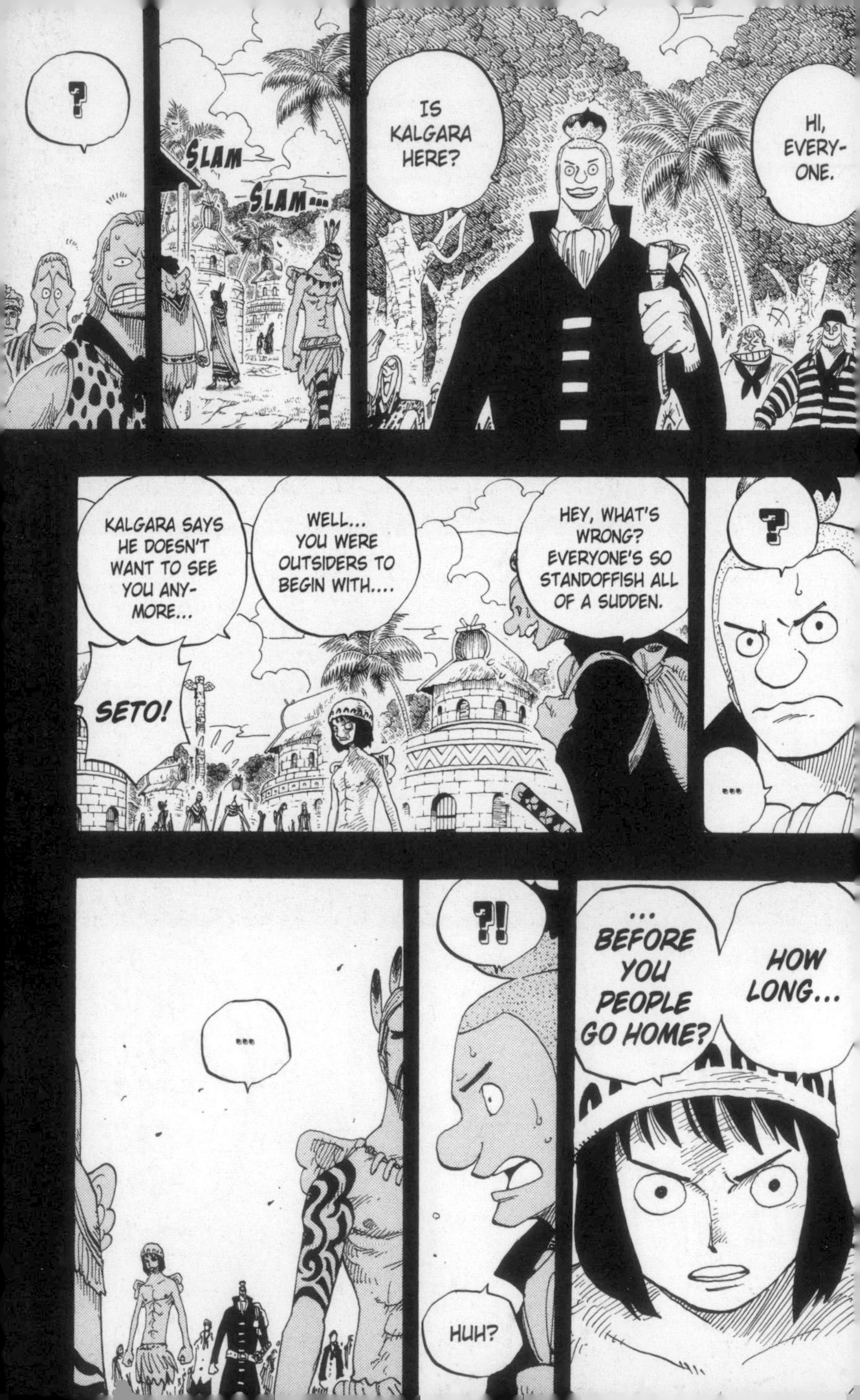
HI, EVERY-ONE.
IS KALGARA HERE?
SLAM
SLAM...
?
?
...
HEY, WHAT'S WRONG? EVERYONE'S SO STANDOFFISH ALL OF A SUDDEN.
WELL... YOU WERE OUTSIDERS TO BEGIN WITH....
KALGARA SAYS HE DOESN'T WANT TO SEE YOU ANY-MORE...
SETO!
HOW LONG...
...BEFORE YOU PEOPLE GO HOME?
?!
HUH?
...

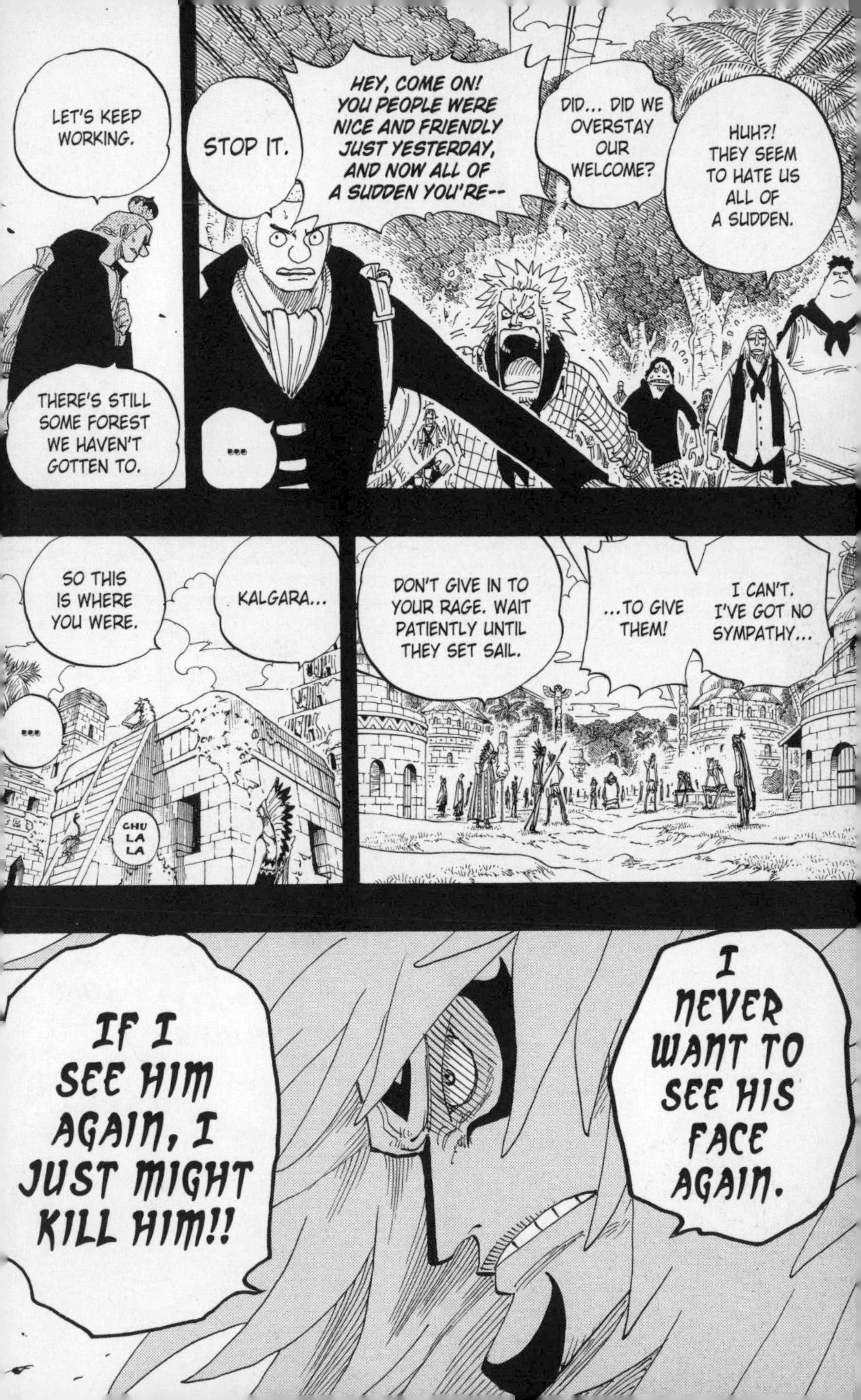
HUH?! THEY SEEM TO HATE US ALL OF A SUDDEN.
DID... DID WE OVERSTAY OUR WELCOME?
HEY, COME ON! YOU PEOPLE WERE NICE AND FRIENDLY JUST YESTERDAY, AND NOW ALL OF A SUDDEN YOU'RE--
STOP IT.
...
LET'S KEEP WORKING.
THERE'S STILL SOME FOREST WE HAVEN'T GOTTEN TO.
I CAN'T. I'VE GOT NO SYMPATHY...
...TO GIVE THEM!
DON'T GIVE IN TO YOUR RAGE. WAIT PATIENTLY UNTIL THEY SET SAIL.
KALGARA...
SO THIS IS WHERE YOU WERE.
...
CHU LA LA
I NEVER WANT TO SEE HIS FACE AGAIN.
IF I SEE HIM AGAIN, I JUST MIGHT KILL HIM!!

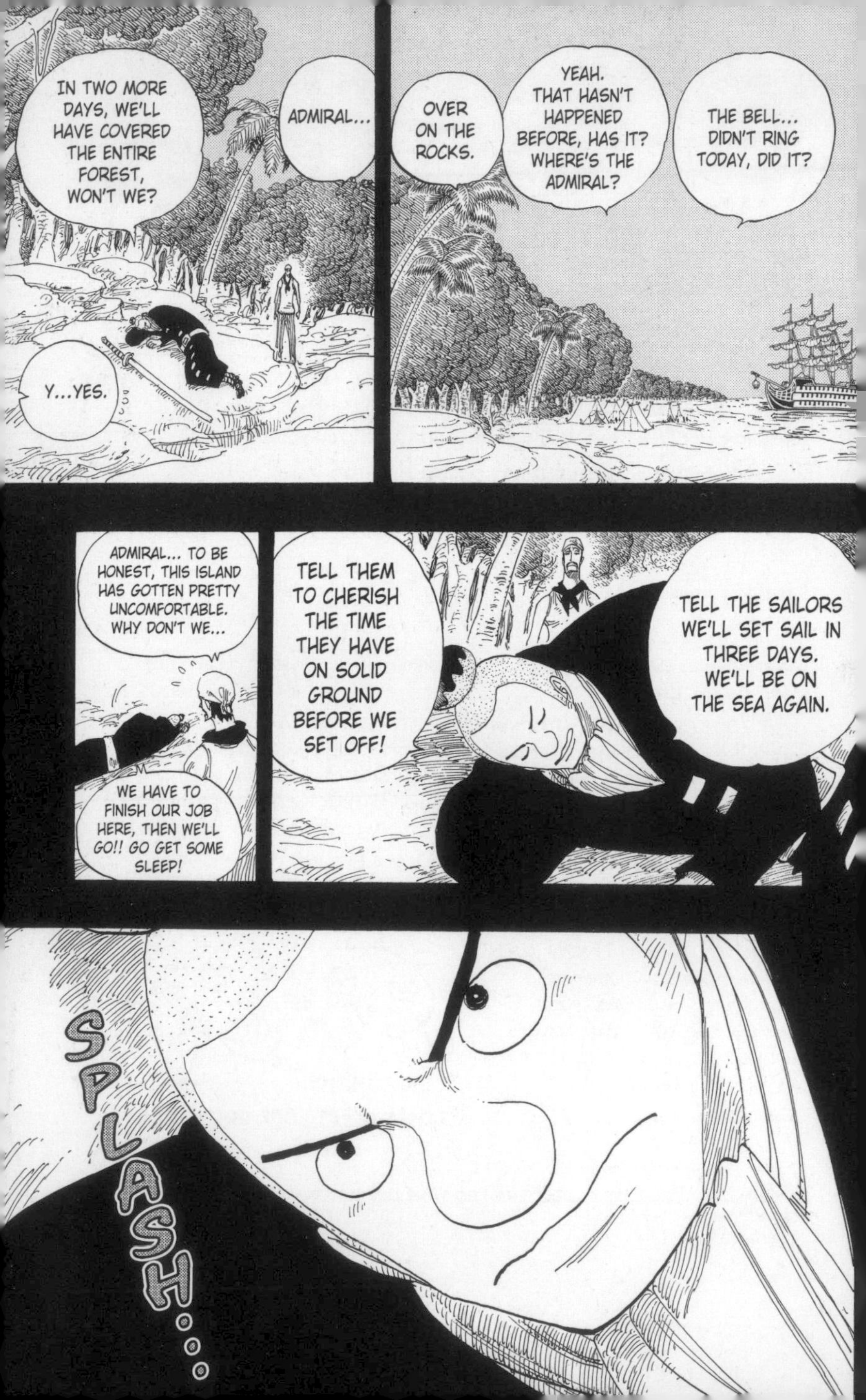
THE BELL... DIDN'T RING TODAY, DID IT?
YEAH. THAT HASN'T HAPPENED BEFORE, HAS IT? WHERE'S THE ADMIRAL?
OVER ON THE ROCKS.
ADMIRAL...
IN TWO MORE DAYS, WE'LL HAVE COVERED THE ENTIRE FOREST, WON'T WE?
Y...YES.
TELL THE SAILORS WE'LL SET SAIL IN THREE DAYS. WE'LL BE ON THE SEA AGAIN.
TELL THEM TO CHERISH THE TIME THEY HAVE ON SOLID GROUND BEFORE WE SET OFF!
ADMIRAL... TO BE HONEST, THIS ISLAND HAS GOTTEN PRETTY UNCOMFORTABLE. WHY DON'T WE...
WE HAVE TO FINISH OUR JOB HERE, THEN WE'LL GO!! GO GET SOME SLEEP!
SPLASH...

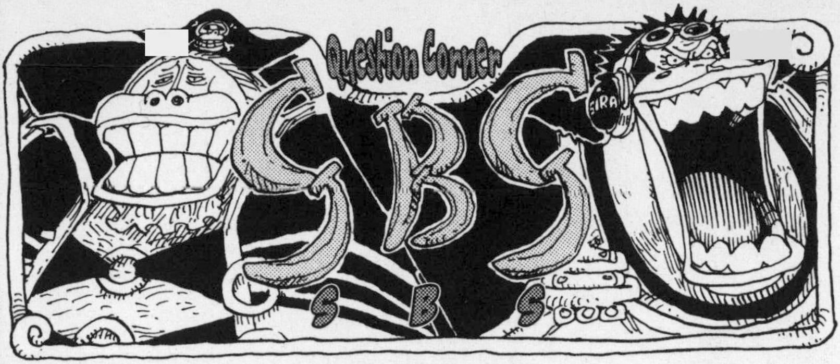
Question Corner
SBS
SBS

Q: Hello, Mr. Eiichiro Oda. Thanks for everything. Lately, I've been rereading *One Piece* from the beginning and I realized something.

The Question Corner used to be decent.

When did it turn into such a whacked-out corner? Whose fault is it? It's been bothering me so much I can't control Gaimon's growth! (My son is bothered as well.) Help me!

P.S. Did you know that there's a person inside Gachapin?

A: Whoa, hang on there. That P.S. concerns me more than the main question.

That's just how Gachapin is. (I swear.)

There's no person in there. Please don't lie. Hmph! By the way, apparently Gachapin is a dinosaur child, and Mukku is a yeti. Well, okay, I can accept "dinosaur child." But a "yeti"? He's red! A bright red yeti on a pure white, snowy mountain?

He'd stand out too much. Don't get me wrong, I like Mukku.

Japanese children grow up watching "Ponkiki." Now, what was the question again? Ah, why is the Question Corner the way it is now? All I know for sure is that it's not my fault.

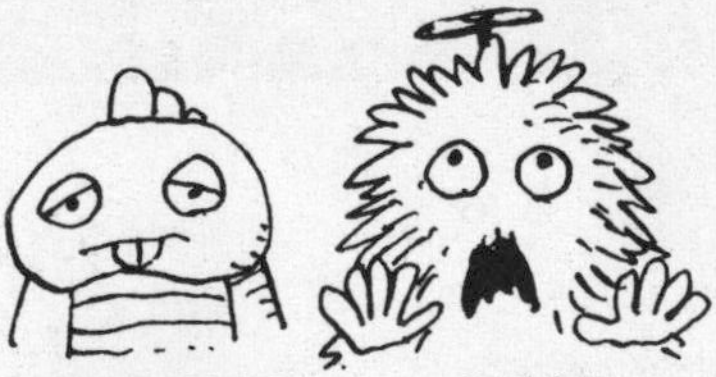

GACHAPIN MUKKU

(THEY DON'T LOOK QUITE RIGHT...)

GACHAPIN AND MUKKU ARE CHARACTERS FROM THE LIVE-ACTION KIDS' SHOW "HIRAKE! PONKIKI." --ED.

Chapter 291:
WE'LL BE HERE

SAIL SAYS "TOP SECRET" --ED.

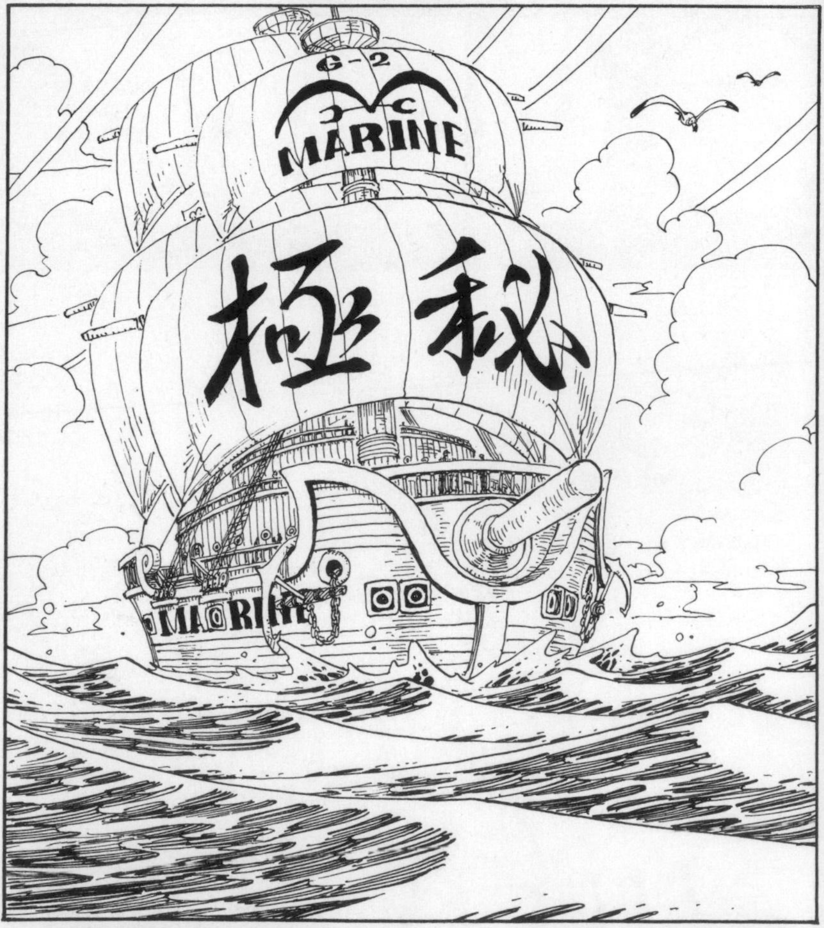
G-2
MARINE
極秘

ACE'S GREAT SEARCH FOR BLACKBEARD, VOL. 17: "THE TOP SECRET NAVAL RECONNAISSANCE SHIP RETURNS TO PORT"

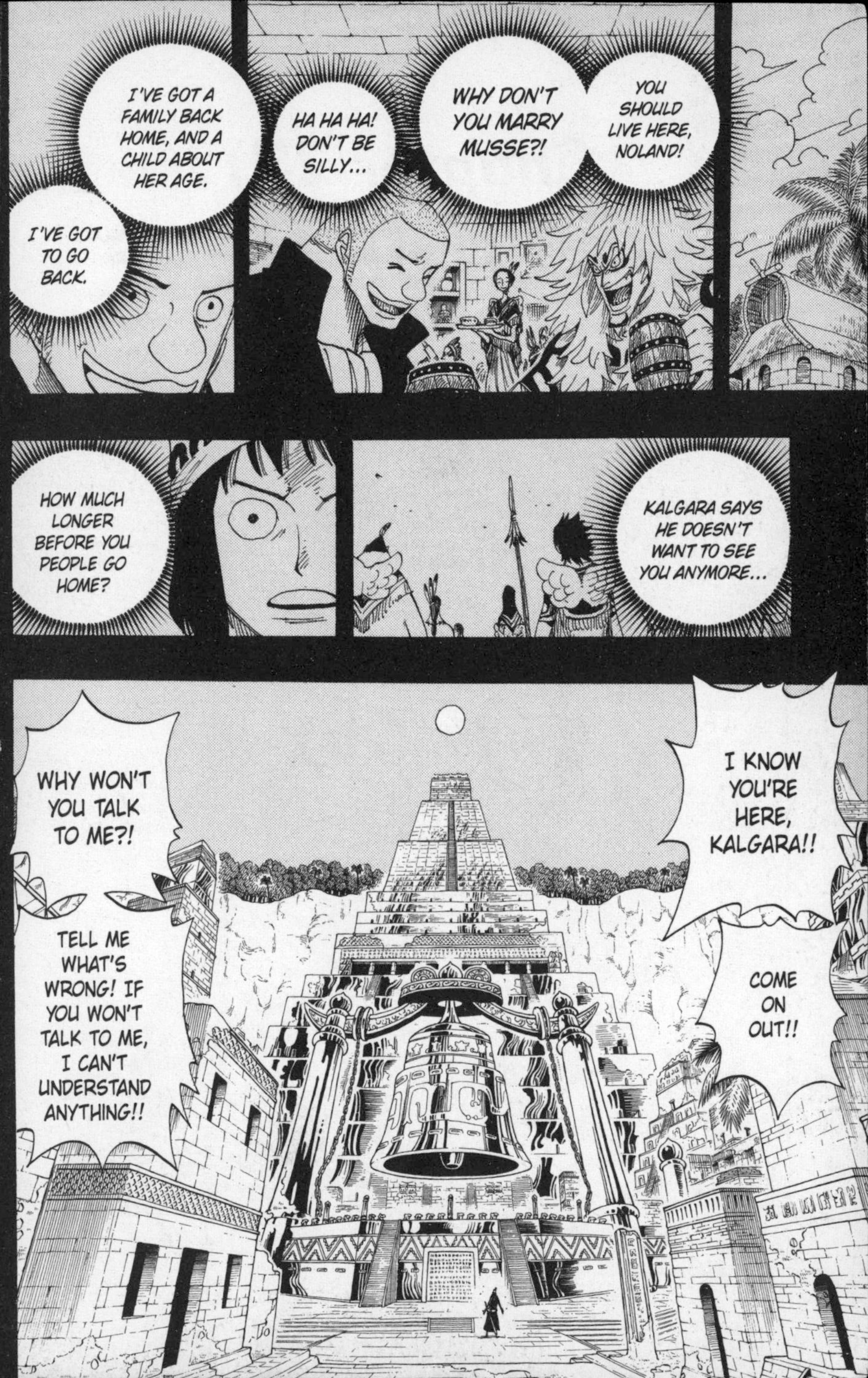
YOU SHOULD LIVE HERE, NOLAND!
WHY DON'T YOU MARRY MUSSE?!
HA HA HA! DON'T BE SILLY...
I'VE GOT A FAMILY BACK HOME, AND A CHILD ABOUT HER AGE.
I'VE GOT TO GO BACK.
KALGARA SAYS HE DOESN'T WANT TO SEE YOU ANYMORE...
HOW MUCH LONGER BEFORE YOU PEOPLE GO HOME?
I KNOW YOU'RE HERE, KALGARA!!
COME ON OUT!!
WHY WON'T YOU TALK TO ME?!
TELL ME WHAT'S WRONG! IF YOU WON'T TALK TO ME, I CAN'T UNDERSTAND ANYTHING!!

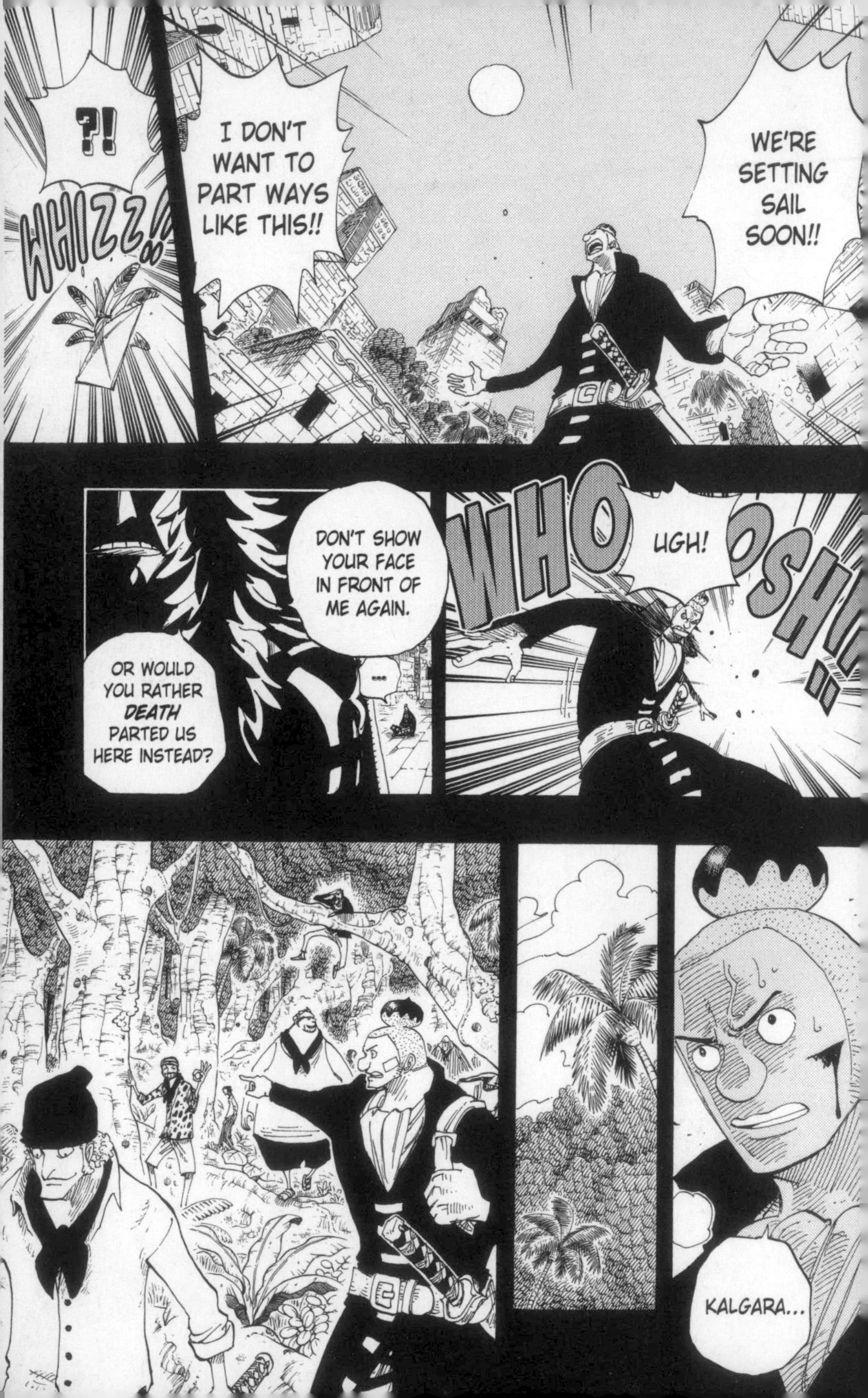
WE'RE SETTING SAIL SOON!!
I DON'T WANT TO PART WAYS LIKE THIS!!
?!
WHIZZZ!!
WHOOSH!!
UGH!
DON'T SHOW YOUR FACE IN FRONT OF ME AGAIN.
...
OR WOULD YOU RATHER *DEATH* PARTED US HERE INSTEAD?
KALGARA...

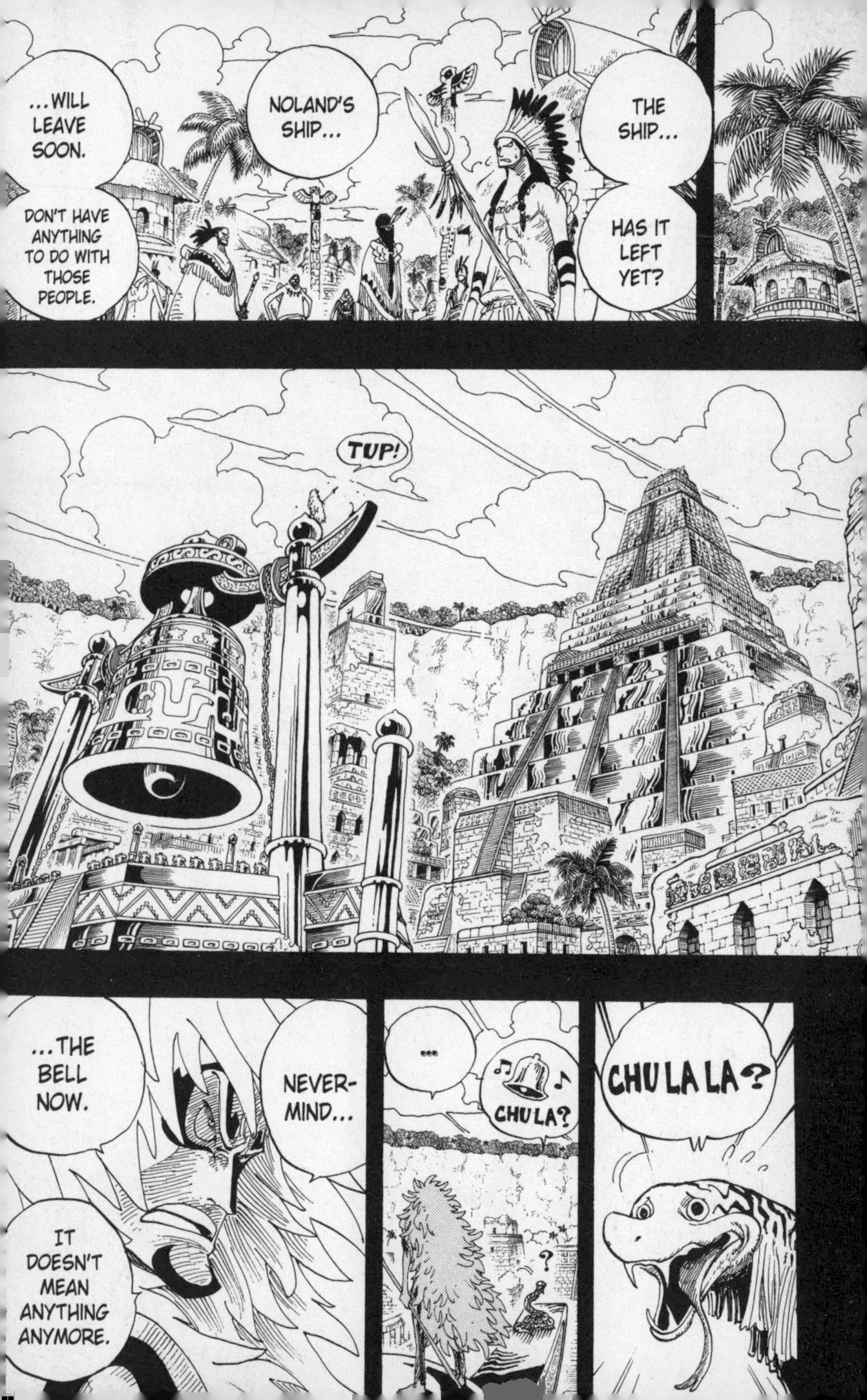
THE SHIP...
HAS IT LEFT YET?
NOLAND'S SHIP...
...WILL LEAVE SOON.
DON'T HAVE ANYTHING TO DO WITH THOSE PEOPLE.
TUP!
CHU LA LA?
...
CHU LA?
?
NEVER-MIND...
...THE BELL NOW.
IT DOESN'T MEAN ANYTHING ANYMORE.

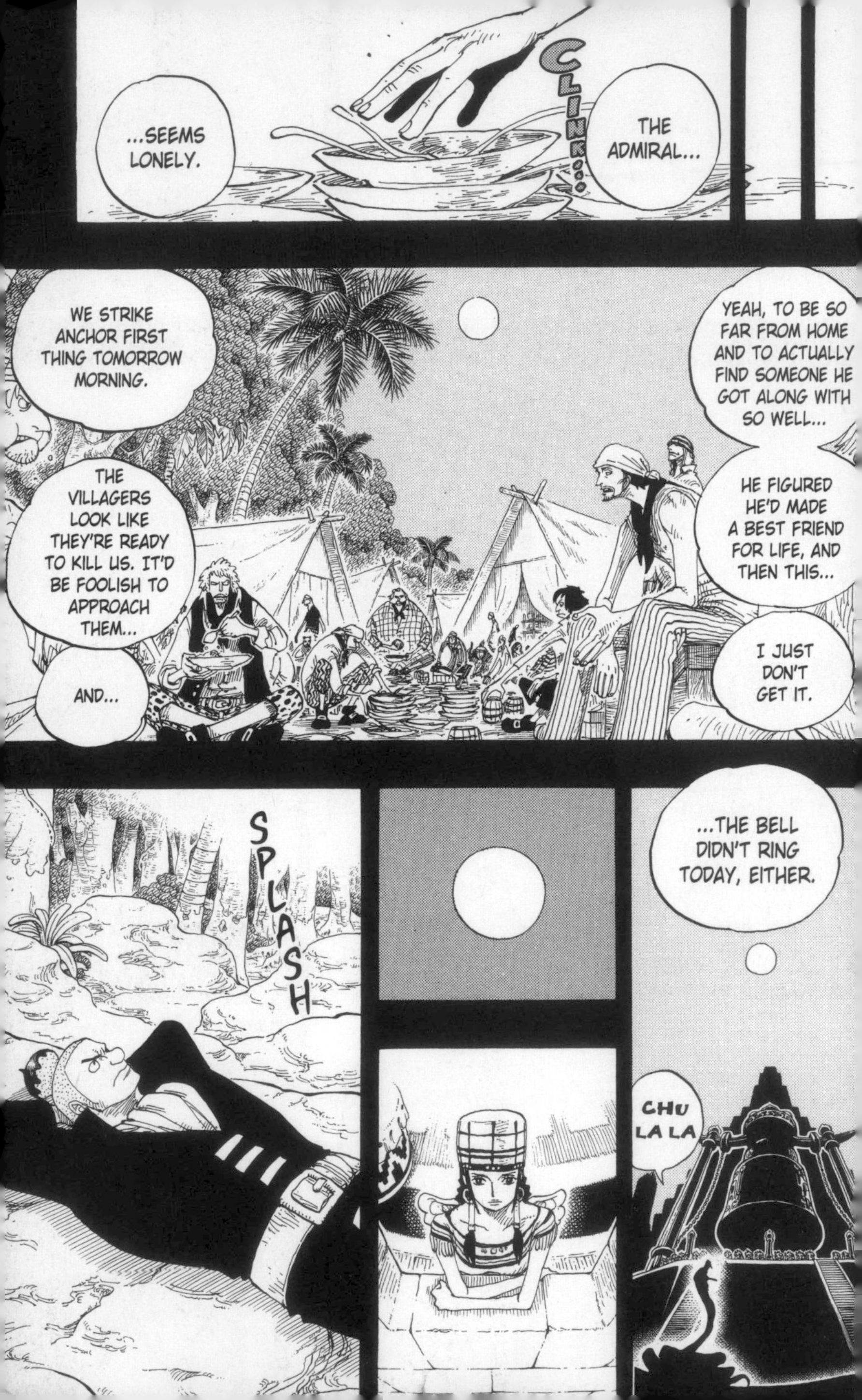
THE ADMIRAL...
CLINK...
...SEEMS LONELY.
YEAH, TO BE SO FAR FROM HOME AND TO ACTUALLY FIND SOMEONE HE GOT ALONG WITH SO WELL...
HE FIGURED HE'D MADE A BEST FRIEND FOR LIFE, AND THEN THIS...
I JUST DON'T GET IT.
WE STRIKE ANCHOR FIRST THING TOMORROW MORNING.
THE VILLAGERS LOOK LIKE THEY'RE READY TO KILL US. IT'D BE FOOLISH TO APPROACH THEM...
AND...
...THE BELL DIDN'T RING TODAY, EITHER.
CHU LA LA
SPLASH

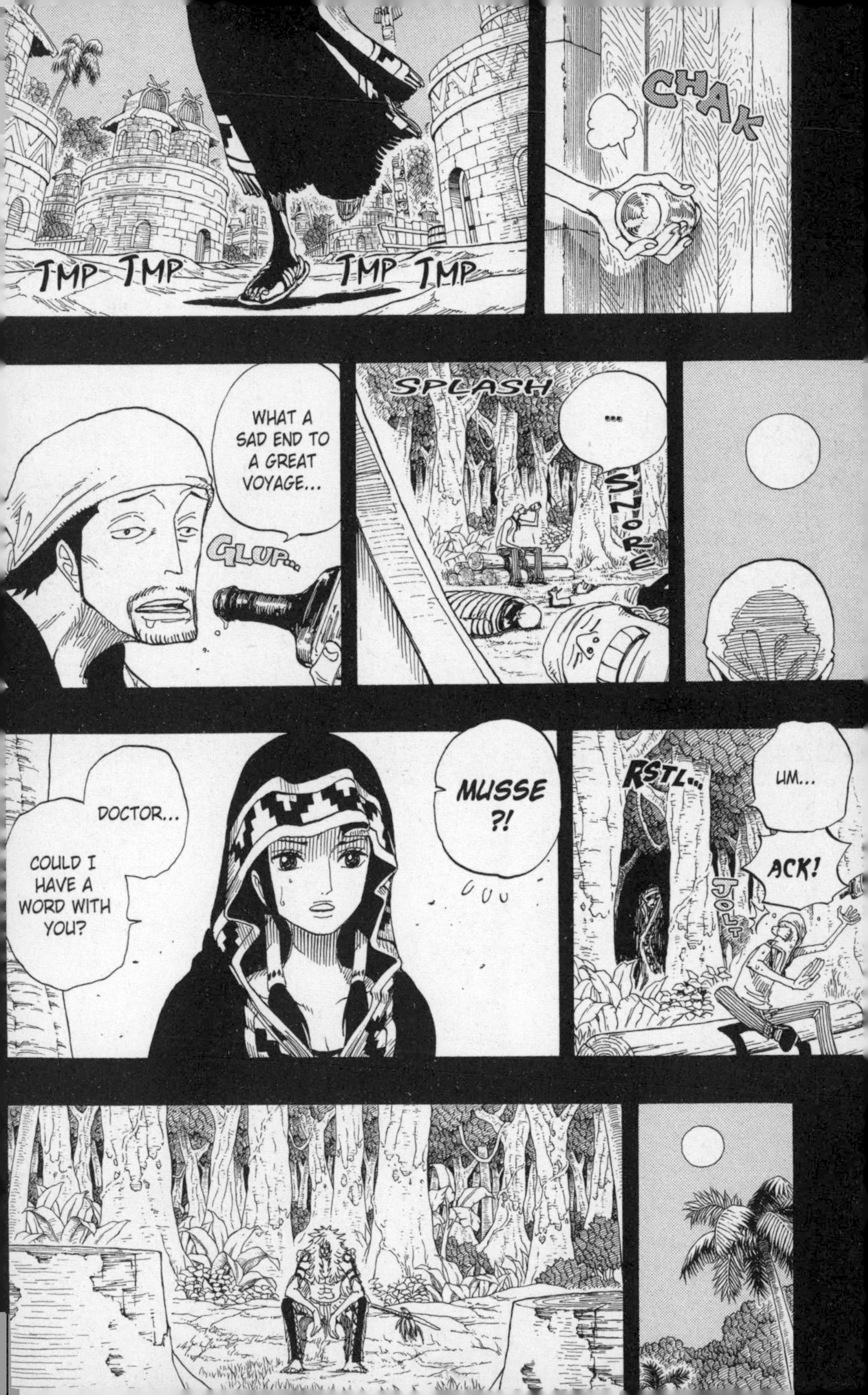
CHAK
TMP TMP TMP TMP
SPLASH
...
SNORE
WHAT A SAD END TO A GREAT VOYAGE...
GLUP...
RSTL...
UM...
ACK!
JOLT
MUSSE ?!
DOCTOR...
COULD I HAVE A WORD WITH YOU?

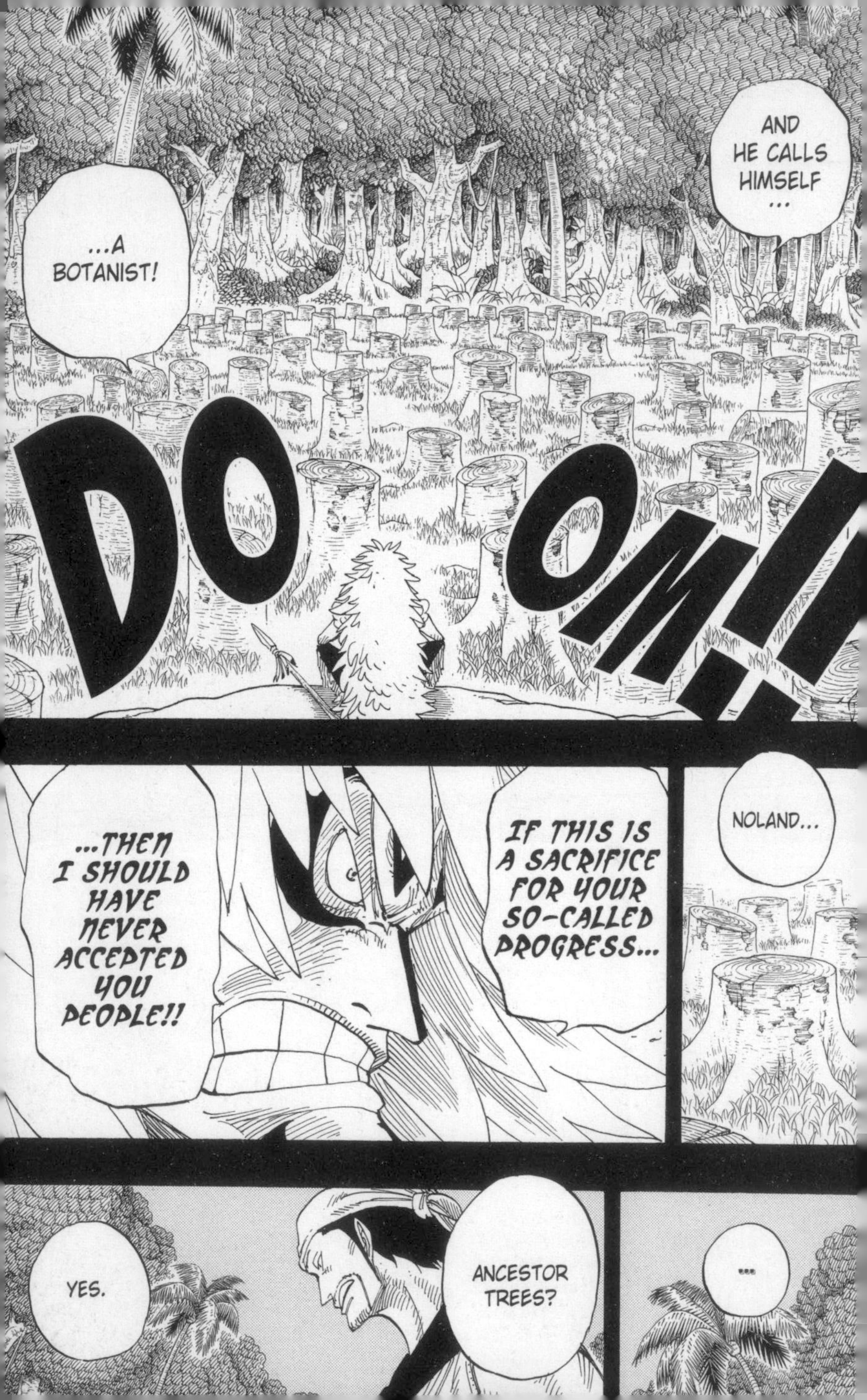
AND HE CALLS HIMSELF ...
...A BOTANIST!
DOON!!
NOLAND...
IF THIS IS A SACRIFICE FOR YOUR SO-CALLED PROGRESS...
...THEN I SHOULD HAVE NEVER ACCEPTED YOU PEOPLE!!
...
ANCESTOR TREES?
YES.

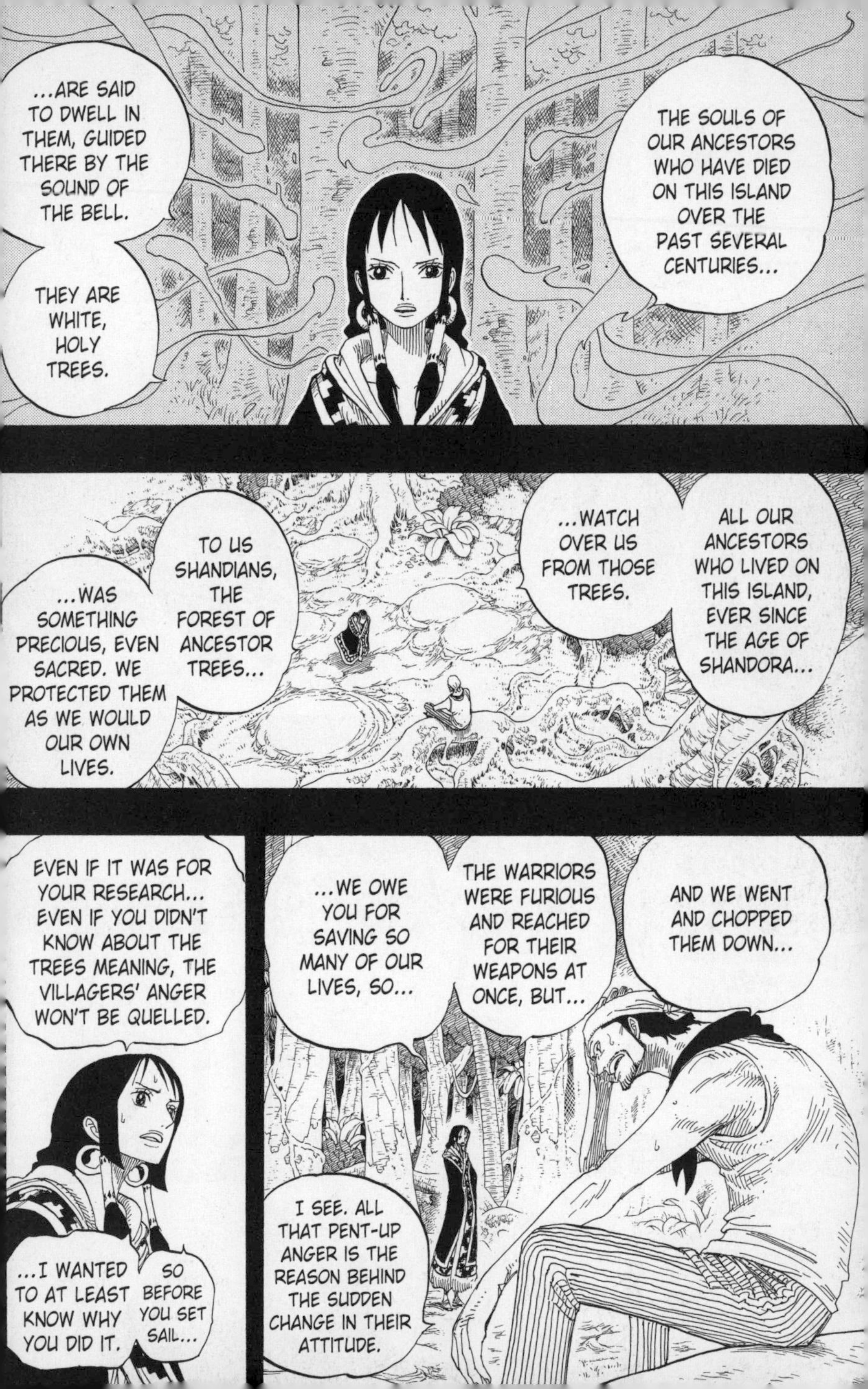
THE SOULS OF OUR ANCESTORS WHO HAVE DIED ON THIS ISLAND OVER THE PAST SEVERAL CENTURIES...
...ARE SAID TO DWELL IN THEM, GUIDED THERE BY THE SOUND OF THE BELL.
THEY ARE WHITE, HOLY TREES.
ALL OUR ANCESTORS WHO LIVED ON THIS ISLAND, EVER SINCE THE AGE OF SHANDORA...
...WATCH OVER US FROM THOSE TREES.
TO US SHANDIANS, THE FOREST OF ANCESTOR TREES...
...WAS SOMETHING PRECIOUS, EVEN SACRED. WE PROTECTED THEM AS WE WOULD OUR OWN LIVES.
AND WE WENT AND CHOPPED THEM DOWN...
THE WARRIORS WERE FURIOUS AND REACHED FOR THEIR WEAPONS AT ONCE, BUT...
...WE OWE YOU FOR SAVING SO MANY OF OUR LIVES, SO...
I SEE. ALL THAT PENT-UP ANGER IS THE REASON BEHIND THE SUDDEN CHANGE IN THEIR ATTITUDE.
EVEN IF IT WAS FOR YOUR RESEARCH... EVEN IF YOU DIDN'T KNOW ABOUT THE TREES MEANING, THE VILLAGERS' ANGER WON'T BE QUELLED.
SO BEFORE YOU SET SAIL...
...I WANTED TO AT LEAST KNOW WHY YOU DID IT.

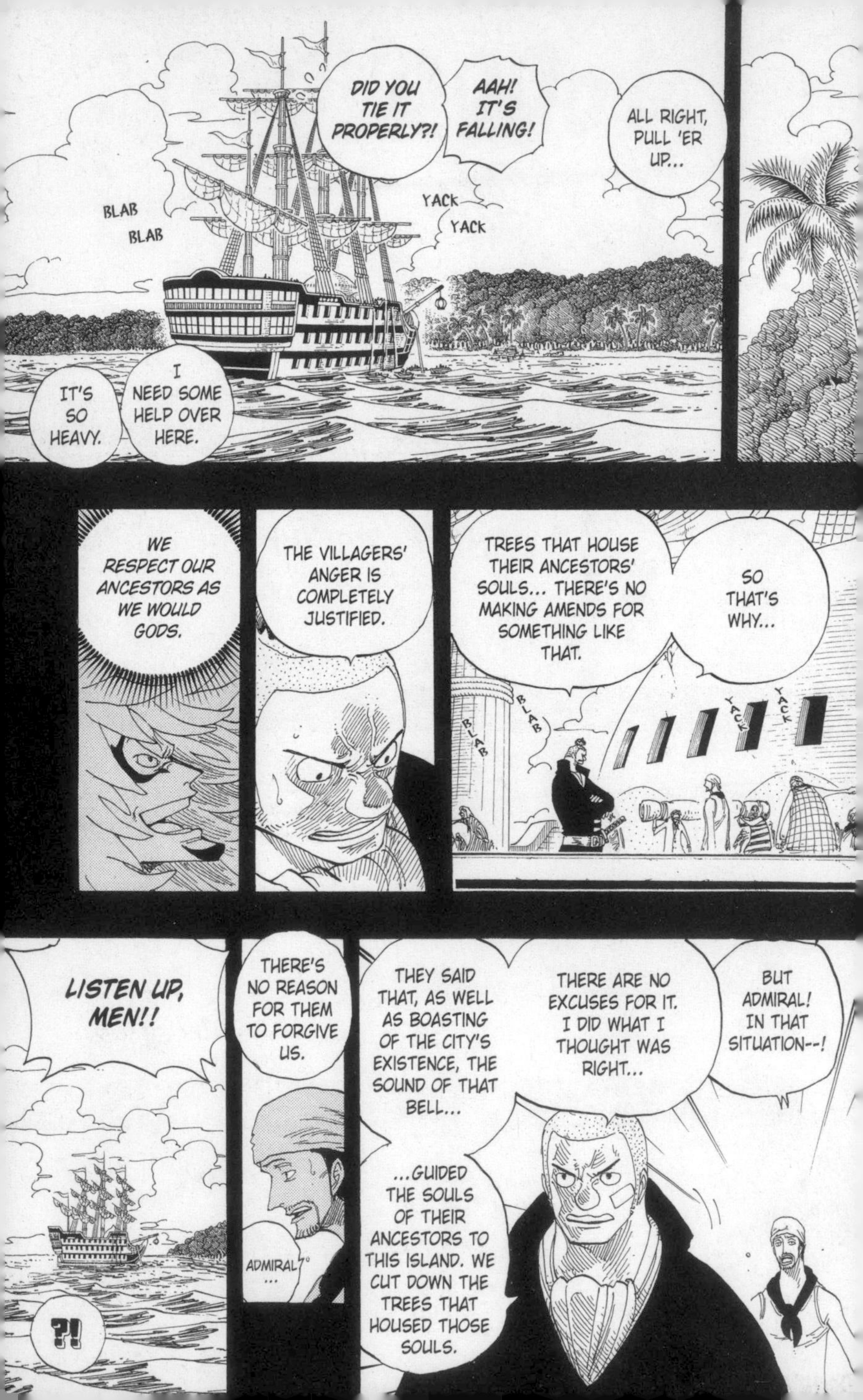
ALL RIGHT, PULL 'ER UP...
AAH! IT'S FALLING!
DID YOU TIE IT PROPERLY?!
YACK YACK
BLAB BLAB
I NEED SOME HELP OVER HERE.
IT'S SO HEAVY.
SO THAT'S WHY...
TREES THAT HOUSE THEIR ANCESTORS' SOULS... THERE'S NO MAKING AMENDS FOR SOMETHING LIKE THAT.
BLAB
BLAB
YACK
YACK
THE VILLAGERS' ANGER IS COMPLETELY JUSTIFIED.
WE RESPECT OUR ANCESTORS AS WE WOULD GODS.
BUT ADMIRAL! IN THAT SITUATION--!
THERE ARE NO EXCUSES FOR IT. I DID WHAT I THOUGHT WAS RIGHT...
THEY SAID THAT, AS WELL AS BOASTING OF THE CITY'S EXISTENCE, THE SOUND OF THAT BELL...
...GUIDED THE SOULS OF THEIR ANCESTORS TO THIS ISLAND. WE CUT DOWN THE TREES THAT HOUSED THOSE SOULS.
THERE'S NO REASON FOR THEM TO FORGIVE US.
ADMIRAL...
LISTEN UP, MEN!!
?!

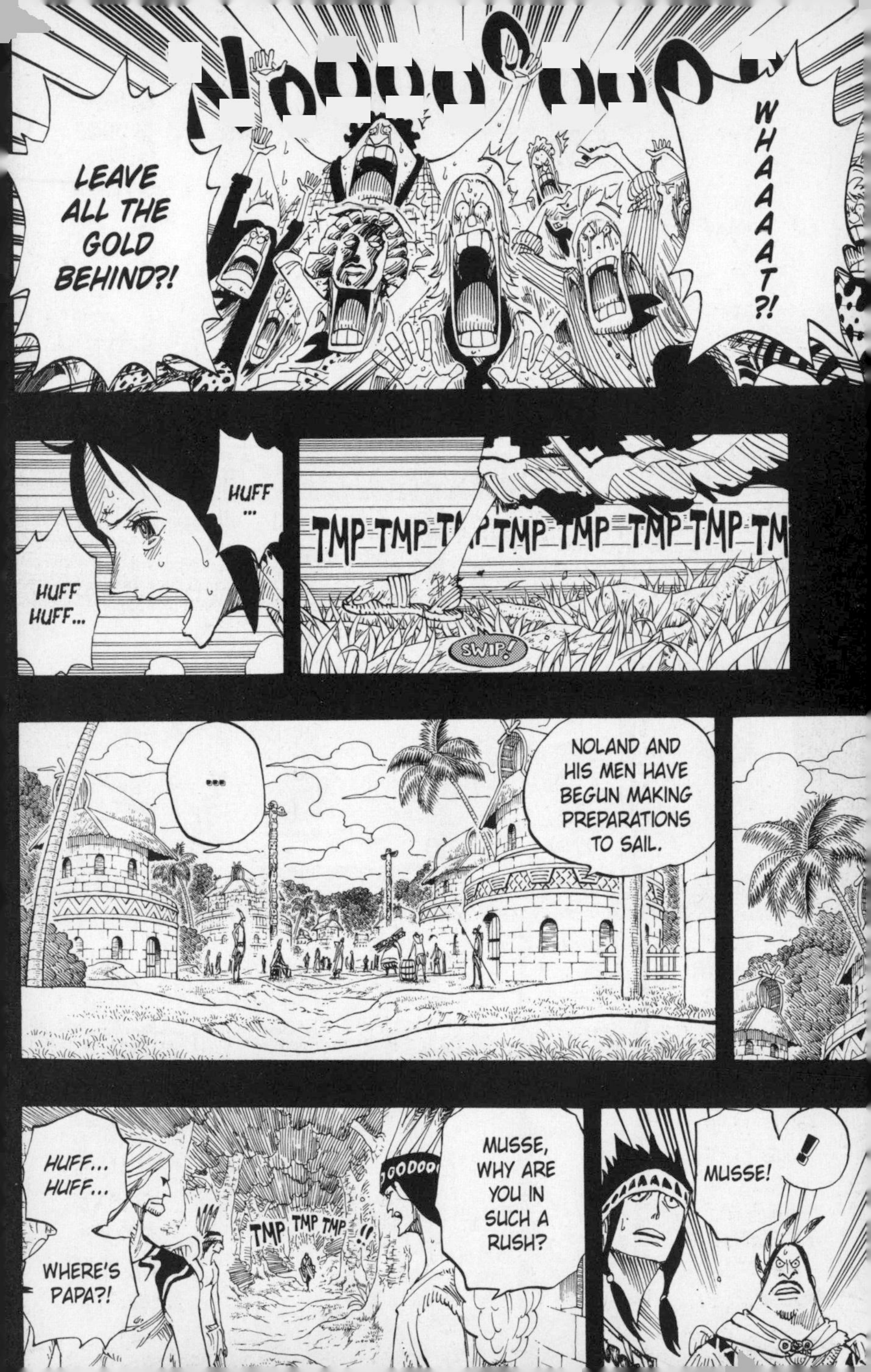
WHAAAAAT?!
LEAVE ALL THE GOLD BEHIND?!
TMP TMP TMP TMP TMP TMP TMP TM
SWIP!
HUFF ...
HUFF HUFF...
NOLAND AND HIS MEN HAVE BEGUN MAKING PREPARATIONS TO SAIL.
...
!
MUSSE!
MUSSE, WHY ARE YOU IN SUCH A RUSH?
GODOOO
TMP TMP TMP
!!
HUFF... HUFF...
WHERE'S PAPA?!

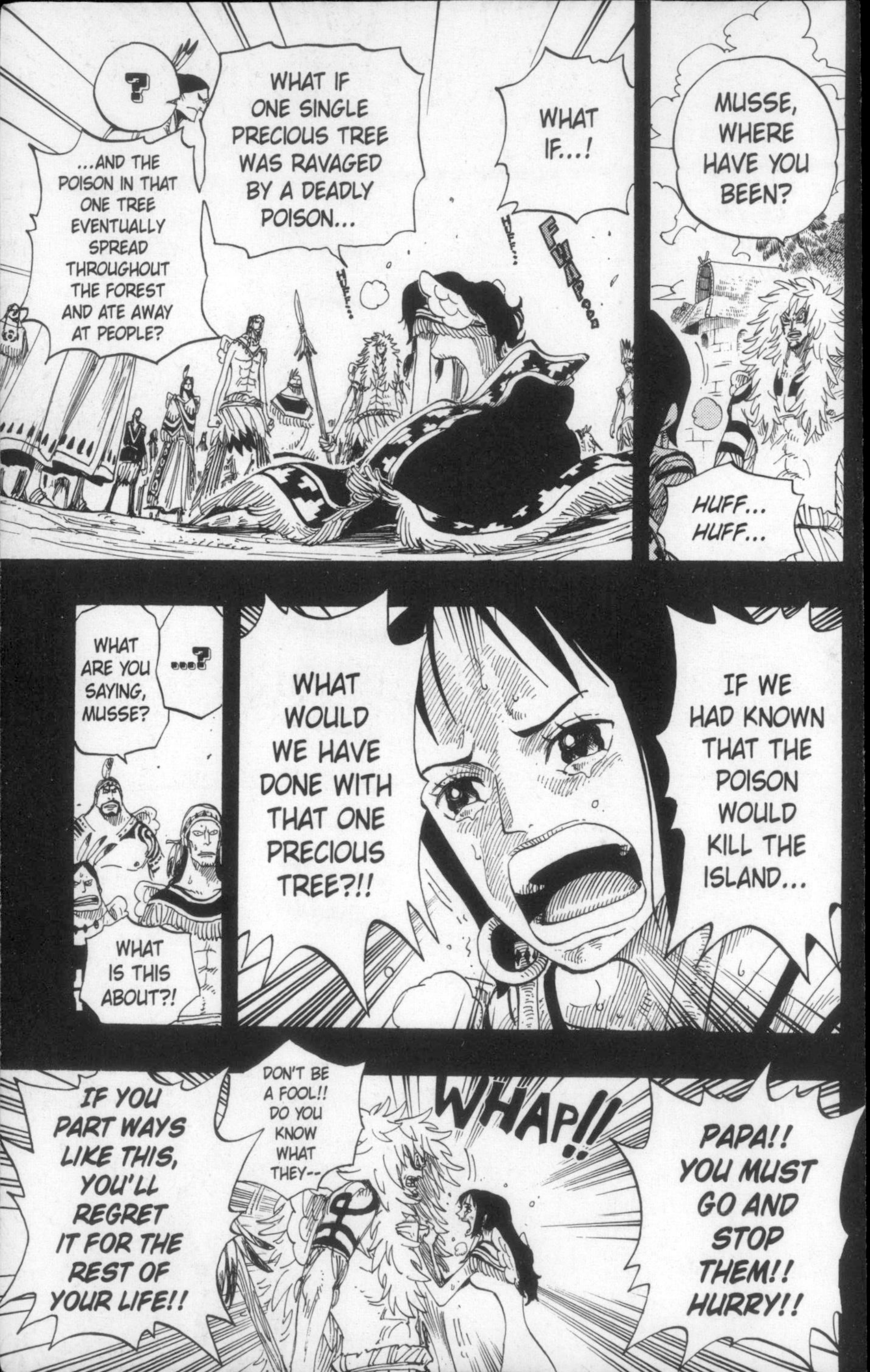
MUSSE, WHERE HAVE YOU BEEN?
HUFF... HUFF...
WHAT IF...!
WHAT IF ONE SINGLE PRECIOUS TREE WAS RAVAGED BY A DEADLY POISON...
...AND THE POISON IN THAT ONE TREE EVENTUALLY SPREAD THROUGHOUT THE FOREST AND ATE AWAY AT PEOPLE?
?
IF WE HAD KNOWN THAT THE POISON WOULD KILL THE ISLAND...
WHAT WOULD WE HAVE DONE WITH THAT ONE PRECIOUS TREE?!!
...?
WHAT ARE YOU SAYING, MUSSE?
WHAT IS THIS ABOUT?!
PAPA!! YOU MUST GO AND STOP THEM!! HURRY!!
WHAP!!
DON'T BE A FOOL!! DO YOU KNOW WHAT THEY--
IF YOU PART WAYS LIKE THIS, YOU'LL REGRET IT FOR THE REST OF YOUR LIFE!!

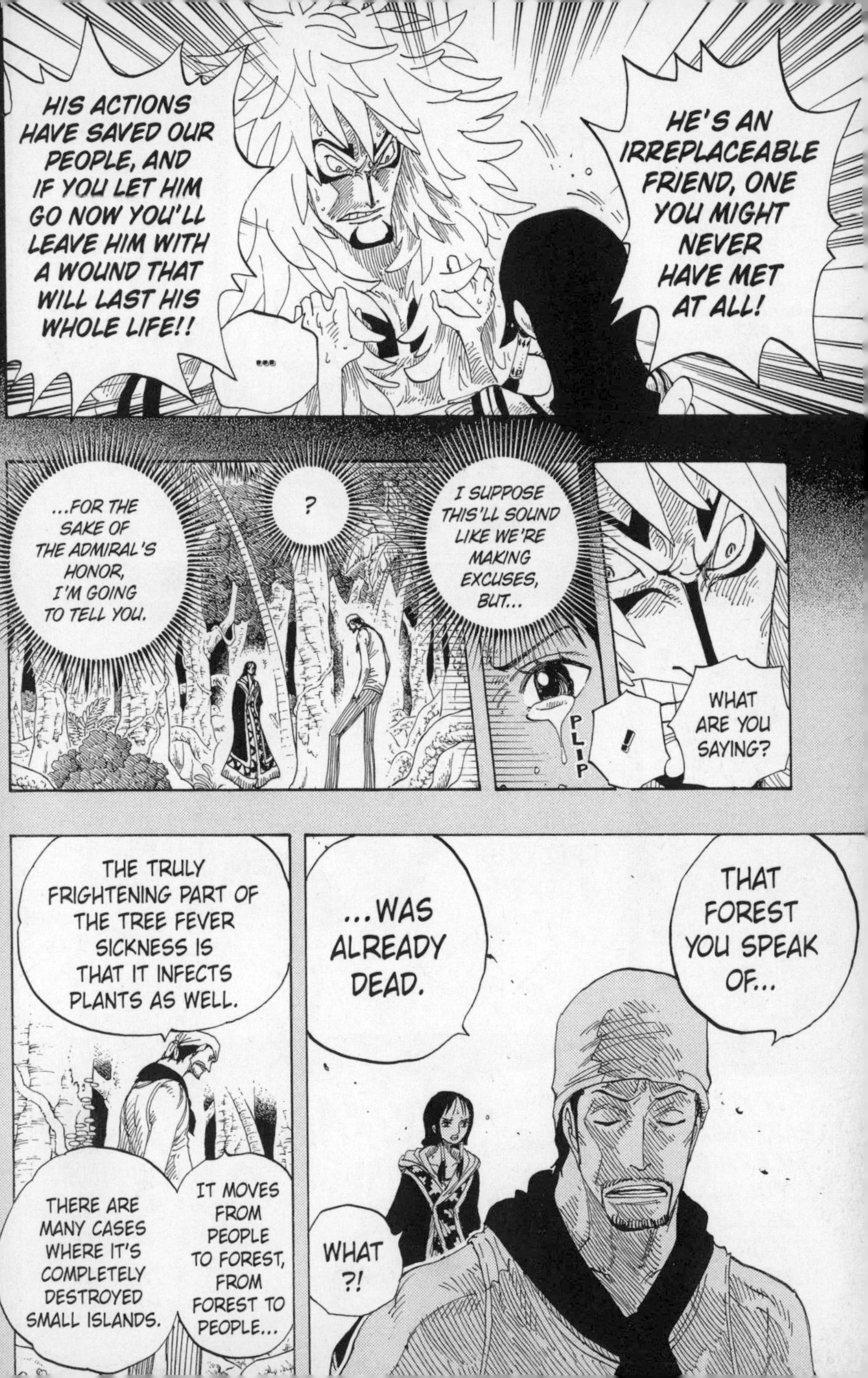
HE'S AN IRREPLACEABLE FRIEND, ONE YOU MIGHT NEVER HAVE MET AT ALL!
HIS ACTIONS HAVE SAVED OUR PEOPLE, AND IF YOU LET HIM GO NOW YOU'LL LEAVE HIM WITH A WOUND THAT WILL LAST HIS WHOLE LIFE!!
...
WHAT ARE YOU SAYING?
!
PLIP
I SUPPOSE THIS'LL SOUND LIKE WE'RE MAKING EXCUSES, BUT...
?
...FOR THE SAKE OF THE ADMIRAL'S HONOR, I'M GOING TO TELL YOU.
THAT FOREST YOU SPEAK OF...
...WAS ALREADY DEAD.
WHAT?!
THE TRULY FRIGHTENING PART OF THE TREE FEVER SICKNESS IS THAT IT INFECTS PLANTS AS WELL.
IT MOVES FROM PEOPLE TO FOREST, FROM FOREST TO PEOPLE...
THERE ARE MANY CASES WHERE IT'S COMPLETELY DESTROYED SMALL ISLANDS.

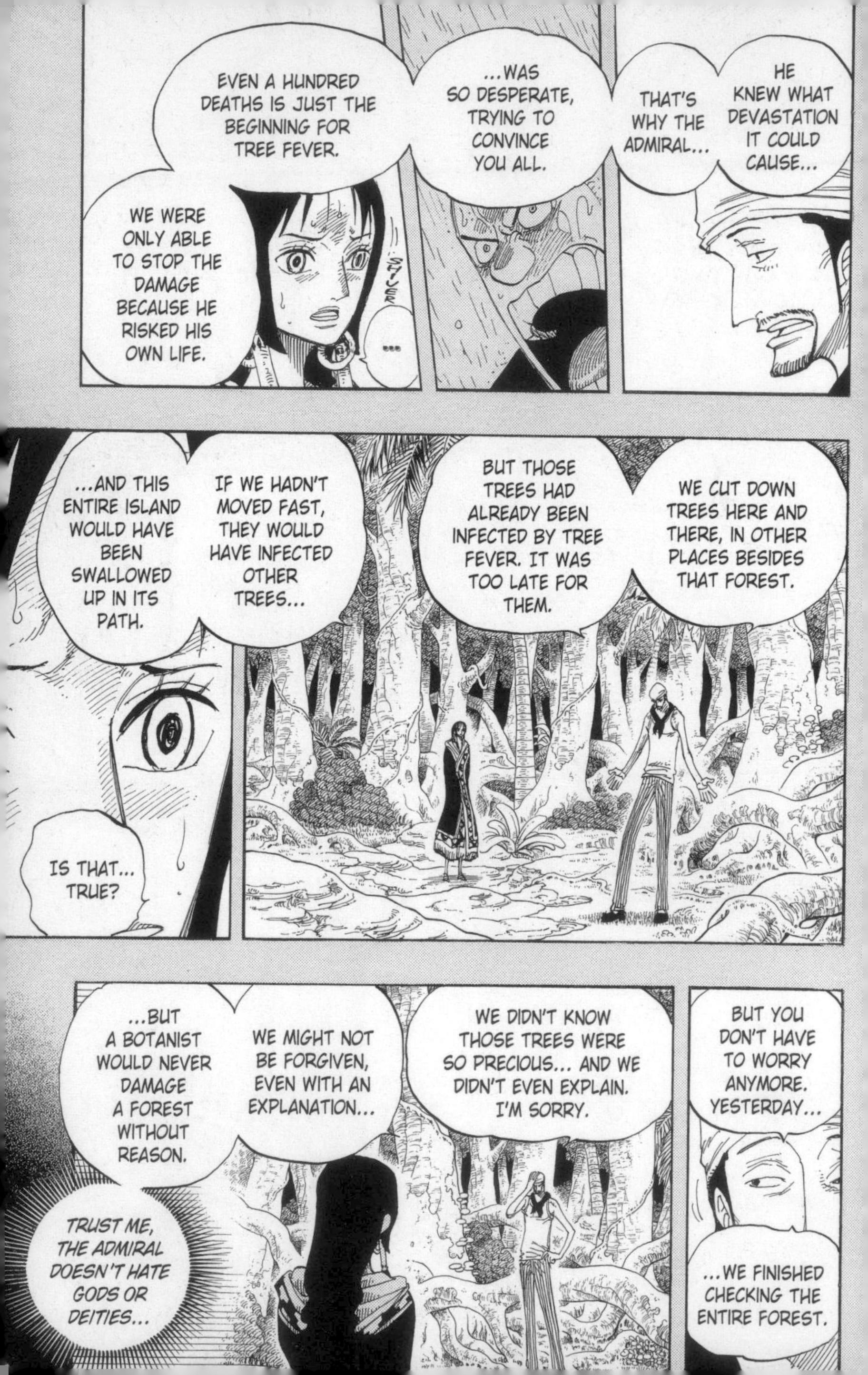
HE KNEW WHAT DEVASTATION IT COULD CAUSE...
THAT'S WHY THE ADMIRAL...
...WAS SO DESPERATE, TRYING TO CONVINCE YOU ALL.
EVEN A HUNDRED DEATHS IS JUST THE BEGINNING FOR TREE FEVER.
WE WERE ONLY ABLE TO STOP THE DAMAGE BECAUSE HE RISKED HIS OWN LIFE.
SHIVER
...
WE CUT DOWN TREES HERE AND THERE, IN OTHER PLACES BESIDES THAT FOREST.
BUT THOSE TREES HAD ALREADY BEEN INFECTED BY TREE FEVER. IT WAS TOO LATE FOR THEM.
IF WE HADN'T MOVED FAST, THEY WOULD HAVE INFECTED OTHER TREES...
...AND THIS ENTIRE ISLAND WOULD HAVE BEEN SWALLOWED UP IN ITS PATH.
IS THAT... TRUE?
BUT YOU DON'T HAVE TO WORRY ANYMORE. YESTERDAY...
...WE FINISHED CHECKING THE ENTIRE FOREST.
WE DIDN'T KNOW THOSE TREES WERE SO PRECIOUS... AND WE DIDN'T EVEN EXPLAIN. I'M SORRY.
WE MIGHT NOT BE FORGIVEN, EVEN WITH AN EXPLANATION...
...BUT A BOTANIST WOULD NEVER DAMAGE A FOREST WITHOUT REASON.
TRUST ME, THE ADMIRAL DOESN'T HATE GODS OR DEITIES...

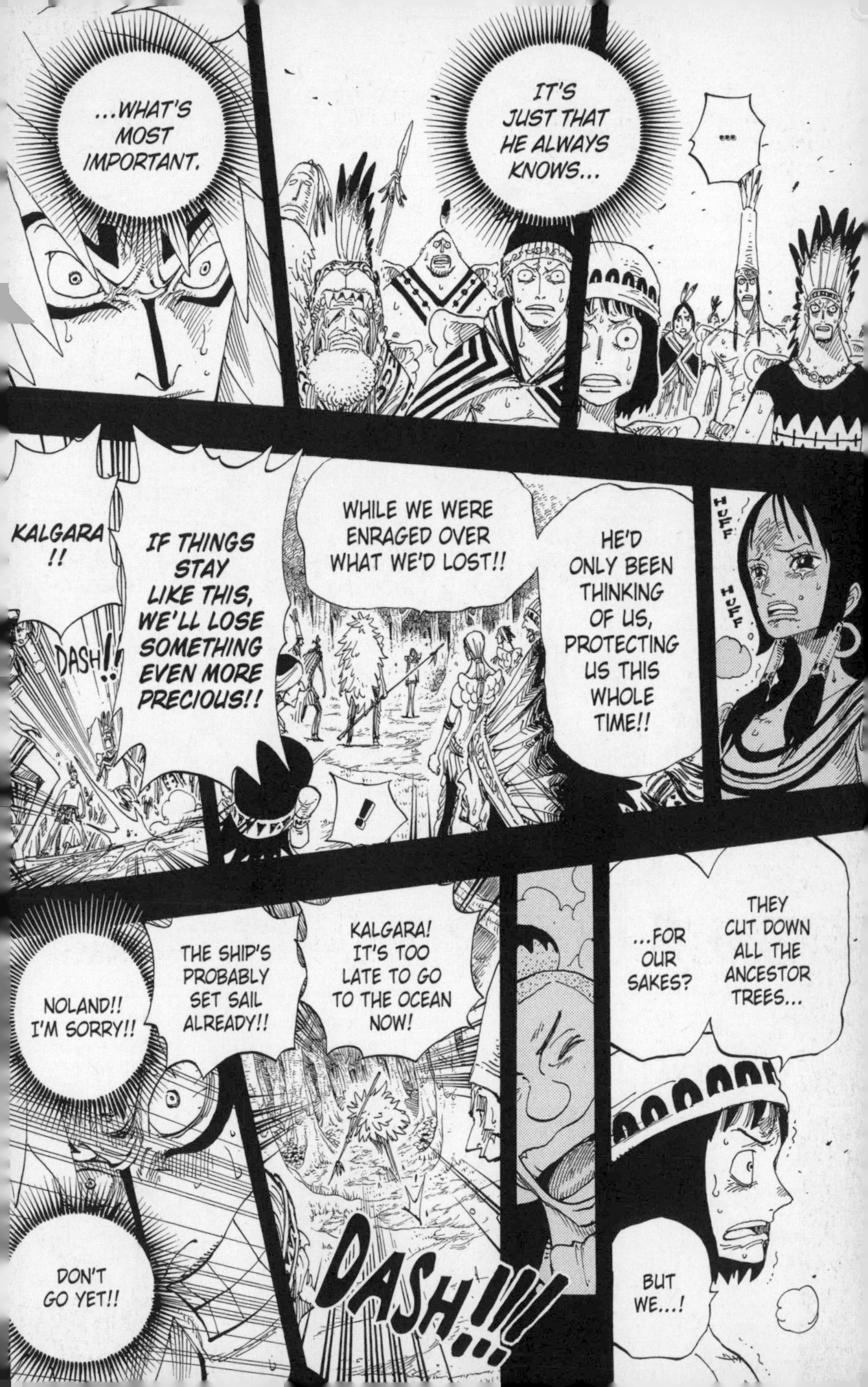
...
IT'S JUST THAT HE ALWAYS KNOWS...
...WHAT'S MOST IMPORTANT.
HUFF HUFF
WHILE WE WERE ENRAGED OVER WHAT WE'D LOST!!
HE'D ONLY BEEN THINKING OF US, PROTECTING US THIS WHOLE TIME!!
!
IF THINGS STAY LIKE THIS, WE'LL LOSE SOMETHING EVEN MORE PRECIOUS!!
KALGARA!!
DASH!!
THEY CUT DOWN ALL THE ANCESTOR TREES...
...FOR OUR SAKES?
BUT WE...!
KALGARA! IT'S TOO LATE TO GO TO THE OCEAN NOW!
THE SHIP'S PROBABLY SET SAIL ALREADY!!
NOLAND!! I'M SORRY!!
DASH!!!!
DON'T GO YET!!

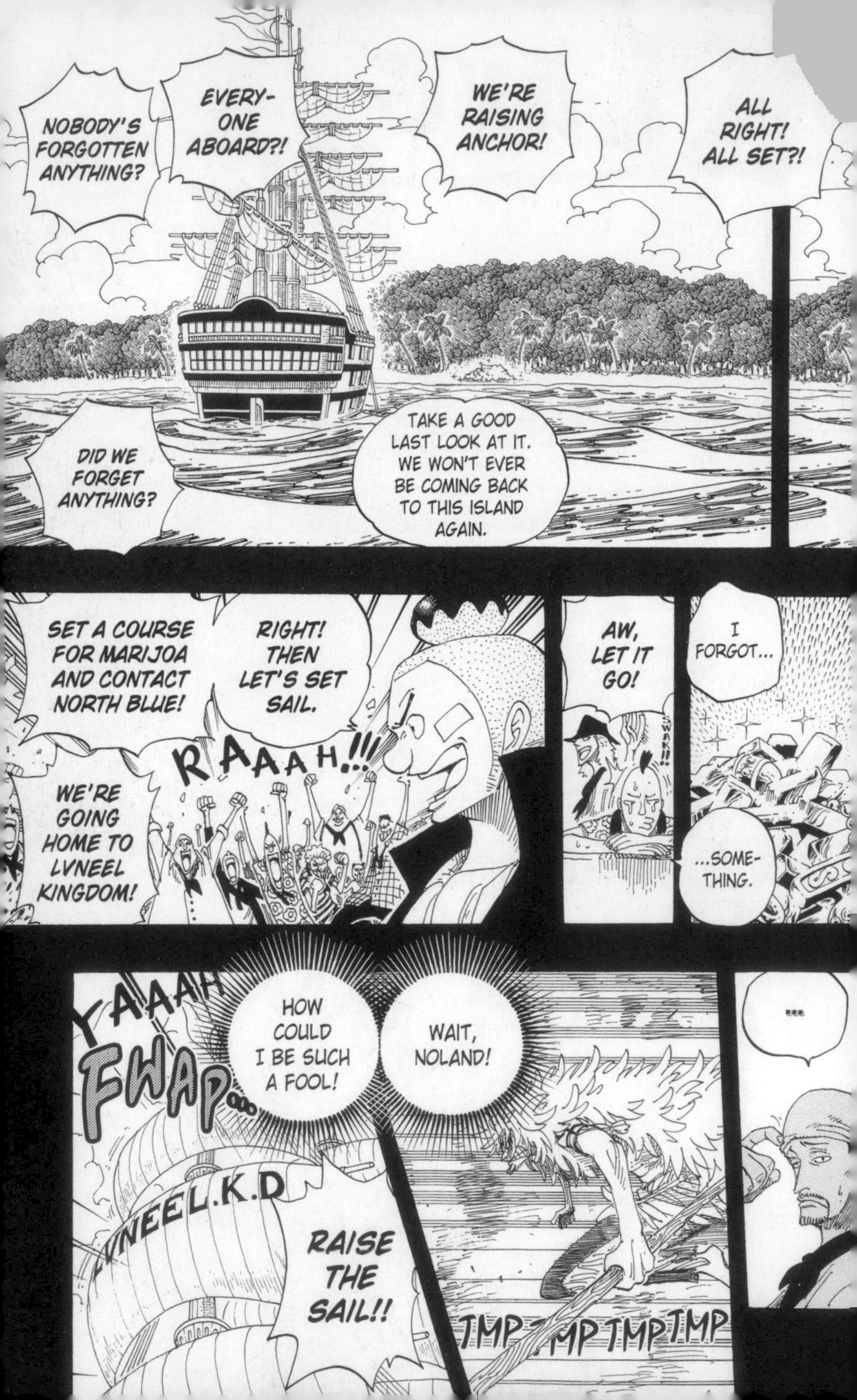
ALL RIGHT! ALL SET?!
WE'RE RAISING ANCHOR!
EVERY-ONE ABOARD?!
NOBODY'S FORGOTTEN ANYTHING?
TAKE A GOOD LAST LOOK AT IT. WE WON'T EVER BE COMING BACK TO THIS ISLAND AGAIN.
DID WE FORGET ANYTHING?
I FORGOT...
...SOME-THING.
AW, LET IT GO!
SWAK!!
RIGHT! THEN LET'S SET SAIL.
SET A COURSE FOR MARIJOA AND CONTACT NORTH BLUE!
RAAAH!!!
WE'RE GOING HOME TO LVNEEL KINGDOM!
...
WAIT, NOLAND!
HOW COULD I BE SUCH A FOOL!
YAAAH
FWAP...
LVNEEL.K.D
RAISE THE SAIL!!
TMP TMP TMP TMP

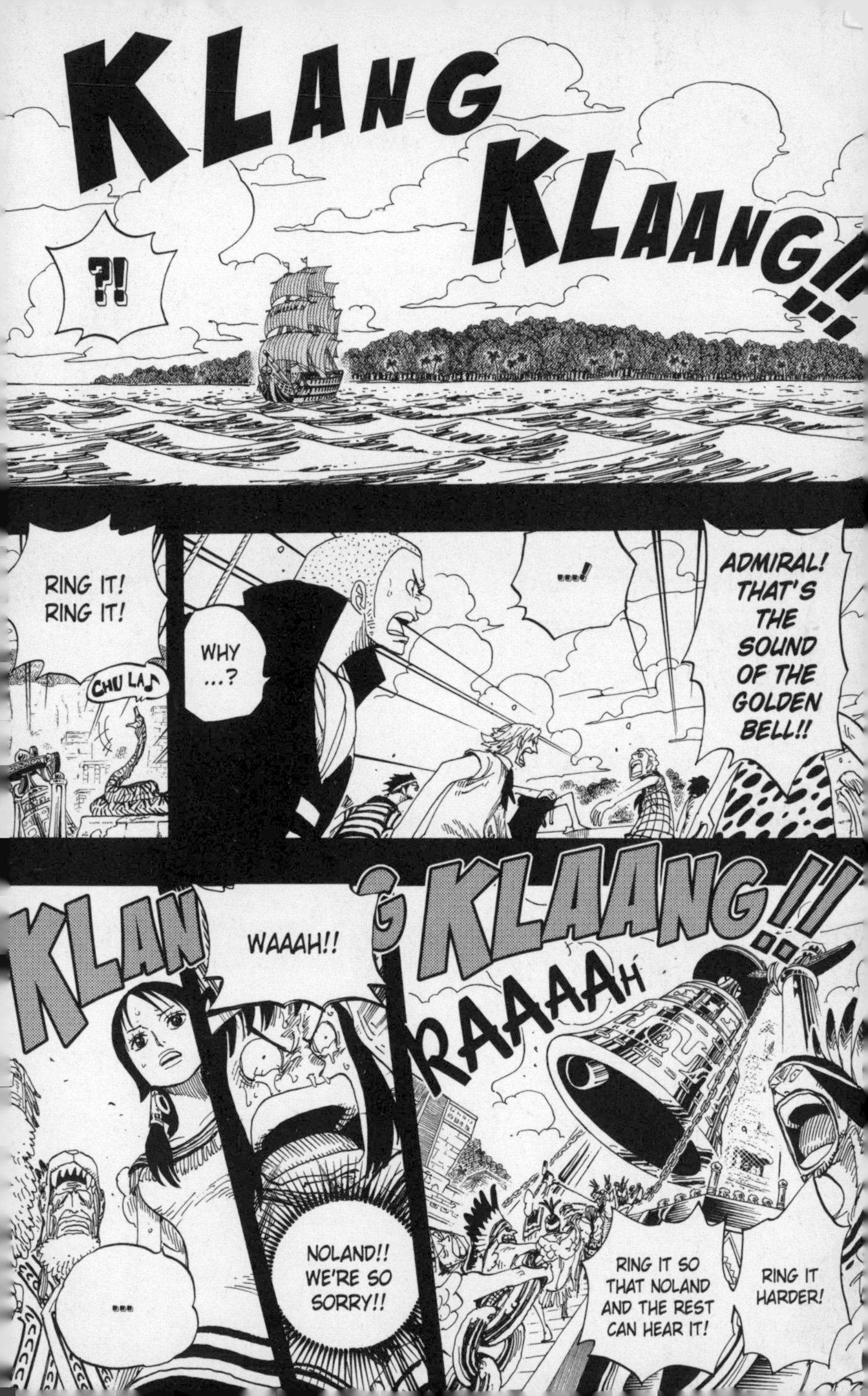

KLANG
KLAANG!!
?!
ADMIRAL! THAT'S THE SOUND OF THE GOLDEN BELL!!
...!
WHY ...?
RING IT! RING IT!
CHU LA♪
KLANG KLAANG!!
RING IT HARDER!
RING IT SO THAT NOLAND AND THE REST CAN HEAR IT!
RAAAAH
WAAAH!!
NOLAND!! WE'RE SO SORRY!!
...

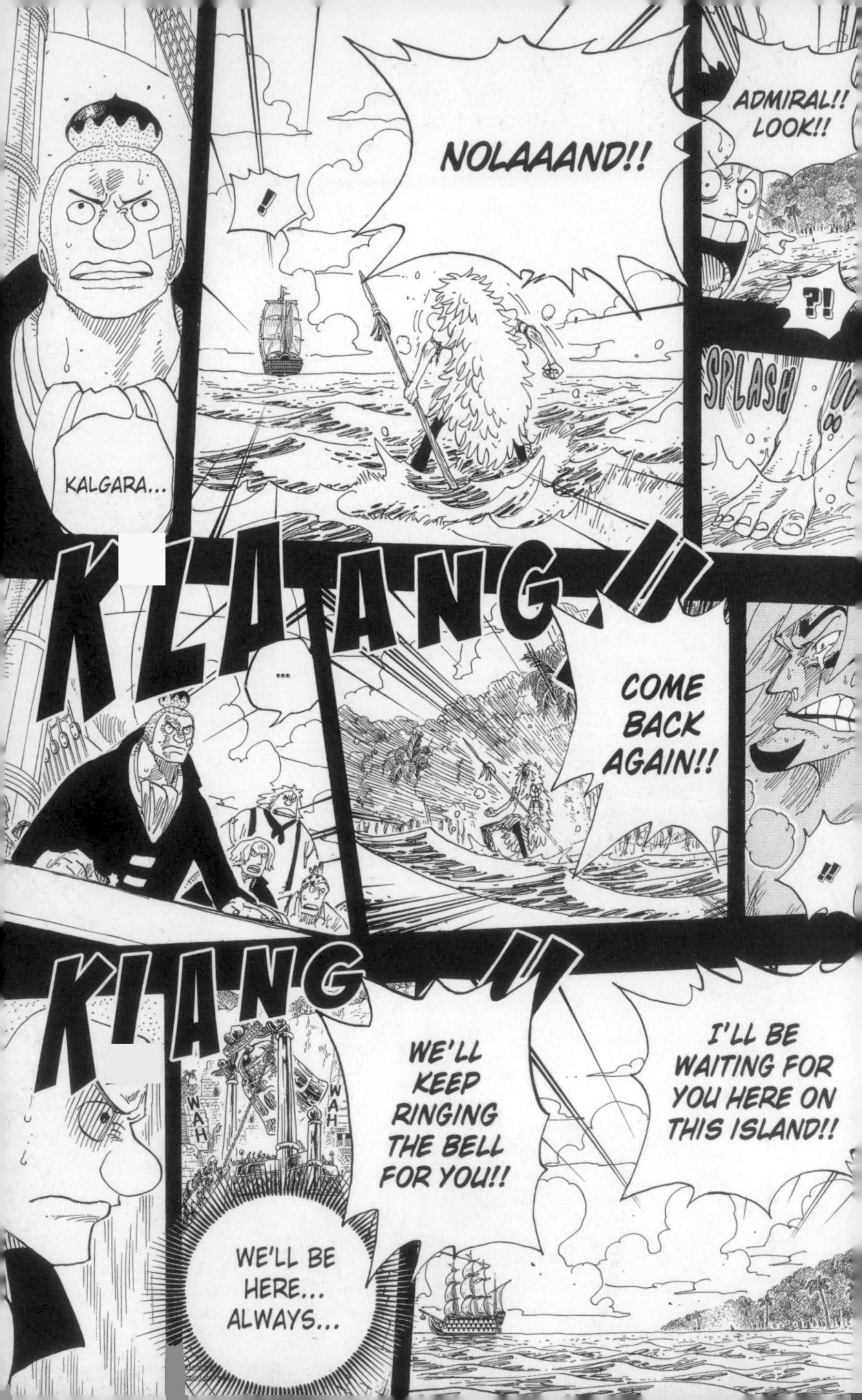
ADMIRAL!! LOOK!!
?!
SPLASH
NOLAAAND!!
!
KALGARA...
KLATANG
!!
COME BACK AGAIN!!
...
KLANG
I'LL BE WAITING FOR YOU HERE ON THIS ISLAND!!
WE'LL KEEP RINGING THE BELL FOR YOU!!
WAH
WAH
WE'LL BE HERE... ALWAYS...

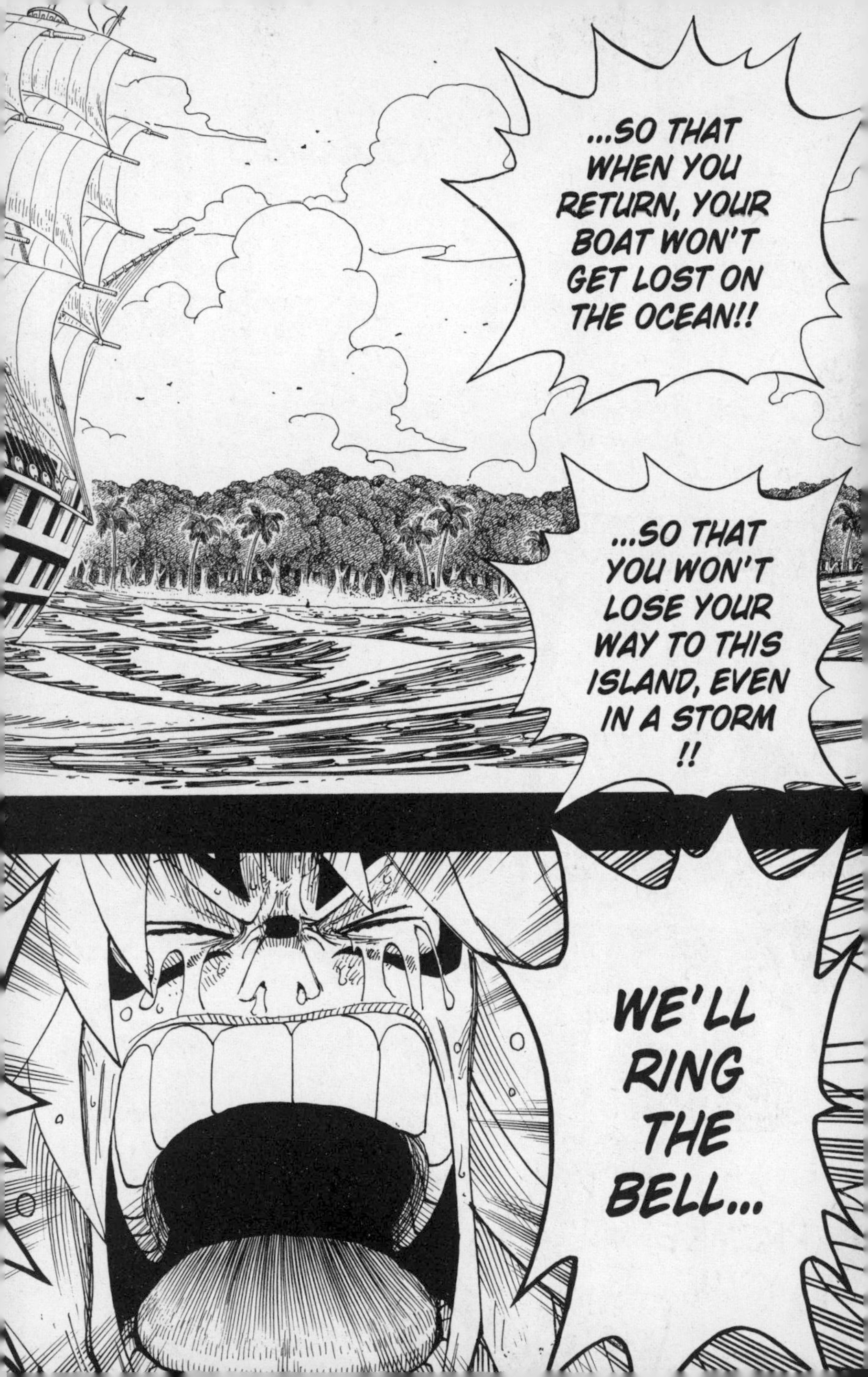
...SO THAT WHEN YOU RETURN, YOUR BOAT WON'T GET LOST ON THE OCEAN!!
...SO THAT YOU WON'T LOSE YOUR WAY TO THIS ISLAND, EVEN IN A STORM !!
WE'LL RING THE BELL...

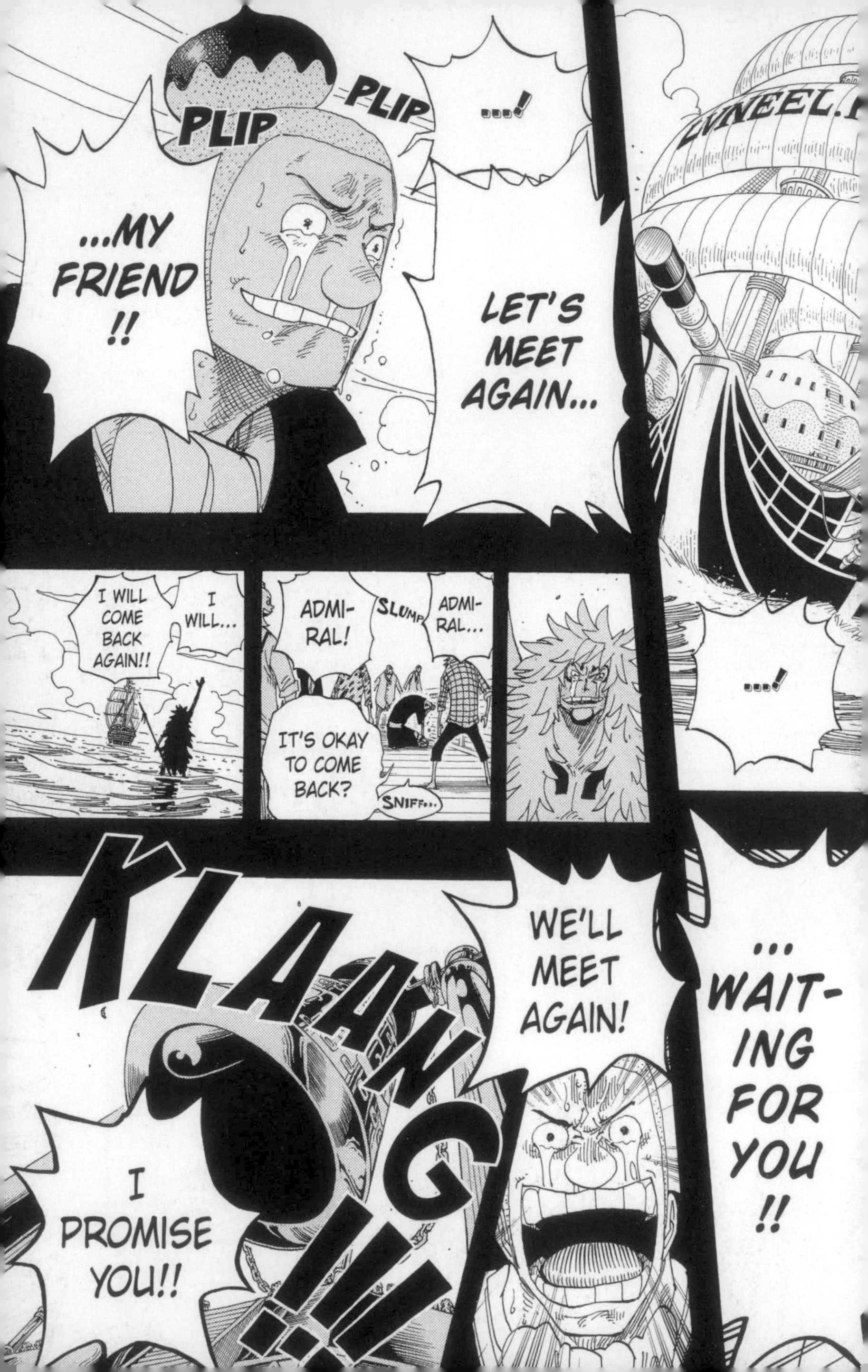
...!
...!
PLIP
PLIP
LET'S MEET AGAIN...
...MY FRIEND!!
ADMI-RAL...
SLUMP
ADMI-RAL!
IT'S OKAY TO COME BACK?
SNIFF...
I WILL...
I WILL COME BACK AGAIN!!
...WAIT-ING FOR YOU!!
WE'LL MEET AGAIN!
KLAANG!!!!
I PROMISE YOU!!

Chapter 292:
TO MEET, LIKE THE HALF-MOON HIDDEN BY CLOUDS

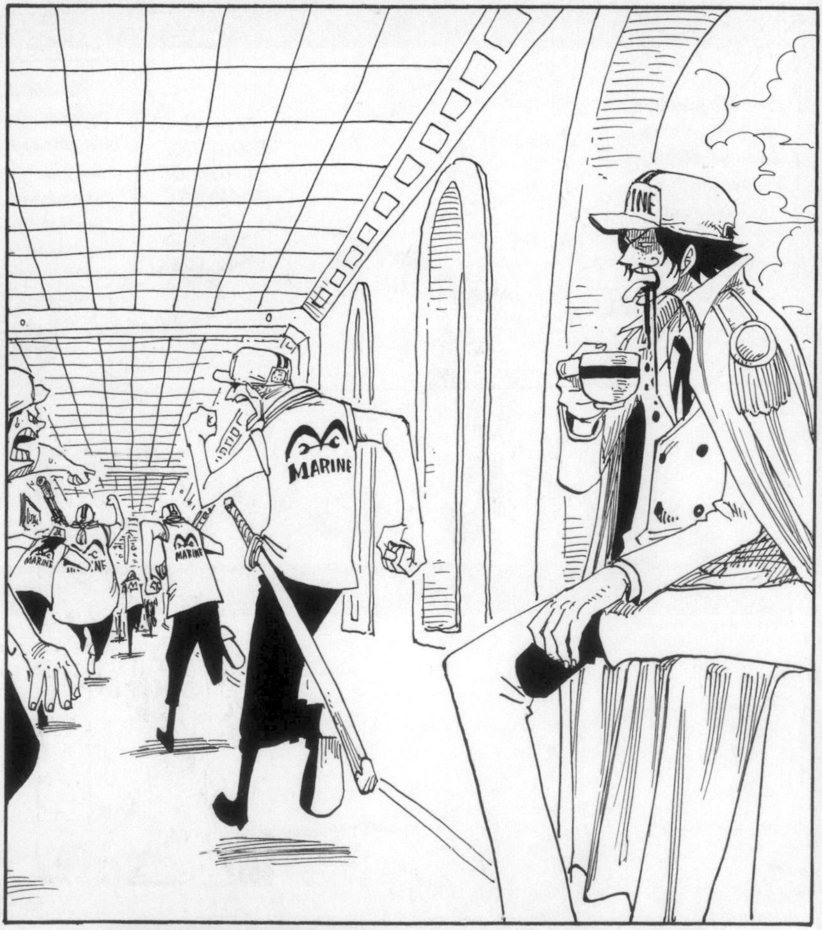

MARINE
MARINE
MARINE

ACE'S GREAT SEARCH FOR BLACKBEARD, VOL. 18:
"AN ARSON INCIDENT FLARES UP ON THE TOP SECRET NAVAL RECONNAISSANCE SHIP"

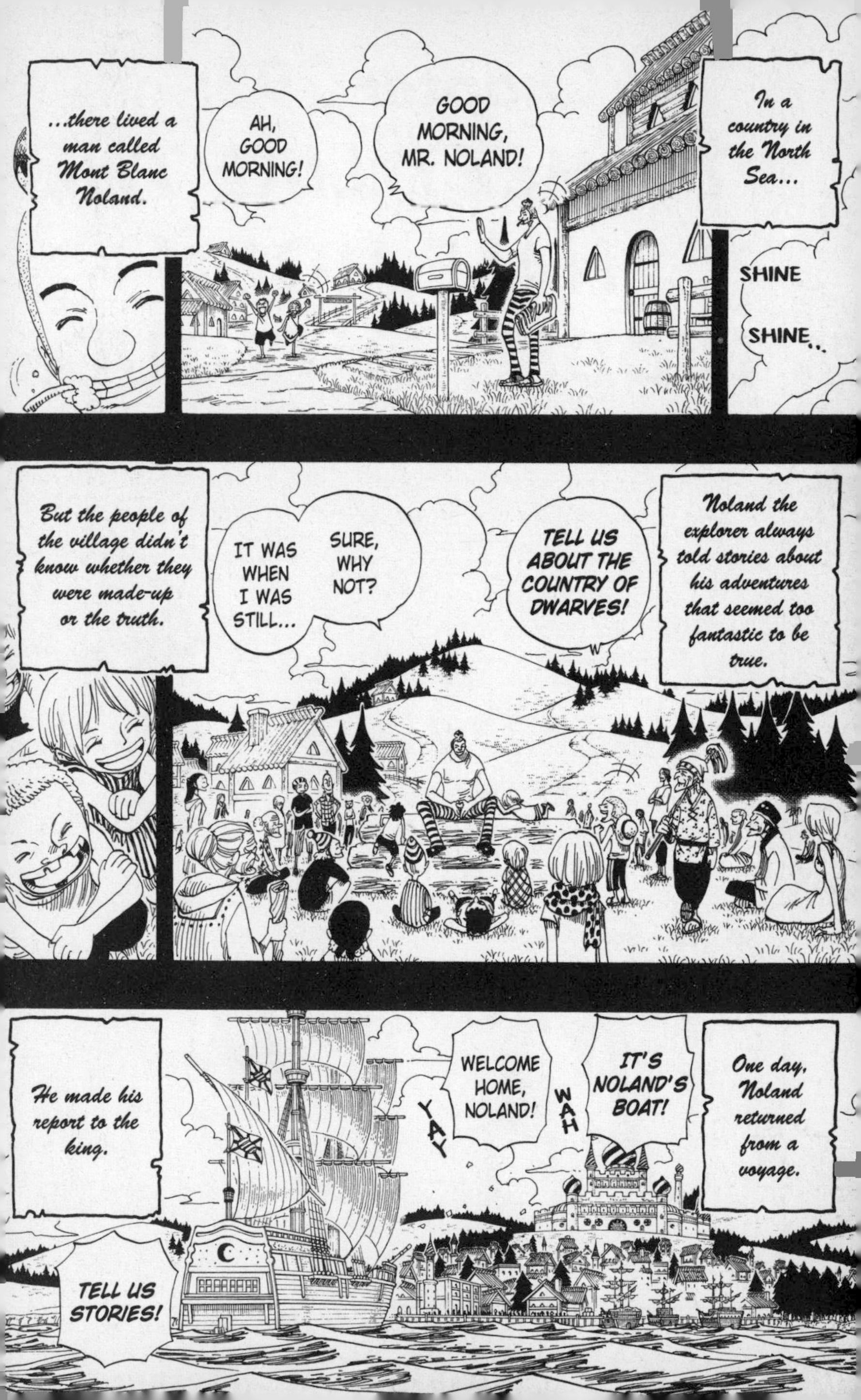
In a country in the North Sea...
SHINE
SHINE...
GOOD MORNING, MR. NOLAND!
AH, GOOD MORNING!
...there lived a man called Mont Blanc Noland.
Noland the explorer always told stories about his adventures that seemed too fantastic to be true.
TELL US ABOUT THE COUNTRY OF DWARVES!
SURE, WHY NOT?
IT WAS WHEN I WAS STILL...
But the people of the village didn't know whether they were made-up or the truth.
One day, Noland returned from a voyage.
IT'S NOLAND'S BOAT!
WAH
WELCOME HOME, NOLAND!
YAY
He made his report to the king.
TELL US STORIES!

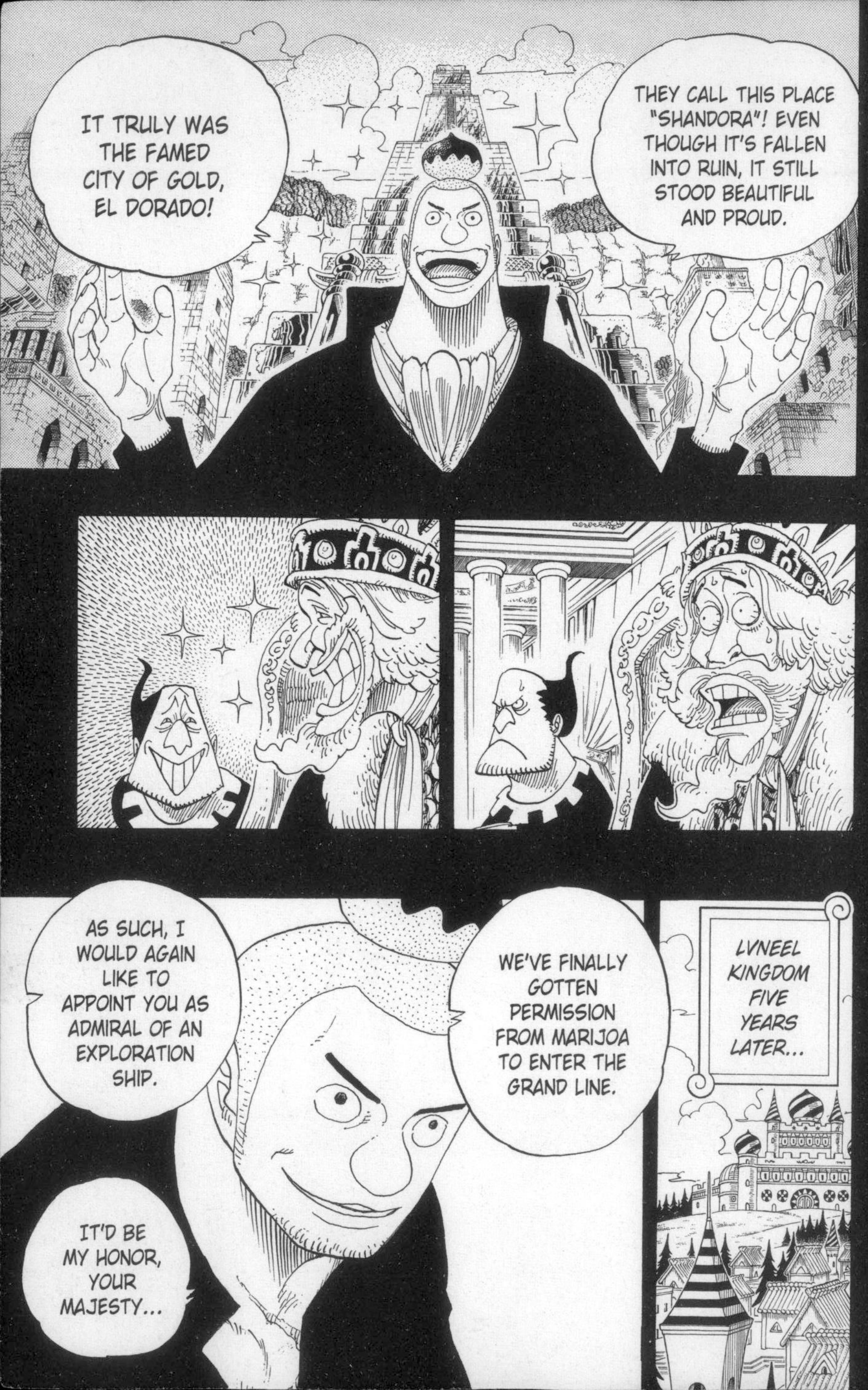
THEY CALL THIS PLACE "SHANDORA"! EVEN THOUGH IT'S FALLEN INTO RUIN, IT STILL STOOD BEAUTIFUL AND PROUD.
IT TRULY WAS THE FAMED CITY OF GOLD, EL DORADO!
LVNEEL KINGDOM FIVE YEARS LATER...
WE'VE FINALLY GOTTEN PERMISSION FROM MARIJOA TO ENTER THE GRAND LINE.
AS SUCH, I WOULD AGAIN LIKE TO APPOINT YOU AS ADMIRAL OF AN EXPLORATION SHIP.
IT'D BE MY HONOR, YOUR MAJESTY...

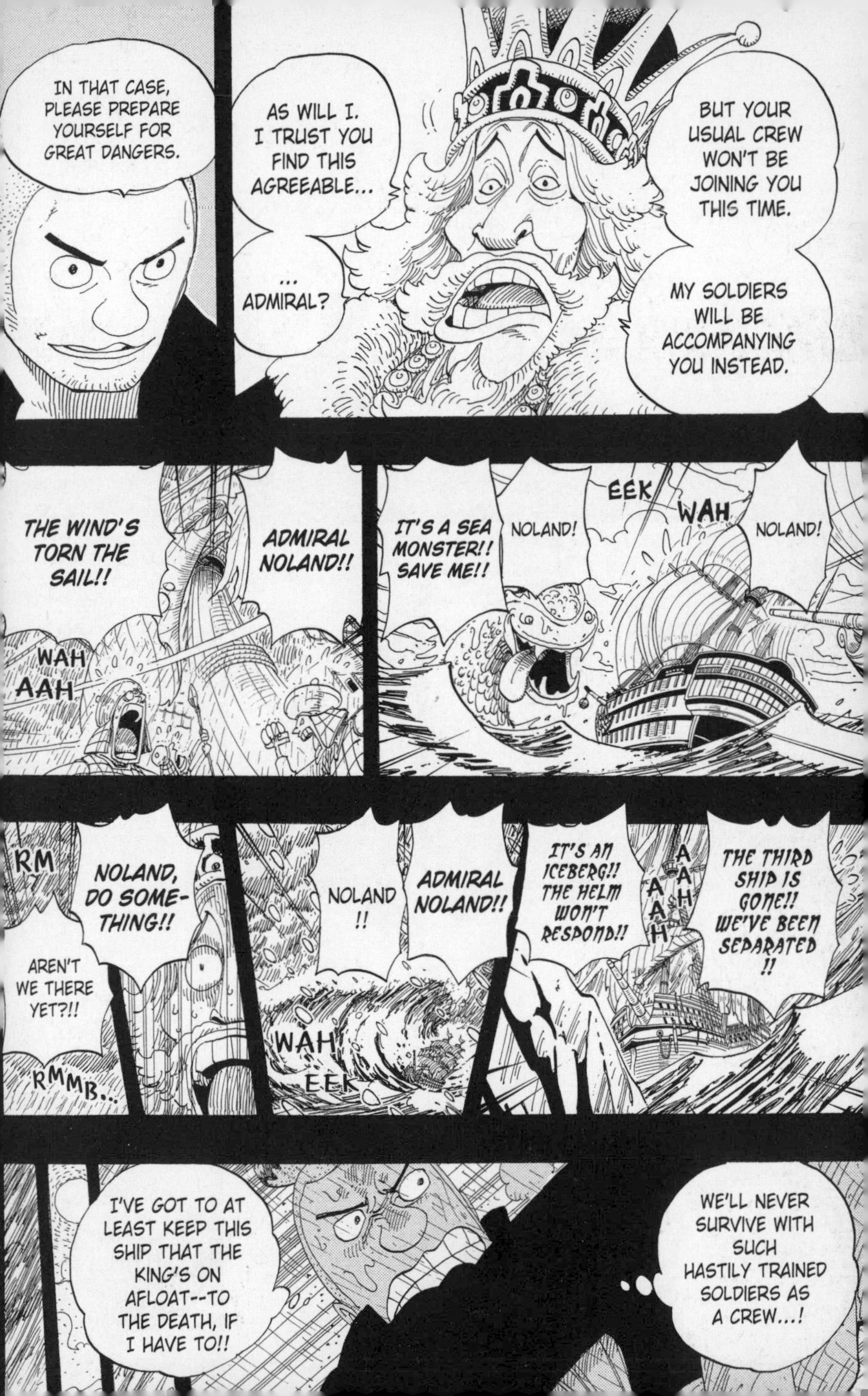
BUT YOUR USUAL CREW WON'T BE JOINING YOU THIS TIME.
MY SOLDIERS WILL BE ACCOMPANYING YOU INSTEAD.
AS WILL I. I TRUST YOU FIND THIS AGREEABLE...
... ADMIRAL?
IN THAT CASE, PLEASE PREPARE YOURSELF FOR GREAT DANGERS.
NOLAND!
WAH
EEK
NOLAND!
IT'S A SEA MONSTER!! SAVE ME!!
ADMIRAL NOLAND!!
THE WIND'S TORN THE SAIL!!
WAH
AAH
THE THIRD SHIP IS GONE!! WE'VE BEEN SEPARATED!!
AAH
AAAH
IT'S AN ICEBERG!! THE HELM WON'T RESPOND!!
ADMIRAL NOLAND!!
NOLAND!!
WAH
EEK
NOLAND, DO SOME-THING!!
RM
AREN'T WE THERE YET?!!
RMMB...
WE'LL NEVER SURVIVE WITH SUCH HASTILY TRAINED SOLDIERS AS A CREW...!
I'VE GOT TO AT LEAST KEEP THIS SHIP THAT THE KING'S ON AFLOAT--TO THE DEATH, IF I HAVE TO!!

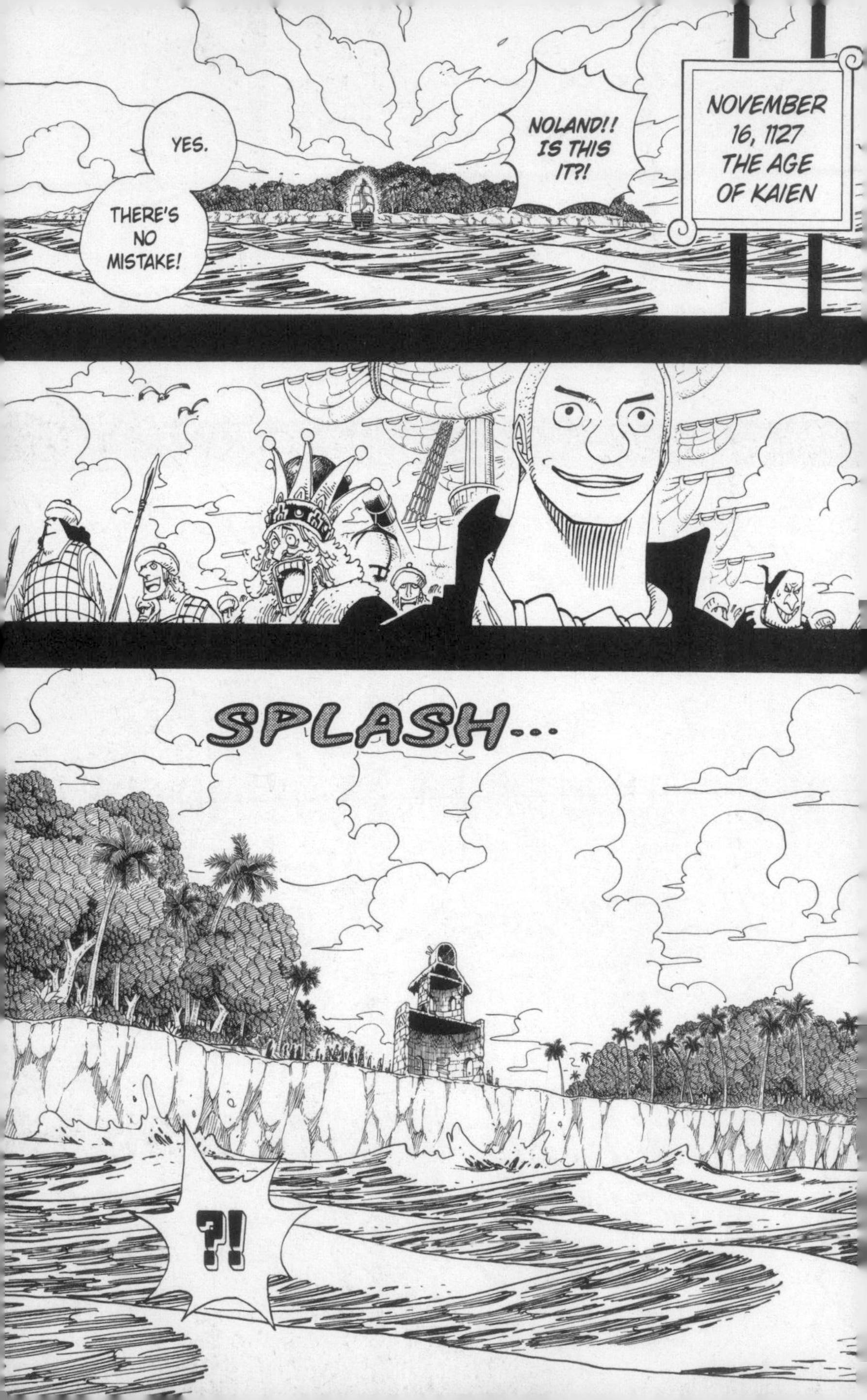
NOVEMBER 16, 1127 THE AGE OF KAIEN
NOLAND!! IS THIS IT?!
YES.
THERE'S NO MISTAKE!
SPLASH...
?!

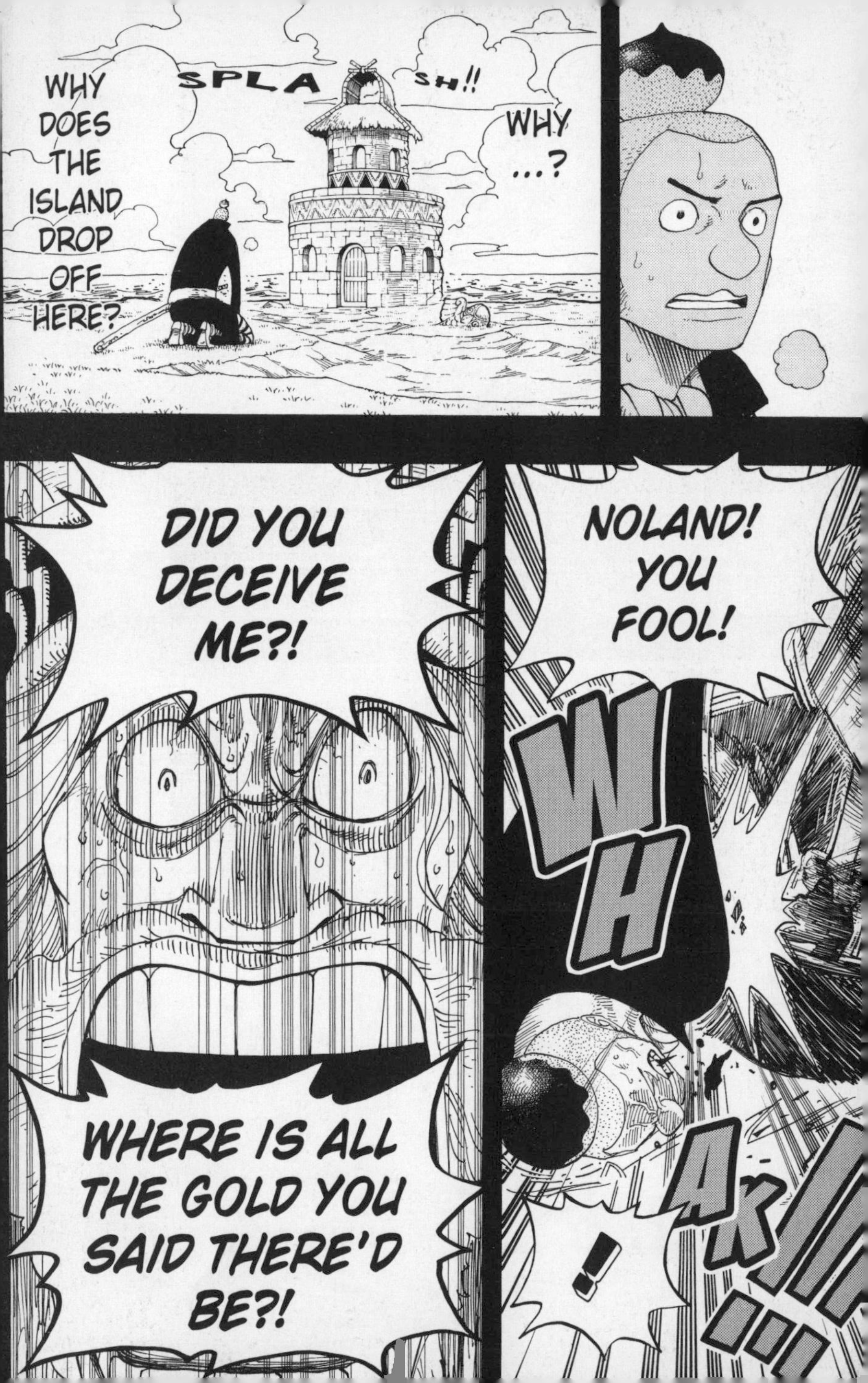
SPLASH!!
WHY ...?
WHY DOES THE ISLAND DROP OFF HERE?
NOLAND! YOU FOOL!
WHACK!!!
DID YOU DECEIVE ME?!
WHERE IS ALL THE GOLD YOU SAID THERE'D BE?!

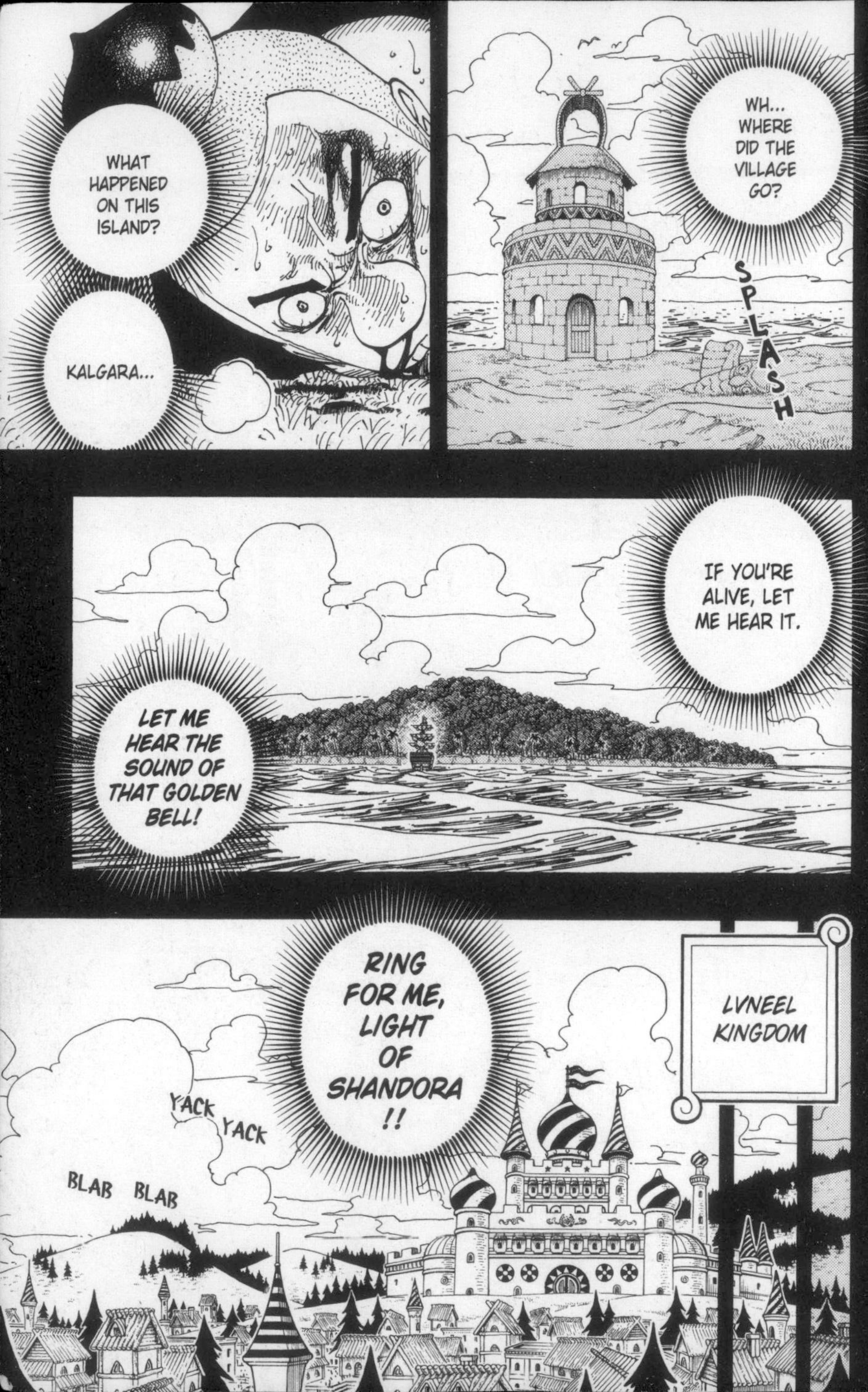
WH... WHERE DID THE VILLAGE GO?
SPLASH
WHAT HAPPENED ON THIS ISLAND?
KALGARA...
IF YOU'RE ALIVE, LET ME HEAR IT.
LET ME HEAR THE SOUND OF THAT GOLDEN BELL!
LVNEEL KINGDOM
RING FOR ME, LIGHT OF SHANDORA !!
YACK YACK
BLAB BLAB

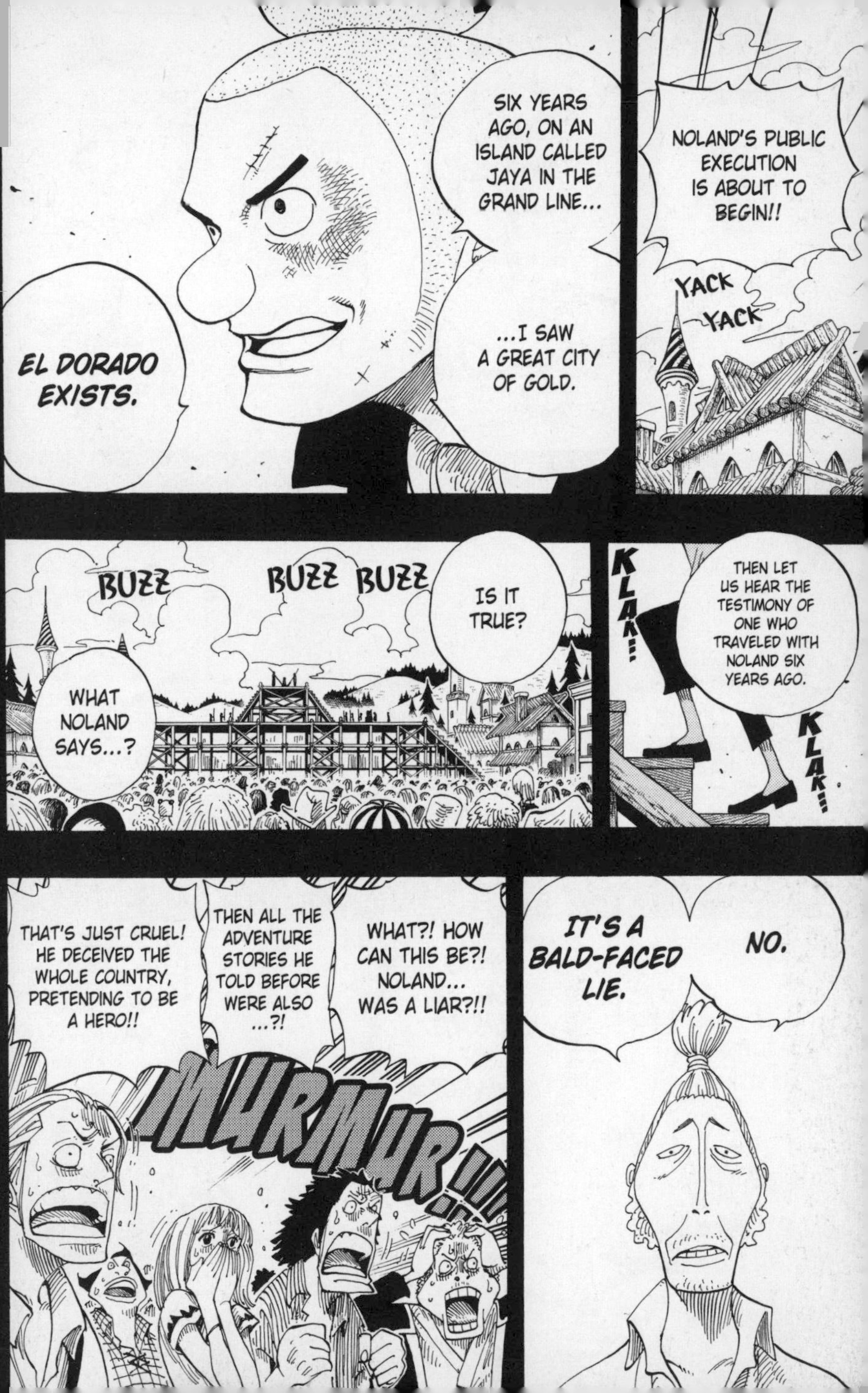
NOLAND'S PUBLIC EXECUTION IS ABOUT TO BEGIN!!
YACK YACK
SIX YEARS AGO, ON AN ISLAND CALLED JAYA IN THE GRAND LINE...
...I SAW A GREAT CITY OF GOLD.
EL DORADO EXISTS.
KLAK!!
THEN LET US HEAR THE TESTIMONY OF ONE WHO TRAVELED WITH NOLAND SIX YEARS AGO.
KLAK!!
IS IT TRUE?
BUZZ BUZZ
BUZZ
WHAT NOLAND SAYS...?
NO.
IT'S A BALD-FACED LIE.
WHAT?! HOW CAN THIS BE?! NOLAND... WAS A LIAR?!!
THEN ALL THE ADVENTURE STORIES HE TOLD BEFORE WERE ALSO ...?!
THAT'S JUST CRUEL! HE DECEIVED THE WHOLE COUNTRY, PRETENDING TO BE A HERO!!
MURMUR!!!

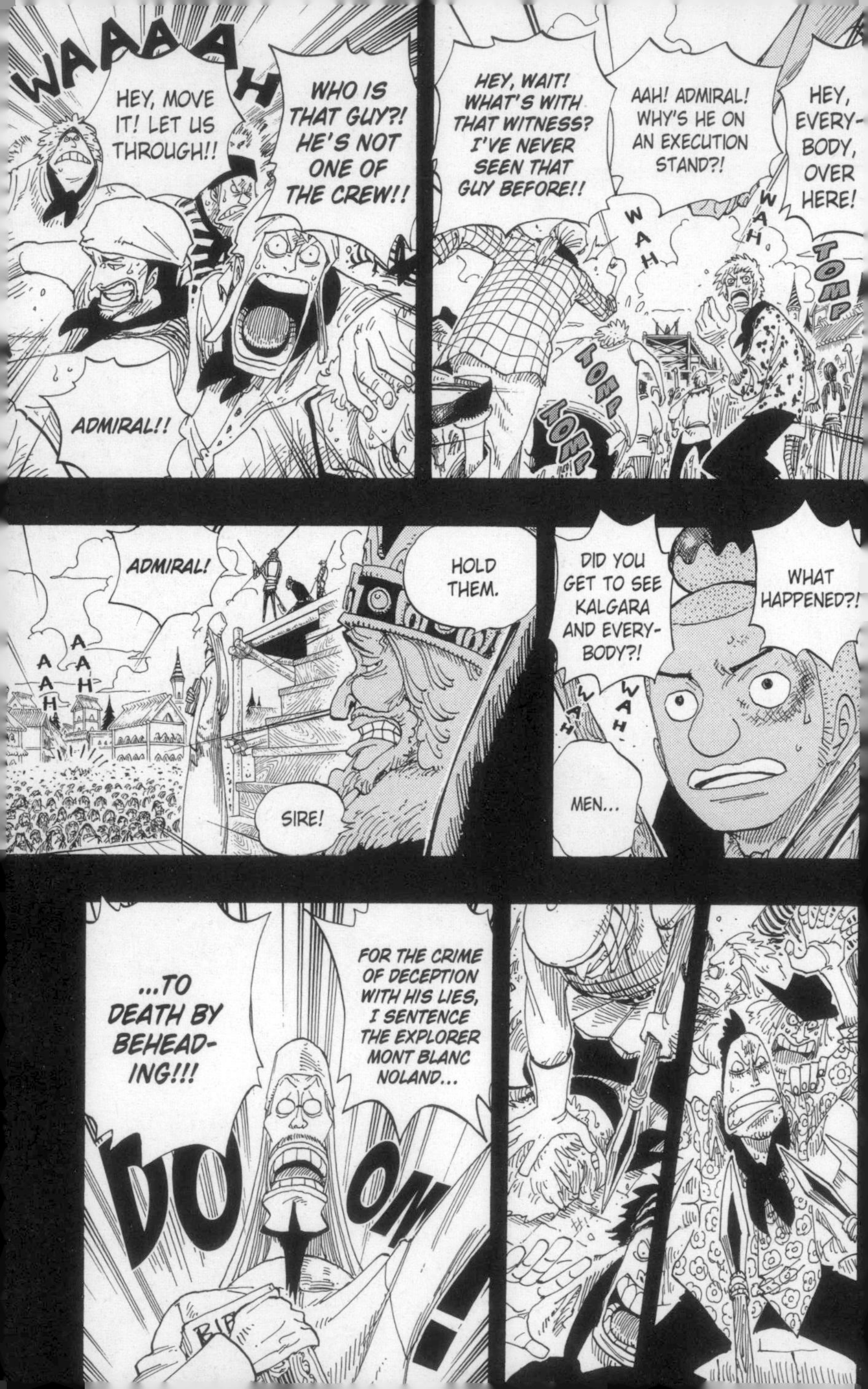
HEY, EVERY-BODY, OVER HERE!
AAH! ADMIRAL! WHY'S HE ON AN EXECUTION STAND?!
HEY, WAIT! WHAT'S WITH THAT WITNESS? I'VE NEVER SEEN THAT GUY BEFORE!!
WAH
WAH
TOMP
WHO IS THAT GUY?! HE'S NOT ONE OF THE CREW!!
HEY, MOVE IT! LET US THROUGH!!
WAAAAH
ADMIRAL!!
WHAT HAPPENED?!
DID YOU GET TO SEE KALGARA AND EVERY-BODY?!
WAH
WAH
MEN...
HOLD THEM.
ADMIRAL!
AAH
AAH
SIRE!
FOR THE CRIME OF DECEPTION WITH HIS LIES, I SENTENCE THE EXPLORER MONT BLANC NOLAND...
...TO DEATH BY BEHEAD-ING!!!
DOOM!

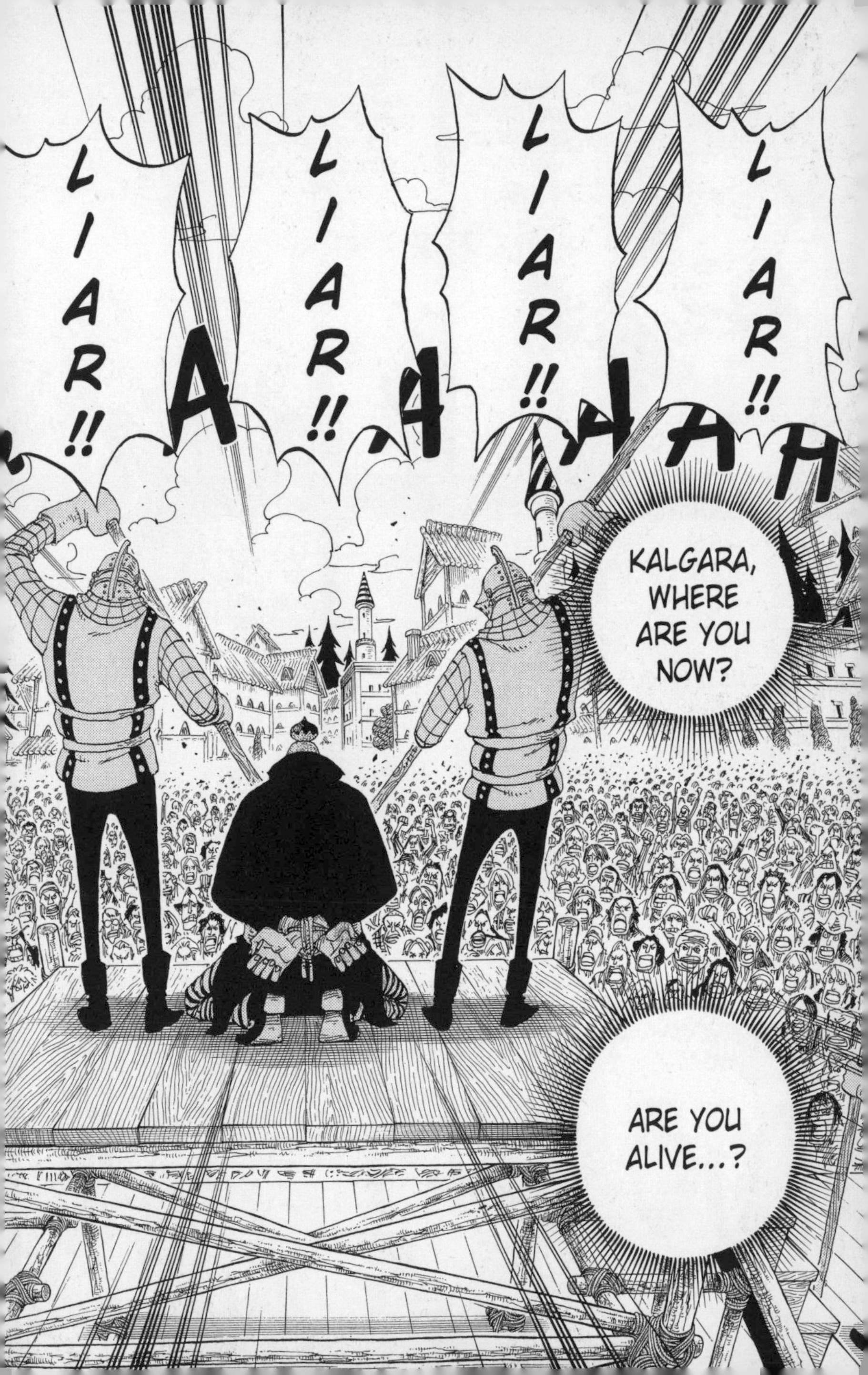
LIAR!!
LIAR!!
LIAR!!
LIAR!!
KALGARA, WHERE ARE YOU NOW?
ARE YOU ALIVE...?

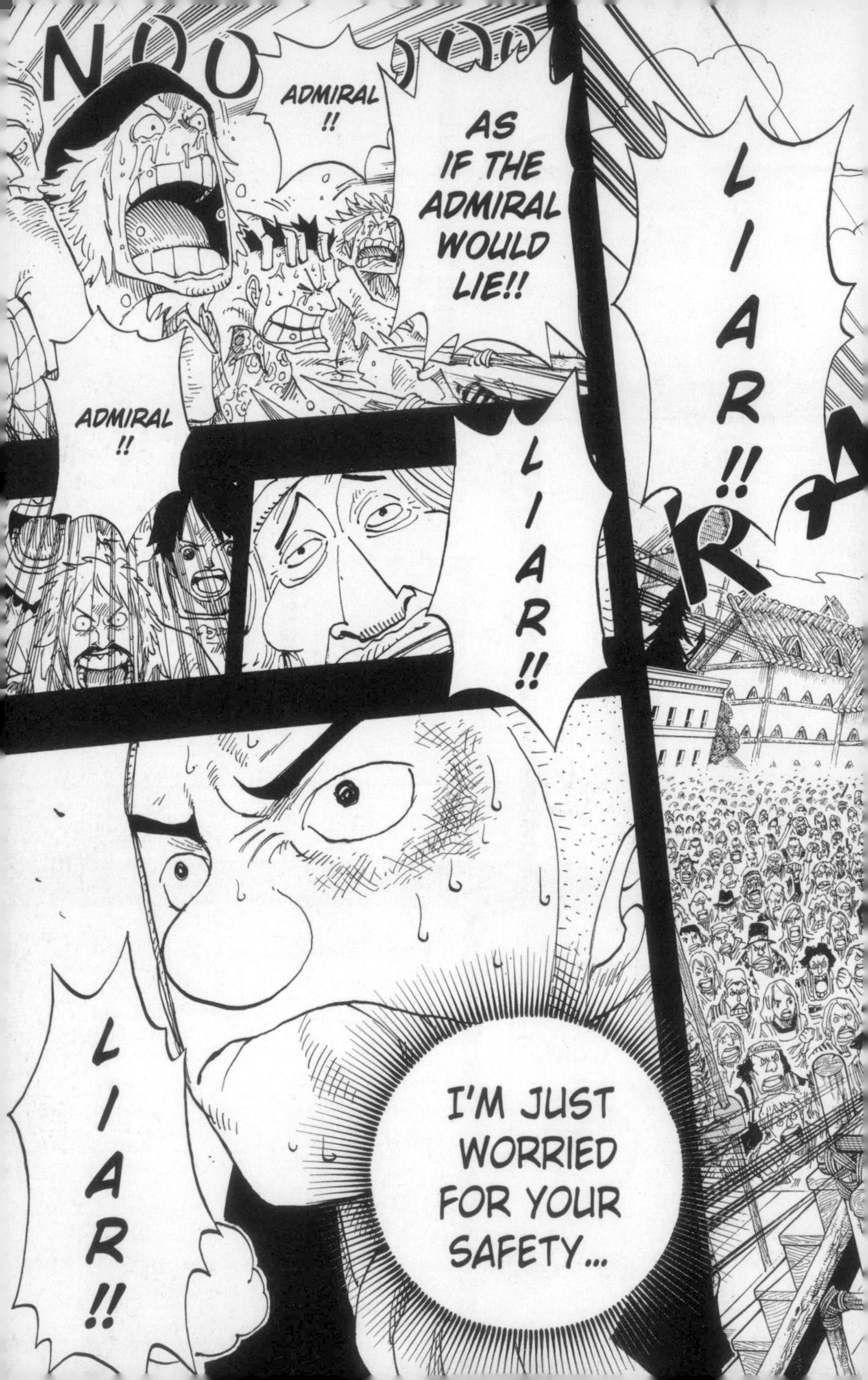
LIAR!!
NOOOOO
AS IF THE ADMIRAL WOULD LIE!!
ADMIRAL!!
ADMIRAL!!
LIAR!!
I'M JUST WORRIED FOR YOUR SAFETY...
LIAR!!

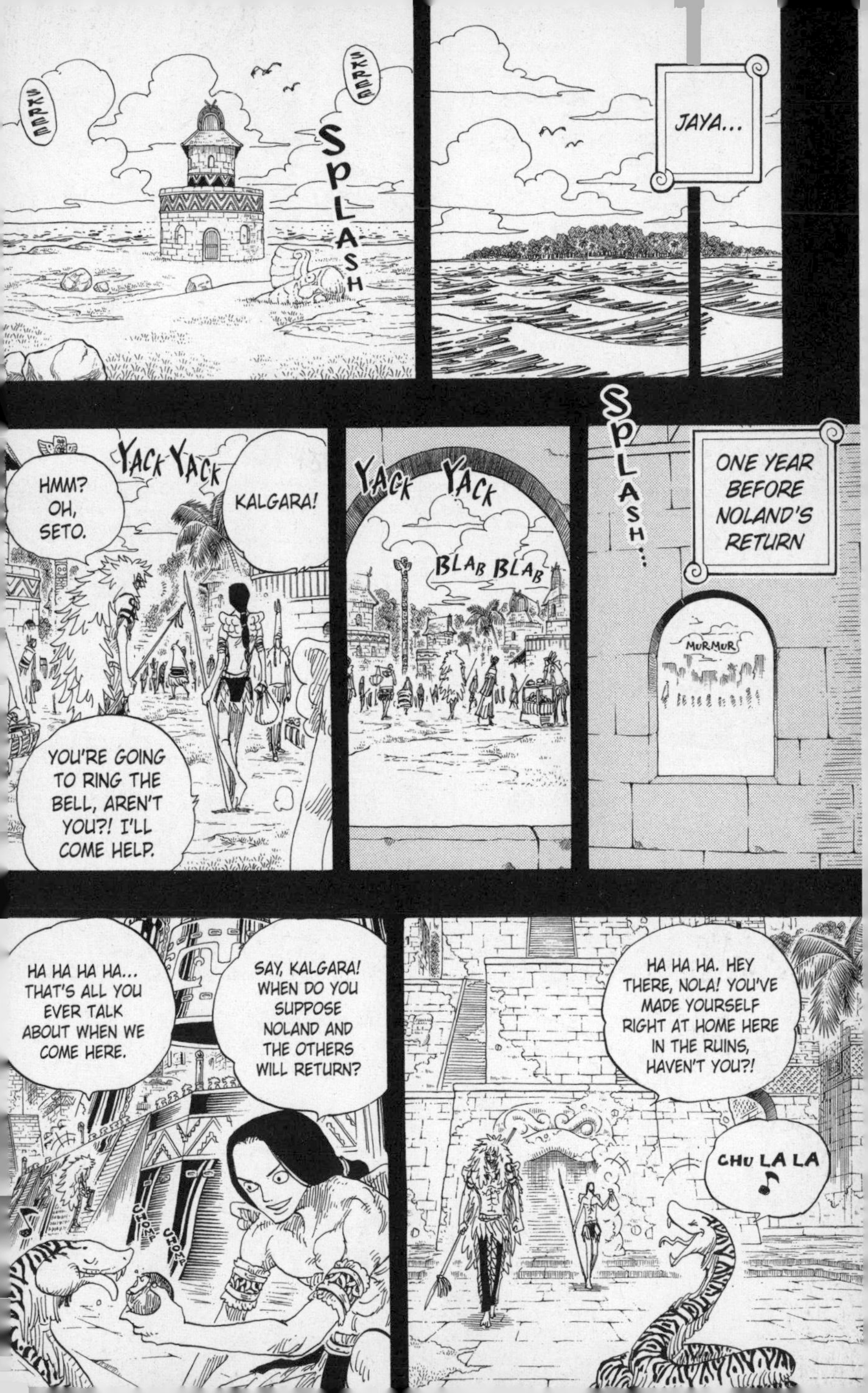
JAYA...
SKREE
SPLASH
SKREE
ONE YEAR BEFORE NOLAND'S RETURN
SPLASH...
MURMUR
YACK YACK
BLAB BLAB
KALGARA!
YACK YACK
HMM? OH, SETO.
YOU'RE GOING TO RING THE BELL, AREN'T YOU?! I'LL COME HELP.
HA HA HA. HEY THERE, NOLA! YOU'VE MADE YOURSELF RIGHT AT HOME HERE IN THE RUINS, HAVEN'T YOU?!
CHU LA LA
SAY, KALGARA! WHEN DO YOU SUPPOSE NOLAND AND THE OTHERS WILL RETURN?
HA HA HA HA... THAT'S ALL YOU EVER TALK ABOUT WHEN WE COME HERE.
CHOMP
CHOMP

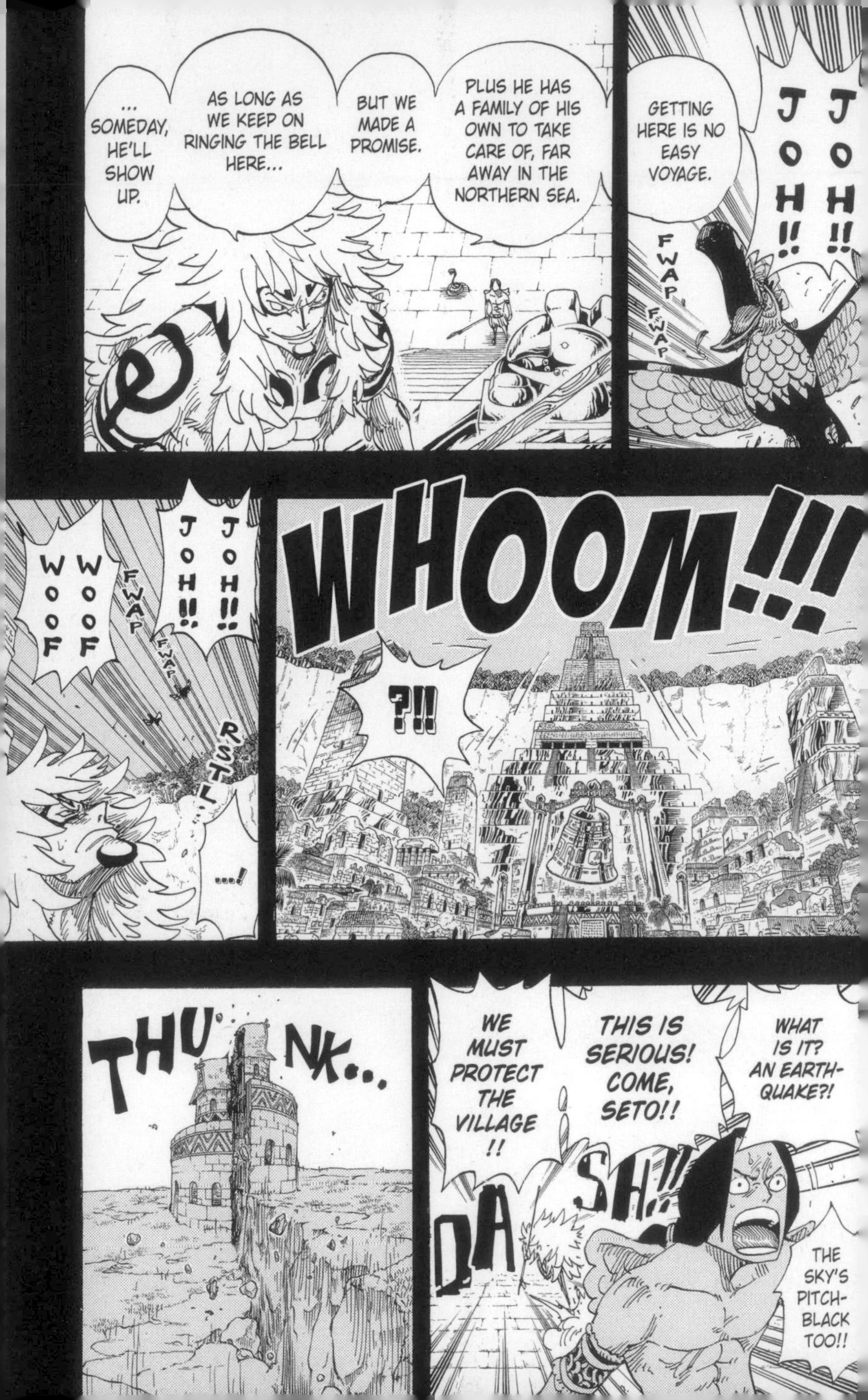
GETTING HERE IS NO EASY VOYAGE.
JOH!!
JOH!!
FWAP
FWAP
PLUS HE HAS A FAMILY OF HIS OWN TO TAKE CARE OF, FAR AWAY IN THE NORTHERN SEA.
BUT WE MADE A PROMISE.
AS LONG AS WE KEEP ON RINGING THE BELL HERE...
... SOMEDAY, HE'LL SHOW UP.
WHOOM!!!
?!!
JOH!!
JOH!!
FWAP
FWAP
WOOF
WOOF
RSTL
...!
WHAT IS IT? AN EARTH-QUAKE?!
THE SKY'S PITCH-BLACK TOO!!
THIS IS SERIOUS! COME, SETO!!
WE MUST PROTECT THE VILLAGE!!
DASH!!
THUNK...

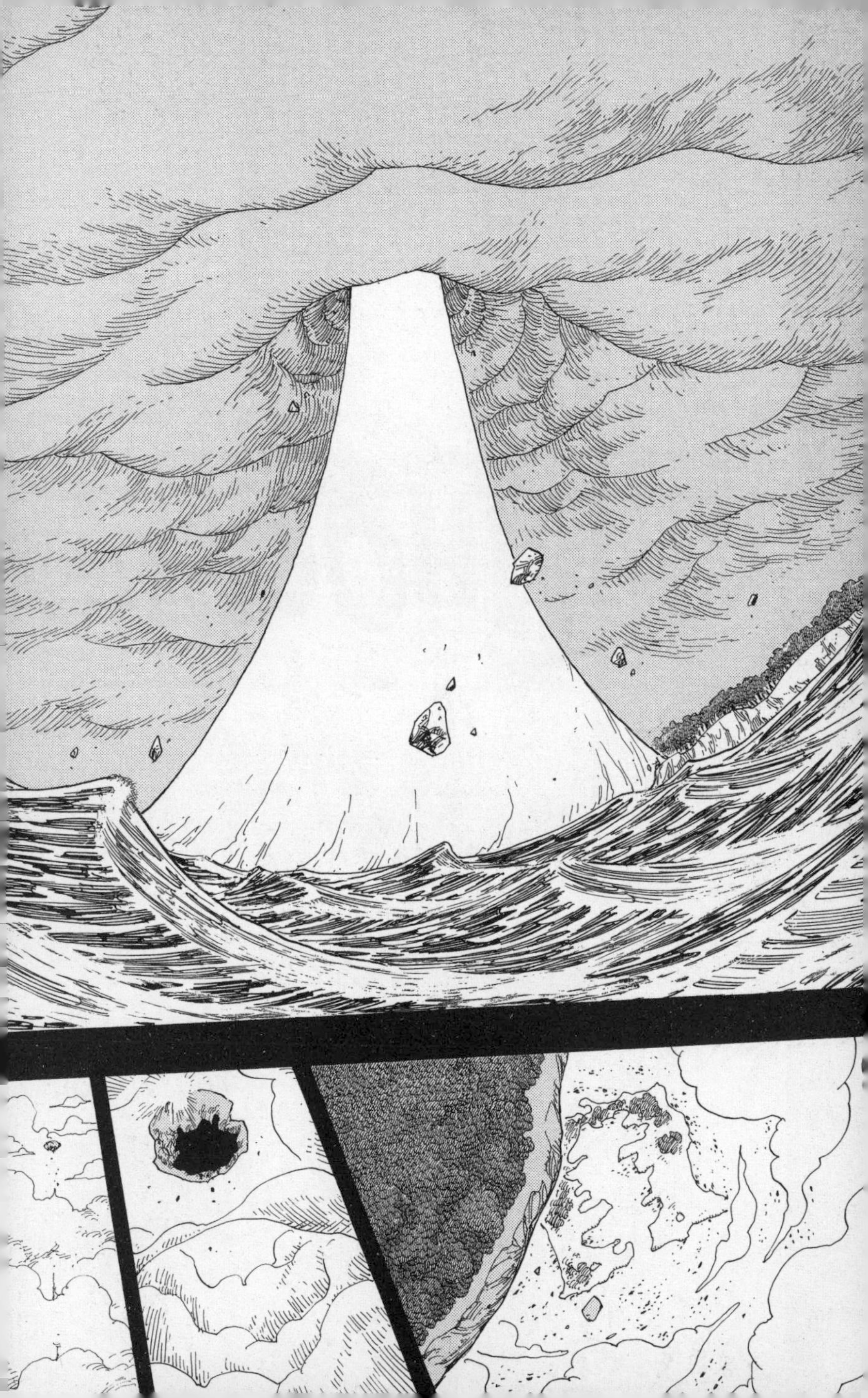

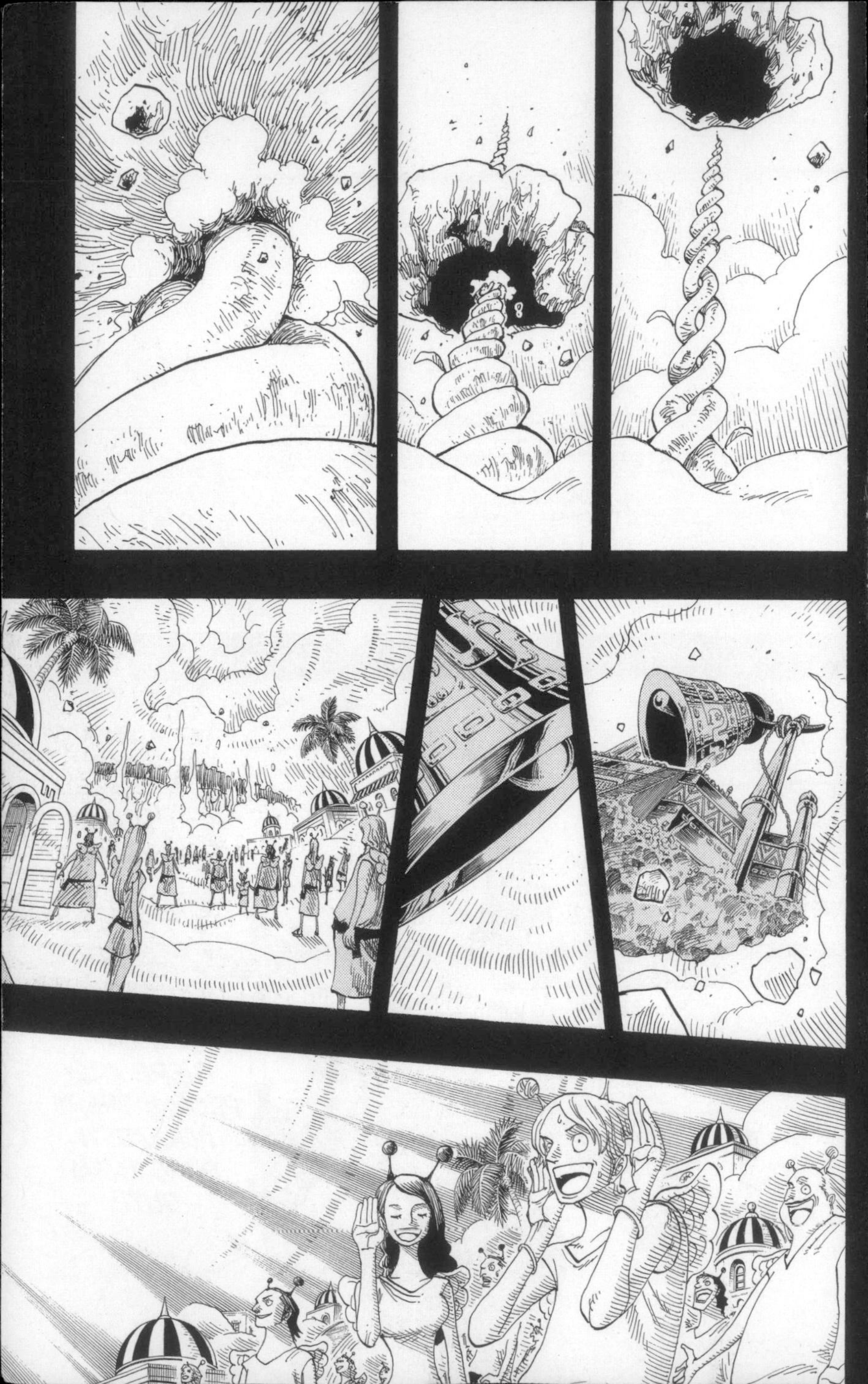

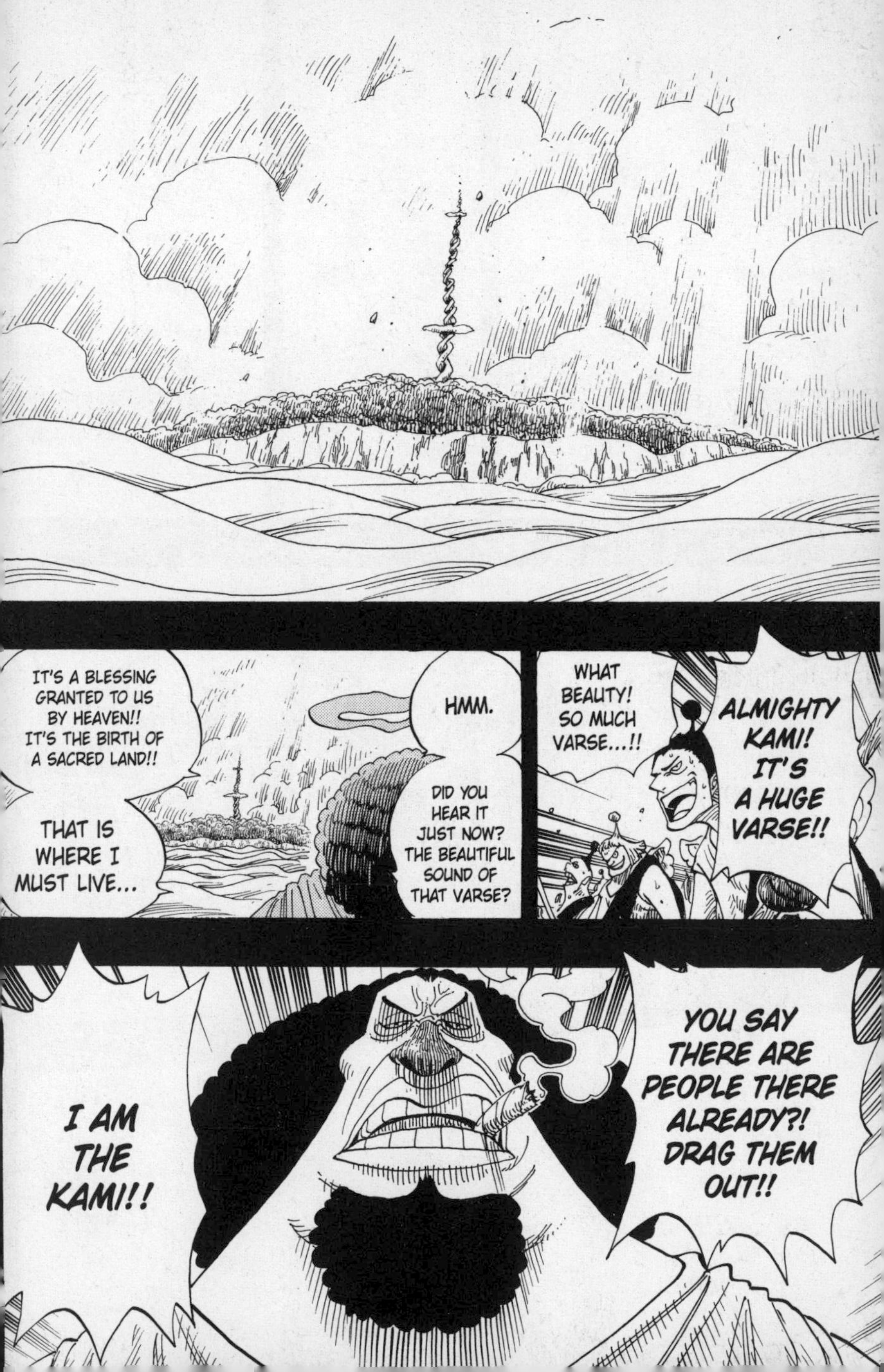

ALMIGHTY KAMI! IT'S A HUGE VARSE!!
WHAT BEAUTY! SO MUCH VARSE...!!
HMM.
DID YOU HEAR IT JUST NOW? THE BEAUTIFUL SOUND OF THAT VARSE?
IT'S A BLESSING GRANTED TO US BY HEAVEN!! IT'S THE BIRTH OF A SACRED LAND!!
THAT IS WHERE I MUST LIVE...
YOU SAY THERE ARE PEOPLE THERE ALREADY?! DRAG THEM OUT!!
I AM THE KAMI!!

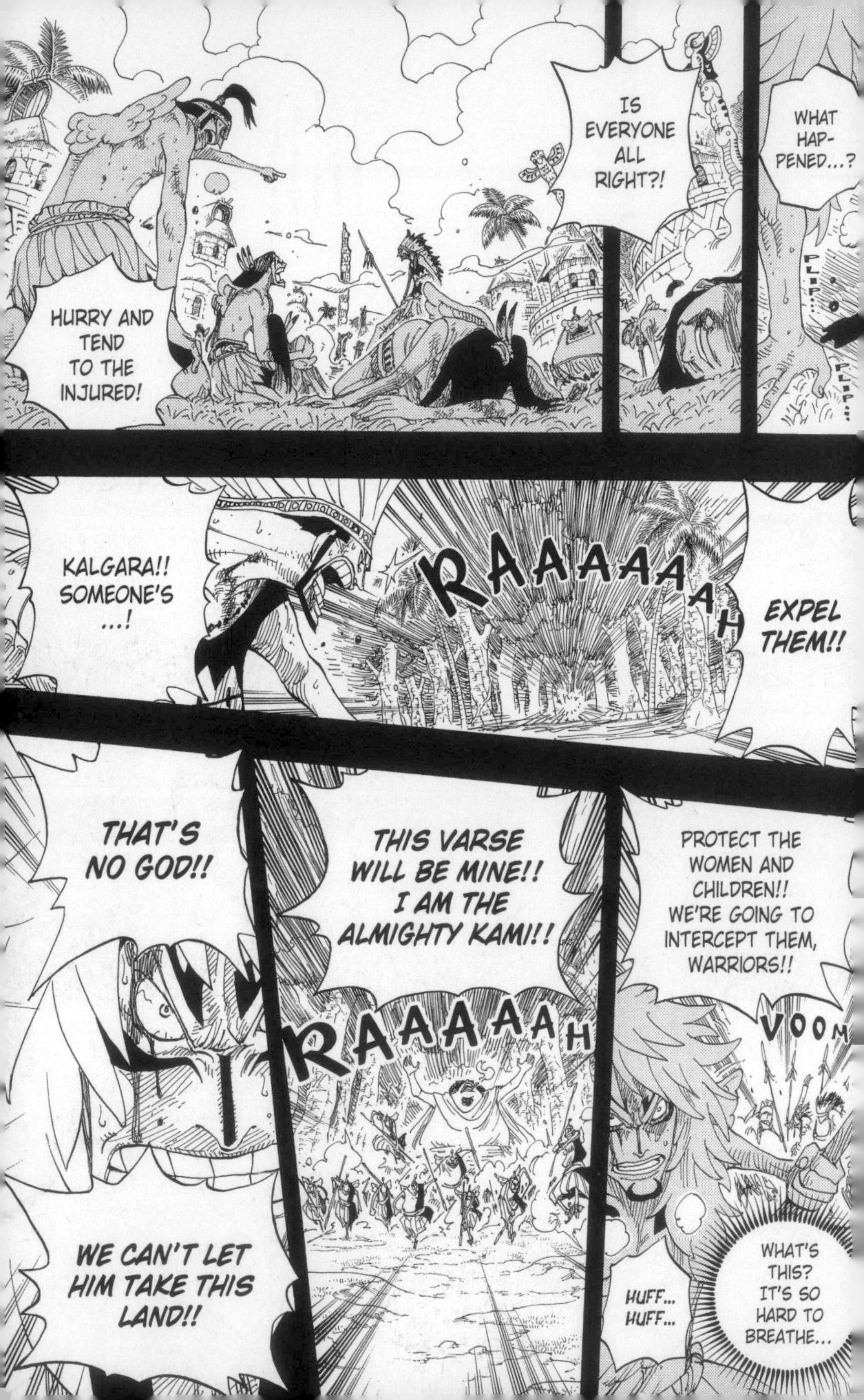
WHAT HAP-PENED...?
PLIP... PLIP...
IS EVERYONE ALL RIGHT?!
HURRY AND TEND TO THE INJURED!
EXPEL THEM!!
RAAAAAAAH
KALGARA!! SOMEONE'S ...!
PROTECT THE WOMEN AND CHILDREN!! WE'RE GOING TO INTERCEPT THEM, WARRIORS!!
VOOM
WHAT'S THIS? IT'S SO HARD TO BREATHE...
HUFF... HUFF...
THIS VARSE WILL BE MINE!! I AM THE ALMIGHTY KAMI!!
RAAAAAAH
THAT'S NO GOD!!
WE CAN'T LET HIM TAKE THIS LAND!!

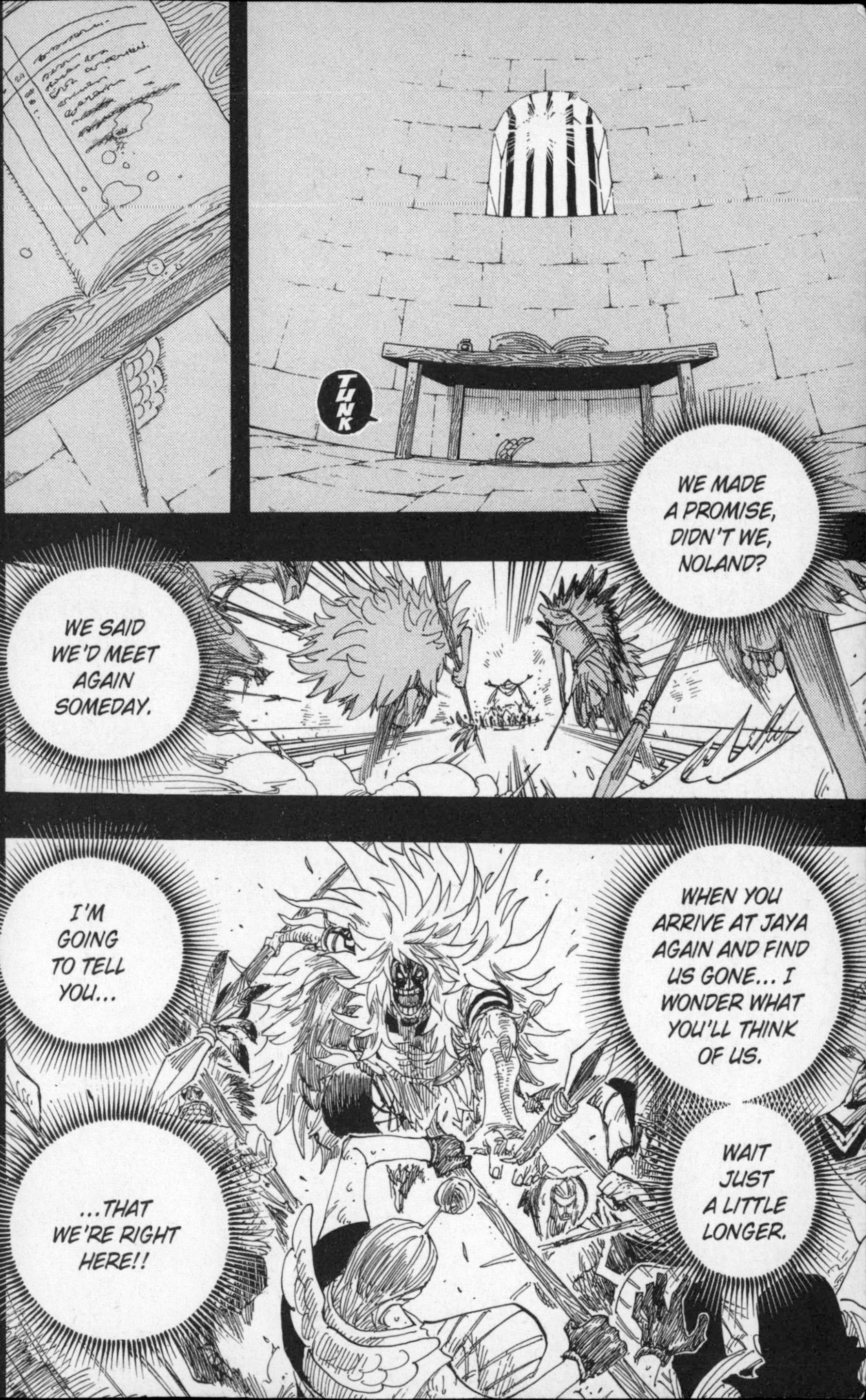
TUNK
WE MADE A PROMISE, DIDN'T WE, NOLAND?
WE SAID WE'D MEET AGAIN SOMEDAY.
WHEN YOU ARRIVE AT JAYA AGAIN AND FIND US GONE... I WONDER WHAT YOU'LL THINK OF US.
I'M GOING TO TELL YOU...
WAIT JUST A LITTLE LONGER.
...THAT WE'RE RIGHT HERE!!

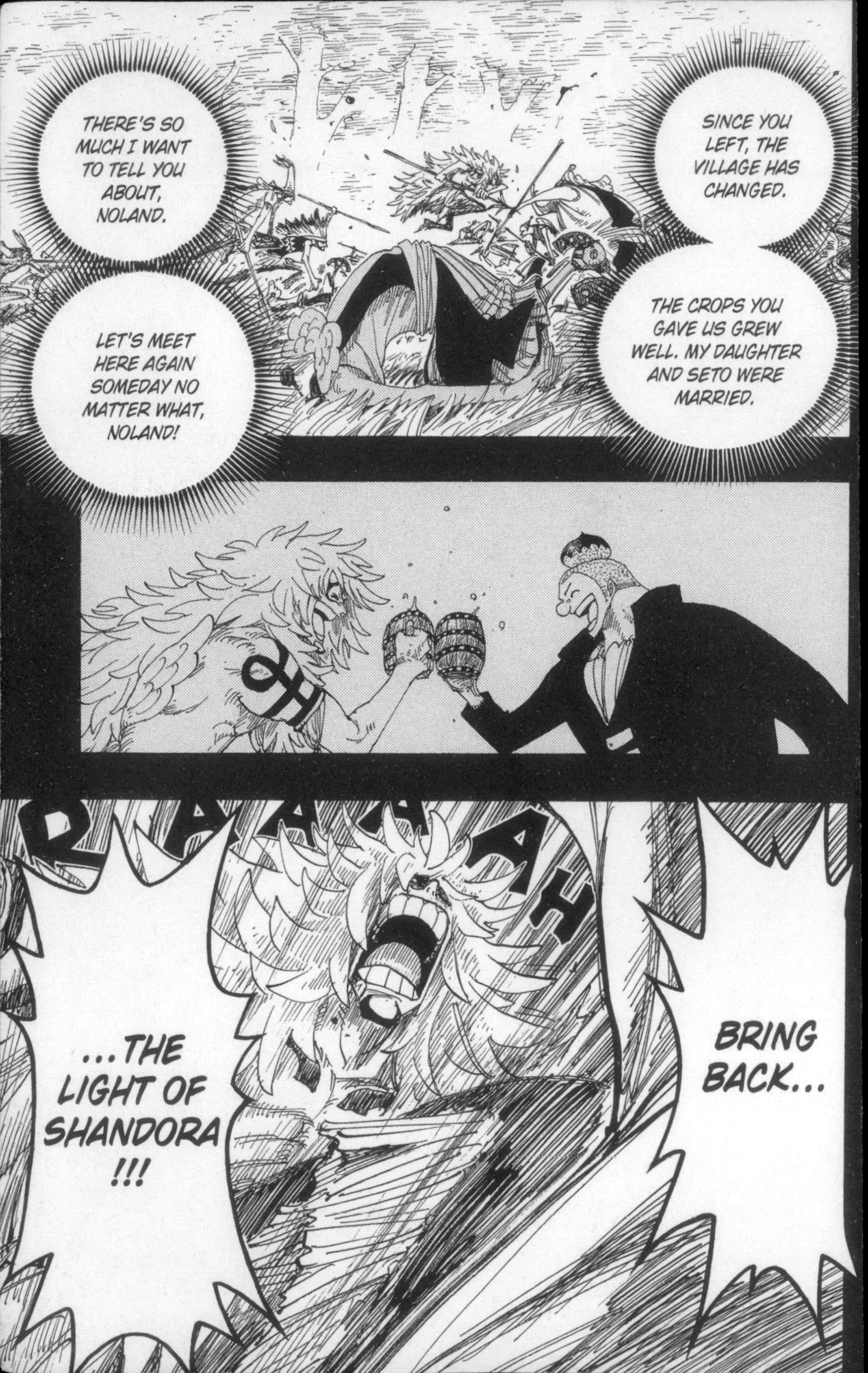
SINCE YOU LEFT, THE VILLAGE HAS CHANGED.
THE CROPS YOU GAVE US GREW WELL. MY DAUGHTER AND SETO WERE MARRIED.
THERE'S SO MUCH I WANT TO TELL YOU ABOUT, NOLAND.
LET'S MEET HERE AGAIN SOMEDAY NO MATTER WHAT, NOLAND!
RAAAAH
BRING BACK...
...THE LIGHT OF SHANDORA !!!

Chapter 293: BOLERO

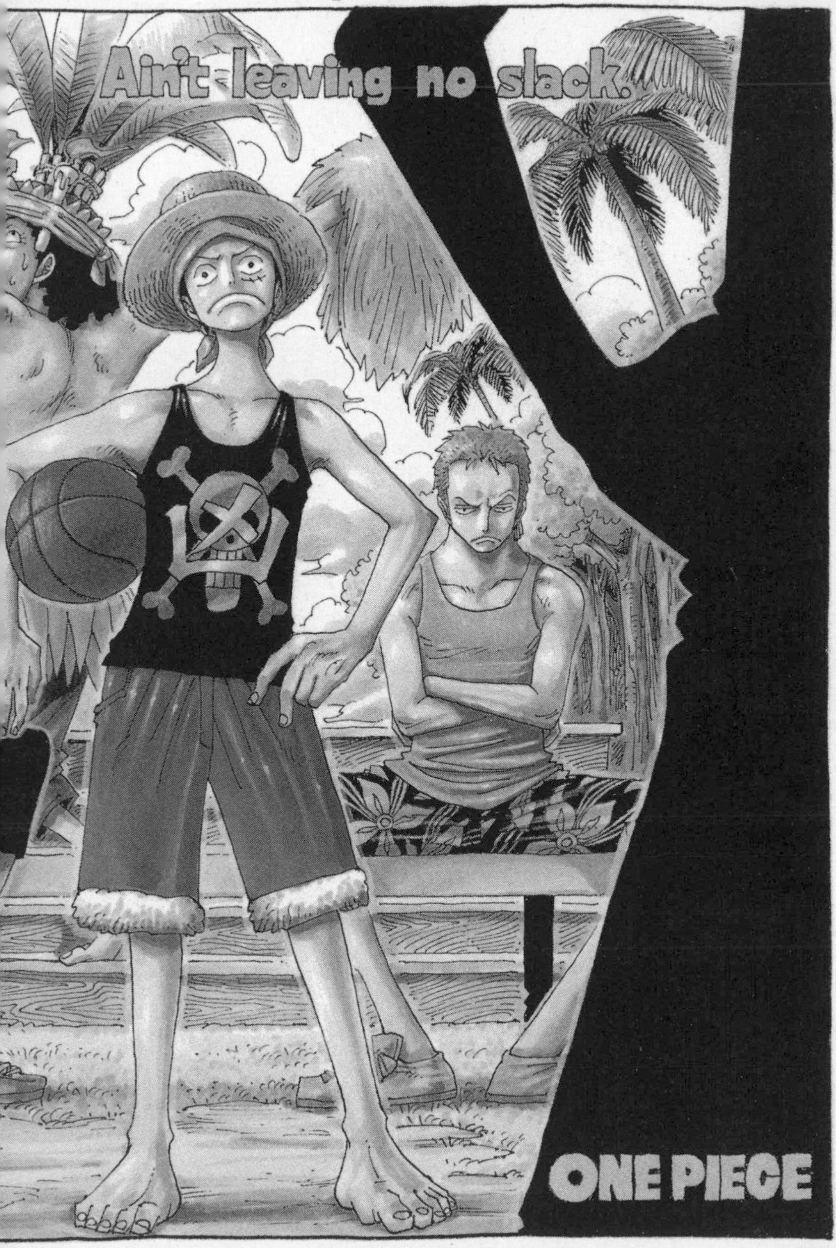
Ain't leaving no slack.
ONE PIECE

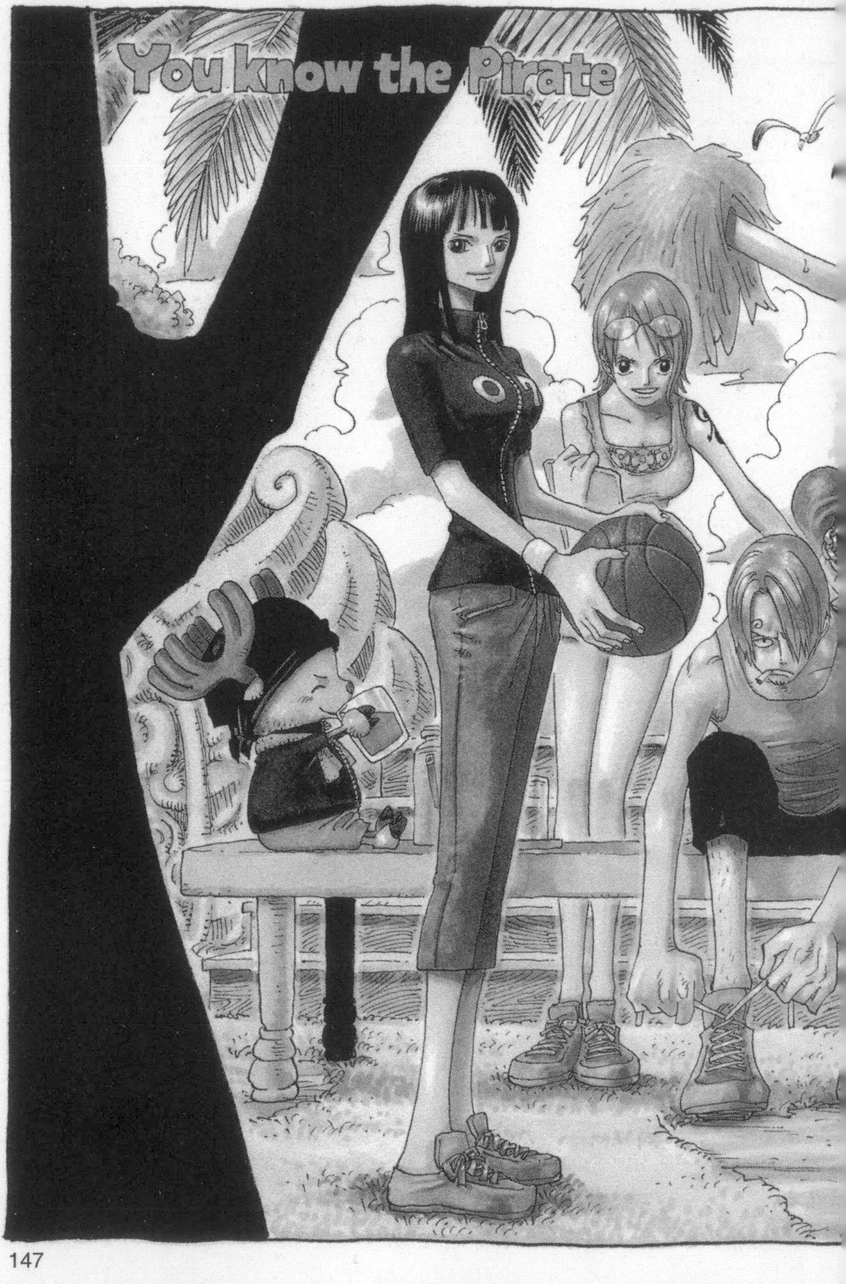
You know the Pirate

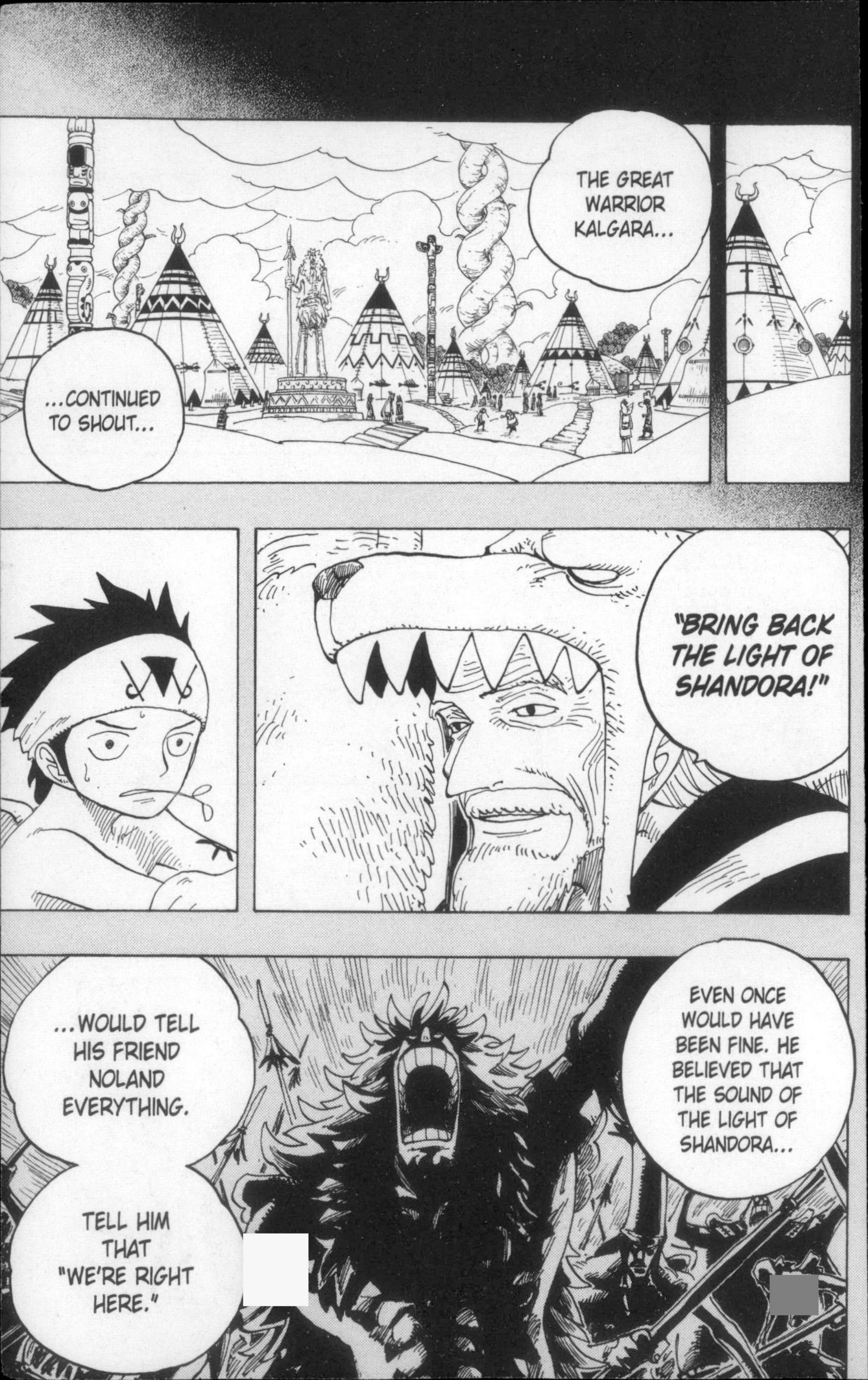
THE GREAT WARRIOR KALGARA...
...CONTINUED TO SHOUT...
"BRING BACK THE LIGHT OF SHANDORA!"
EVEN ONCE WOULD HAVE BEEN FINE. HE BELIEVED THAT THE SOUND OF THE LIGHT OF SHANDORA...
...WOULD TELL HIS FRIEND NOLAND EVERYTHING.
TELL HIM THAT "WE'RE RIGHT HERE."

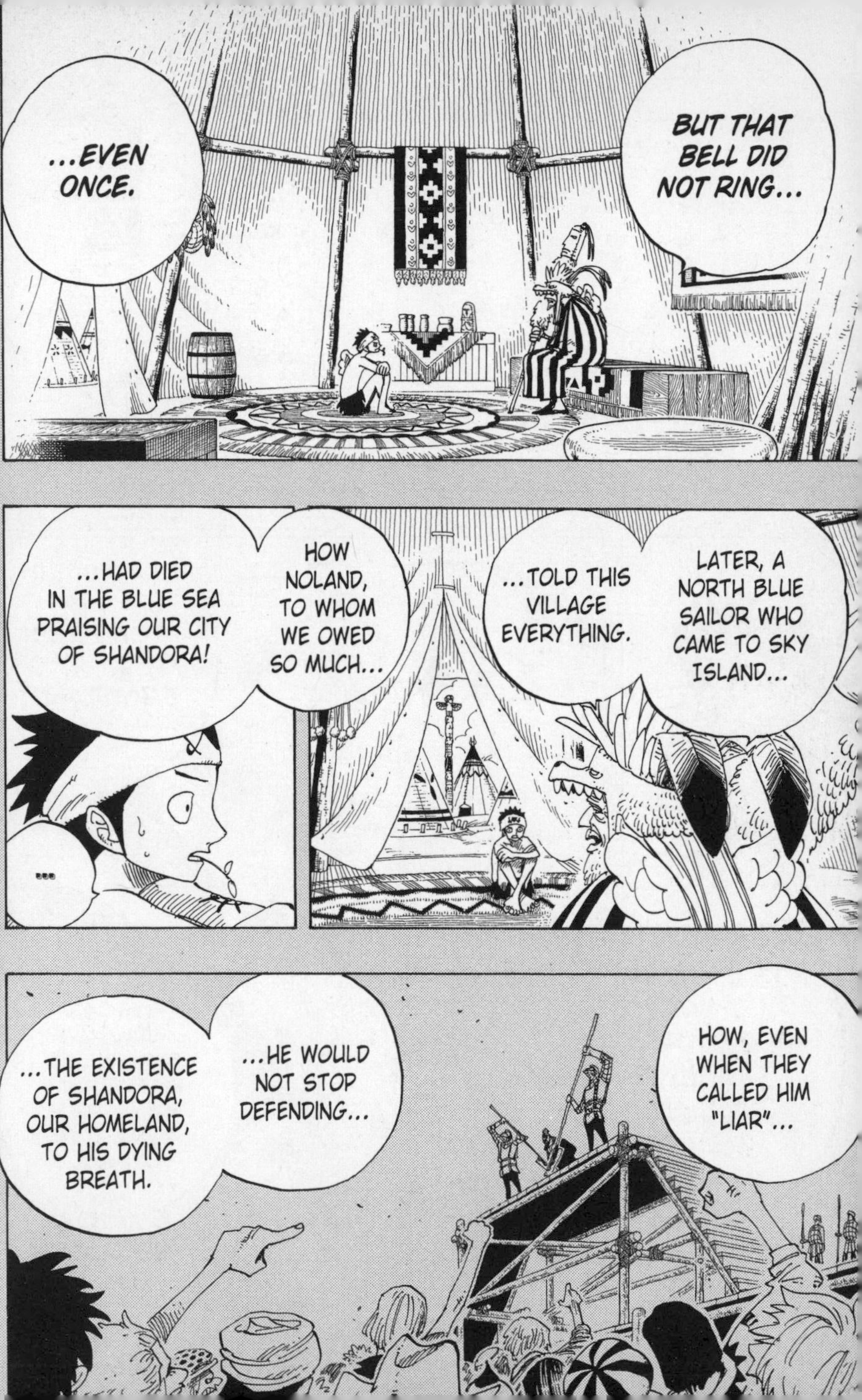
BUT THAT BELL DID NOT RING...
...EVEN ONCE.
LATER, A NORTH BLUE SAILOR WHO CAME TO SKY ISLAND...
...TOLD THIS VILLAGE EVERYTHING.
HOW NOLAND, TO WHOM WE OWED SO MUCH...
...HAD DIED IN THE BLUE SEA PRAISING OUR CITY OF SHANDORA!
...
HOW, EVEN WHEN THEY CALLED HIM "LIAR"...
...HE WOULD NOT STOP DEFENDING...
...THE EXISTENCE OF SHANDORA, OUR HOMELAND, TO HIS DYING BREATH.

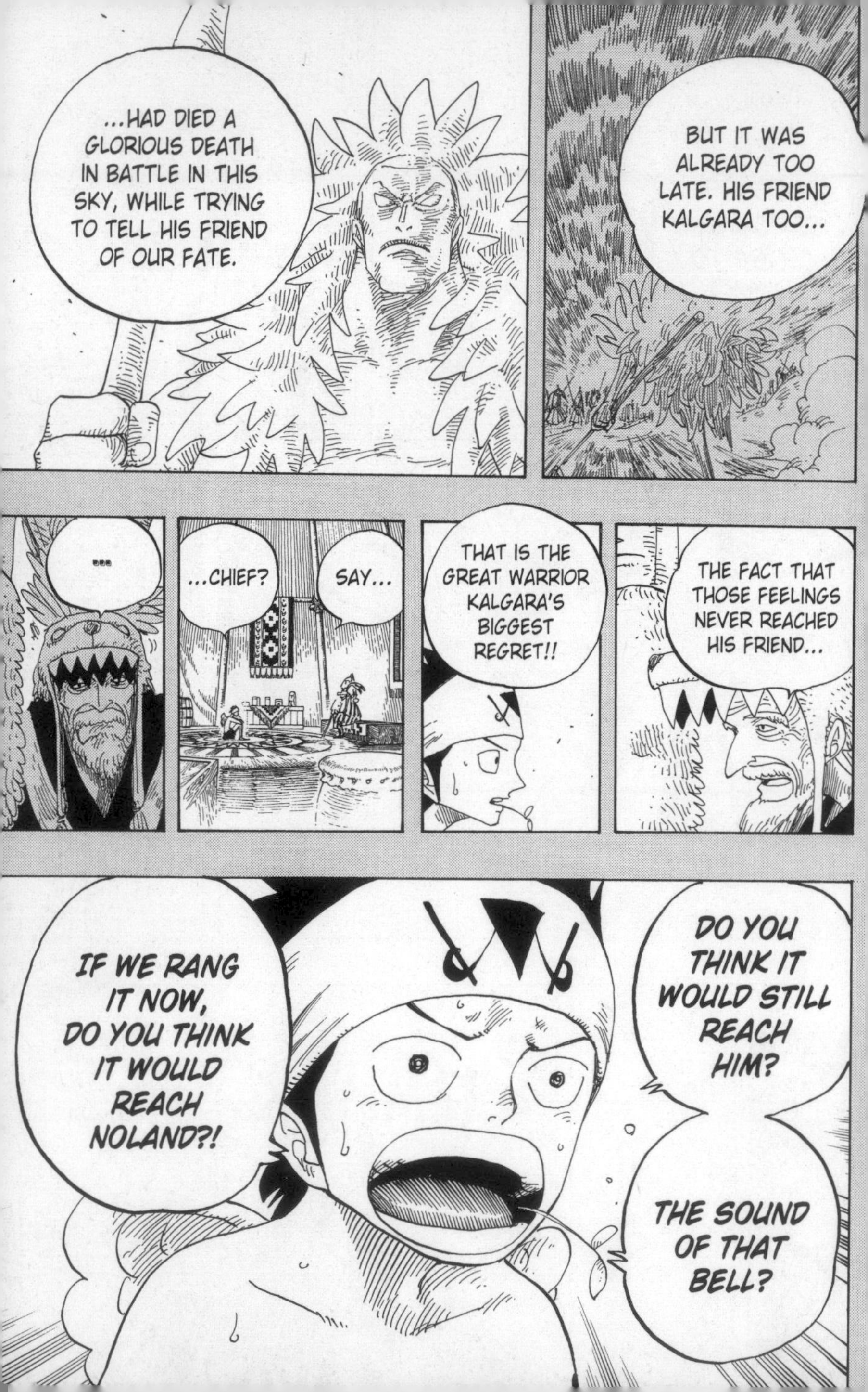
BUT IT WAS ALREADY TOO LATE. HIS FRIEND KALGARA TOO...
...HAD DIED A GLORIOUS DEATH IN BATTLE IN THIS SKY, WHILE TRYING TO TELL HIS FRIEND OF OUR FATE.
THE FACT THAT THOSE FEELINGS NEVER REACHED HIS FRIEND...
THAT IS THE GREAT WARRIOR KALGARA'S BIGGEST REGRET!!
SAY...
...CHIEF?
...
DO YOU THINK IT WOULD STILL REACH HIM?
THE SOUND OF THAT BELL?
IF WE RANG IT NOW, DO YOU THINK IT WOULD REACH NOLAND?!

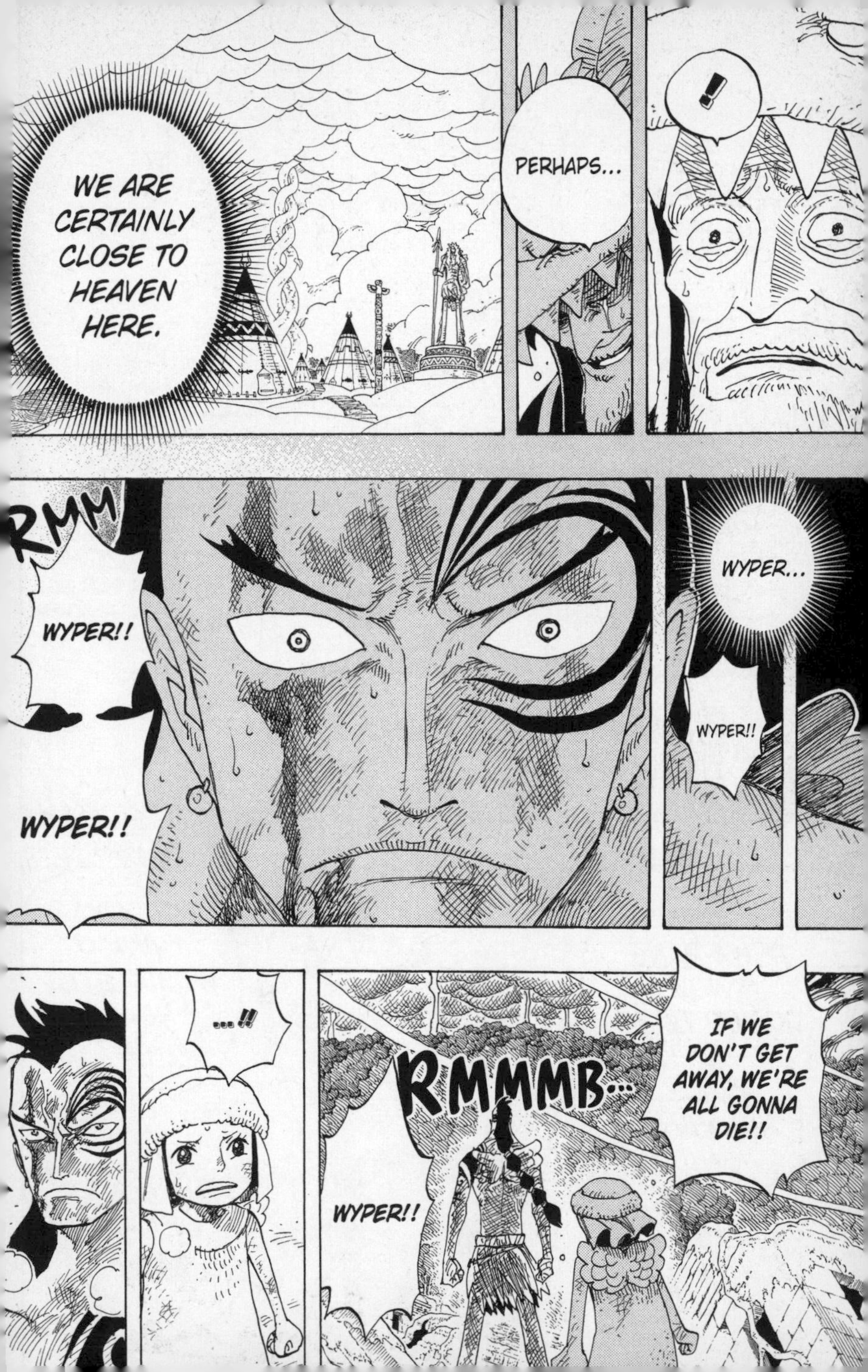
!
PERHAPS...
WE ARE CERTAINLY CLOSE TO HEAVEN HERE.
WYPER...
WYPER!!
RMM
WYPER!!
WYPER!!
IF WE DON'T GET AWAY, WE'RE ALL GONNA DIE!!
RMMMB...
WYPER!!
...!!

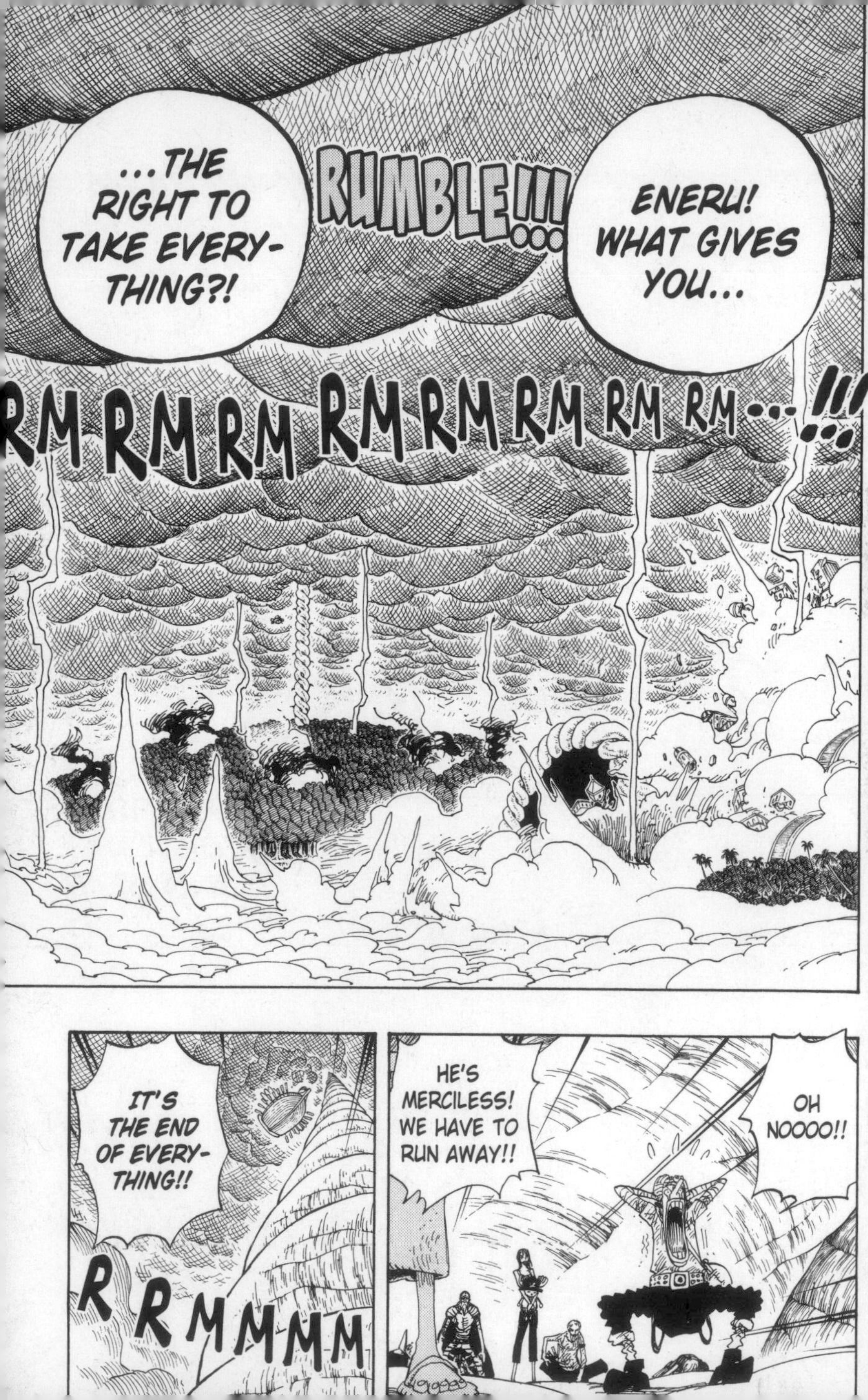
ENERU! WHAT GIVES YOU...
RUMBLE!!!...
...THE RIGHT TO TAKE EVERY-THING?!
RM RM RM RM RM RM RM RM RM RM...!!!
OH NOOOO!!
HE'S MERCILESS! WE HAVE TO RUN AWAY!!
IT'S THE END OF EVERY-THING!!
RRMMMMM

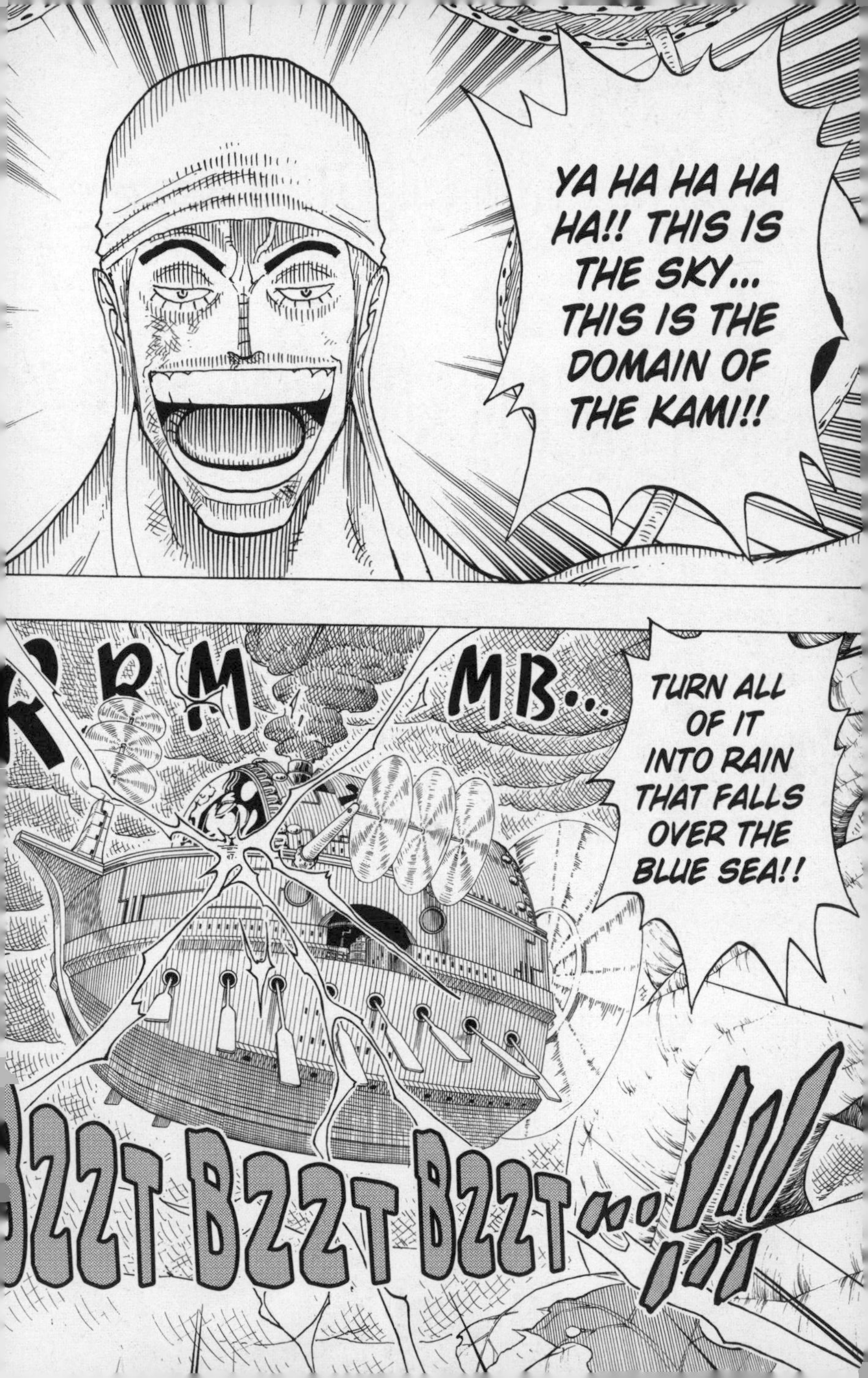
YA HA HA HA HA!! THIS IS THE SKY... THIS IS THE DOMAIN OF THE KAMI!!
TURN ALL OF IT INTO RAIN THAT FALLS OVER THE BLUE SEA!!
RRM MB...
ZZT BZZT BZZT...!!!

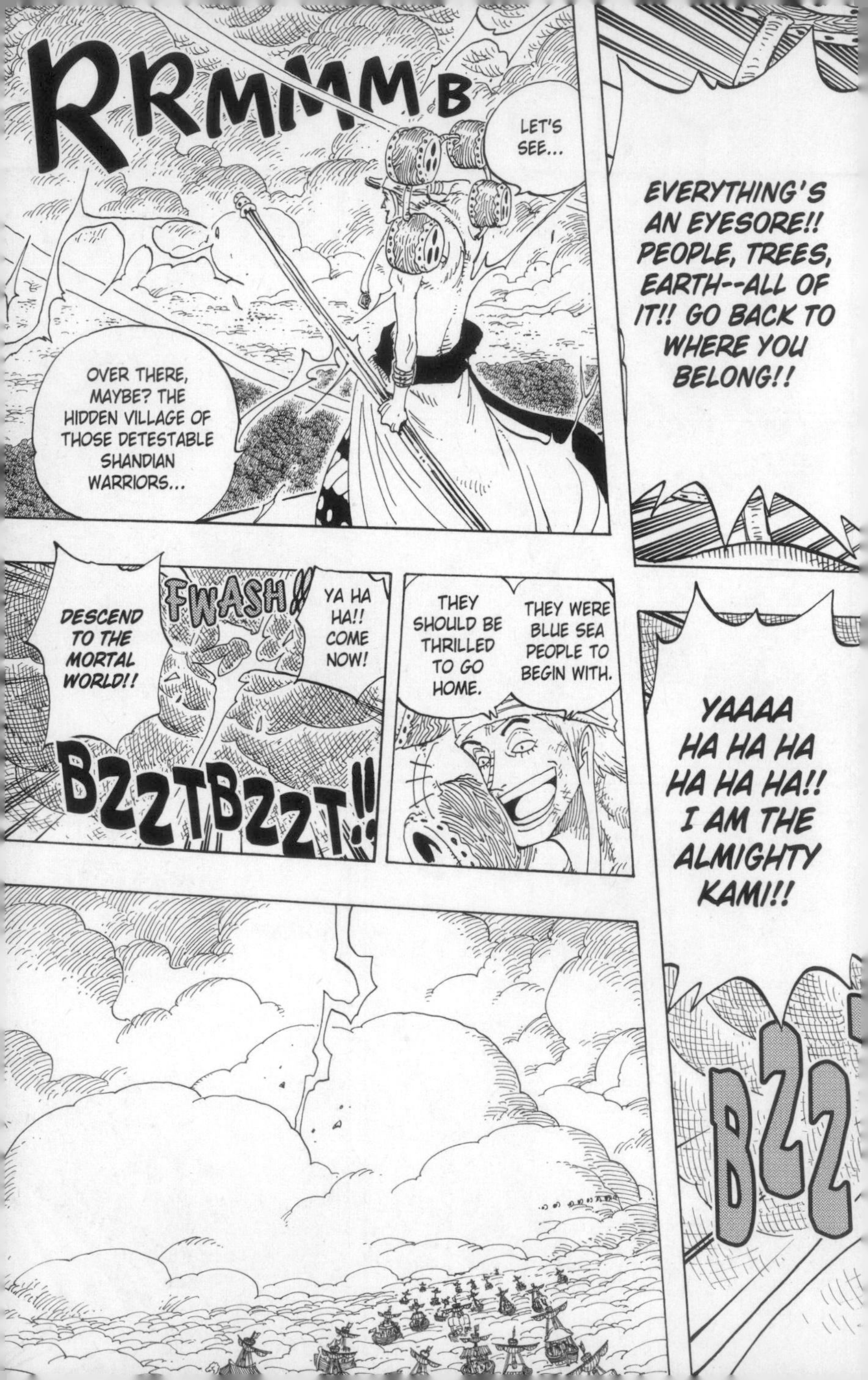
EVERYTHING'S AN EYESORE!! PEOPLE, TREES, EARTH--ALL OF IT!! GO BACK TO WHERE YOU BELONG!!
LET'S SEE...
RRMMMB
OVER THERE, MAYBE? THE HIDDEN VILLAGE OF THOSE DETESTABLE SHANDIAN WARRIORS...
YAAAA HA HA HA HA HA HA!! I AM THE ALMIGHTY KAMI!!
BZZ
THEY WERE BLUE SEA PEOPLE TO BEGIN WITH.
THEY SHOULD BE THRILLED TO GO HOME.
YA HA HA!! COME NOW!
FWASH!!
DESCEND TO THE MORTAL WORLD!!
BZZTBZZT!!

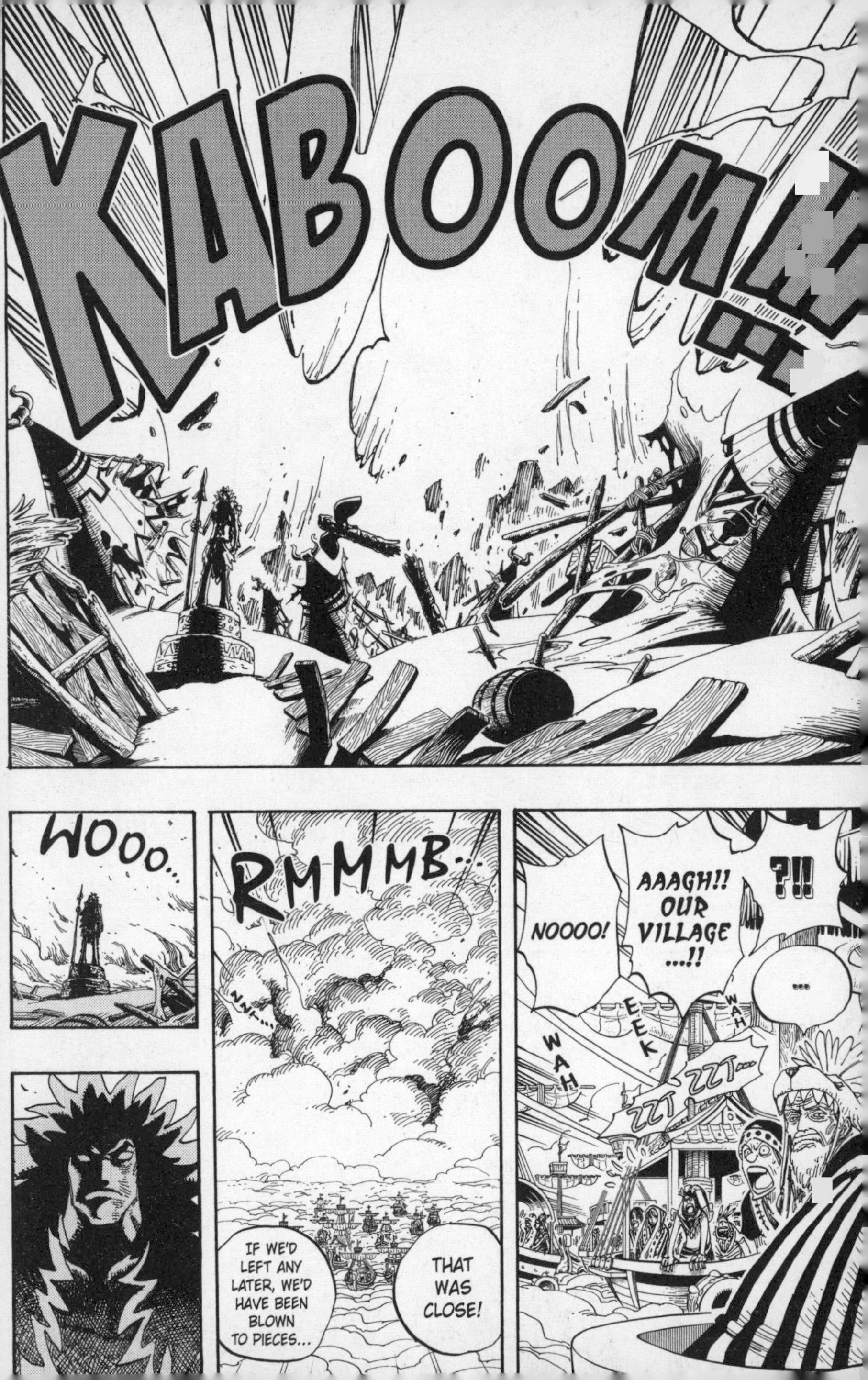
KABOOM!!
?!!
AAAGH!! OUR VILLAGE ...!!
NOOOO!
...
WAH
EEEK
WAH
ZZT ZZT...
RMMMB...
NNN...
THAT WAS CLOSE!
IF WE'D LEFT ANY LATER, WE'D HAVE BEEN BLOWN TO PIECES...
WOOO...

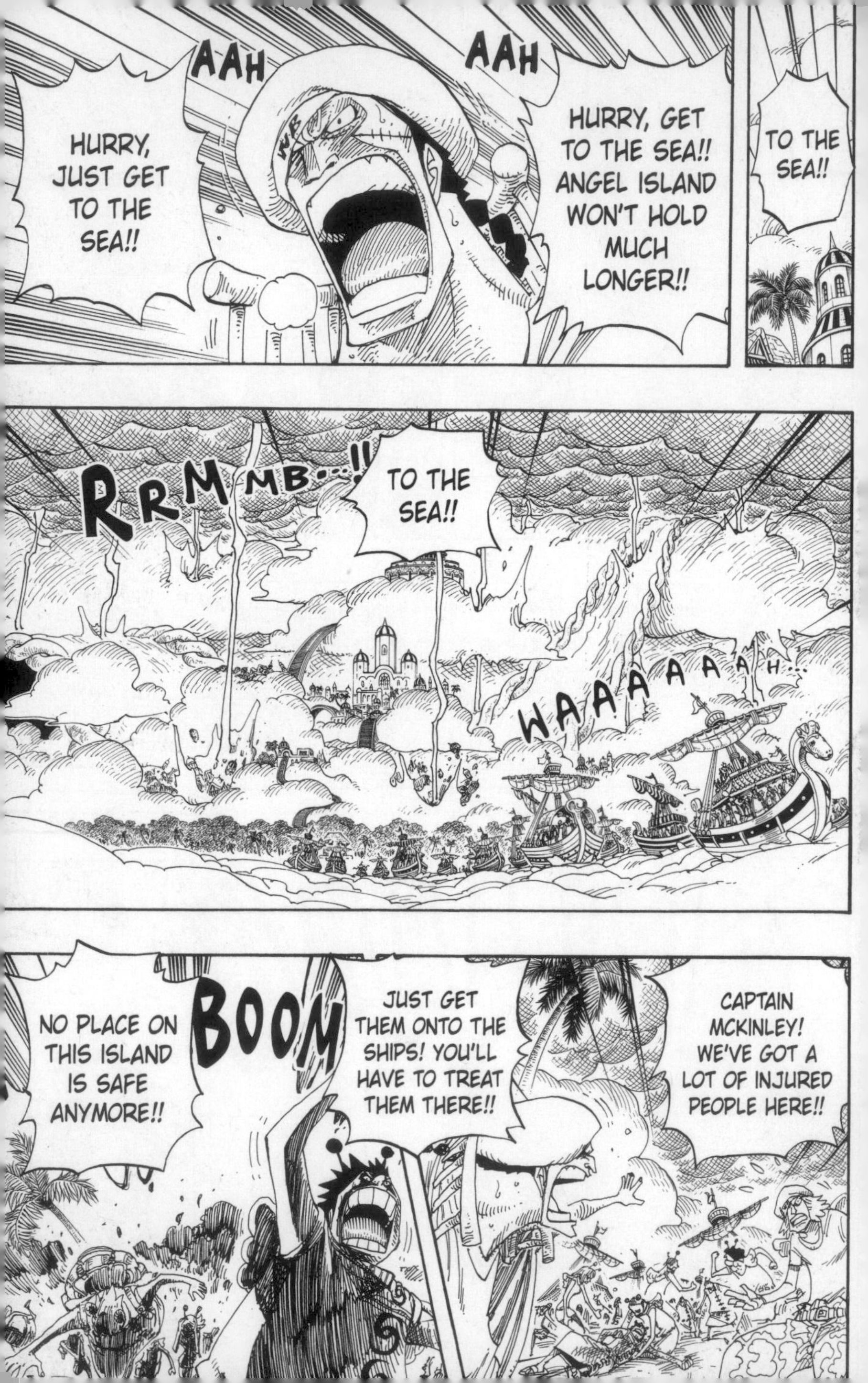
TO THE SEA!!
AAH
HURRY, GET TO THE SEA!! ANGEL ISLAND WON'T HOLD MUCH LONGER!!
AAH
HURRY, JUST GET TO THE SEA!!
TO THE SEA!!
WAAAAAAAH...
RRMMB...!!
CAPTAIN MCKINLEY! WE'VE GOT A LOT OF INJURED PEOPLE HERE!!
JUST GET THEM ONTO THE SHIPS! YOU'LL HAVE TO TREAT THEM THERE!!
BOOM
NO PLACE ON THIS ISLAND IS SAFE ANYMORE!!

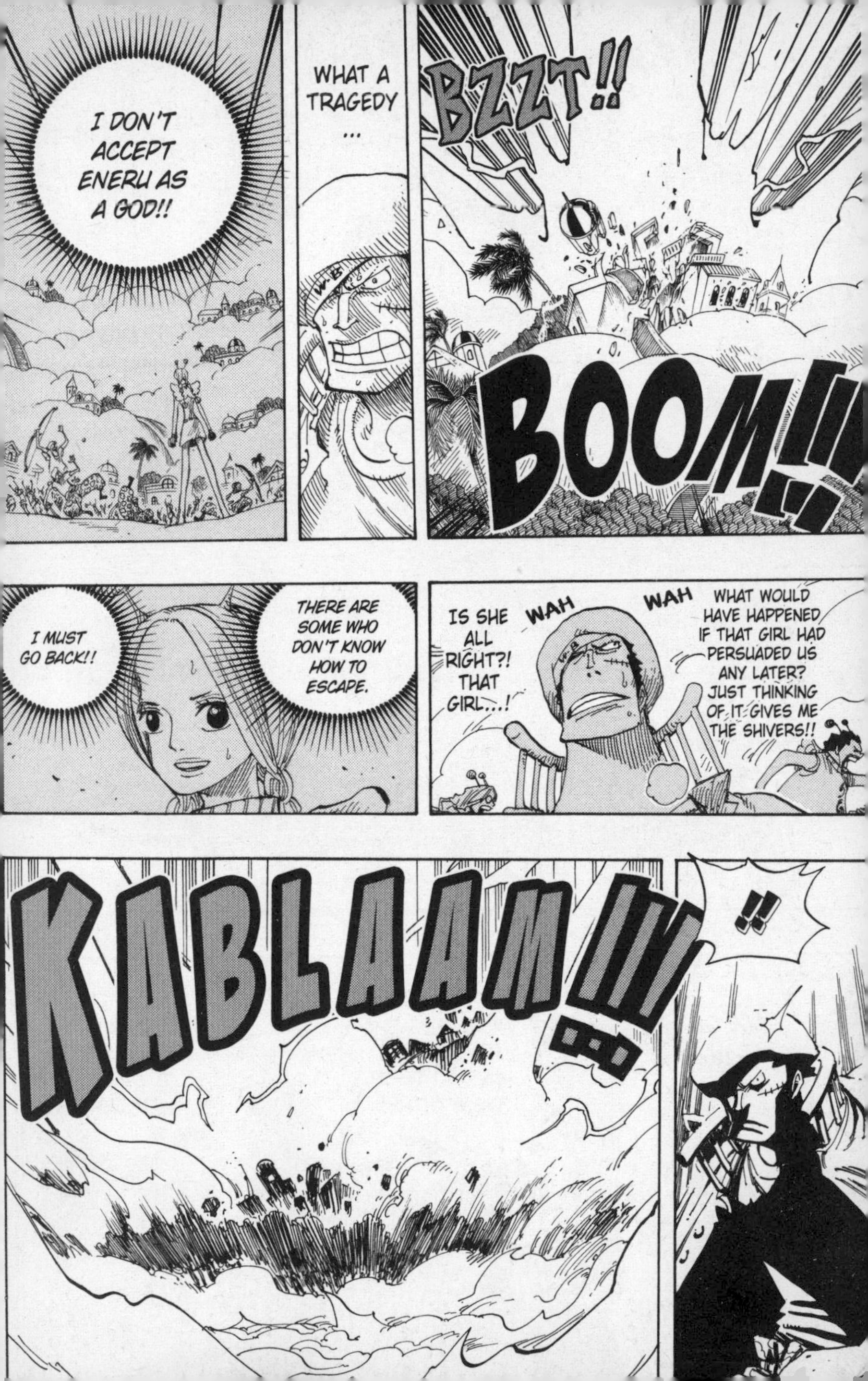
BZZT!!
BOOM!!!
WHAT A TRAGEDY ...
I DON'T ACCEPT ENERU AS A GOD!!
WHAT WOULD HAVE HAPPENED IF THAT GIRL HAD PERSUADED US ANY LATER? JUST THINKING OF IT GIVES ME THE SHIVERS!!
WAH
WAH
IS SHE ALL RIGHT?! THAT GIRL...!
THERE ARE SOME WHO DON'T KNOW HOW TO ESCAPE.
I MUST GO BACK!!
!!
KABLAAM!!!

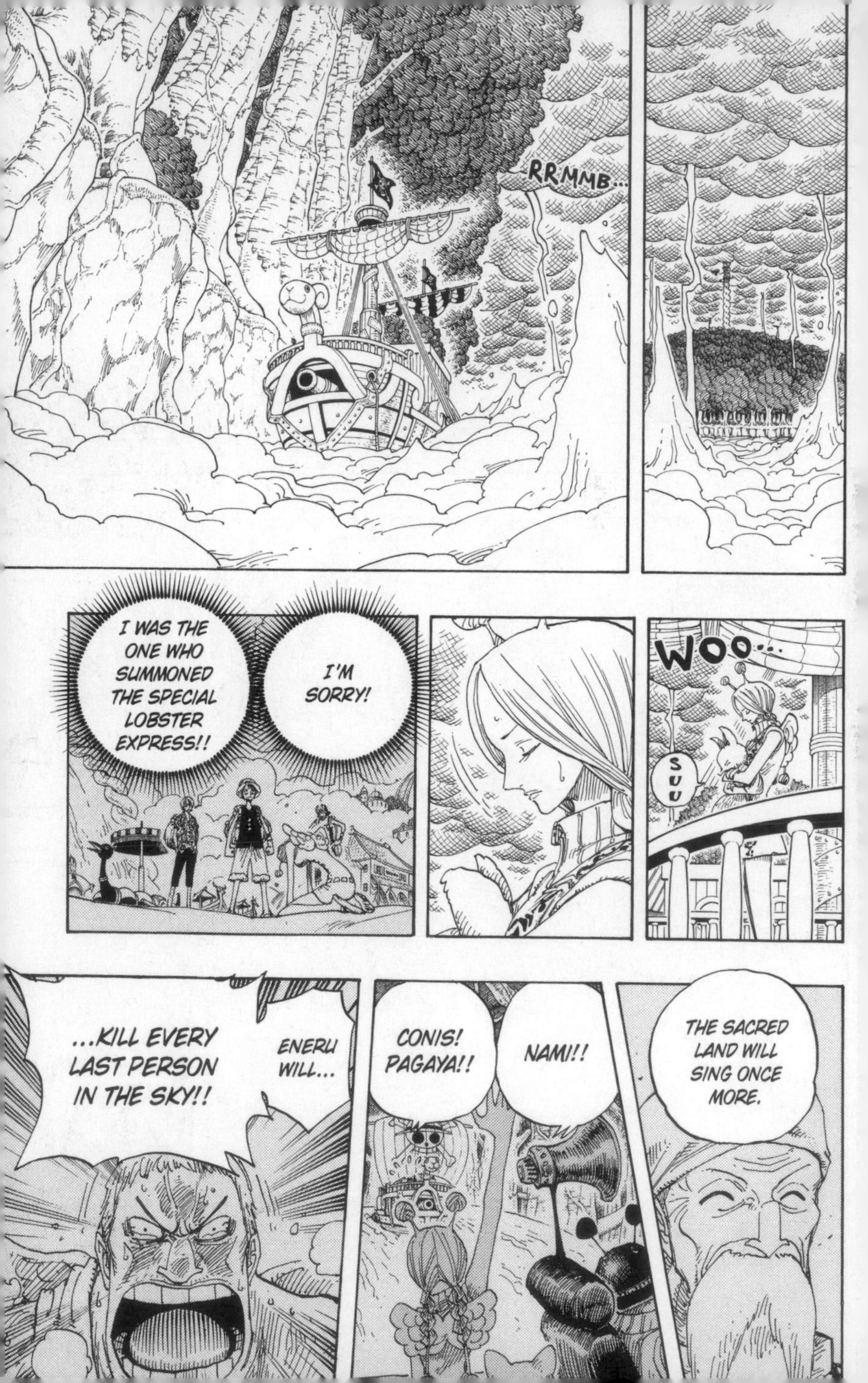
RRMMB...
WOO...
SUU
I'M SORRY!
I WAS THE ONE WHO SUMMONED THE SPECIAL LOBSTER EXPRESS!!
THE SACRED LAND WILL SING ONCE MORE.
NAMI!!
CONIS! PAGAYA!!
ENERU WILL...
...KILL EVERY LAST PERSON IN THE SKY!!

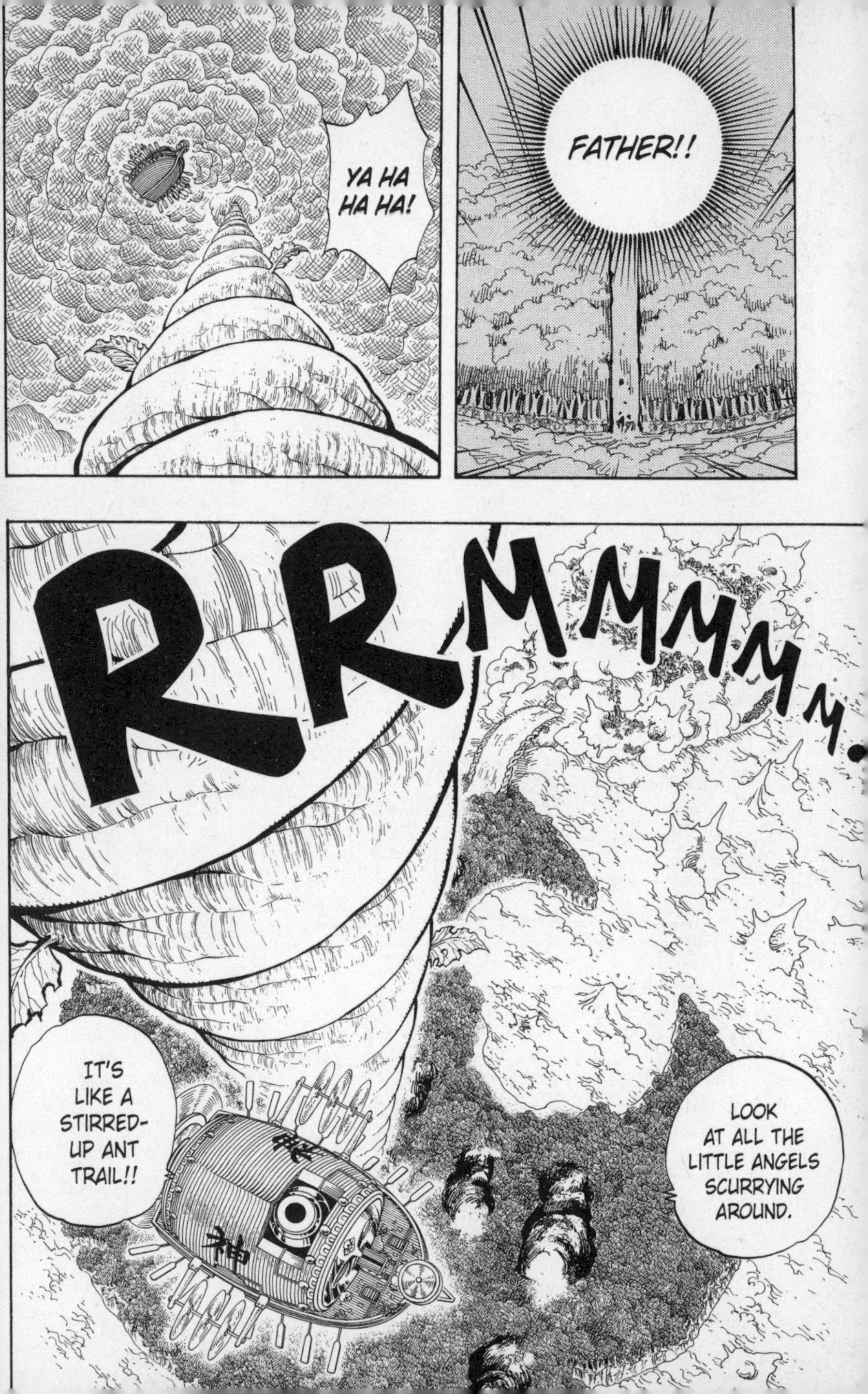
FATHER!!
YA HA HA HA!
RRMMMMMM
LOOK AT ALL THE LITTLE ANGELS SCURRYING AROUND.
IT'S LIKE A STIRRED-UP ANT TRAIL!!

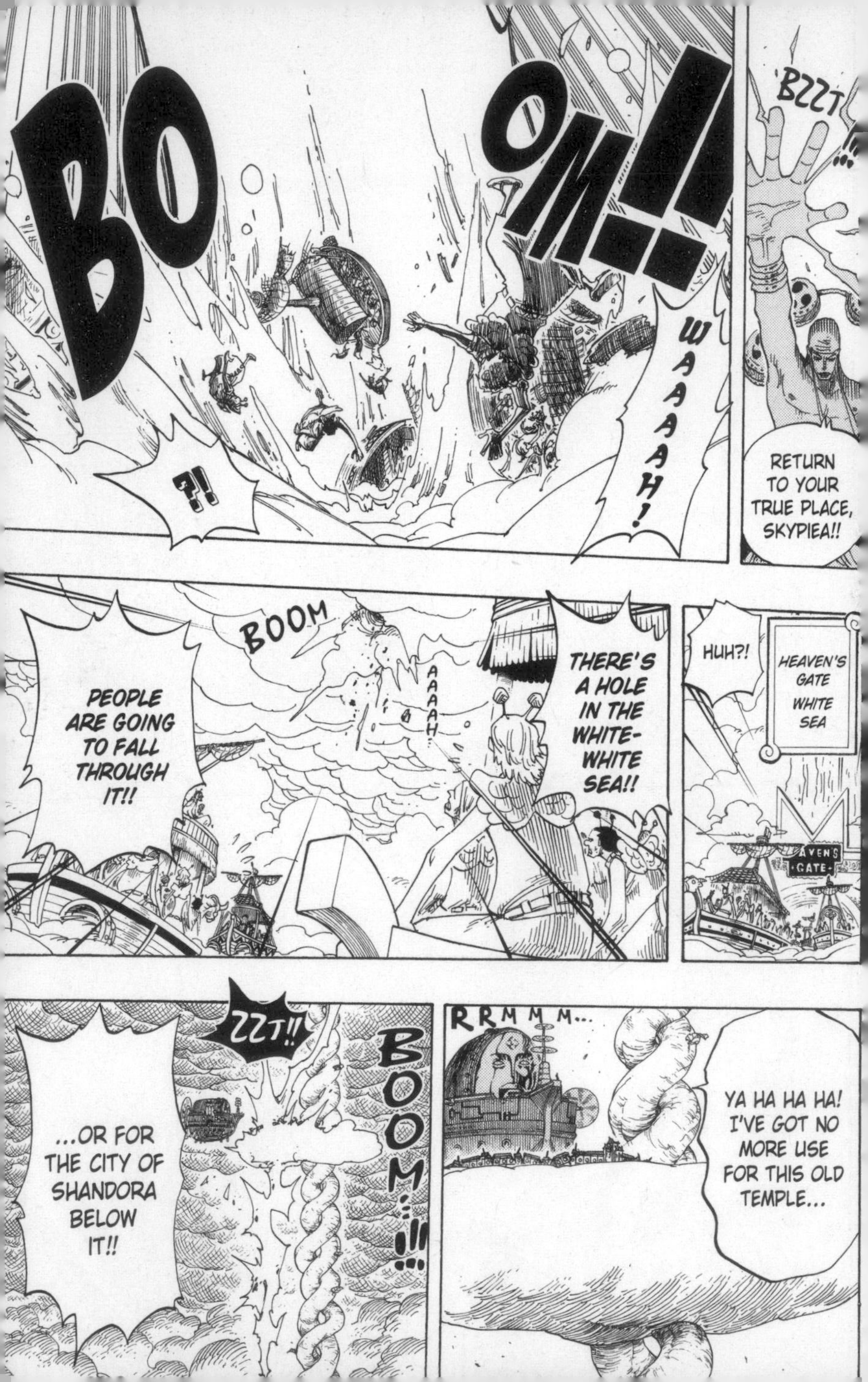
BZZT!!
RETURN TO YOUR TRUE PLACE, SKYPIEA!!
BOOM!!
WAAAAAH!
?!
HUH?!
HEAVEN'S GATE
WHITE SEA
AVEN'S GATE
THERE'S A HOLE IN THE WHITE-WHITE SEA!!
BOOM
AAAAAH
PEOPLE ARE GOING TO FALL THROUGH IT!!
RRMMMM...
YA HA HA HA! I'VE GOT NO MORE USE FOR THIS OLD TEMPLE...
ZZT!!
BOOM!!!
...OR FOR THE CITY OF SHANDORA BELOW IT!!

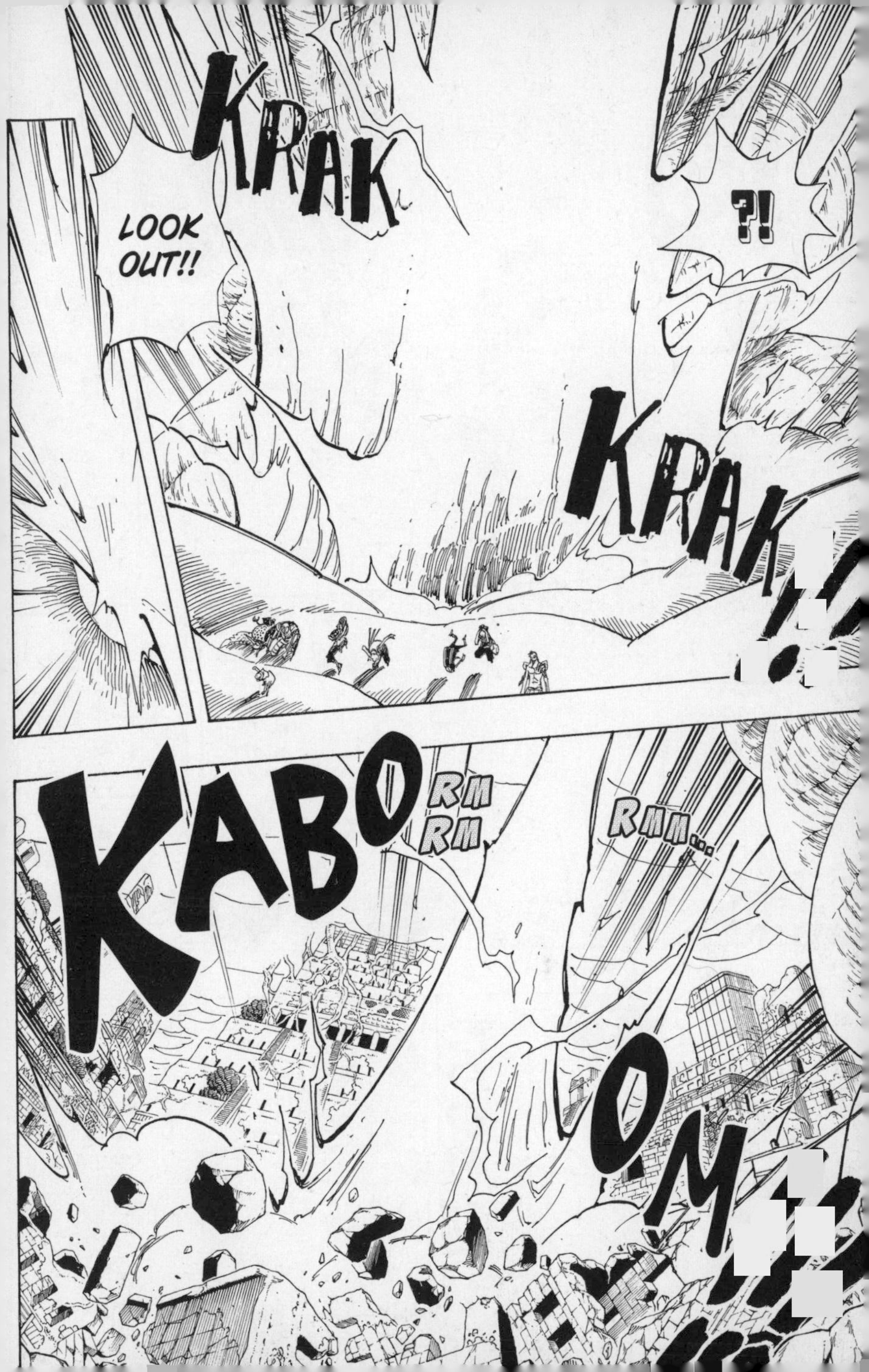
KRAK
?!
LOOK OUT!!
KRAK
KABOOM
RMM...
RM RM

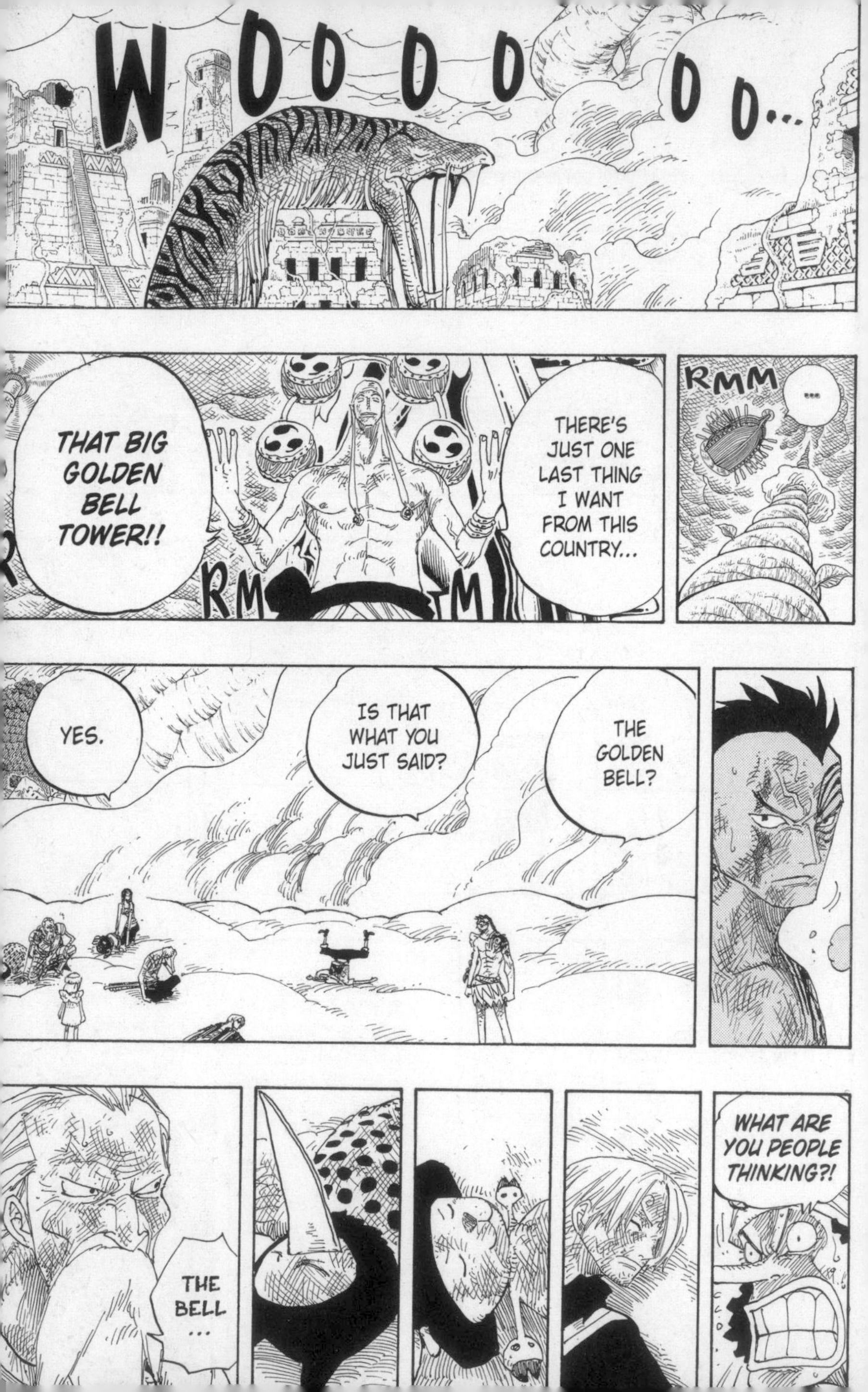
WOOOOOO...
RMM
...
THERE'S JUST ONE LAST THING I WANT FROM THIS COUNTRY...
RM
RM
THAT BIG GOLDEN BELL TOWER!!
THE GOLDEN BELL?
IS THAT WHAT YOU JUST SAID?
YES.
WHAT ARE YOU PEOPLE THINKING?!
THE BELL...

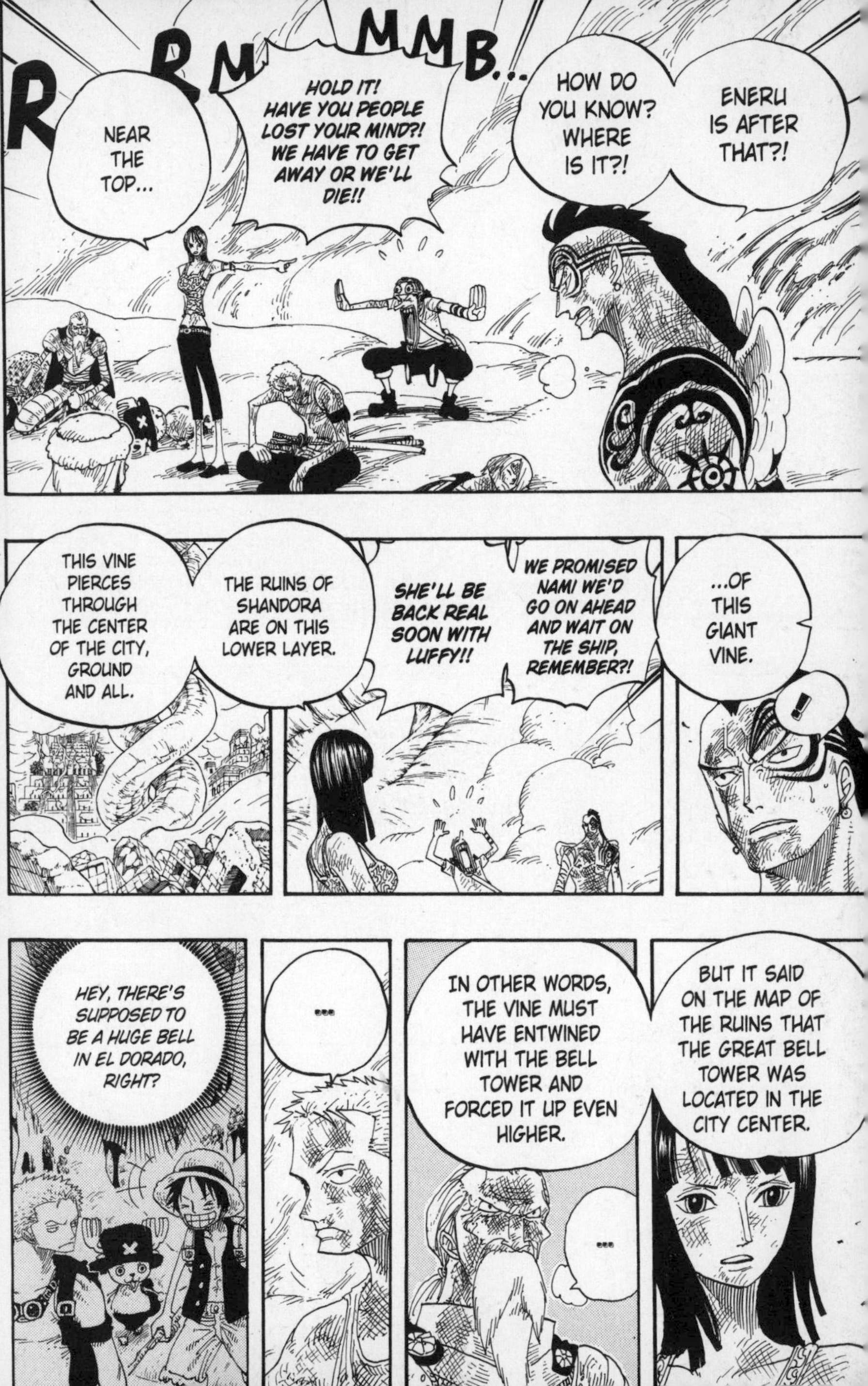
ENERU IS AFTER THAT?!
HOW DO YOU KNOW? WHERE IS IT?!
RRMMMB...
HOLD IT! HAVE YOU PEOPLE LOST YOUR MIND?! WE HAVE TO GET AWAY OR WE'LL DIE!!
NEAR THE TOP...
...OF THIS GIANT VINE.
!
WE PROMISED NAMI WE'D GO ON AHEAD AND WAIT ON THE SHIP, REMEMBER?!
SHE'LL BE BACK REAL SOON WITH LUFFY!!
THE RUINS OF SHANDORA ARE ON THIS LOWER LAYER.
THIS VINE PIERCES THROUGH THE CENTER OF THE CITY, GROUND AND ALL.
BUT IT SAID ON THE MAP OF THE RUINS THAT THE GREAT BELL TOWER WAS LOCATED IN THE CITY CENTER.
IN OTHER WORDS, THE VINE MUST HAVE ENTWINED WITH THE BELL TOWER AND FORCED IT UP EVEN HIGHER.
...
...
HEY, THERE'S SUPPOSED TO BE A HUGE BELL IN EL DORADO, RIGHT?

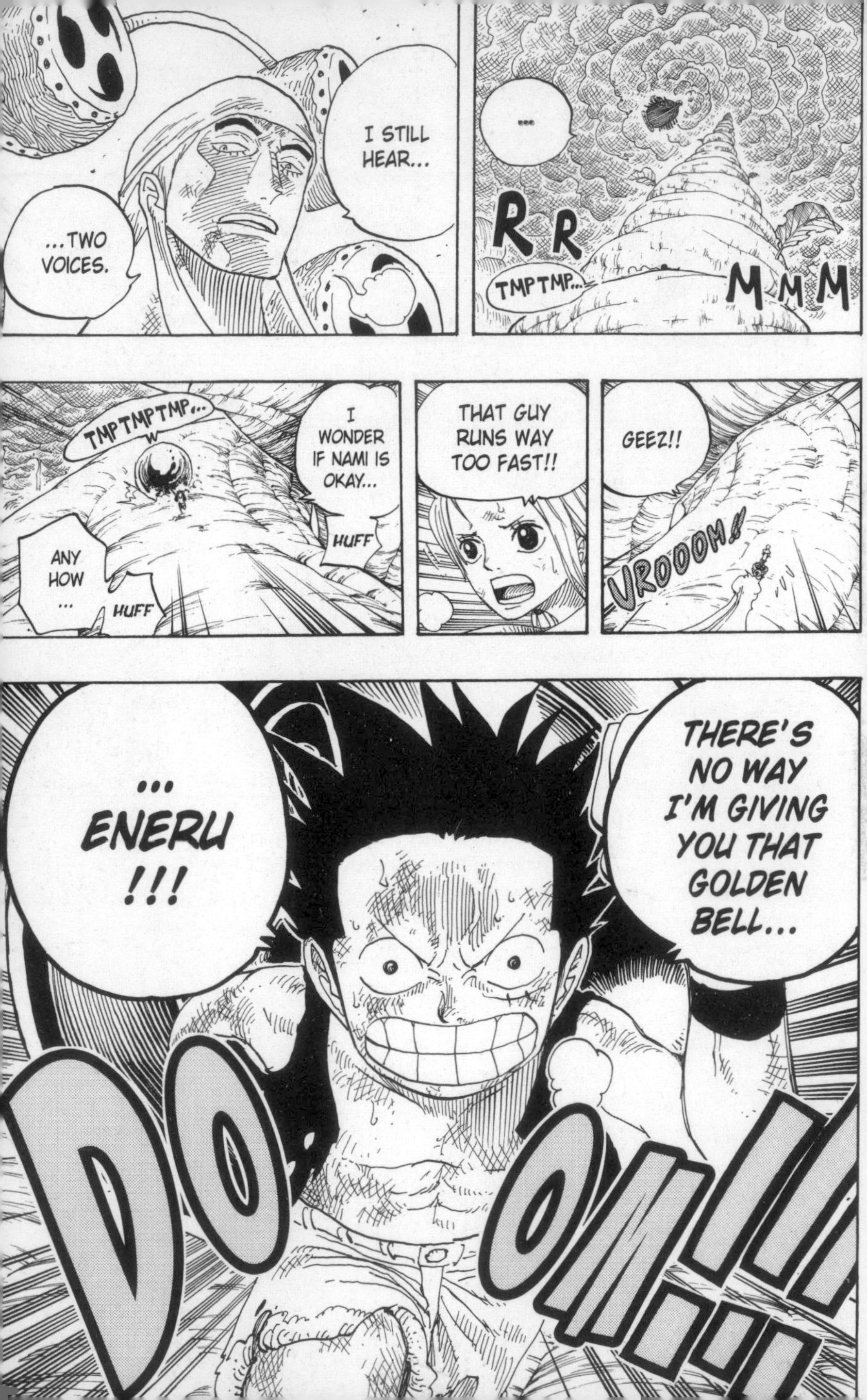
...
RRRMMM
TMPTMP...
I STILL HEAR...
...TWO VOICES.
GEEZ!!
VROOOM!!
THAT GUY RUNS WAY TOO FAST!!
TMPTMPTMP...
I WONDER IF NAMI IS OKAY...
HUFF
ANY HOW...
HUFF
THERE'S NO WAY I'M GIVING YOU THAT GOLDEN BELL...
...ENERU!!!
DOOM!!...

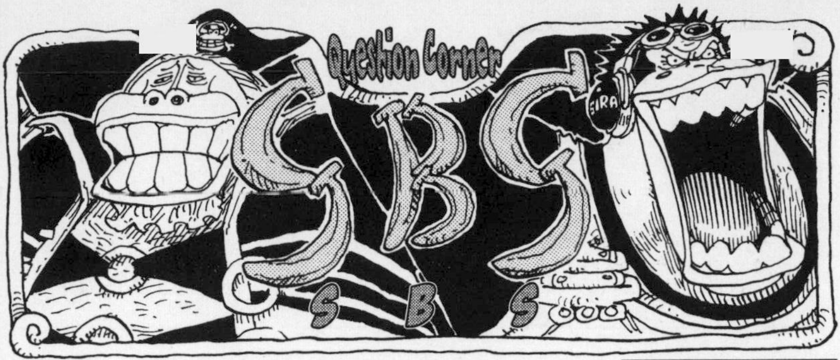
Question Corner
SBS
S B S

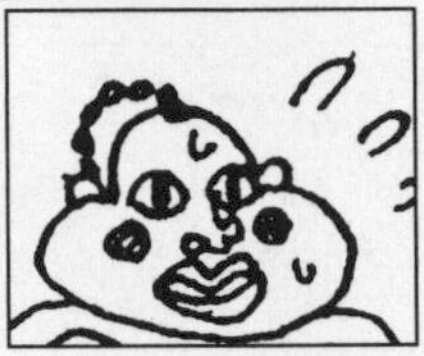

volume 2, page 13

Q: Hewwo, Mr. Oda! Remember those aliens you thought up who are plotting world domination? I want to see Domo-kun's (volume 2, page 13) comrade Nnke-kun so bad you won't even bereave it (believe it), so please tell me about him.

-- Chiiyan

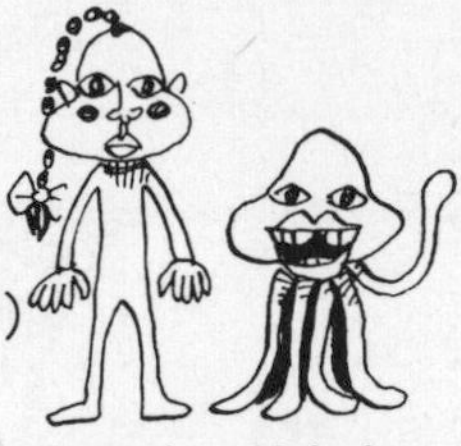

Domo-kun Nnke-kun

A: Right. Um. This is a secret character from a long time ago. I commented that he had comrades in a book called One Piece: *Blue*, and I think that got people curious, so I'll introduce them here! This is Domo-kun and Nnke-kun! (→) Clap clap clap clap I thought these guys up when I was in high school. They're also hiding in a few places in my short story "A Present of the Future from God," which is in my "masterpiece collection" WANTED. Since I went and introduced them here, I might end up drawing them somewhere again (Laugh).

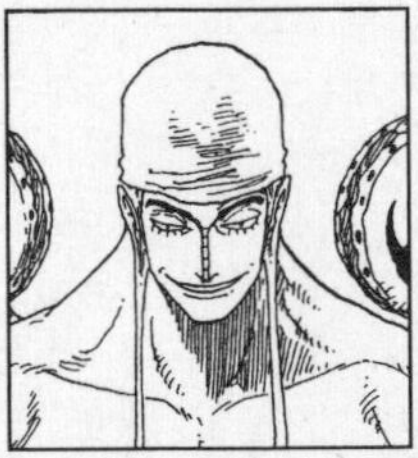

Q: Is that thing Kami Eneru wears on his head a rubber swim cap?

A: Sure... Yeah, that's it. (Whatever.) Ah, no, wait a sec. There isn't any rubber on Sky Island, is there? So... It's cloth. (Yeah, that's it.)

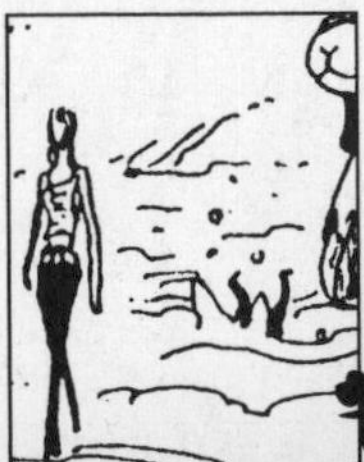

Q: Hello, Oda Sensei. In the right-hand corner of the first panel on page 54 of volume 26, Zolo's just casually diving into the sea of clouds, isn't he? He must really have wanted to goof around, huh!

--Toro

A: Yeah. The guy's not so bright, eh?

Chapter 294:

KINGDOM COME

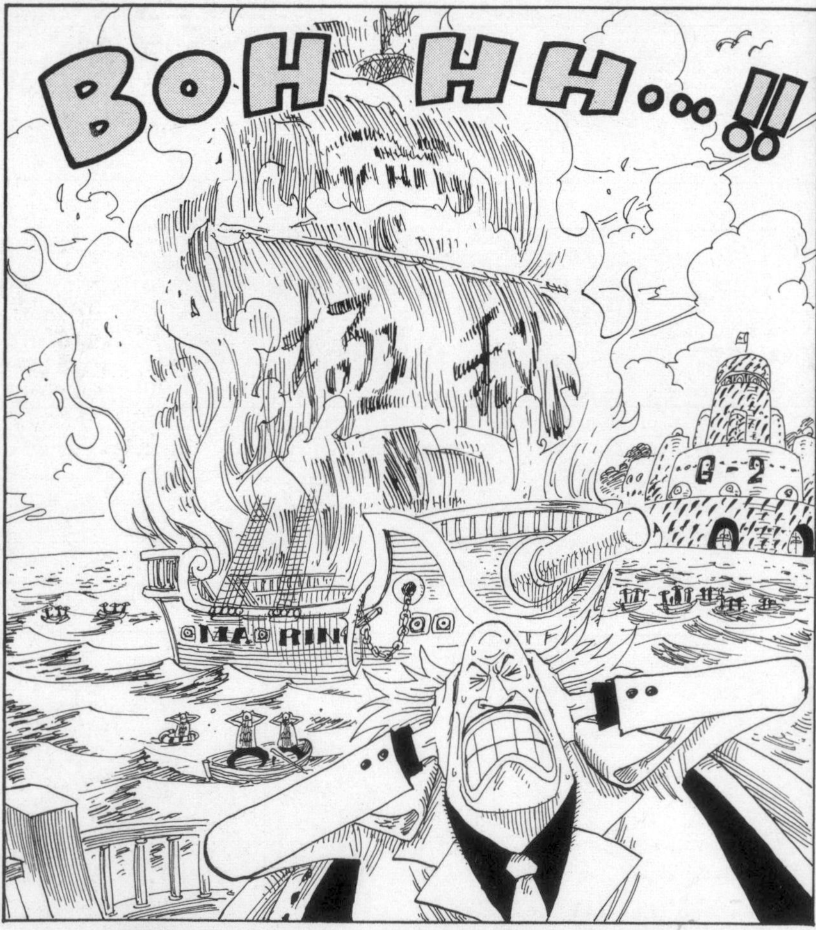
BOH HHH...!!
MARINE
G-2

ACE'S GREAT SEARCH FOR BLACKBEARD, VOL. 19:
"PIRATES SET FIRE TO THE SHIP OUT OF SPITE. THERE'LL BE TROUBLE IF THE TOP SECRET INFORMATION BURNS UP!"

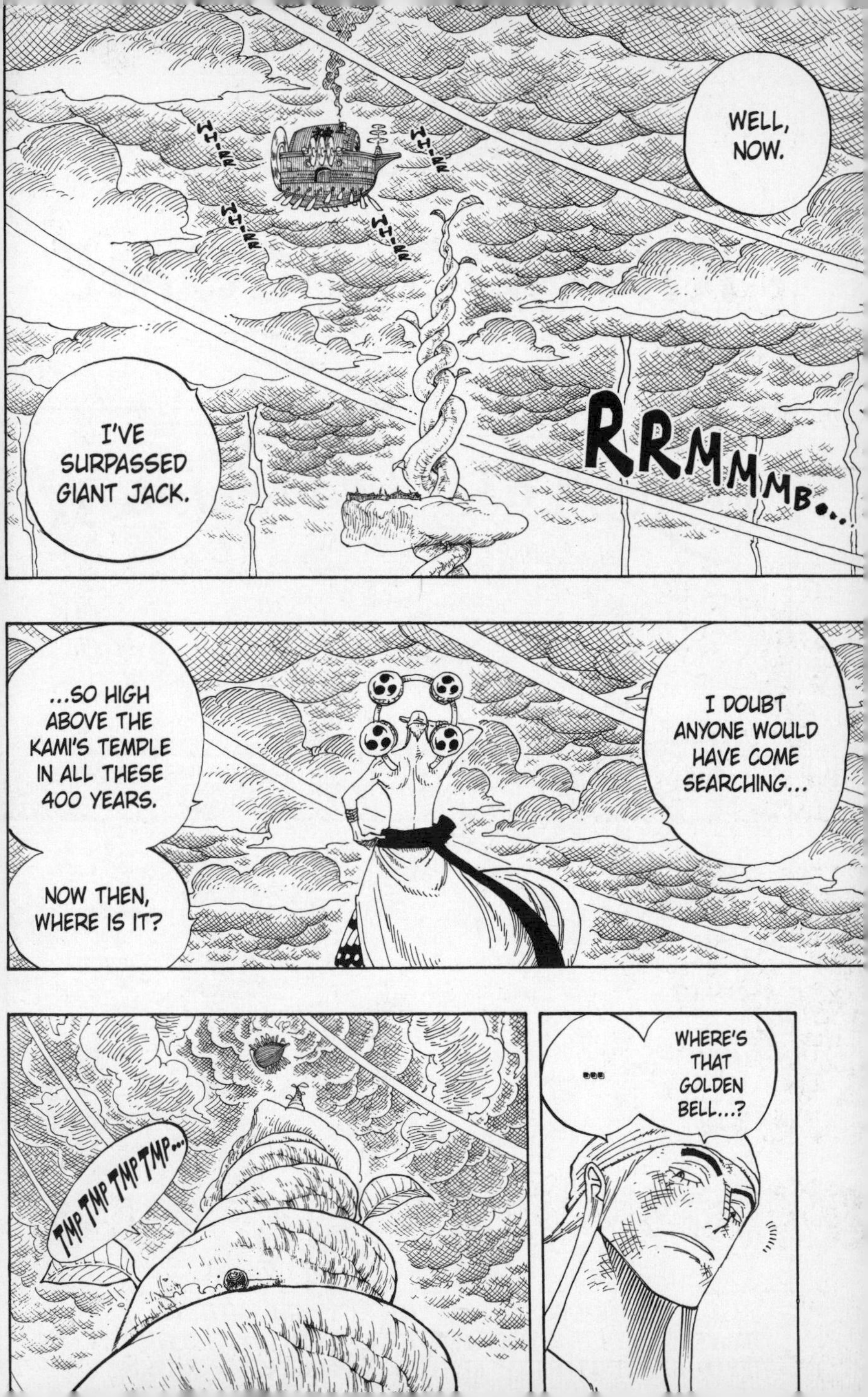
WELL, NOW.
WHIRR
WHIRR
WHIRR
WHIRR
RRMMMMB...
I'VE SURPASSED GIANT JACK.
I DOUBT ANYONE WOULD HAVE COME SEARCHING...
...SO HIGH ABOVE THE KAMI'S TEMPLE IN ALL THESE 400 YEARS.
NOW THEN, WHERE IS IT?
WHERE'S THAT GOLDEN BELL...?
...
TMP TMP TMP TMP...

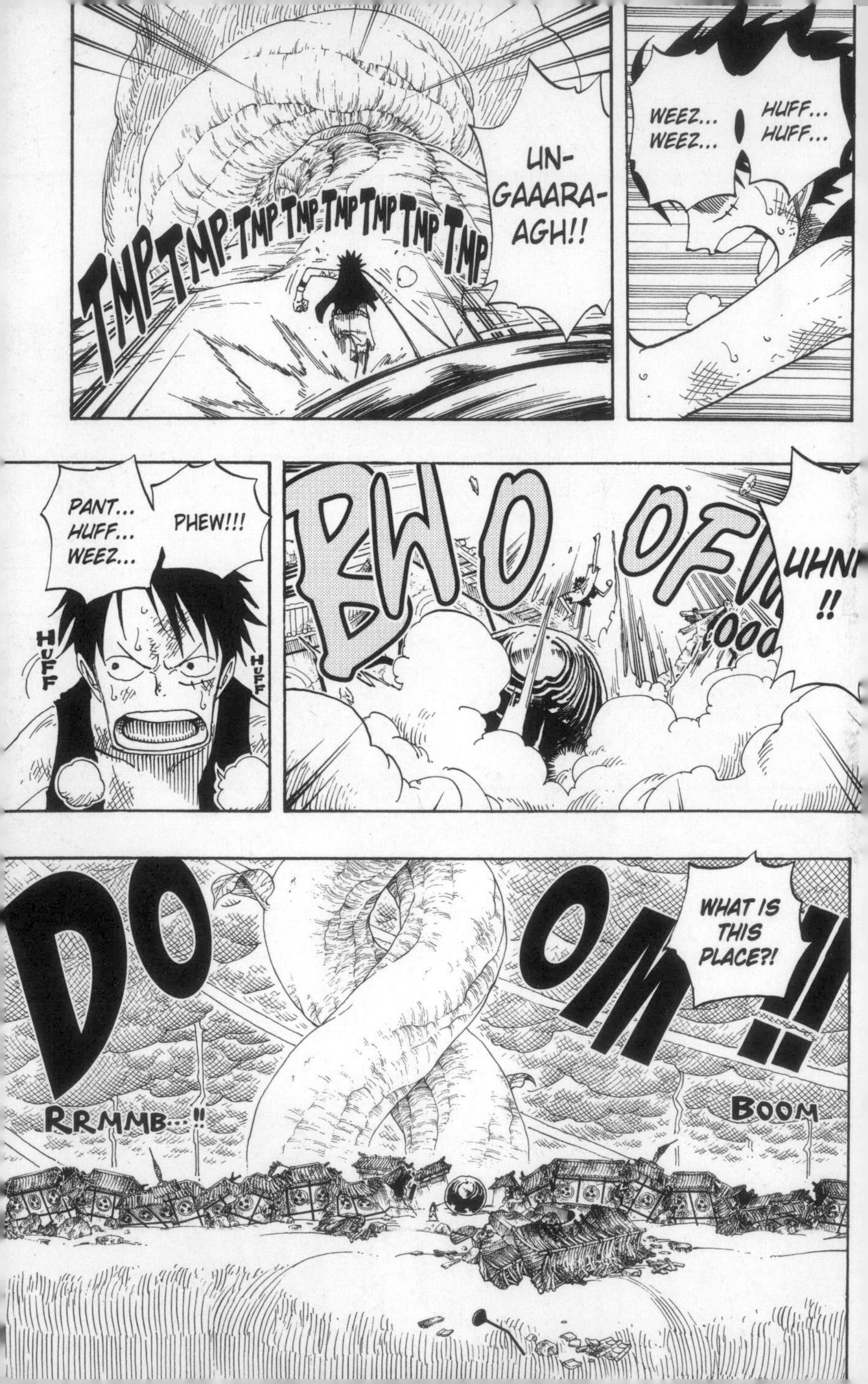
WEEZ... WEEZ...
HUFF... HUFF...
UN-GAAARA-AGH!!
TMP TMP TMP TMP TMP TMP TMP TMP
BWOOF
UHN
!!
PANT... HUFF... WEEZ...
PHEW!!!
HUFF
HUFF
DOOM!!
WHAT IS THIS PLACE?!
RRMMB...!!
BOOM

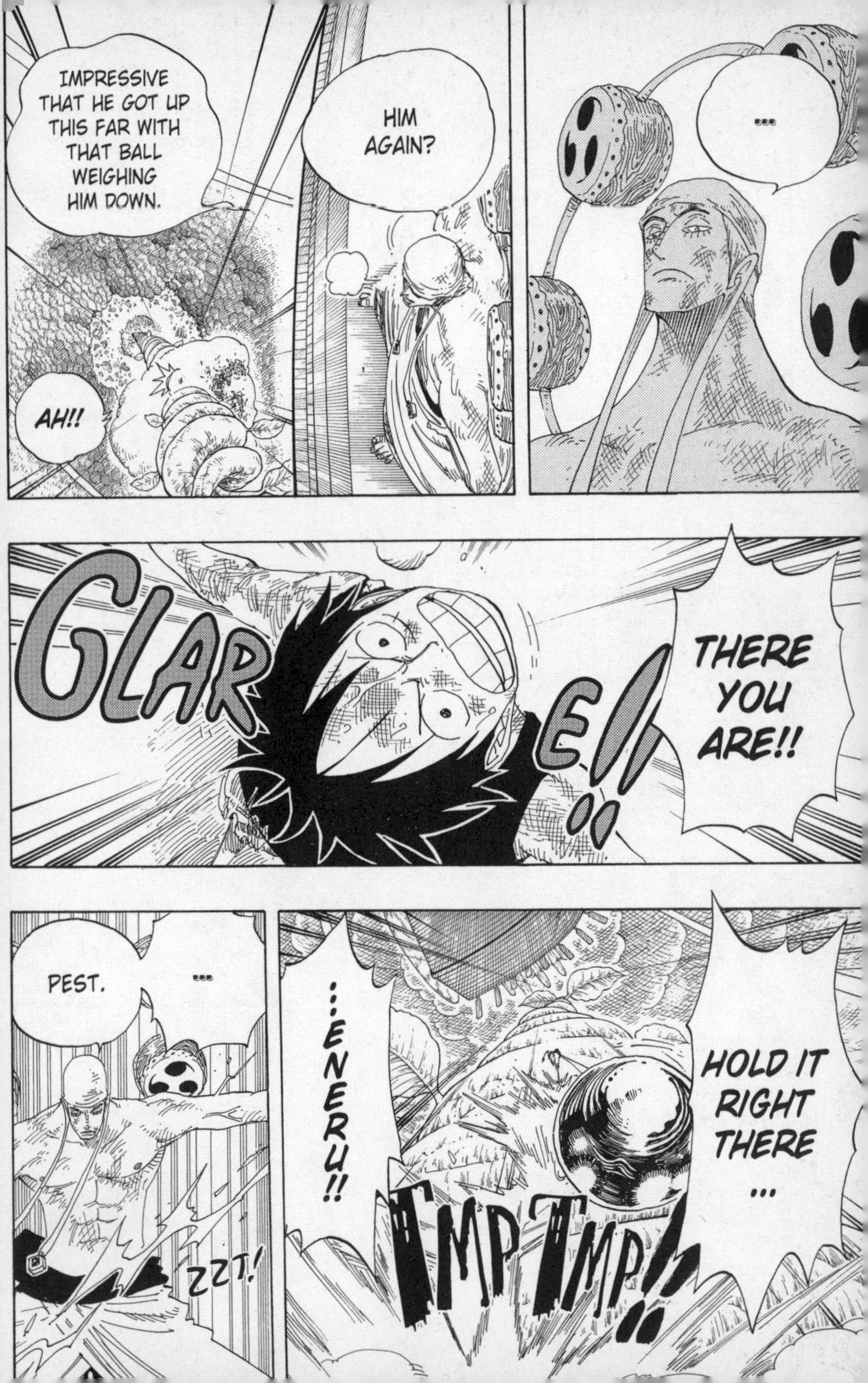
...
HIM AGAIN?
IMPRESSIVE THAT HE GOT UP THIS FAR WITH THAT BALL WEIGHING HIM DOWN.
AH!!
THERE YOU ARE!!
GLARE!!
HOLD IT RIGHT THERE ...
...ENERU!!
TMP TMP!!
...
PEST.
ZZT!

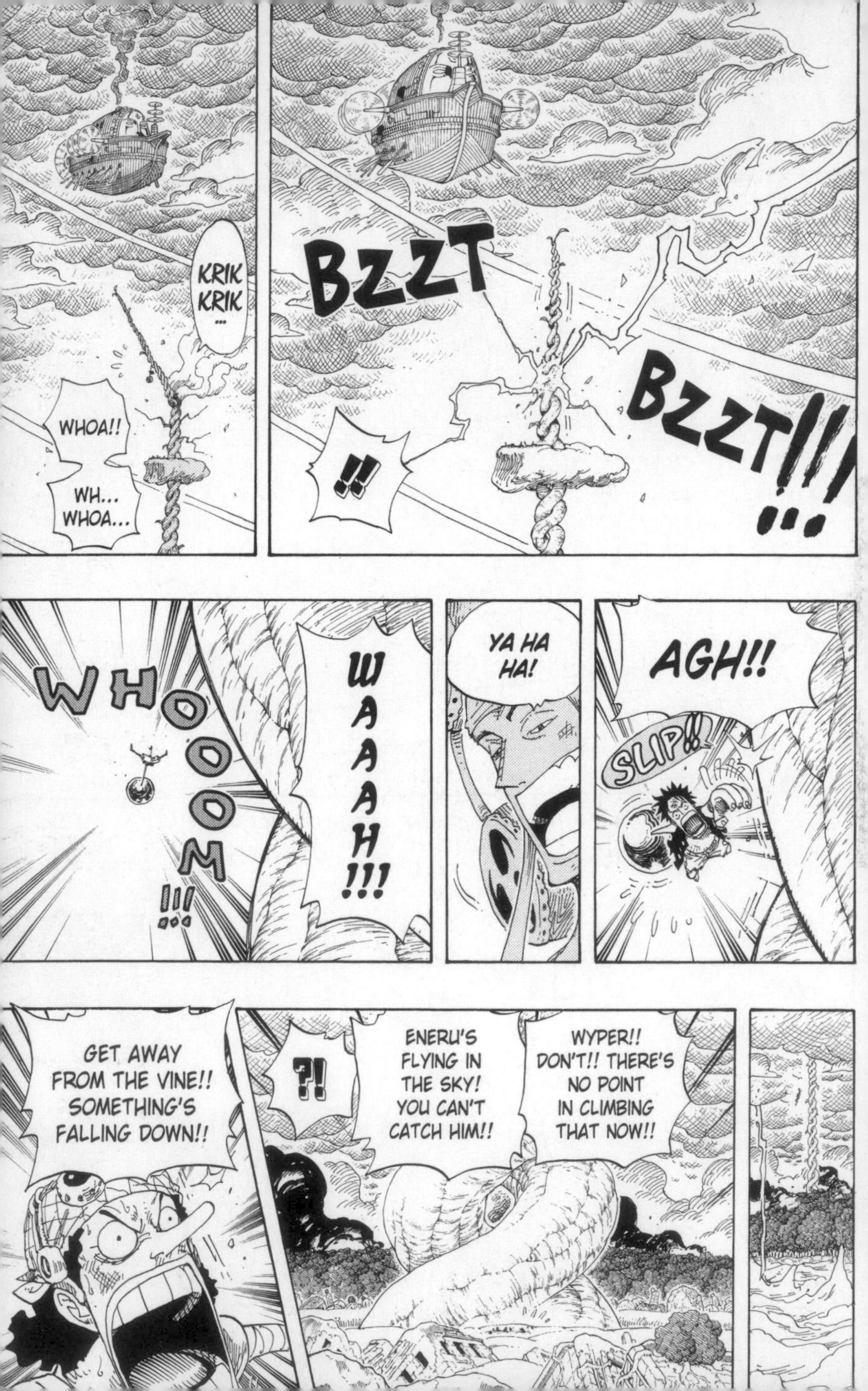
BZZT
!!
BZZT!!!
KRIK KRIK ...
WHOA!!
WH... WHOA...
AGH!!
SLIP!!
YA HA HA!
WAAAAH!!!
WHOOOOM!!!
WYPER!! DON'T!! THERE'S NO POINT IN CLIMBING THAT NOW!!
ENERU'S FLYING IN THE SKY! YOU CAN'T CATCH HIM!!
?!
GET AWAY FROM THE VINE!! SOMETHING'S FALLING DOWN!!

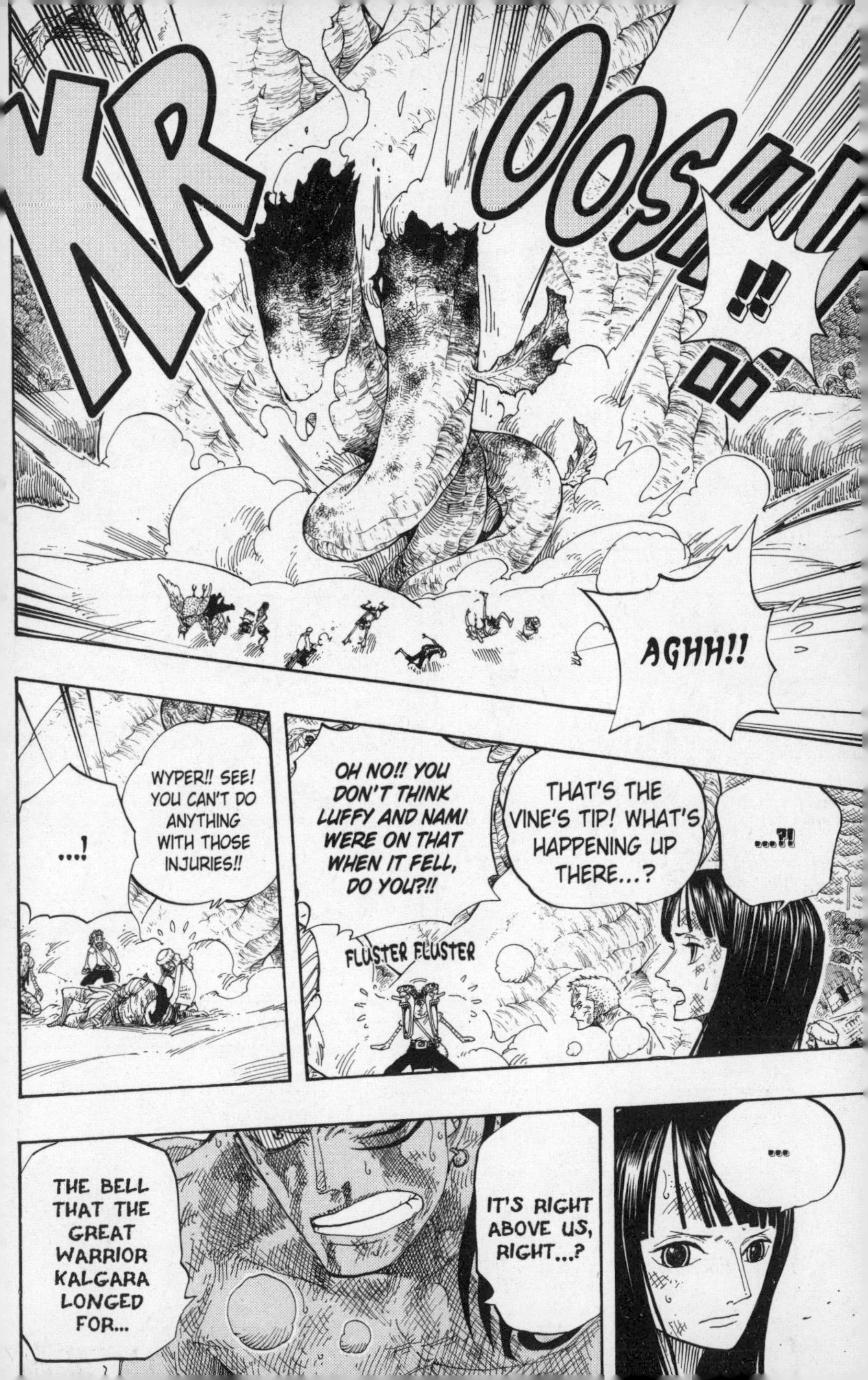
KROOSH!!
AGHH!!
...?!
THAT'S THE VINE'S TIP! WHAT'S HAPPENING UP THERE...?
OH NO!! YOU DON'T THINK LUFFY AND NAMI WERE ON THAT WHEN IT FELL, DO YOU?!!
FLUSTER FLUSTER
WYPER!! SEE! YOU CAN'T DO ANYTHING WITH THOSE INJURIES!!
...!
...
IT'S RIGHT ABOVE US, RIGHT...?
THE BELL THAT THE GREAT WARRIOR KALGARA LONGED FOR...

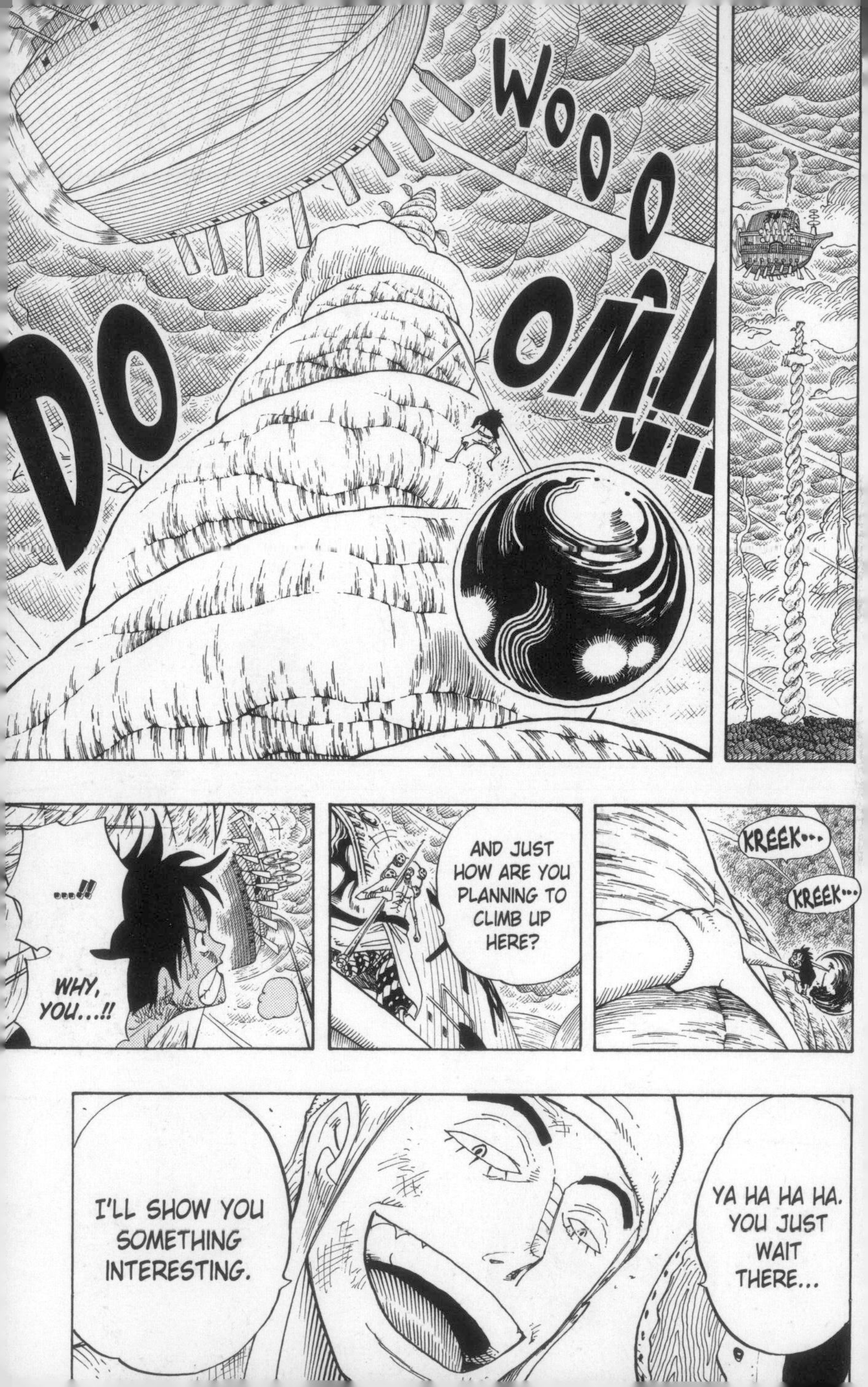
WOOOO
DOOM!!
KREEK...
KREEK...
AND JUST HOW ARE YOU PLANNING TO CLIMB UP HERE?
...!!
WHY, YOU...!!
YA HA HA HA. YOU JUST WAIT THERE...
I'LL SHOW YOU SOMETHING INTERESTING.

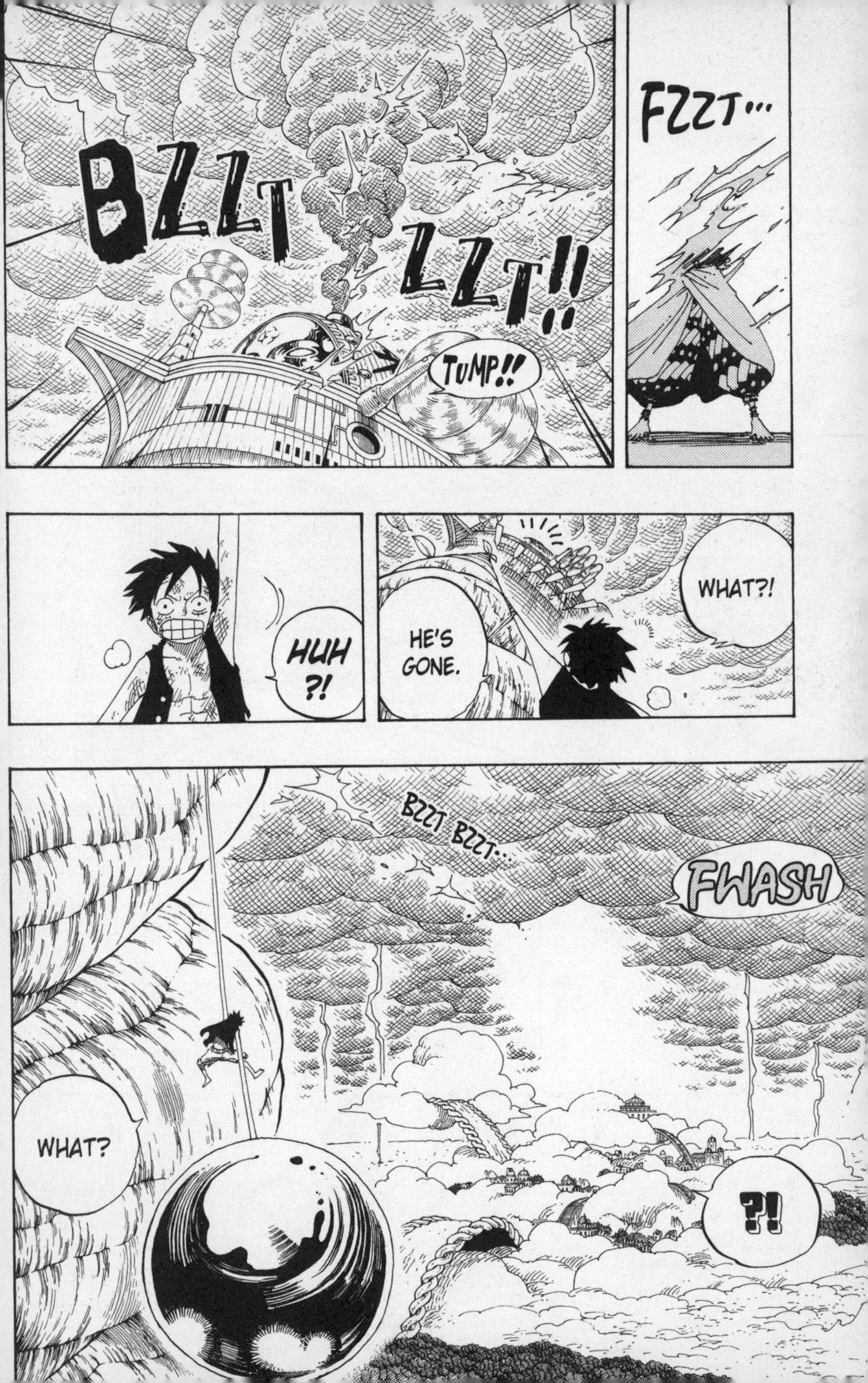
FZZT...
BZZT
ZZZT!!
TUMP!!
WHAT?!
HE'S GONE.
HUH ?!
FWASH
BZZT BZZT...
?!
WHAT?

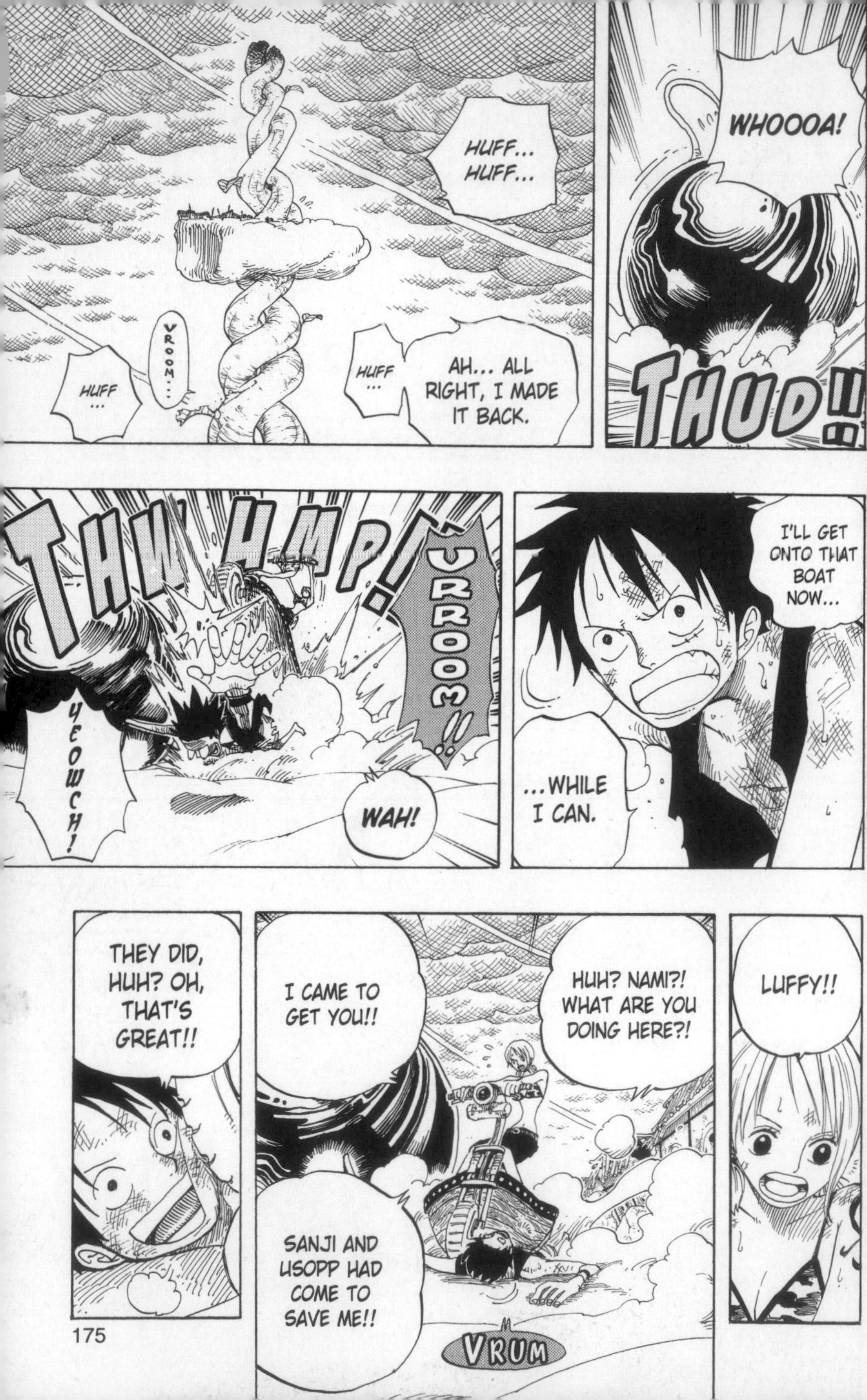
WHOOOA!
THUD!!
HUFF... HUFF...
AH... ALL RIGHT, I MADE IT BACK.
HUFF ...
VROOM...
HUFF ...
I'LL GET ONTO THAT BOAT NOW...
...WHILE I CAN.
VROOM!!
THWUMP!
WAH!
YEOWCH!
LUFFY!!
HUH? NAMI?! WHAT ARE YOU DOING HERE?!
I CAME TO GET YOU!!
SANJI AND USOPP HAD COME TO SAVE ME!!
VRUM
THEY DID, HUH? OH, THAT'S GREAT!!

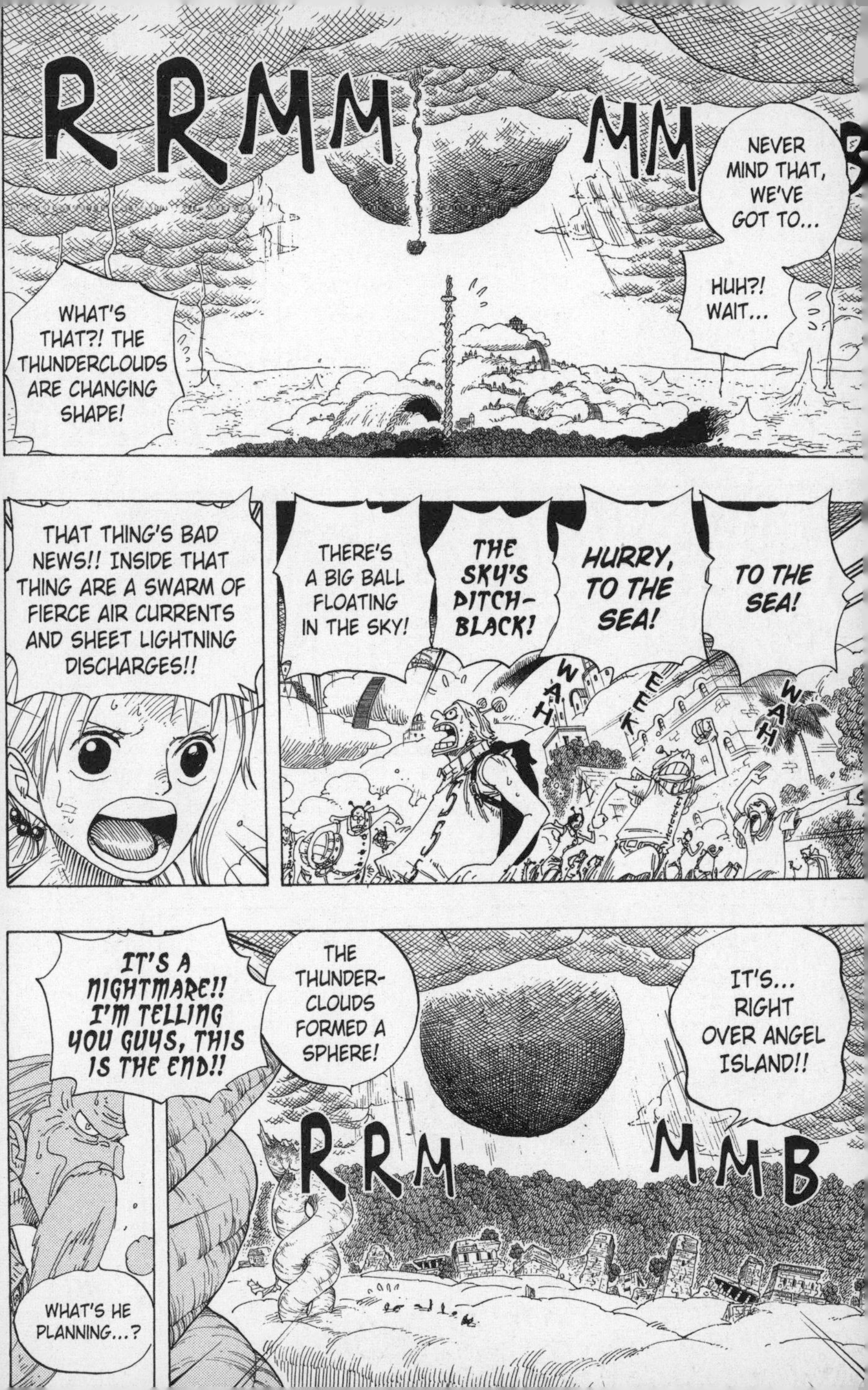
RRMM MM
NEVER MIND THAT, WE'VE GOT TO...
HUH?! WAIT...
WHAT'S THAT?! THE THUNDERCLOUDS ARE CHANGING SHAPE!
TO THE SEA!
HURRY, TO THE SEA!
THE SKY'S PITCH-BLACK!
THERE'S A BIG BALL FLOATING IN THE SKY!
WAH
EEEK
WAH
THAT THING'S BAD NEWS!! INSIDE THAT THING ARE A SWARM OF FIERCE AIR CURRENTS AND SHEET LIGHTNING DISCHARGES!!
IT'S... RIGHT OVER ANGEL ISLAND!!
THE THUNDER-CLOUDS FORMED A SPHERE!
RRM MMB
IT'S A NIGHTMARE!! I'M TELLING YOU GUYS, THIS IS THE END!!
WHAT'S HE PLANNING...?

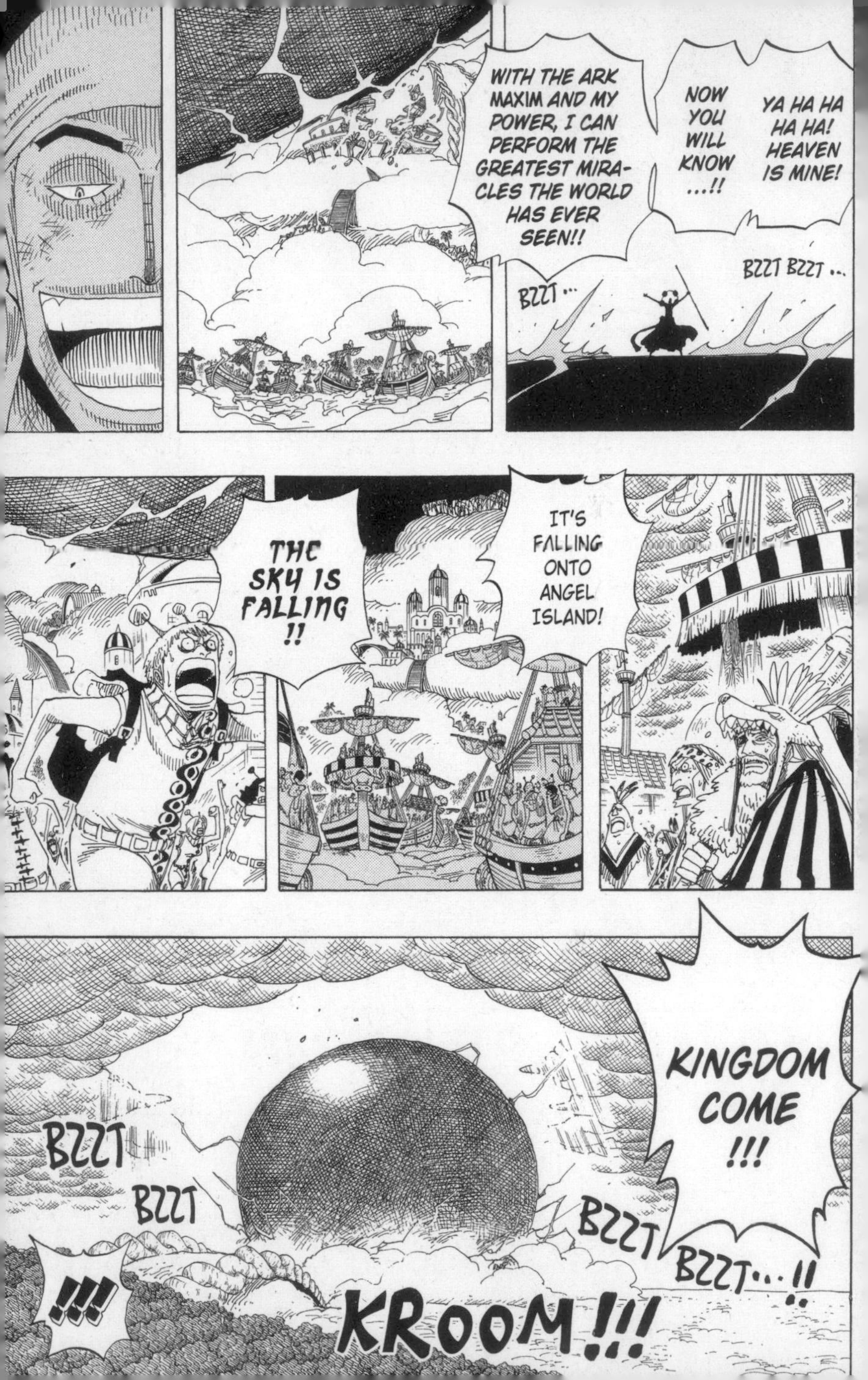
YA HA HA HA HA! HEAVEN IS MINE!
NOW YOU WILL KNOW ...!!
WITH THE ARK MAXIM AND MY POWER, I CAN PERFORM THE GREATEST MIRACLES THE WORLD HAS EVER SEEN!!
BZZT BZZT ...
BZZT ...
IT'S FALLING ONTO ANGEL ISLAND!
THE SKY IS FALLING !!
KINGDOM COME !!!
BZZT
BZZT...!!
BZZT
BZZT
!!!
KROOM!!!

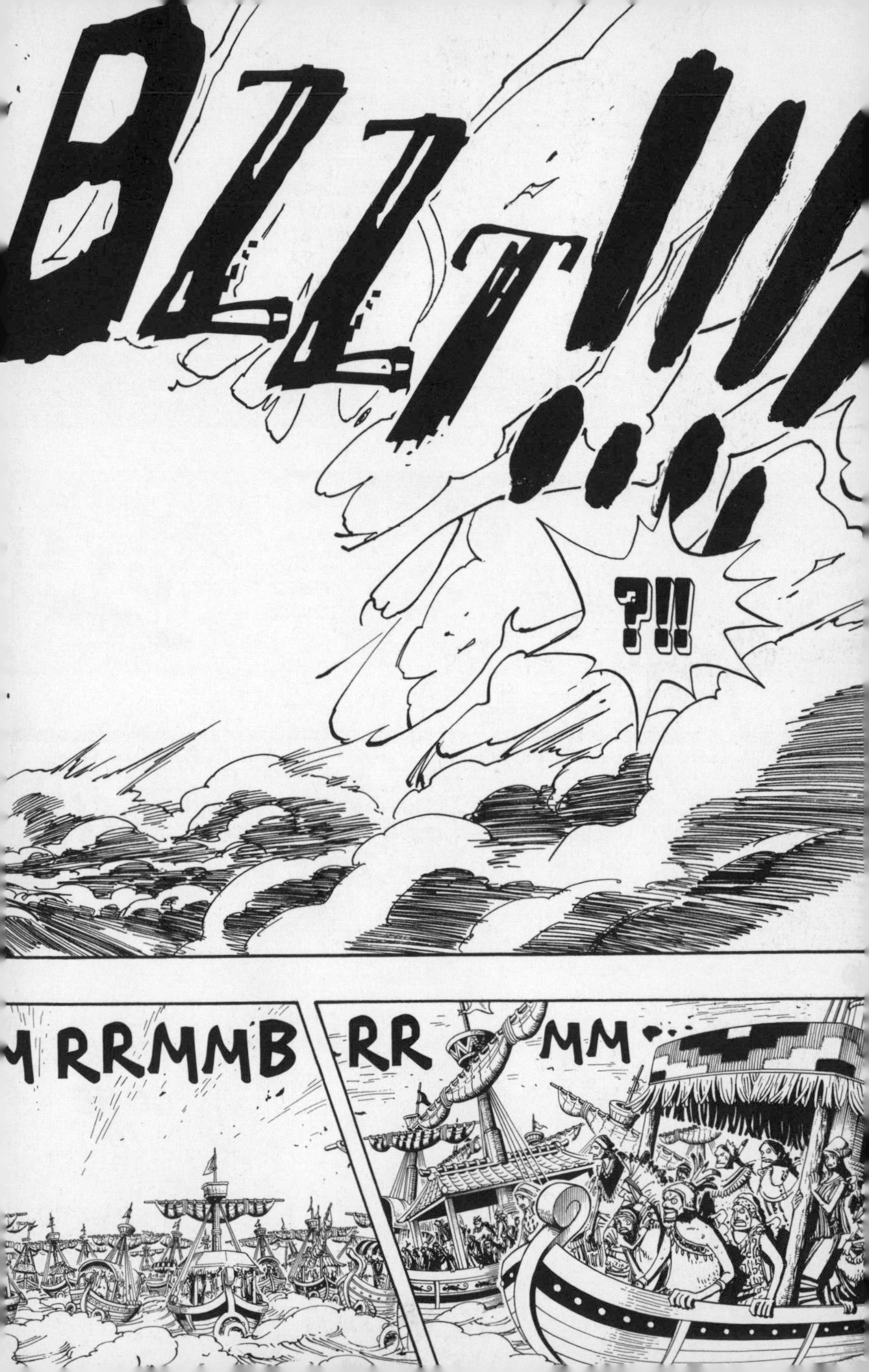
BZZT!!!!
?!!
RR MM
M RRMMB

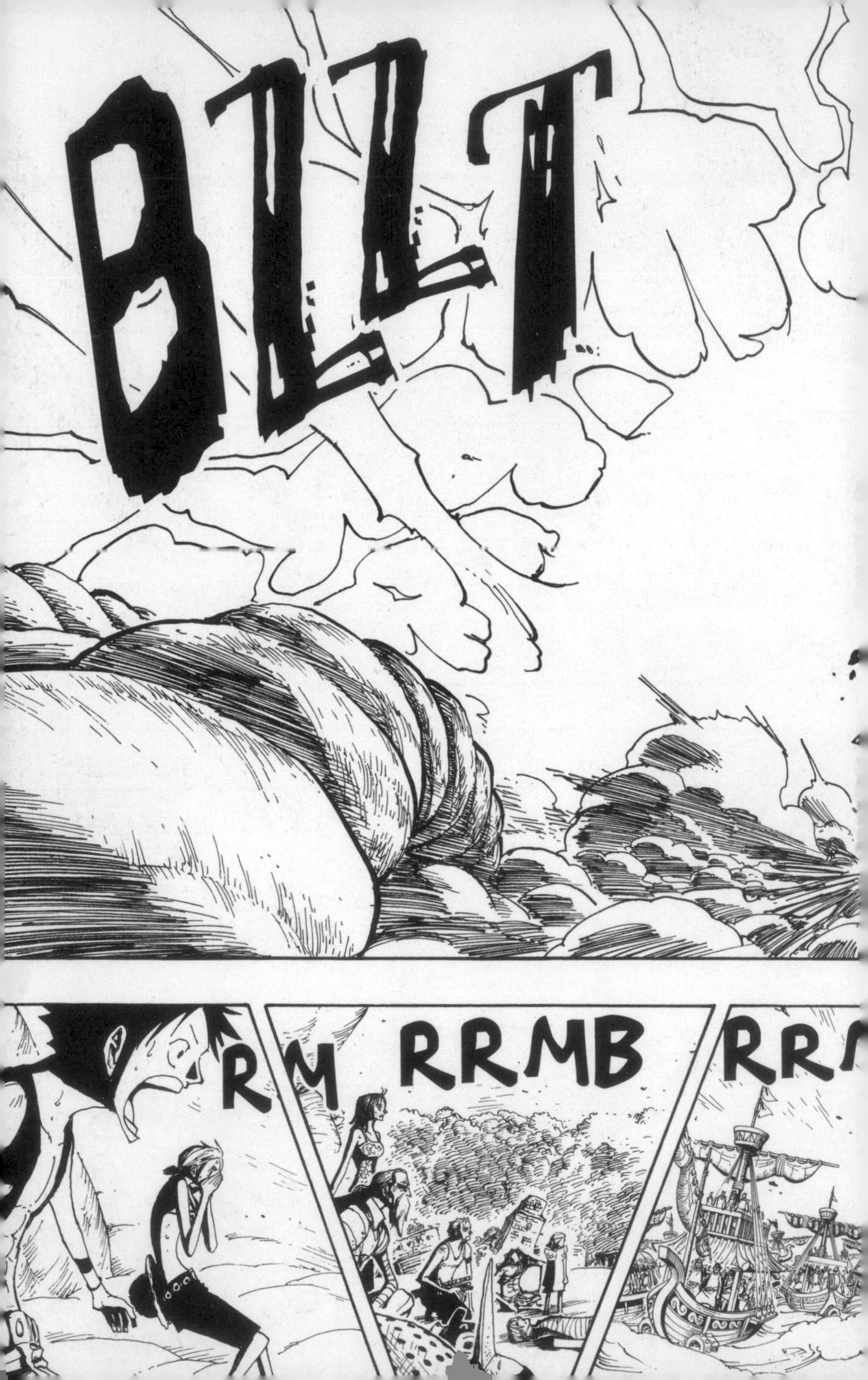
BZZT
RM RRMB RR

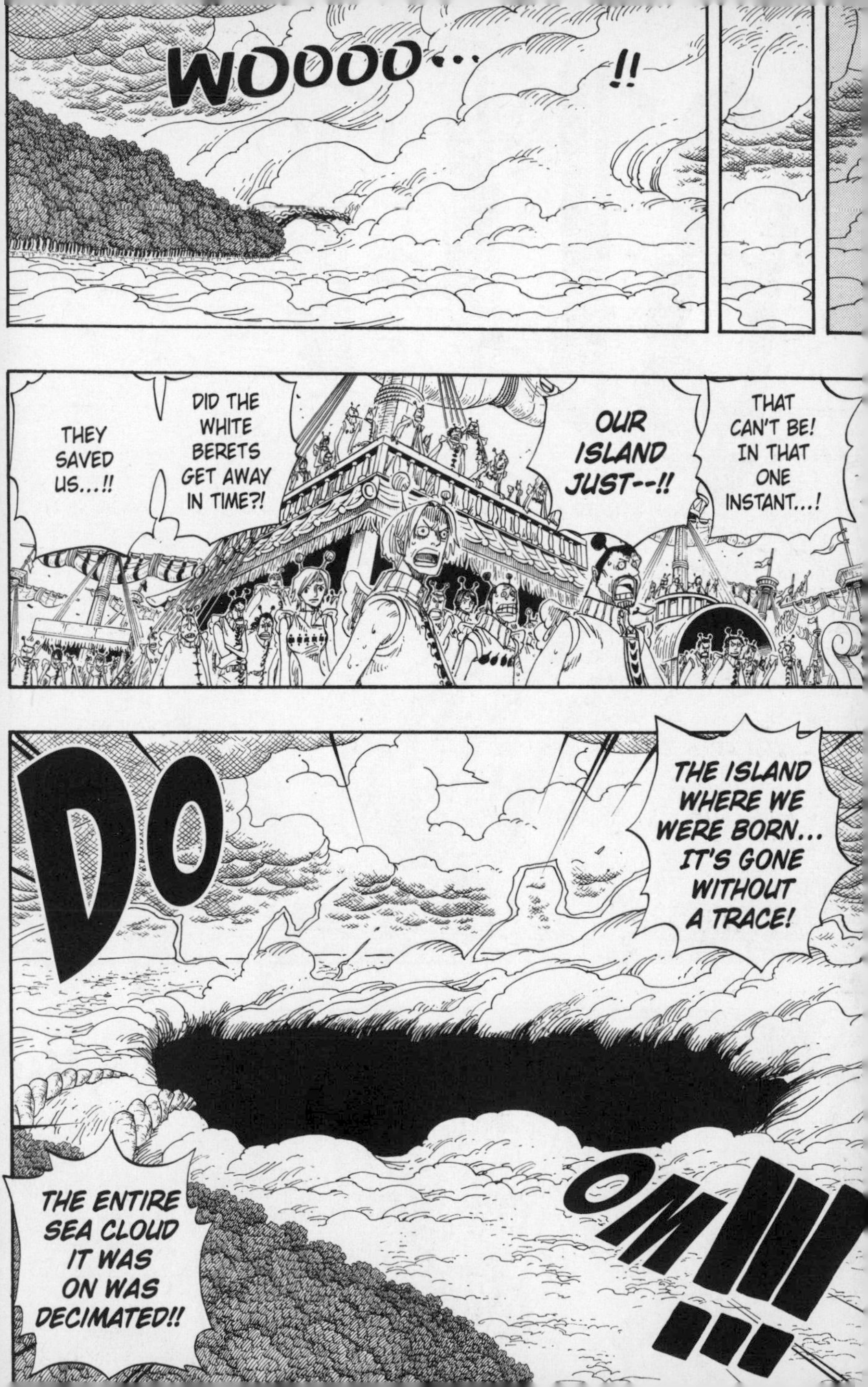
WOOOO...!!
THAT CAN'T BE! IN THAT ONE INSTANT...!
OUR ISLAND JUST--!!
DID THE WHITE BERETS GET AWAY IN TIME?!
THEY SAVED US...!!
THE ISLAND WHERE WE WERE BORN... IT'S GONE WITHOUT A TRACE!
DO
THE ENTIRE SEA CLOUD IT WAS ON WAS DECIMATED!!
OM!!!!!!

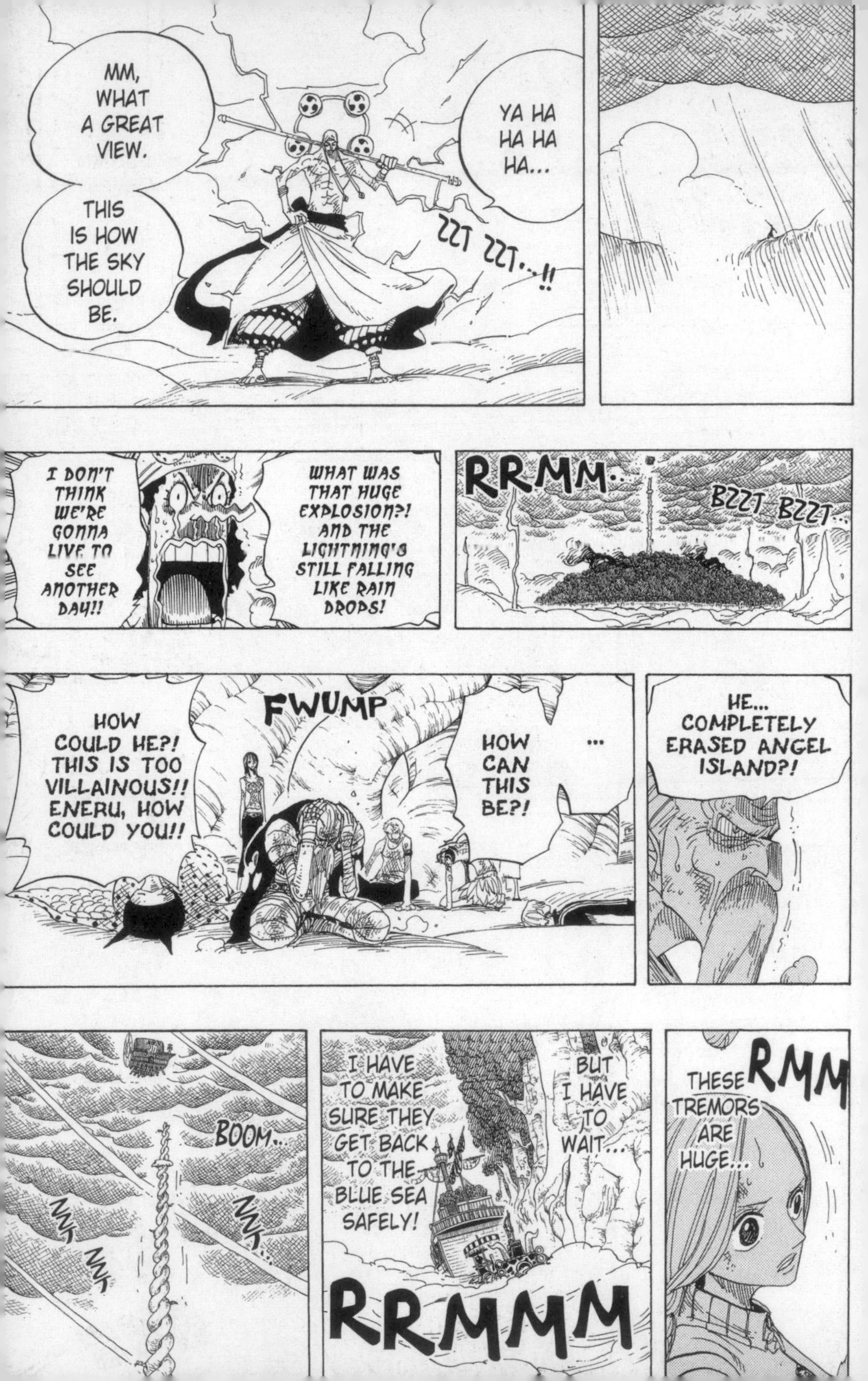
YA HA HA HA HA...
MM, WHAT A GREAT VIEW.
ZZT ZZT...!!
THIS IS HOW THE SKY SHOULD BE.
RRMM...
BZZT BZZT...
WHAT WAS THAT HUGE EXPLOSION?! AND THE LIGHTNING'S STILL FALLING LIKE RAIN DROPS!
I DON'T THINK WE'RE GONNA LIVE TO SEE ANOTHER DAY!!
HE... COMPLETELY ERASED ANGEL ISLAND?!
FWUMP
...
HOW CAN THIS BE?!
HOW COULD HE?! THIS IS TOO VILLAINOUS!! ENERU, HOW COULD YOU!!
RMM
THESE TREMORS ARE HUGE...
BUT I HAVE TO WAIT...
I HAVE TO MAKE SURE THEY GET BACK TO THE BLUE SEA SAFELY!
RRMMMM
BOOM...

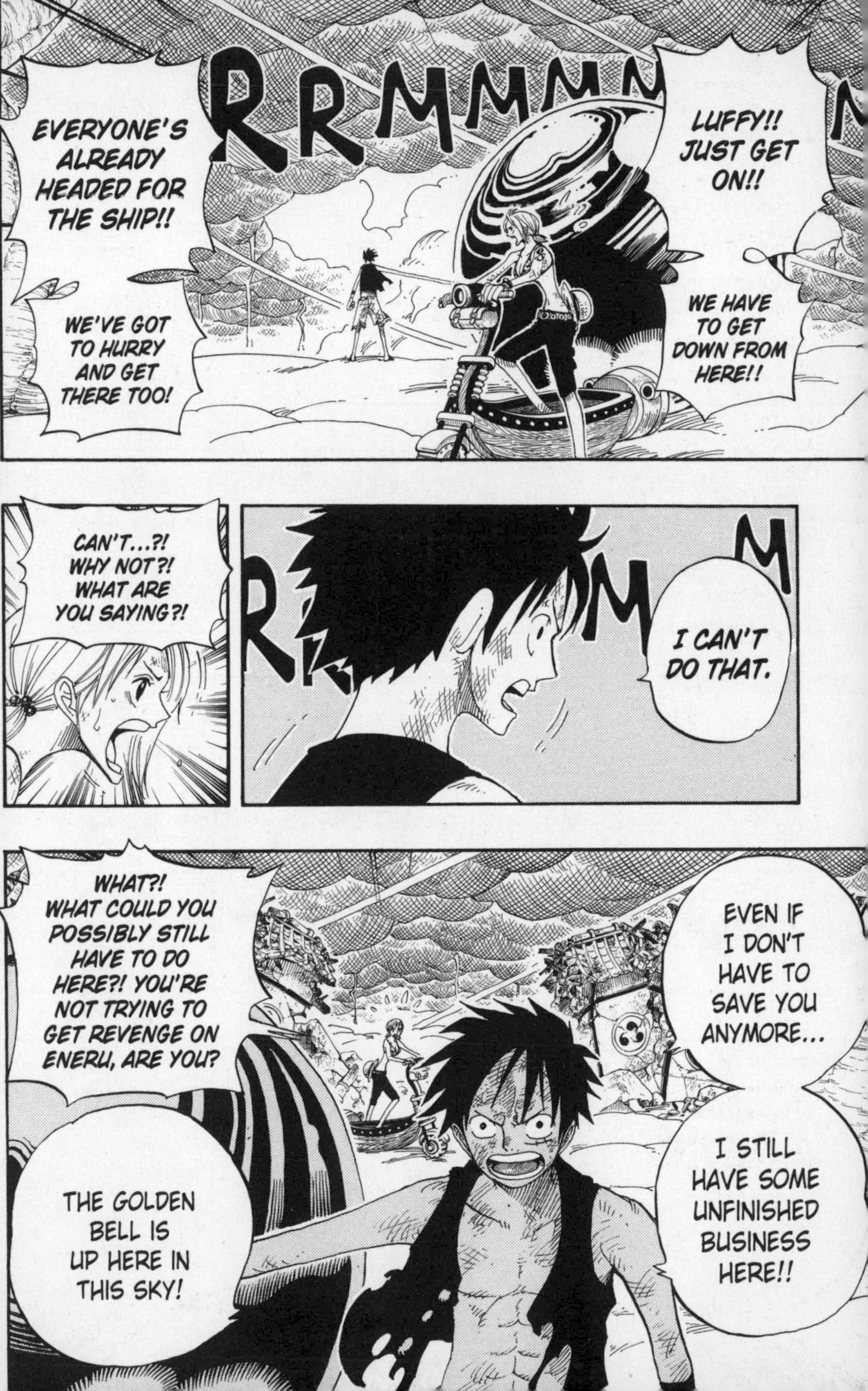
RRMMMMM
LUFFY!! JUST GET ON!!
WE HAVE TO GET DOWN FROM HERE!!
EVERYONE'S ALREADY HEADED FOR THE SHIP!!
WE'VE GOT TO HURRY AND GET THERE TOO!
RMM
I CAN'T DO THAT.
CAN'T...?! WHY NOT?! WHAT ARE YOU SAYING?!
WHAT?! WHAT COULD YOU POSSIBLY STILL HAVE TO DO HERE?! YOU'RE NOT TRYING TO GET REVENGE ON ENERU, ARE YOU?
EVEN IF I DON'T HAVE TO SAVE YOU ANYMORE...
I STILL HAVE SOME UNFINISHED BUSINESS HERE!!
THE GOLDEN BELL IS UP HERE IN THIS SKY!

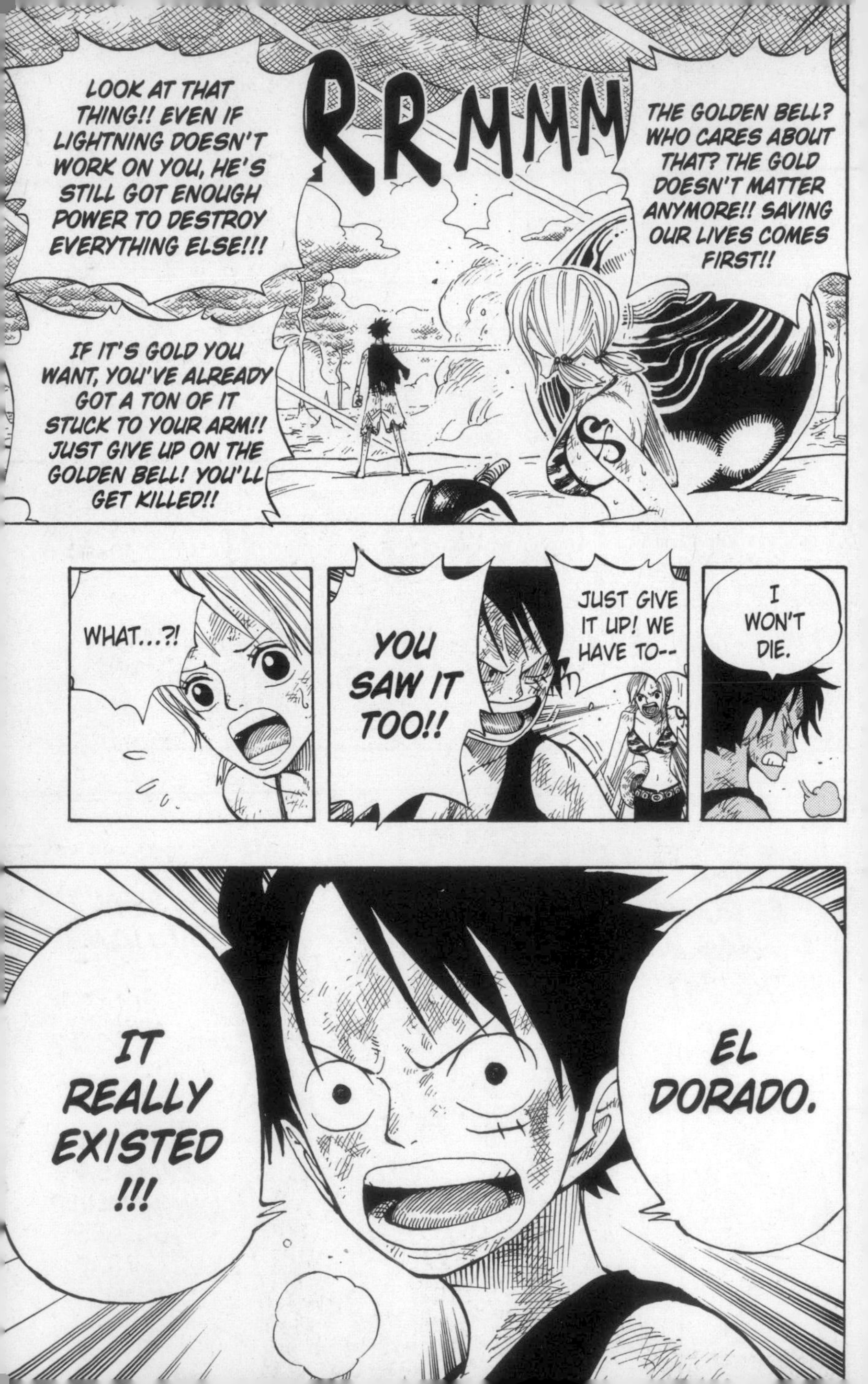
THE GOLDEN BELL? WHO CARES ABOUT THAT? THE GOLD DOESN'T MATTER ANYMORE!! SAVING OUR LIVES COMES FIRST!!
RRMMM
LOOK AT THAT THING!! EVEN IF LIGHTNING DOESN'T WORK ON YOU, HE'S STILL GOT ENOUGH POWER TO DESTROY EVERYTHING ELSE!!!
IF IT'S GOLD YOU WANT, YOU'VE ALREADY GOT A TON OF IT STUCK TO YOUR ARM!! JUST GIVE UP ON THE GOLDEN BELL! YOU'LL GET KILLED!!
I WON'T DIE.
JUST GIVE IT UP! WE HAVE TO--
YOU SAW IT TOO!!
WHAT...?!
EL DORADO.
IT REALLY EXISTED!!!

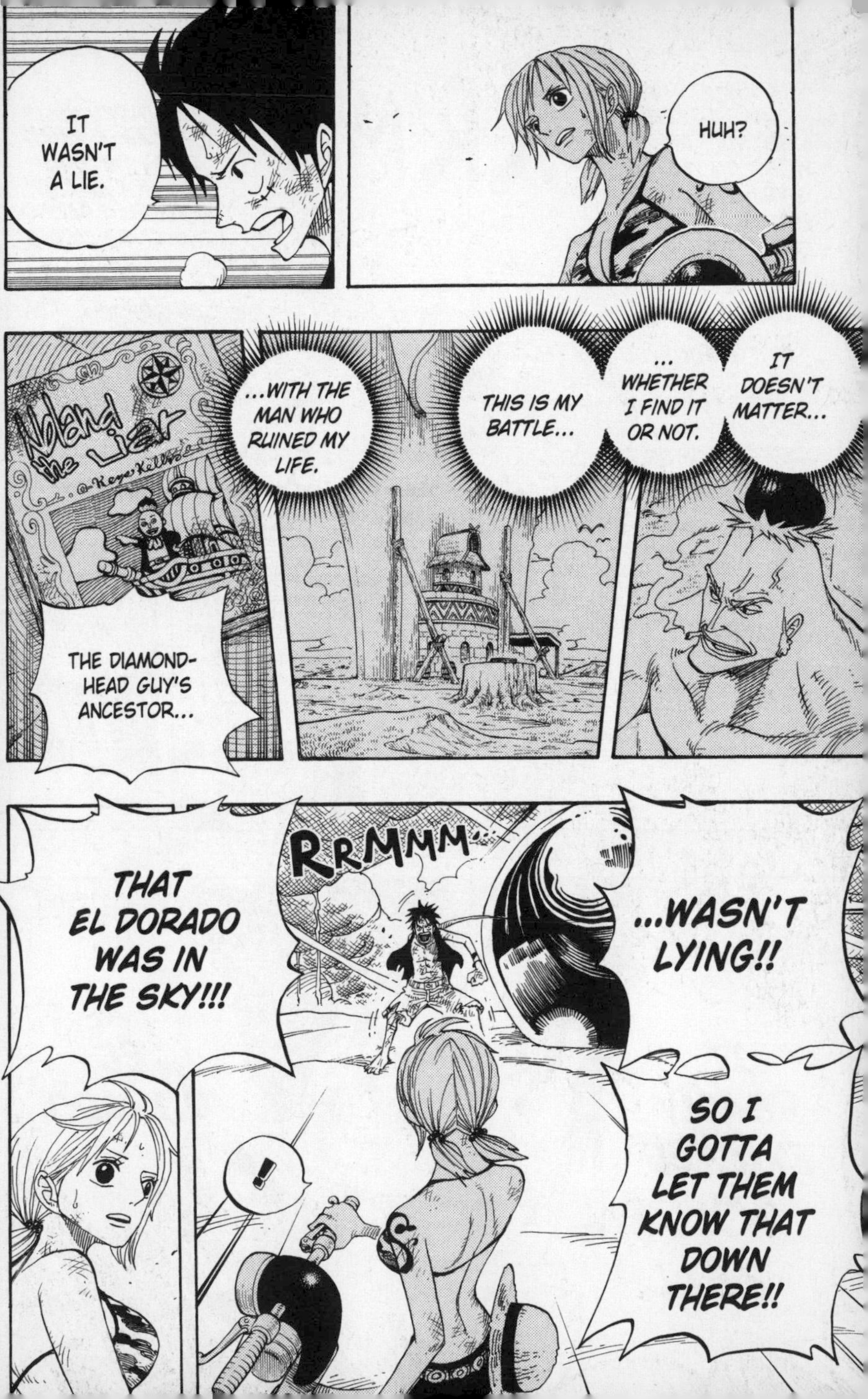
HUH?
IT WASN'T A LIE.
IT DOESN'T MATTER...
...WHETHER I FIND IT OR NOT.
THIS IS MY BATTLE...
...WITH THE MAN WHO RUINED MY LIFE.
Noland the Liar
THE DIAMOND-HEAD GUY'S ANCESTOR...
...WASN'T LYING!!
SO I GOTTA LET THEM KNOW THAT DOWN THERE!!
THAT EL DORADO WAS IN THE SKY!!!
RRMMM
!

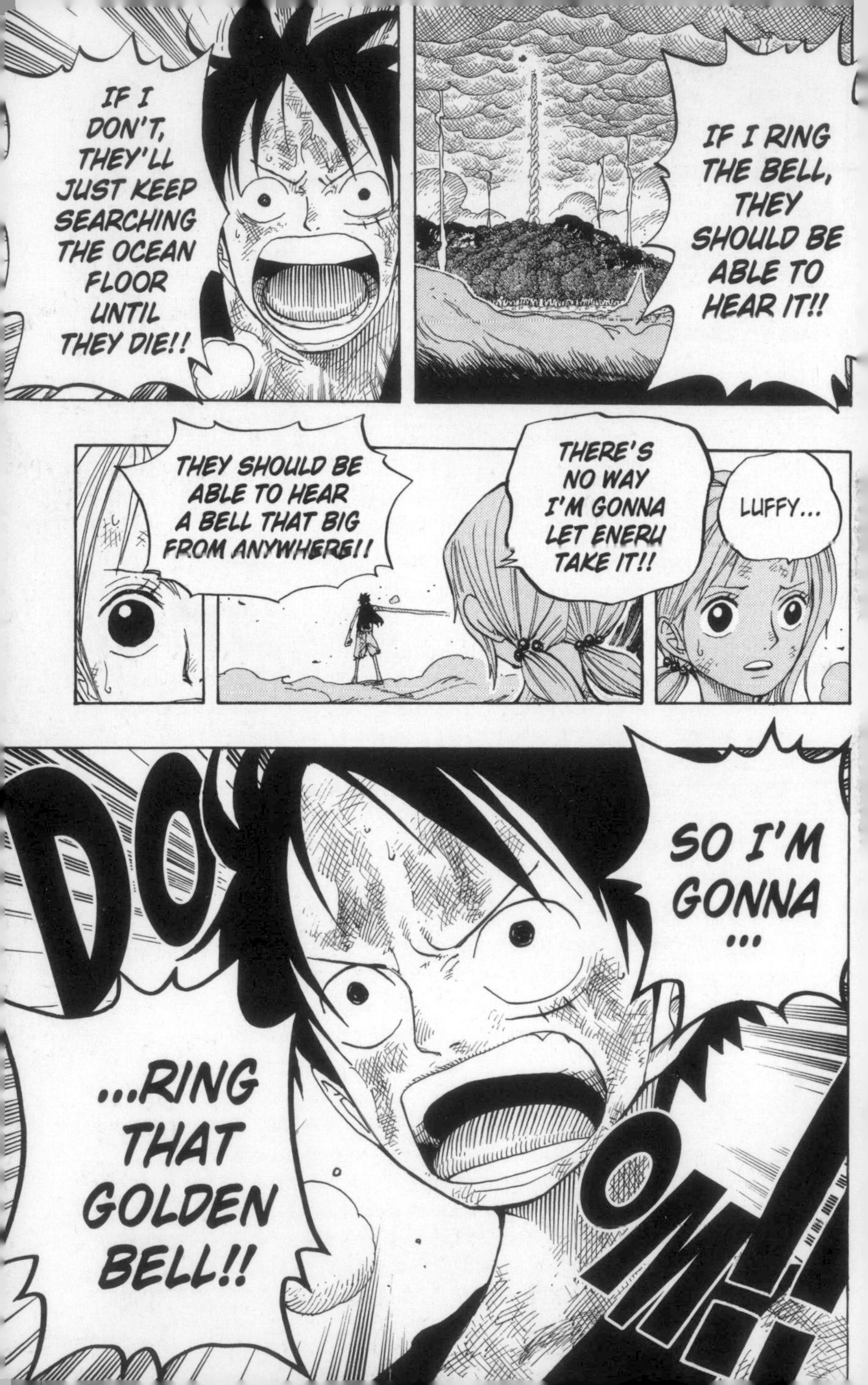
IF I RING THE BELL, THEY SHOULD BE ABLE TO HEAR IT!!
IF I DON'T, THEY'LL JUST KEEP SEARCHING THE OCEAN FLOOR UNTIL THEY DIE!!
LUFFY...
THERE'S NO WAY I'M GONNA LET ENERU TAKE IT!!
THEY SHOULD BE ABLE TO HEAR A BELL THAT BIG FROM ANYWHERE!!
SO I'M GONNA...
...RING THAT GOLDEN BELL!!
DOOM!!

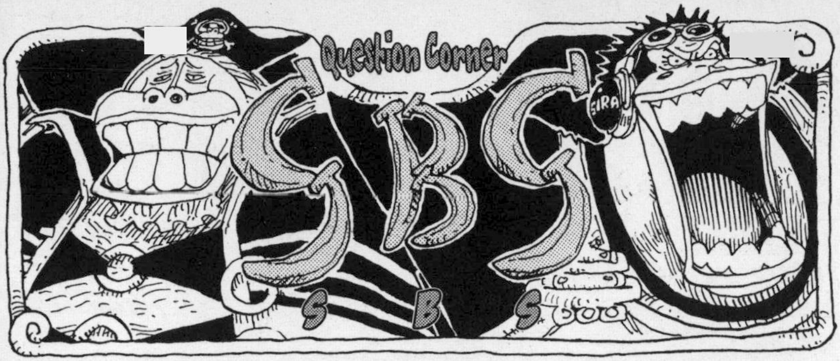
Question Corner
SBS
SIRA
S B S

Q: Hello. My name is Akihiko. This is sudden, but, Oda Sensei, I've found a mistake on page 155 of volume 28! I assume you've gotten a lot of postcards telling you already. I'm sure you're very busy, so I've thought of an answer you can give. The answer is that during the Surprise Dial Illusion, Hotori and Kotori's necks became able to spin around, right?! Ah, yes, it all makes sense now…

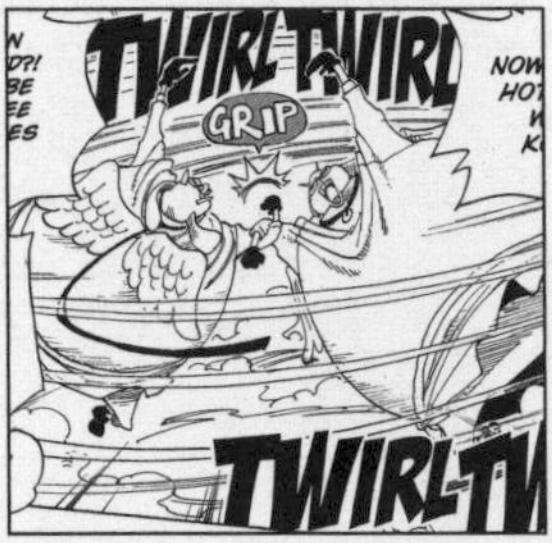
TWIRL TWIRL
GRIP
TWIRL TW

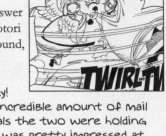

A: Whoa! Akihiko! You're such a nice guy! (I'm so happy!) You're right. I got an incredible amount of mail pointing that out. Somehow, the dials the two were holding got all mixed up (Sorry 'bout that). I was pretty impressed at how carefully people were looking, and at the same time I was trying to figure out what to do. And just as I was thinking I'd ignore it (hey now), there was your postcard. It brought tears to my eyes. Thank you. Good job, Akihiko! Everybody, so that's what happened! (Right...)

Q: Hello, Oda Sensei, it's nice to meet you! Getting right to the point, I've been watching the *One Piece* anime and I've got a question. It's about him… Panda Man! He shows up in the same scenes in the anime as he does in the manga. Does that mean you remind the anime people where he shows up?

A: No, no. I've never mentioned it to them. Actually, even if I don't draw him, he tends to show up. That's just the animators having some fun. I've told the voice actors to play around and ad lib, and except for the important plot points, I'd like them to keep having fun with the story. When they have fun, that emotion communicates itself to the viewers too. And that wraps up the Question Corner. See you in the next volume!!

Chapter 295:
GIANT JACK

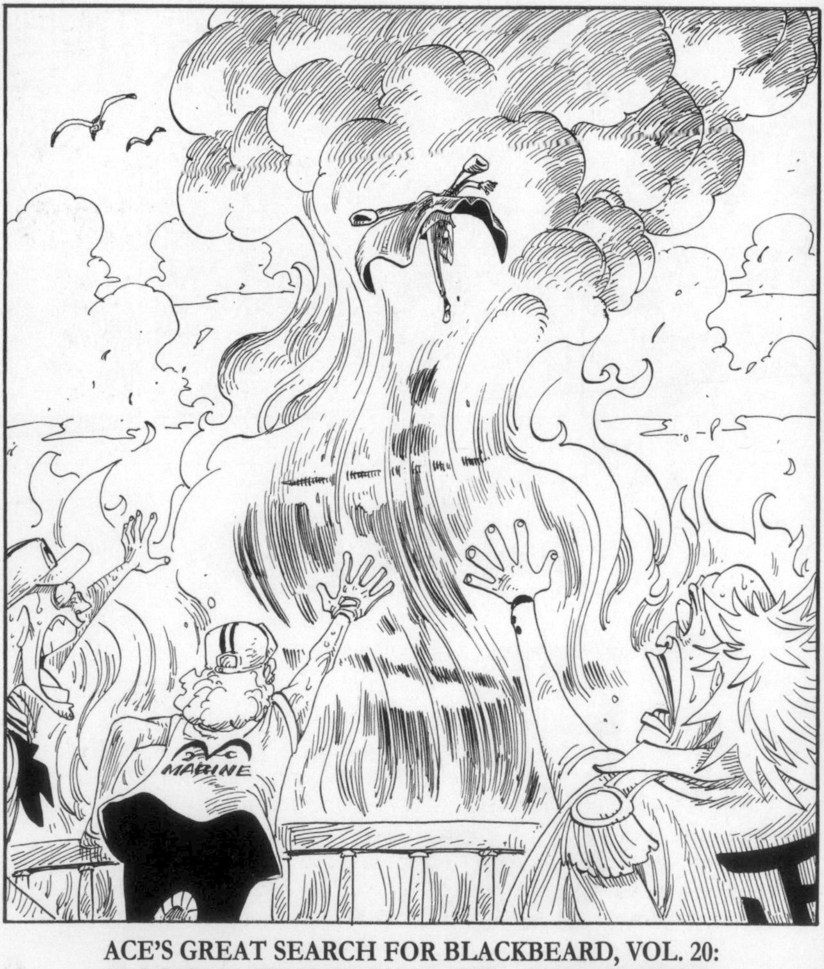
MARINE

ACE'S GREAT SEARCH FOR BLACKBEARD, VOL. 20:
"A LONE NAVY MAN DIVES INTO THE INFERNO"

FWASH!!

RRMMB

NGHHHH!!

...!

MADE IT!!

HUFF...
HUFF...

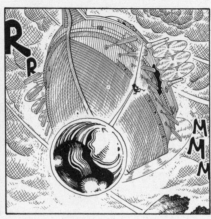

R
R

M
M
M

WHA?!!!

YA HA HA!

ENERU!!

WHO GAVE YOU PERMISSION TO BOARD THIS BOAT, HM?

TUP...

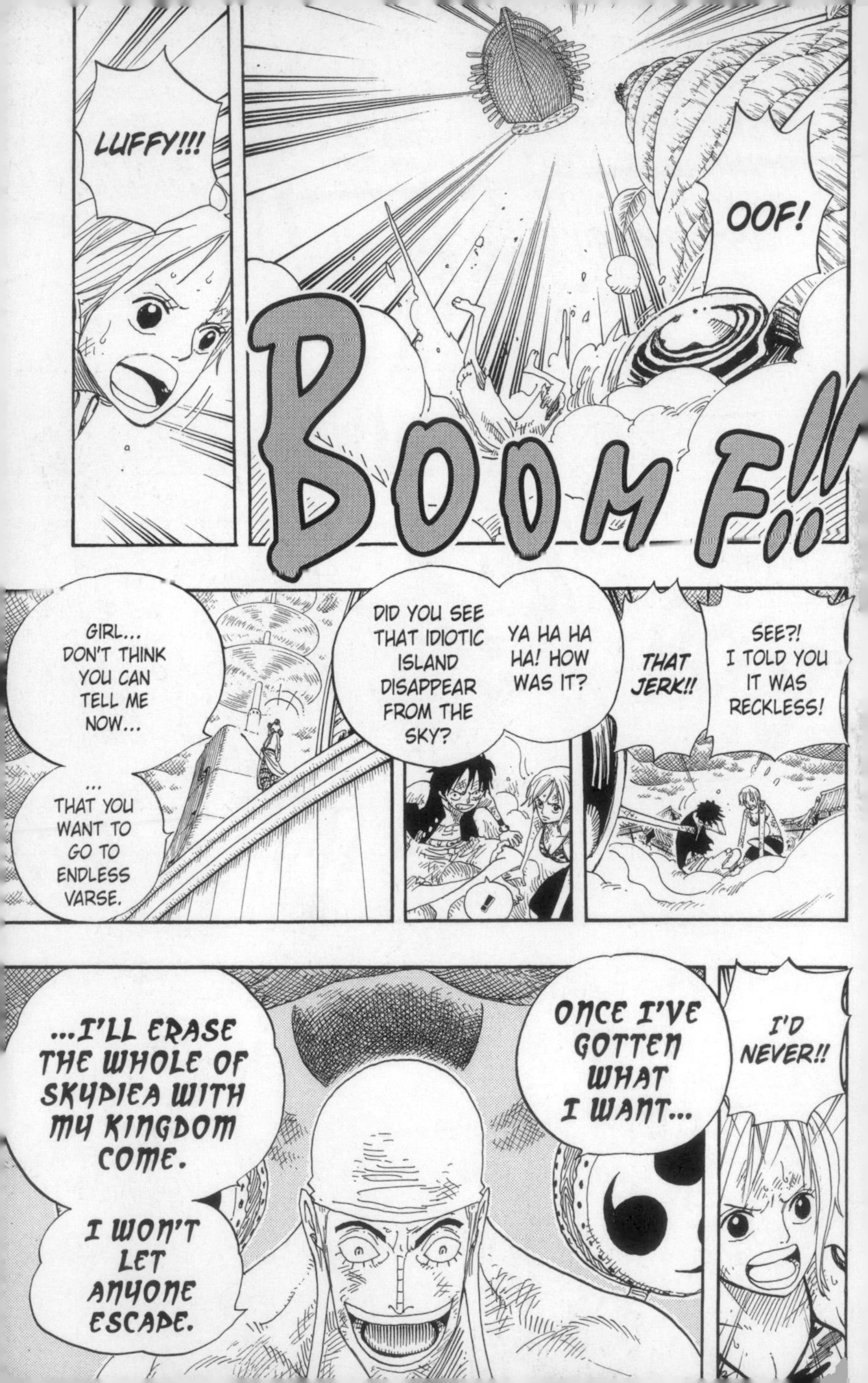
OOF!
BOOMF!!
LUFFY!!!
SEE?! I TOLD YOU IT WAS RECKLESS!
THAT JERK!!
YA HA HA HA! HOW WAS IT?
DID YOU SEE THAT IDIOTIC ISLAND DISAPPEAR FROM THE SKY?
GIRL... DON'T THINK YOU CAN TELL ME NOW...
... THAT YOU WANT TO GO TO ENDLESS VARSE.
I'D NEVER!!
ONCE I'VE GOTTEN WHAT I WANT...
...I'LL ERASE THE WHOLE OF SKYPIEA WITH MY KINGDOM COME.
I WON'T LET ANYONE ESCAPE.

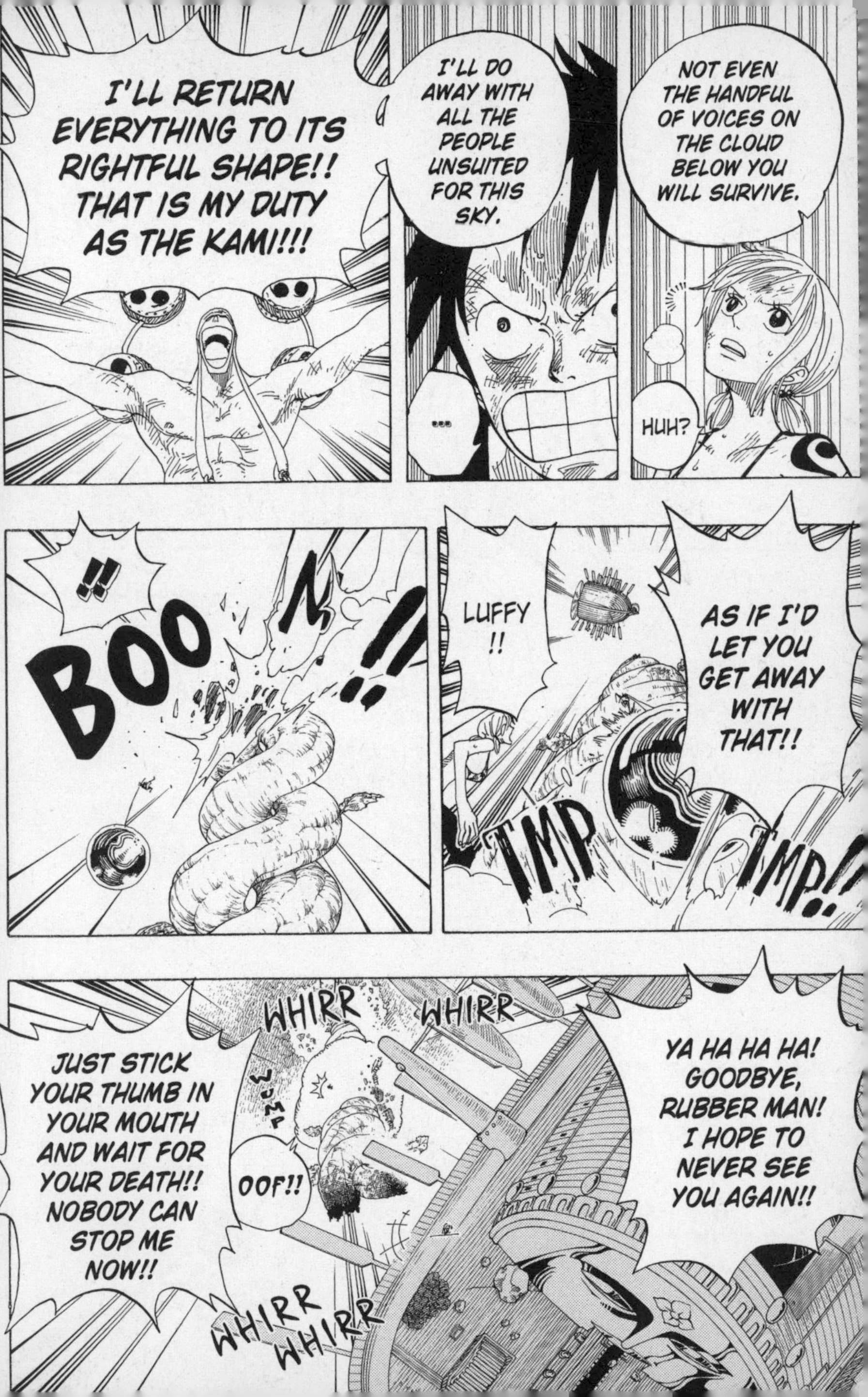
NOT EVEN THE HANDFUL OF VOICES ON THE CLOUD BELOW YOU WILL SURVIVE.
HUH?
I'LL DO AWAY WITH ALL THE PEOPLE UNSUITED FOR THIS SKY.
...
I'LL RETURN EVERYTHING TO ITS RIGHTFUL SHAPE!! THAT IS MY DUTY AS THE KAMI!!!
AS IF I'D LET YOU GET AWAY WITH THAT!!
LUFFY !!
TMP
TMP!!
!!
BOOM!!
YA HA HA HA! GOODBYE, RUBBER MAN! I HOPE TO NEVER SEE YOU AGAIN!!
WHIRR WHIRR
WUMP
OOF!!
JUST STICK YOUR THUMB IN YOUR MOUTH AND WAIT FOR YOUR DEATH!! NOBODY CAN STOP ME NOW!!
WHIRR WHIRR

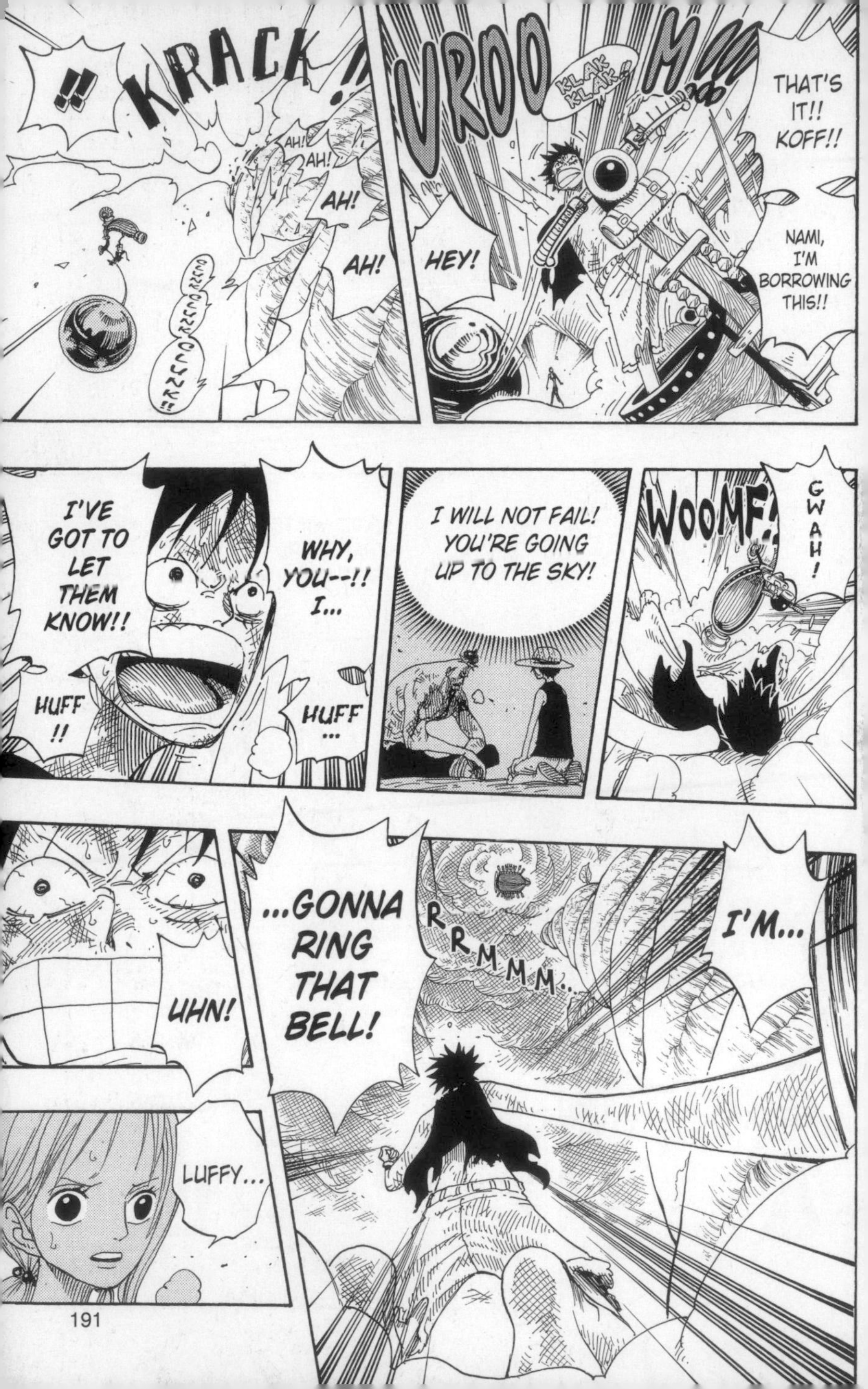
VROOOM!!
KLAK KLAK
THAT'S IT!! KOFF!!
NAMI, I'M BORROWING THIS!!
HEY!
!!
KRACK!!
AH! AH! AH! AH!
CLUNK CLUNK CLUNK!!
WOOMF!
GWAH!
I WILL NOT FAIL! YOU'RE GOING UP TO THE SKY!
WHY, YOU--!! I...
HUFF...
I'VE GOT TO LET THEM KNOW!!
HUFF!!
I'M...
RRRMMM...
...GONNA RING THAT BELL!
UHN!
LUFFY...

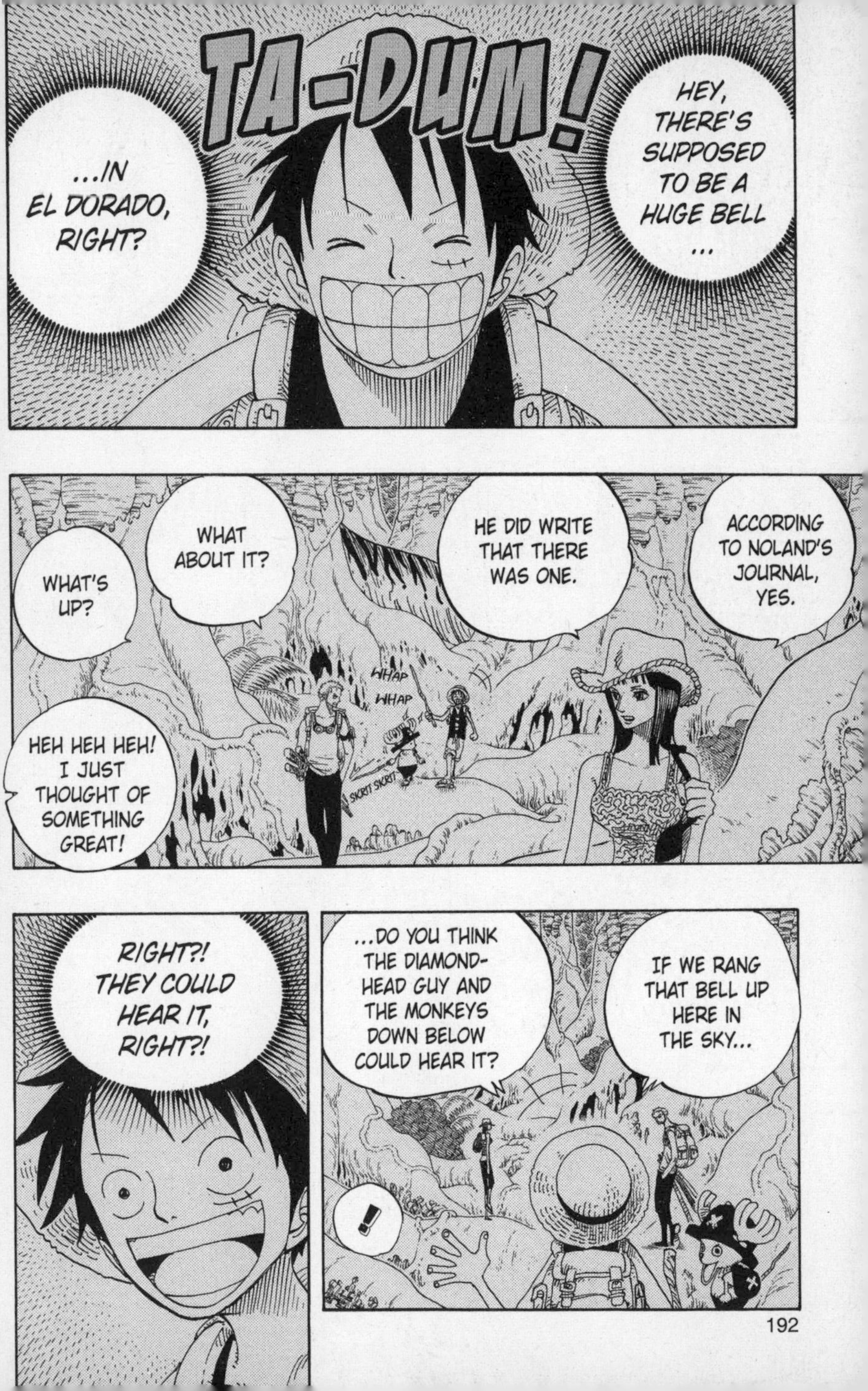
HEY, THERE'S SUPPOSED TO BE A HUGE BELL ...
TA-DUM!
...IN EL DORADO, RIGHT?
ACCORDING TO NOLAND'S JOURNAL, YES.
HE DID WRITE THAT THERE WAS ONE.
WHAT ABOUT IT?
WHAT'S UP?
WHAP WHAP
SKRIT SKRIT
HEH HEH HEH! I JUST THOUGHT OF SOMETHING GREAT!
IF WE RANG THAT BELL UP HERE IN THE SKY...
...DO YOU THINK THE DIAMOND-HEAD GUY AND THE MONKEYS DOWN BELOW COULD HEAR IT?
!
RIGHT?! THEY COULD HEAR IT, RIGHT?!

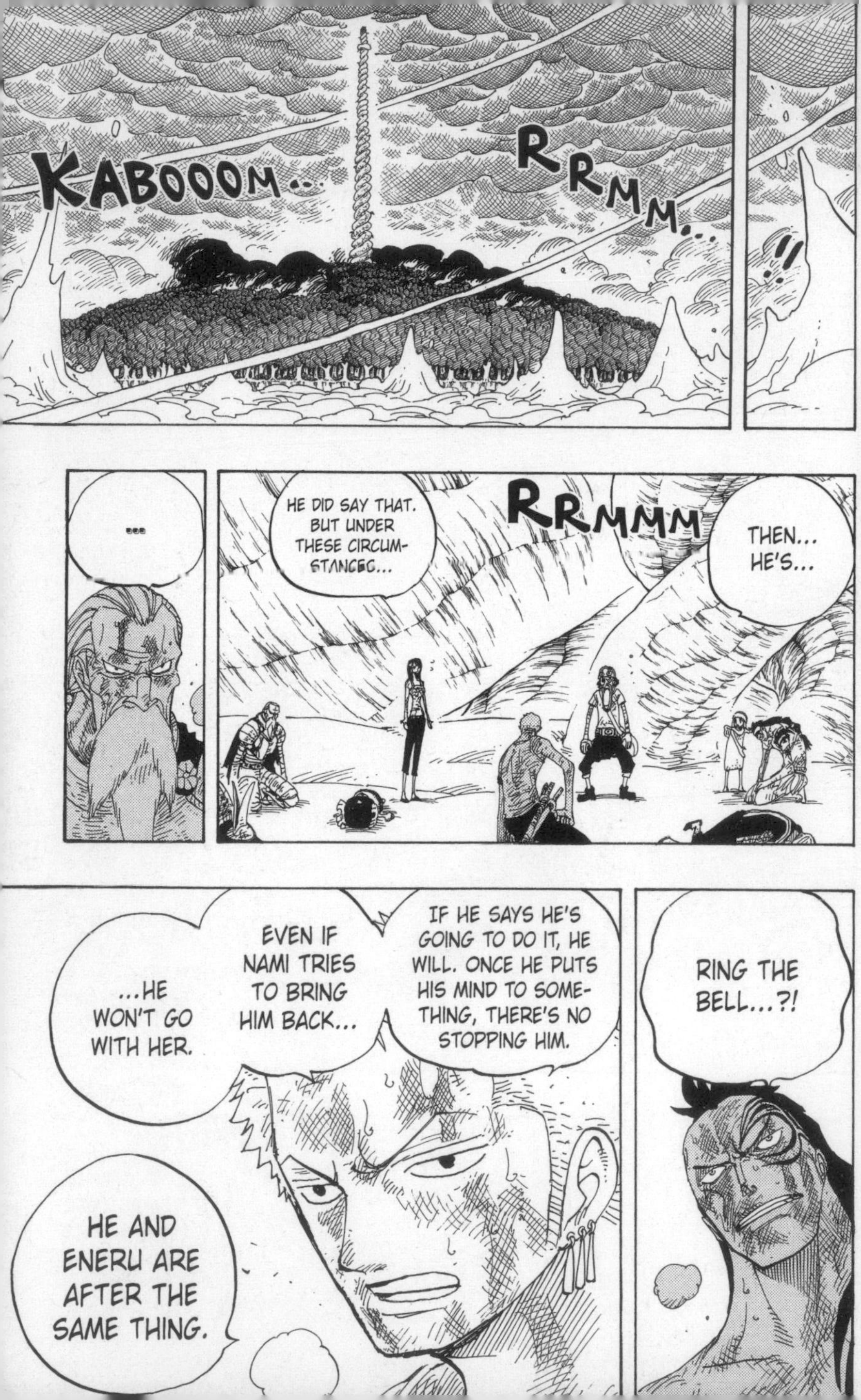
!!
RRMM...
KABOOOM...
THEN... HE'S...
RRMMM
HE DID SAY THAT. BUT UNDER THESE CIRCUM-STANCES...
...
RING THE BELL...?!
IF HE SAYS HE'S GOING TO DO IT, HE WILL. ONCE HE PUTS HIS MIND TO SOME-THING, THERE'S NO STOPPING HIM.
EVEN IF NAMI TRIES TO BRING HIM BACK...
...HE WON'T GO WITH HER.
HE AND ENERU ARE AFTER THE SAME THING.

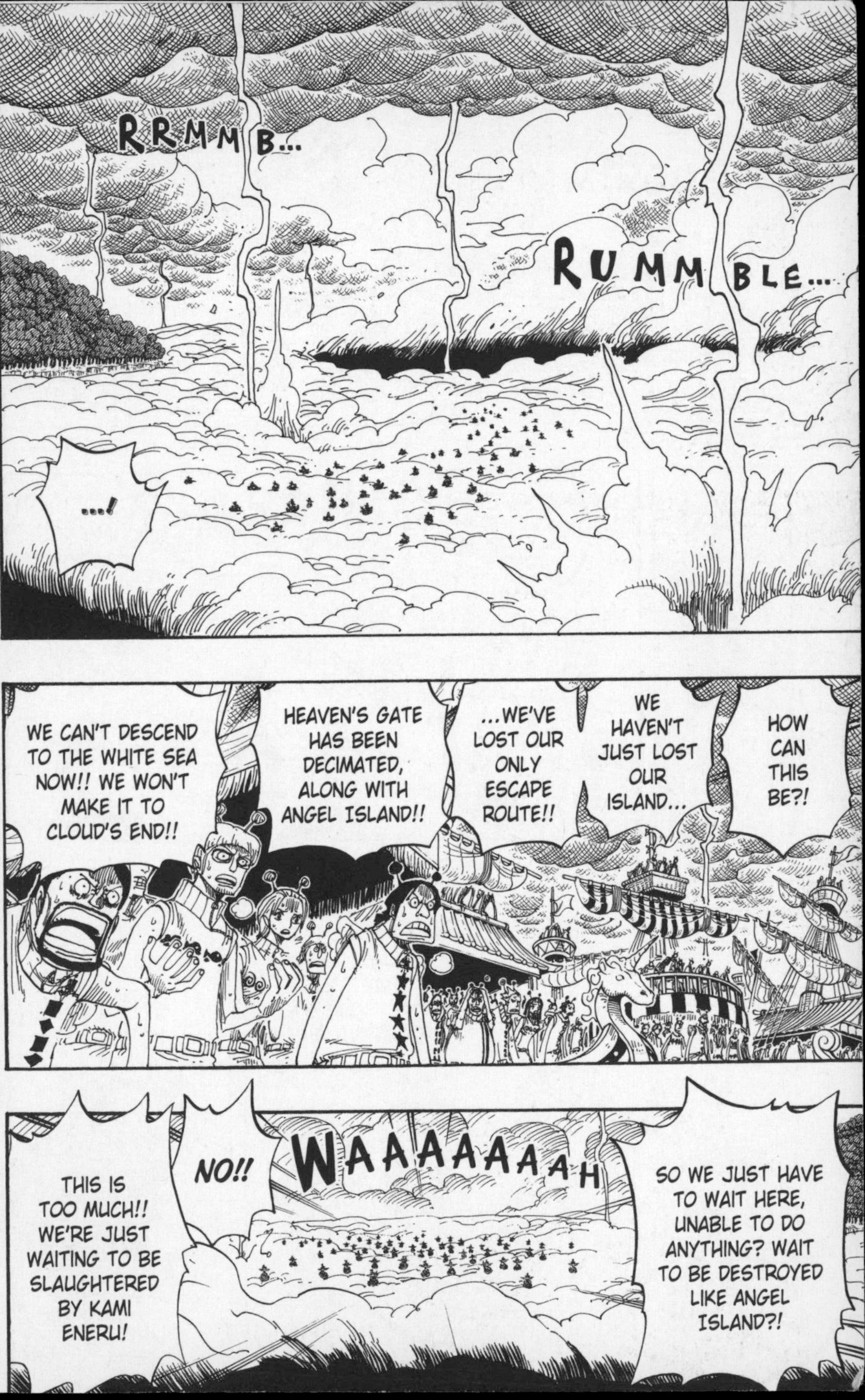
RRMMB...
RUMMBLE...
...!
HOW CAN THIS BE?!
WE HAVEN'T JUST LOST OUR ISLAND...
...WE'VE LOST OUR ONLY ESCAPE ROUTE!!
HEAVEN'S GATE HAS BEEN DECIMATED, ALONG WITH ANGEL ISLAND!!
WE CAN'T DESCEND TO THE WHITE SEA NOW!! WE WON'T MAKE IT TO CLOUD'S END!!
SO WE JUST HAVE TO WAIT HERE, UNABLE TO DO ANYTHING? WAIT TO BE DESTROYED LIKE ANGEL ISLAND?!
WAAAAAAAAH
NO!!
THIS IS TOO MUCH!! WE'RE JUST WAITING TO BE SLAUGHTERED BY KAMI ENERU!

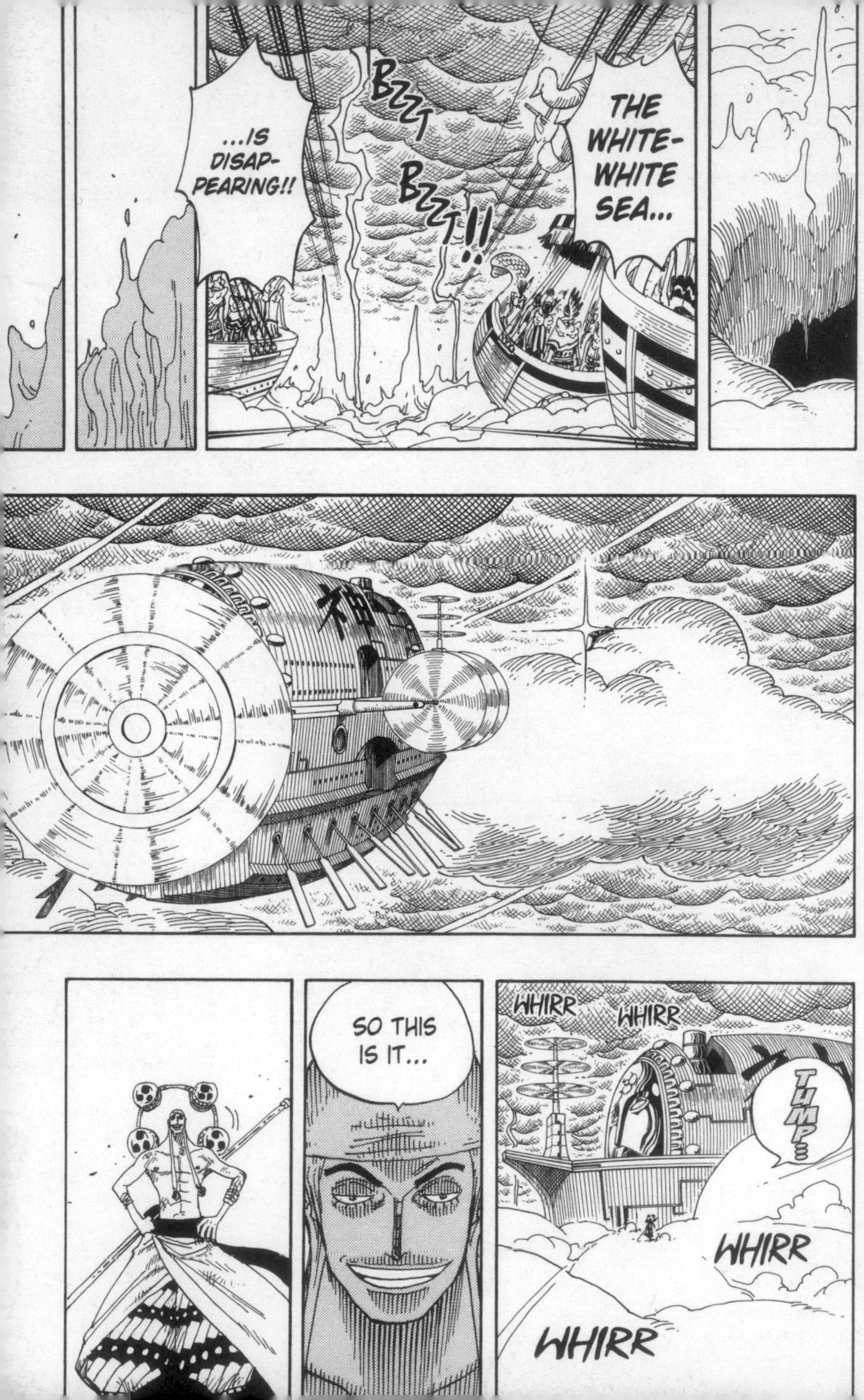
THE WHITE-WHITE SEA...
BZZT
BZZT!!
...IS DISAP-PEARING!!
WHIRR
WHIRR
TUMP!!
WHIRR
WHIRR
SO THIS IS IT...

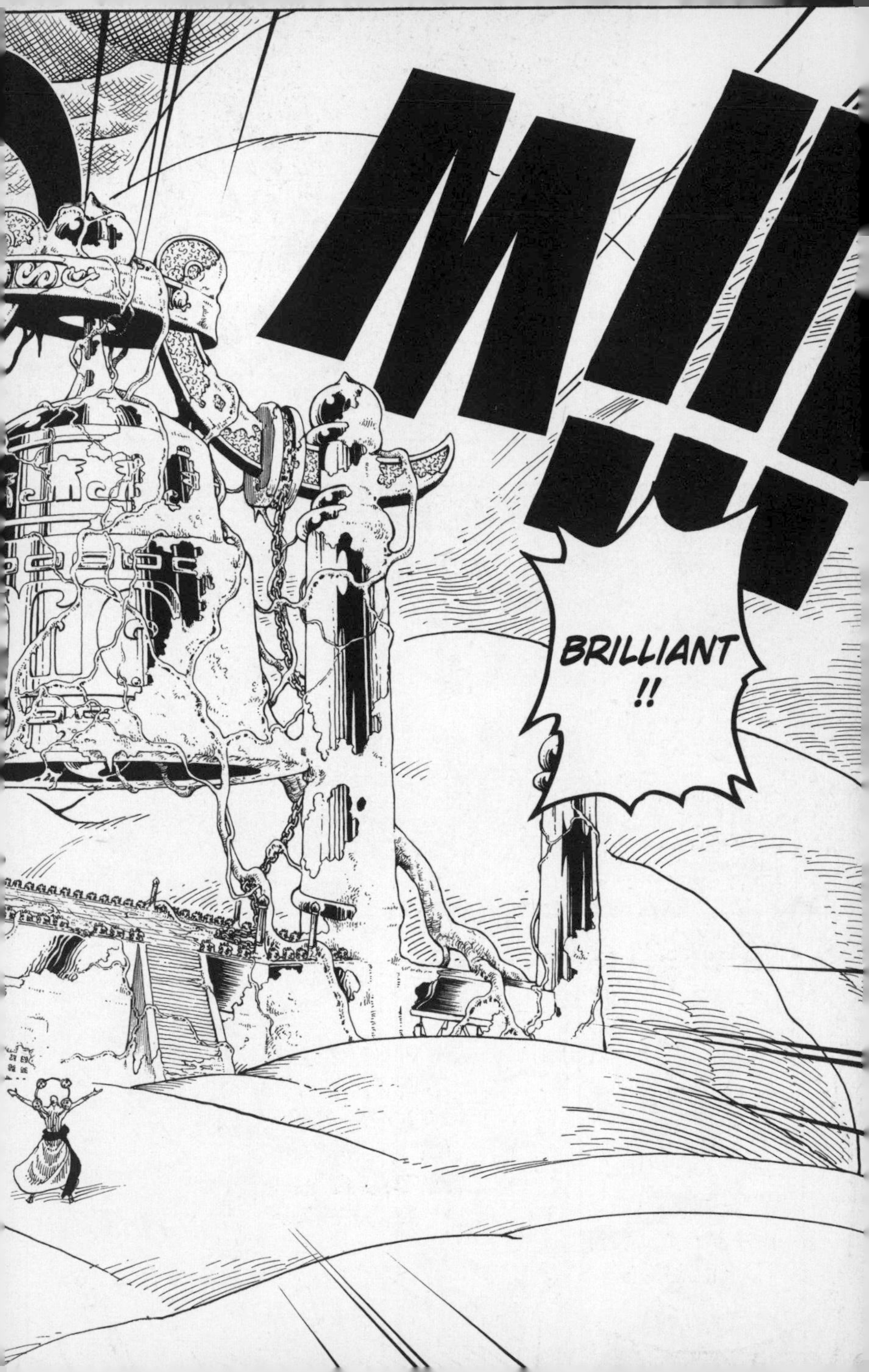
M!!!
BRILLIANT !!

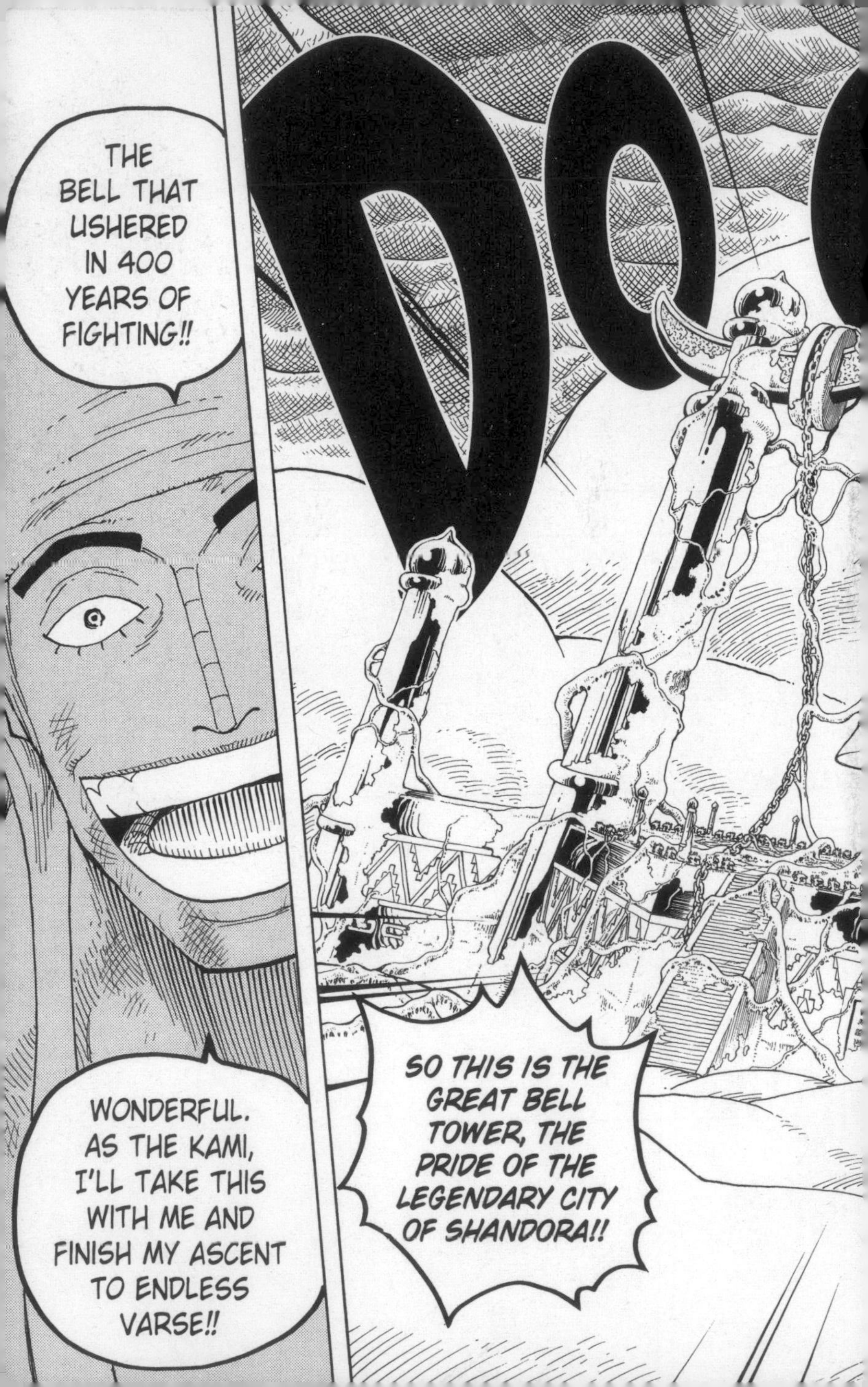
DOO
SO THIS IS THE GREAT BELL TOWER, THE PRIDE OF THE LEGENDARY CITY OF SHANDORA!!
THE BELL THAT USHERED IN 400 YEARS OF FIGHTING!!
WONDERFUL. AS THE KAMI, I'LL TAKE THIS WITH ME AND FINISH MY ASCENT TO ENDLESS VARSE!!

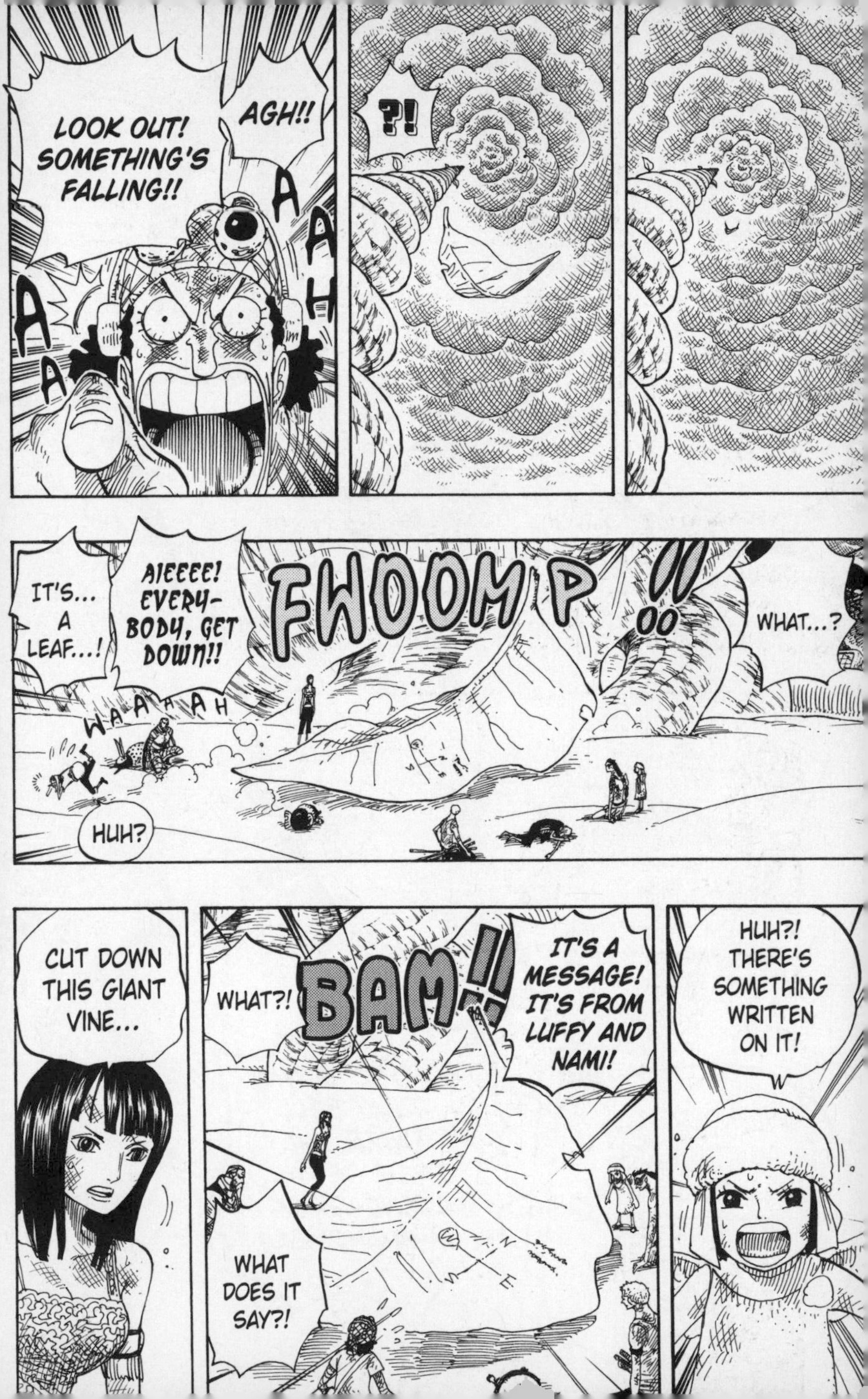
?!
AGH!!
LOOK OUT! SOMETHING'S FALLING!!
AAAH
AAA
WHAT...?
FWOOMP!!
AIEEEE! EVERYBODY, GET DOWN!!
IT'S... A LEAF...!
WAAAAH
HUH?
HUH?! THERE'S SOMETHING WRITTEN ON IT!
IT'S A MESSAGE! IT'S FROM LUFFY AND NAMI!
BAM!!
WHAT?!
WHAT DOES IT SAY?!
CUT DOWN THIS GIANT VINE...

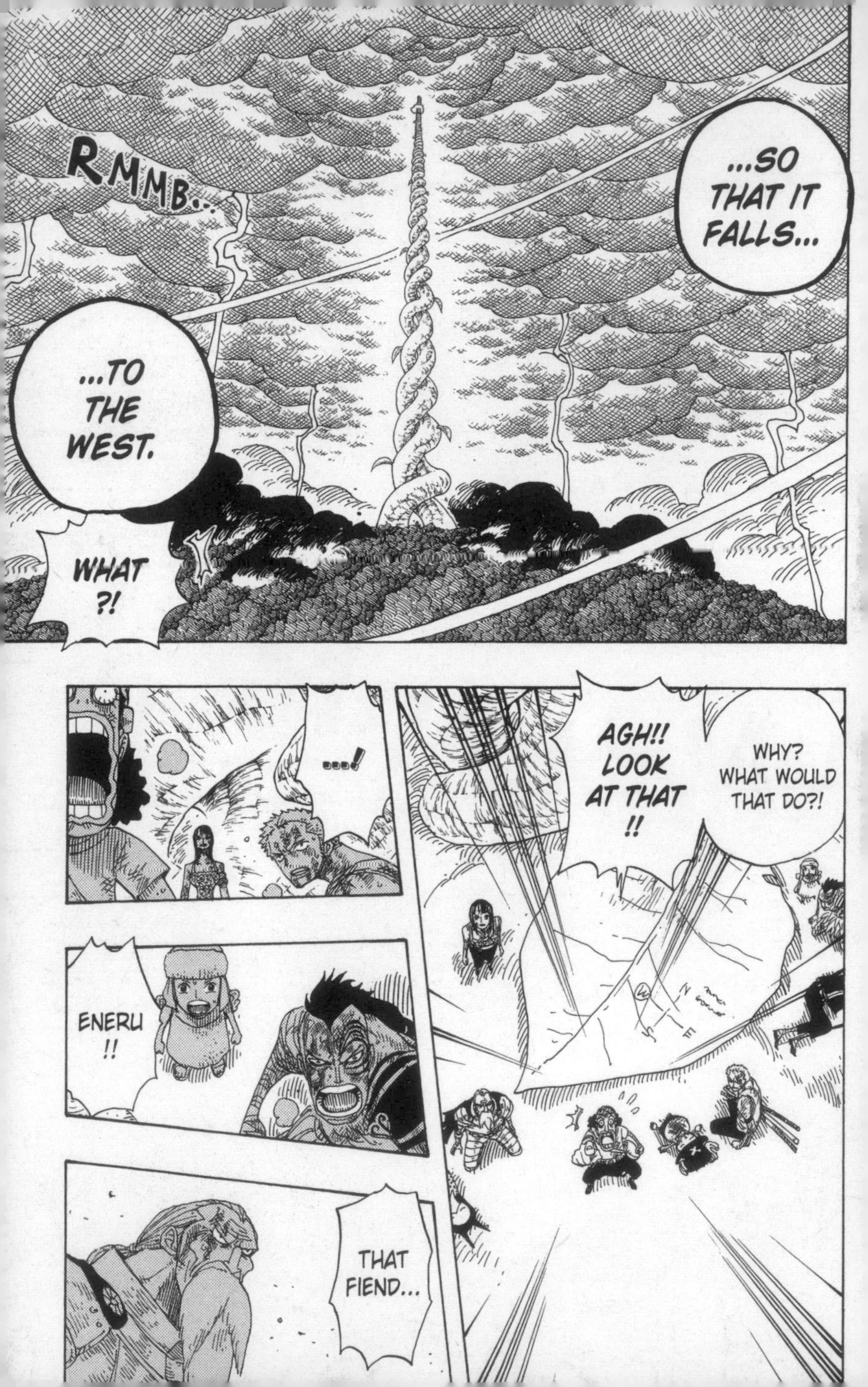
...SO THAT IT FALLS...
RMMB...
...TO THE WEST.
WHAT ?!
WHY? WHAT WOULD THAT DO?!
AGH!! LOOK AT THAT !!
...!
ENERU !!
THAT FIEND...

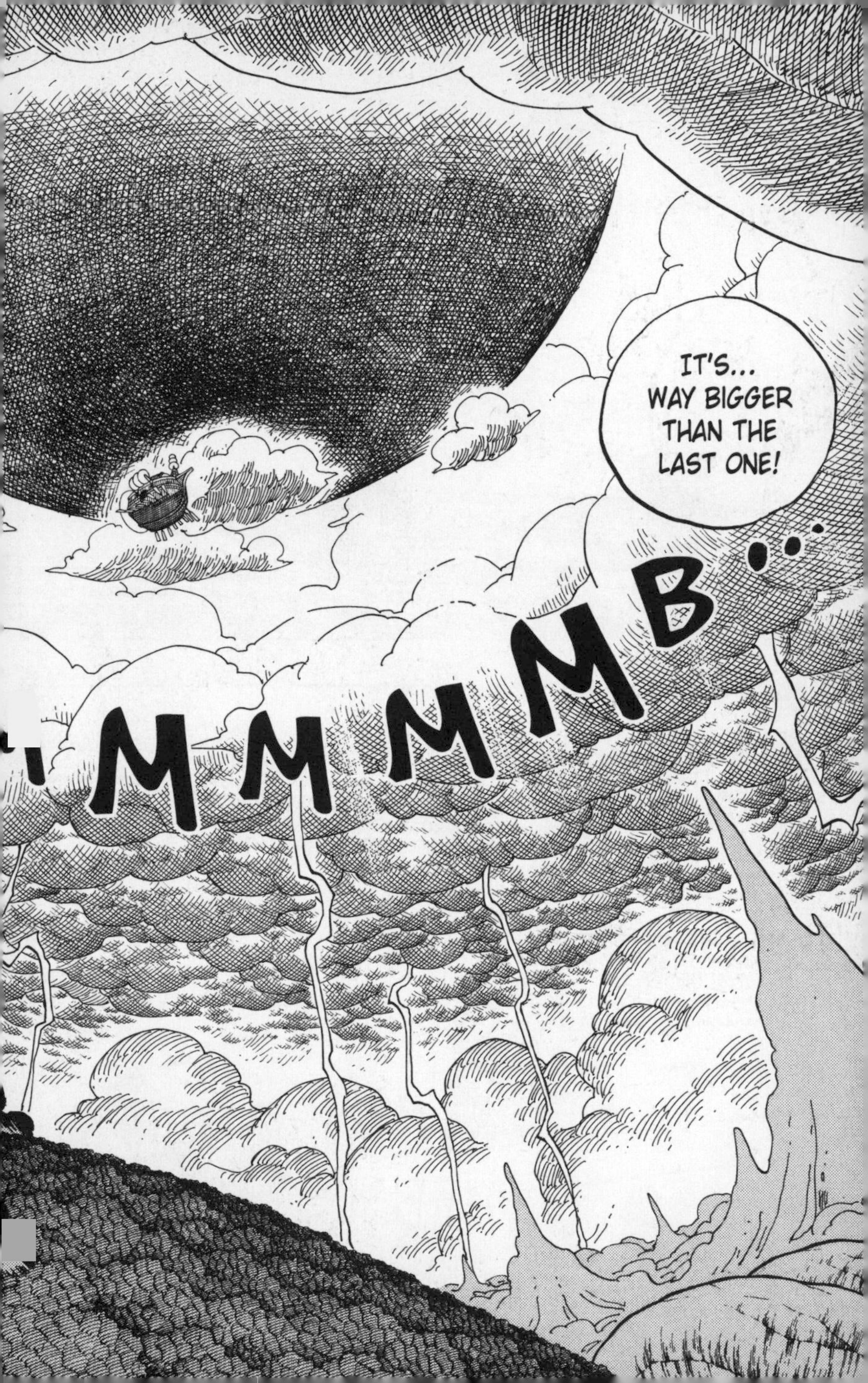
IT'S... WAY BIGGER THAN THE LAST ONE!
MMMMMB

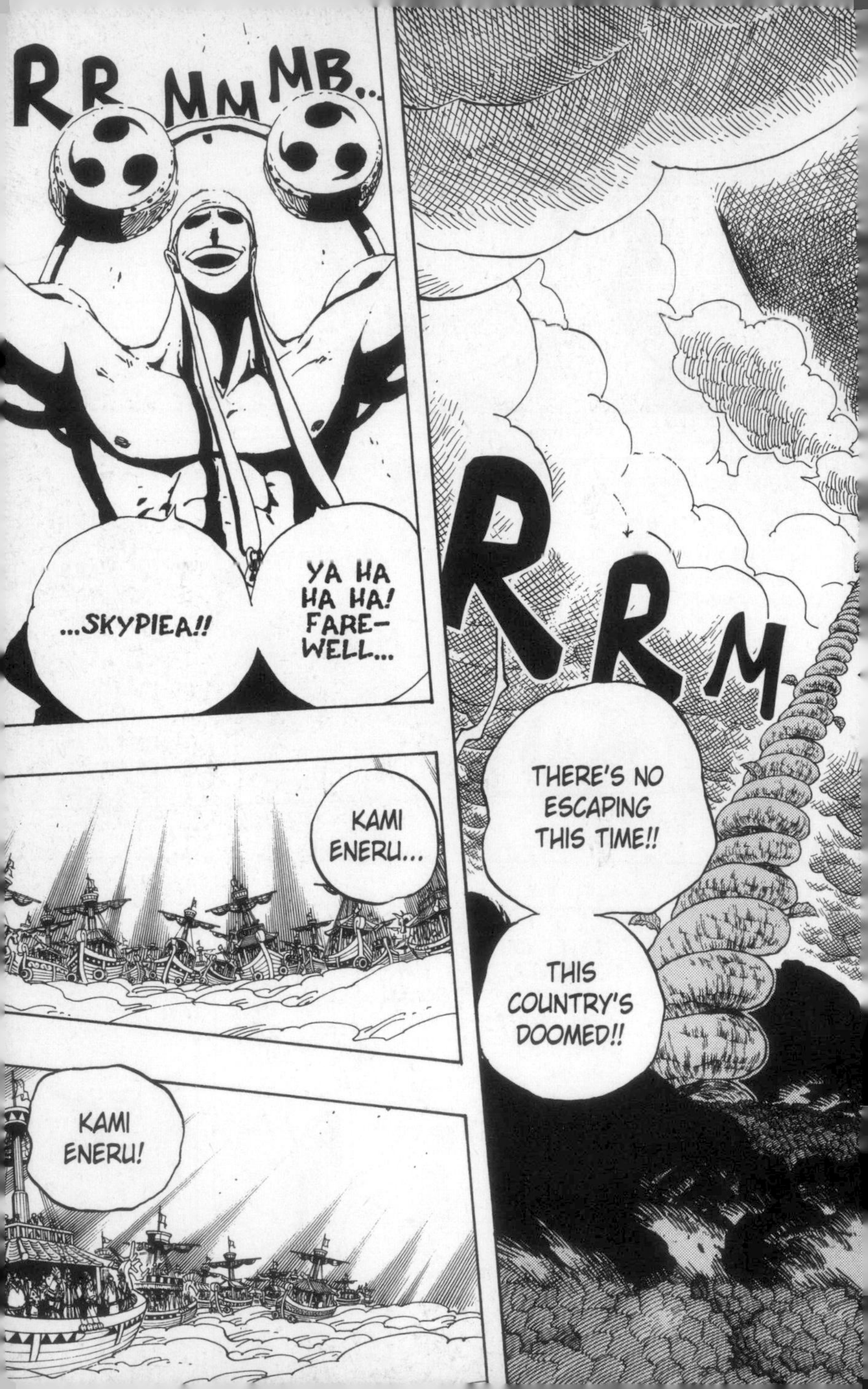
RRRM
THERE'S NO ESCAPING THIS TIME!!
THIS COUNTRY'S DOOMED!!
RRNNMB...
YA HA HA HA! FARE-WELL...
...SKYPIEA!!
KAMI ENERU...
KAMI ENERU!

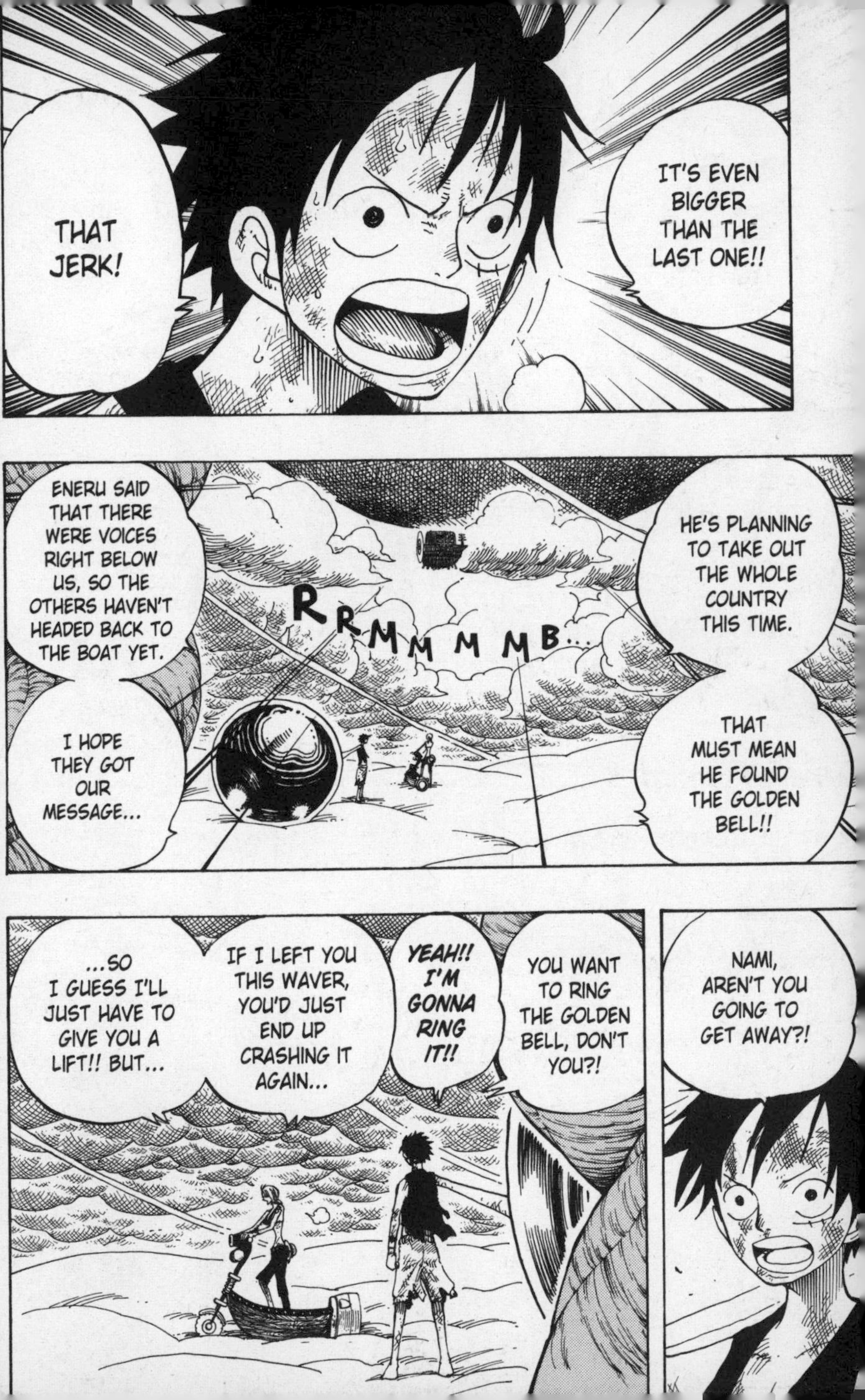
IT'S EVEN BIGGER THAN THE LAST ONE!!
THAT JERK!
HE'S PLANNING TO TAKE OUT THE WHOLE COUNTRY THIS TIME.
THAT MUST MEAN HE FOUND THE GOLDEN BELL!!
RRMMMMB...
ENERU SAID THAT THERE WERE VOICES RIGHT BELOW US, SO THE OTHERS HAVEN'T HEADED BACK TO THE BOAT YET.
I HOPE THEY GOT OUR MESSAGE...
NAMI, AREN'T YOU GOING TO GET AWAY?!
YOU WANT TO RING THE GOLDEN BELL, DON'T YOU?!
YEAH!! I'M GONNA RING IT!!
IF I LEFT YOU THIS WAVER, YOU'D JUST END UP CRASHING IT AGAIN...
...SO I GUESS I'LL JUST HAVE TO GIVE YOU A LIFT!! BUT...

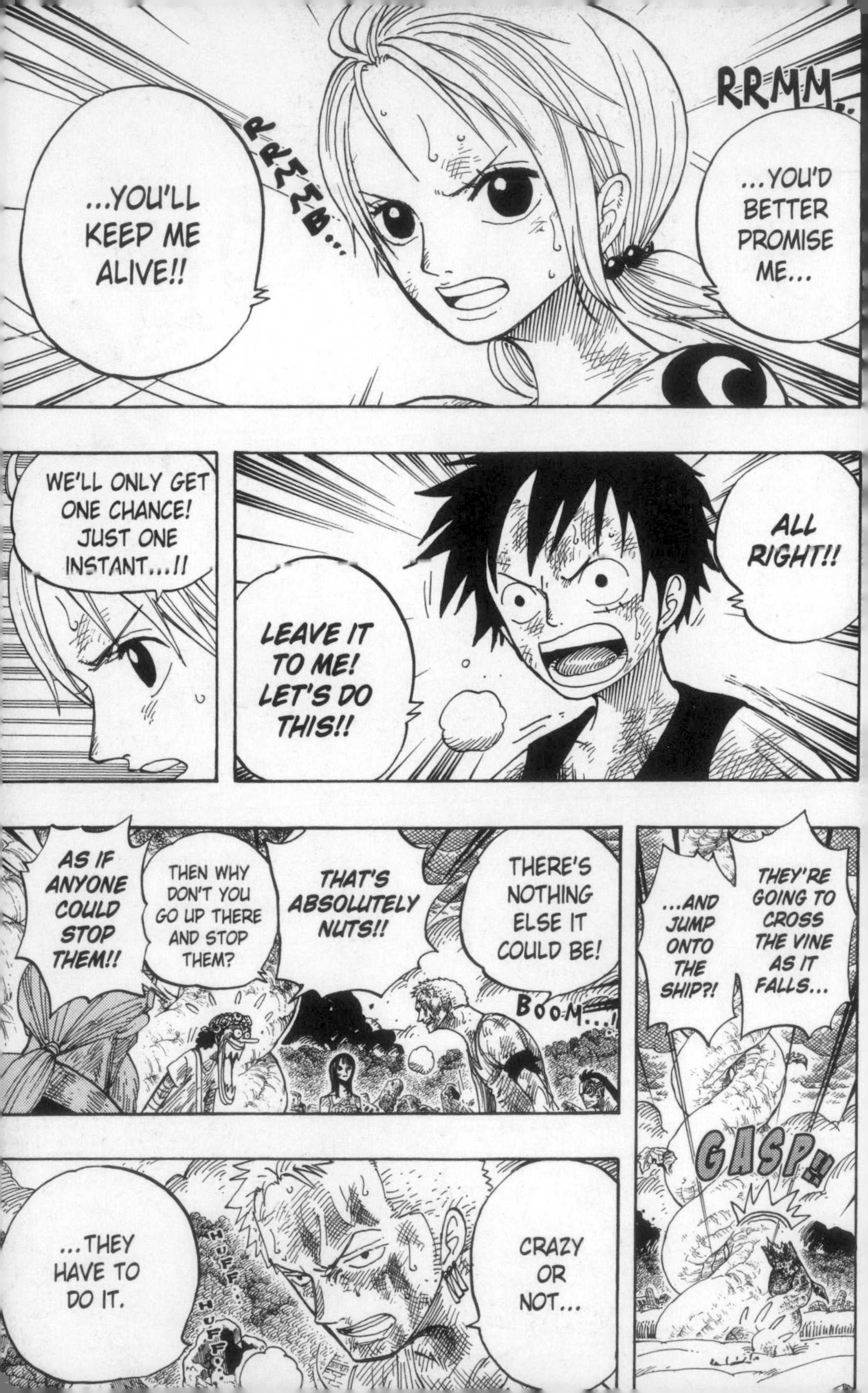
RRMM..
...YOU'D BETTER PROMISE ME...
RRRMB...
...YOU'LL KEEP ME ALIVE!!
ALL RIGHT!!
LEAVE IT TO ME! LET'S DO THIS!!
WE'LL ONLY GET ONE CHANCE! JUST ONE INSTANT...!!
THEY'RE GOING TO CROSS THE VINE AS IT FALLS...
...AND JUMP ONTO THE SHIP?!
GASP!!
THERE'S NOTHING ELSE IT COULD BE!
BOOM...
THAT'S ABSOLUTELY NUTS!!
THEN WHY DON'T YOU GO UP THERE AND STOP THEM?
AS IF ANYONE COULD STOP THEM!!
CRAZY OR NOT...
HUFF... HUFF...
...THEY HAVE TO DO IT.

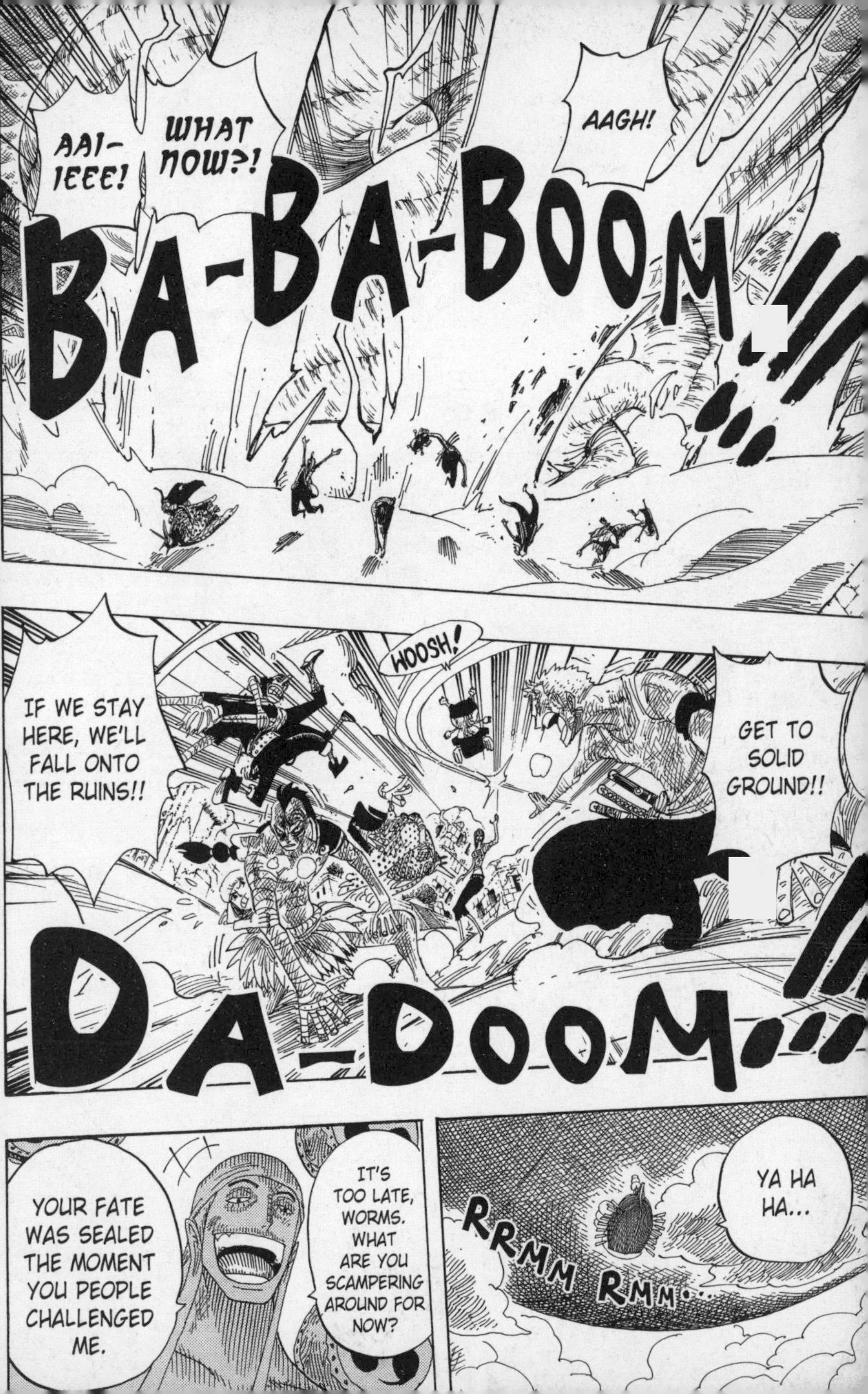
AAGH!
WHAT NOW?!
AAI-IEEE!
BA-BA-BOOM!!!
GET TO SOLID GROUND!!
WOOSH!
IF WE STAY HERE, WE'LL FALL ONTO THE RUINS!!
DA-DOOM...!!
YA HA HA...
RRMM RMM...
IT'S TOO LATE, WORMS. WHAT ARE YOU SCAMPERING AROUND FOR NOW?
YOUR FATE WAS SEALED THE MOMENT YOU PEOPLE CHALLENGED ME.

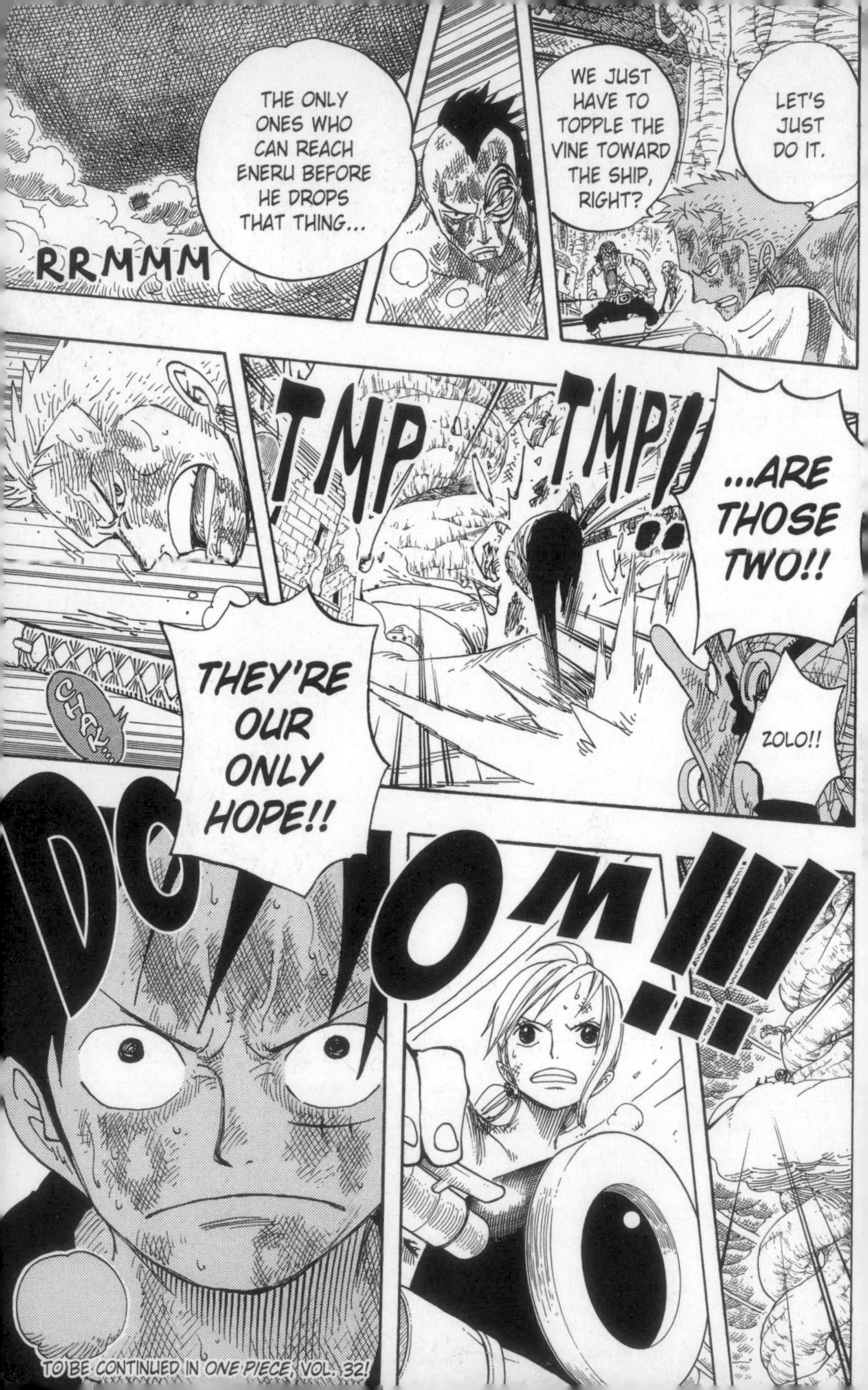
LET'S JUST DO IT.
WE JUST HAVE TO TOPPLE THE VINE TOWARD THE SHIP, RIGHT?
THE ONLY ONES WHO CAN REACH ENERU BEFORE HE DROPS THAT THING...
RRMMM
ZOLO!!
TMP TMP!
...ARE THOSE TWO!!
THEY'RE OUR ONLY HOPE!!
CHAK...
DO OM!!!!
TO BE CONTINUED IN ONE PIECE, VOL. 32!

COMING NEXT VOLUME:

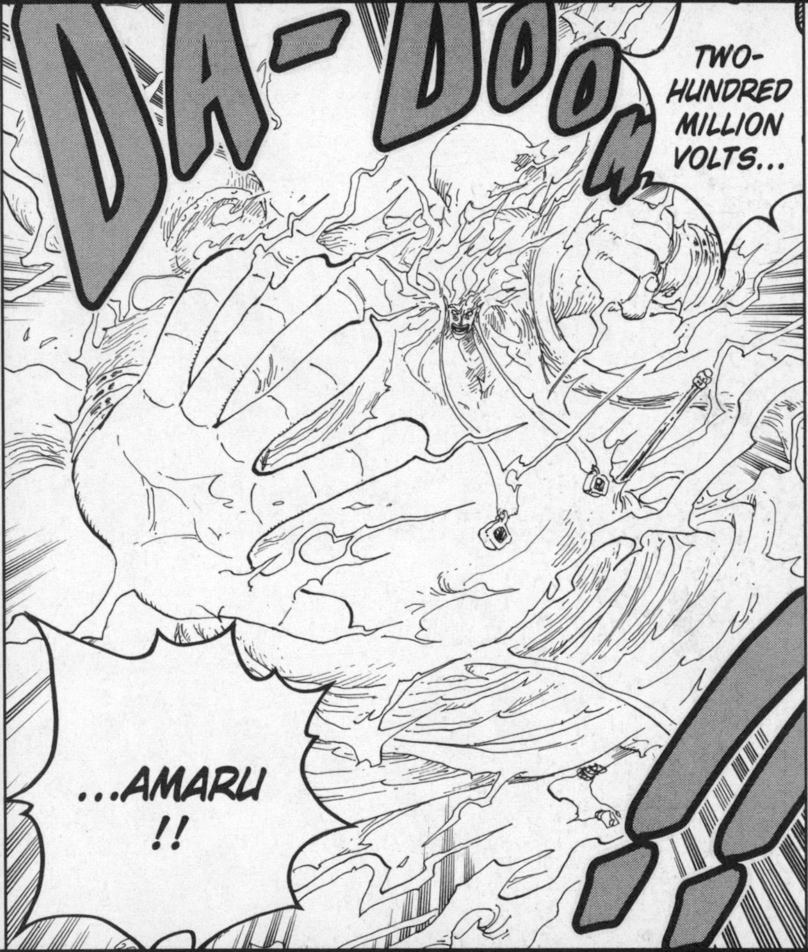
DA-DOOM
TWO-HUNDRED MILLION VOLTS...
...AMARU !!

As Kami Eneru departs for Endless Varse with the Golden Bell in tow, all hope down below turns to a certain rubber man. Not willing to give up the fight to thwart Eneru's evil plan to demolish Skypiea and all its inhabitants, Luffy gives it his all. But can he harness the power to defeat this almighty being, or will lightning strike twice in this epic battle?!

ON SALE NOW!